M?

The Unknown Karen Horney

KAREN HORNEY

The Unknown Karen Horney

ESSAYS ON GENDER, CULTURE, AND PSYCHOANALYSIS

Edited with Introductions
by Bernard J. Paris

Yale University Press
New Haven &
London

Set in Postscript Sabon type by Keystone Typesetting, Inc., Orwigsburg,
Pennsylvania. Printed in the United States of America.

Library of Congress Cataloging-in-Publication Data
The unknown Karen Horney : essays on gender, culture, and
psychoanalysis / edited with introductions by Bernard J. Paris.
        p.   cm.
Includes bibliographical references and index.
ISBN 0-300-08042-5
1. Psychoanalysis.   2. Horney, Karen, 1885–1952.   I. Paris, Bernard J.
BF173.U55   2000
150.19′5 — dc21   99-39715   CIP

A catalogue record for this book is available from the British Library.

The paper in this book meets the guidelines for permanence and durability
of the Committee on Production Guidelines for Book Longevity of the
Council on Library Resources.

10 9 8 7 6 5 4 3 2 1

For Gladys Topkis

Contents

Preface

In the course of working on *Karen Horney: A Psychoanalyst's Search for Self-Understanding* (Paris 1994), I discovered a number of unpublished writings by Horney, most of them in Harold Kelman's papers at the Postgraduate Center for Mental Health. Horney had been Kelman's supervisor when she was on the faculty of the New York Psychoanalytic Institute, and he left with her in 1941 when she resigned and founded the American Institute for Psychoanalysis. He underwent training analysis with her, eventually became her assistant dean, and was her close associate for a number of years (see Paris 1994). He became dean of the institute after Horney's death and took her papers with him when he moved to the Postgraduate Center in 1968. In addition to the writings in Kelman's papers, I discovered Horney's typewritten notes for a series of fourteen lectures on "Pride and Self-Hatred in Neurosis" in the files of the American Institute for Psychoanalysis. All of this material is now in the Karen Horney Papers in the Manuscript and Archives Division of Sterling Library at Yale University.

I found Horney's unpublished writings invaluable for the insight they give into the evolution of her ideas and the history of psychoanalysis, and I made frequent reference to them in *Karen Horney*. They reveal aspects of her thought that we do not find as fully developed elsewhere — about female homosexuality, for example, or why she stopped writing about feminine psychology. Since these manuscripts are so important, I am making them available to others with an interest in Horney's ideas. Some that were first drafts, course notes, or stenographic transcriptions of lectures have required a good deal of editing. In addition to hitherto unpublished writings, this book includes essays by Horney that have never before been collected and are difficult to obtain. Some of these were originally written in German, have not been previously translated, and were omitted from *Feminine Psychology*.

My original plan was to present Horney's unpublished and uncollected writings in a single volume to be entitled *The Unknown Karen Horney,* but as I worked on the project, I found that Horney's writings on clinical issues required a volume of their own. These have now been published as *The Therapeutic Process* (Horney 1999). The remaining unpublished and uncollected writings that I have found to be valuable are included in the present volume.

The book is divided into two parts. Part 1 includes Horney's writings on feminine psychology and the relations between the sexes; Part 2 collects her writings on other aspects of psychoanalytic theory from 1930 to 1952. Except for "Woman's Fear of Action," an essay included as an appendix in *Karen Horney,* Part 1 is made up entirely of previously unpublished and untranslated material. There are several hitherto unpublished items in Part 2, but it consists mainly of previously uncollected essays. In addition to some publications from the 1930s, these include three classic pieces that Horney wrote toward the end of her life: "The Value of Vindictiveness," "On Feeling Abused," and "The Paucity of Inner Experiences." The essays that were published in English are reprinted here in their original form, except that errors have been corrected and punctuation has been modified to conform to current practice.

Especially in Part 2, this volume makes available Horney's unpublished and uncollected writings on a variety of topics that are not always closely related to each other. I shall try to provide a context for these items, but there will inevitably be gaps. For a full account of Horney's thought I refer the reader to *Karen Horney: A Psychoanalyst's Search for Self-Understanding* (Paris 1994).

Acknowledgments

Nineteen items in this book have not been previously published. Of these, twelve were among the Horney writings that I found in Harold Kelman's papers at the Postgraduate Center for Mental Health in New York. I am grateful to Natalie Jaffe, Dr. Kelman's niece and executor, who led me to this material and has kindly placed it in my possession. The remaining previously unpublished items are from the files of the American Institute for Psychoanalysis. My thanks to the institute and to Jeffrey Rubin, who was dean at the time I did my research, for providing me with copies of this material.

The first four essays in this volume were originally published in German and appear here in English for the first time. All translations from the German have been made by Andrea Dlaska, Christa Zorn, and Marian Price, with my occasional editing. The specific contributions of the translators are identified in the headnotes. All three translators worked on the first four essays. Andrea Dlaska provided the initial literal translations, which were then refined by Christa Zorn. Since these translations often reflected Horney's difficult German, I asked Marian Price to polish the style, while remaining faithful to the meaning of the originals. I wish to thank my translators for the excellent results of this collaborative effort. Andrea Dlaska and Christa Zorn, both native speakers of German, also served as my research assistants. I deeply appreciate the many ways in which they have facilitated my work on Karen

Horney. Christa Zorn's assistance was supported by a grant from the Division of Sponsored Research at the University of Florida. The Department of English made the services of Andrea Dlaska available while she was a graduate exchange student from the University of Innsbruck.

The previously published items in this book that are still under copyright have been reprinted with the permission of their original publishers, who are identified in the headnotes. These include the *American Journal of Psychoanalysis* (Human Sciences Press), the *American Journal of Sociology* (University of Chicago Press), *Psychoanalytic Quarterly,* and *Newsweek.* I am grateful to Yale University Press for permitting me to draw on *Karen Horney: A Psychoanalyst's Search for Self-Understanding* (Paris 1994) in the introductions to Parts 1 and 2 of this book, and to reprint "Woman's Fear of Action," originally published as an appendix to *Karen Horney.*

Karen Horney's daughters, Marianne Horney Eckardt and Renate Horney Patterson, have been very helpful from the start, as I have acknowledged more fully in *The Therapeutic Process,* which is dedicated to them. As Horney's literary executors, they have kindly granted me permission to publish her writings. Susan Abel has edited this manuscript with great intelligence and care and has made many improvements. It has truly been a pleasure to work with her. As always, my wife's involvement and concern have sustained me in my labors, and I thank her again for being there.

One of my deepest debts is to my editor at Yale, Gladys Topkis. When I discovered unpublished Horney material in Harold Kelman's papers in the course of working on *Karen Horney,* Gladys immediately suggested that it could be gathered into a volume to be titled *The Unknown Karen Horney.* As things have turned out, Horney's unpublished and uncollected writings have required two volumes, *The Therapeutic Process,* published in 1999, and the present collection. My work on Karen Horney during the past ten years has owed a great deal to Gladys's advice and support, and I dedicate this book to her.

PART I

Feminine Psychology and the Relations Between the Sexes

Introduction

Born Karen Danielsen in a suburb of Hamburg in 1885, Horney studied medicine at the Universities of Freiburg, Göttingen, and Berlin. She married Oskar Horney in 1909, entered analysis with Karl Abraham in 1910, and became a founding member of the Berlin Psychoanalytic Institute in 1920. Having separated from her husband in 1926, she emigrated to the United States in 1932, when Franz Alexander invited her to become associate director of the newly formed Chicago Psychoanalytic Institute. In 1934, she moved to New York and began teaching at the New York Psychoanalytic Institute. She founded the American Institute for Psychoanalysis in 1941 and served as dean until her death in 1952.

Karen Horney's thought went through three phases: in the 1920s and early 1930s, she wrote a series of essays in which she tried to modify orthodox ideas about feminine psychology while staying within the framework of Freudian theory. In *The Neurotic Personality of Our Time* (1937) and *New Ways in Psychoanalysis* (1939), she tried to redefine psychoanalysis by replacing Freud's biological orientation with an emphasis on culture and interpersonal relationships. In *Our Inner Conflicts* (1945) and *Neurosis and Human Growth* (1950), she developed her mature theory, in which individuals cope with the anxiety that results from feeling unsafe, unloved, and unvalued by disowning their spontaneous feelings and developing elaborate strategies of defense.

Although the selections in Part 1 deal with feminine psychology and the relations between the sexes, they represent all three phases of Horney's thought. In the "Educational and Scientific Record" that she prepared as part of her application for immigration in 1932, Horney wrote: "My scientific interest concentrated more and more on female psychology and connected fields such as the differentiation between masculine and feminine psychology, general disturbances in the relations between the two sexes, marriage problems. As psychology has been until now mostly worked at from the side of men, it seems to me to be the given task for a woman psychologist — or at least I think it to be mine — to work out a fuller understanding for specifically female trends and attitudes in life" (Horney Papers). Between 1923 and 1935, a total of nineteen essays by Horney were published on these topics, including the first four essays in this collection, all of which date from 1927. These essays are representative of the first phase of Horney's thought which, despite her growing disagreements with Freud, was based largely on orthodox psychoanalytic premises.

In the second phase of Horney's thought she broke with Freud's biological model and emphasized culture and interpersonal relations. This phase is reflected in "Woman's Fear of Action" (1935), in which she turned away from what she had identified as her "given task" and argued that "we should stop bothering about what is feminine." Horney's growing awareness of the cultural construction of gender had led her to conclude that only when women have been freed from the conceptions of femininity fostered by male-dominated cultures can we discover how they differ from men psychologically.

The remaining selections in Part 1 — "Sadistic Love," "Overemphasis on Love," and lectures from Horney's course "Pride and Self-Hatred in Neuroses" — represent the third phase of Horney's thought, in which she understood human behavior in terms of defenses and inner conflicts that have no inherent relation to gender. She examined some of the same issues that had concerned her in earlier essays, such as difficulties in love and sex life, but from a very different perspective.

Although I have arranged Horney's essays and lectures in a chronological sequence, I shall discuss them here according to topic, looking first at those focused on feminine psychology and then at those dealing with relations between the sexes. The first essay in this collection, "The Masculinity Complex in Women" (1927), explores one of Horney's favorite topics. She addressed women's preference for the masculine role in about a third of the essays she published between 1923 and 1935 and in some unpublished lectures as well. I shall discuss her writings on this and related topics before turning to the three essays on marriage that Horney also published in 1927. These essays are most fruitfully compared with Horney's unpublished writings from the 1940s on relations between the sexes.

Horney defined the masculinity complex as "the entire complex of feelings and fantasies that have for their content the woman's feeling of being discriminated against, her envy of the male, her wish to be a man and to discard the female role" (1926b, 27, 74). Her first two essays on feminine psychology — "On the Genesis of the Castration Complex in Women" (1923) and "The Flight from Womanhood" (1926) — focused on the masculinity complex, and they were immediately followed by two more essays in which it was the central issue: "Inhibited Femininity" (1926) and "The Masculinity Complex in Women" (1927).

Horney began to write about the masculinity complex in response to Karl Abraham's "Manifestations of the Female Castration Complex" (1920), an essay that articulated the psychoanalytic view of women. According to Abraham, most women dislike being female and want to be male because in the early stages of their development they have felt at a disadvantage "on account of the inferiority of their external genitals" (339). When they become aware of their lack of a penis, girls interpret it as the result of castration and look on their genitals as a wound. They are reminded of their castrated state by such later events as menstruation, defloration, and childbirth. Their psychological development is governed by their efforts to compensate for their genital deficiency.

In her rejoinder, "On the Genesis of the Castration Complex in Women," Horney took issue not with Abraham's description of the masculinity complex but with his contention that the complex is "based solely on a dissatisfaction" due to the woman's coveting a penis (1923, 37, 38). She denied the inherent inferiority of the female sex and the causal relationship that Freud and Abraham posited between penis envy and the castration complex.

In explaining why penis envy is a typical occurrence, Horney contended that although the little girl's sense of inferiority is "by no means primary," she is subject to restrictions in comparison with boys in "gratifying certain instinct-components that are of the greatest importance in the pregenital period" (42) — namely, urethral eroticism, the scoptophilic instinct, and onanistic wishes. As a result of these restrictions, the difference "in bodily formation may easily give rise to a bitter feeling of injury," and the resulting penis envy complicates her development (41–42). Her later "repudiation of womanhood" on the grounds that men have greater sexual freedom is based on childhood experiences (42).

But Horney did not believe penis envy to be the source of the female castration complex. She pointed instead to identification with the father as a means of resolving the Oedipus complex. Women whose desire to be men is "glaringly evident have at the very outset of life passed through a phase of extremely strong father fixation" (43). In the oedipal phase, they take the father as a love object and desire a child by him. Disappointment in this hope leads them to relinquish the father as a love object, to identify with him, and to pretend to be a male. The penis envy involved in the castration complex is not the primary penis envy of the preoedipal stage but a much stronger one that is the product of the oedipal girl's identification with the father.

Women are at a disadvantage not only because they suffer from penis envy, first primary and then intensified, but also because they must resolve the Oedipus complex in a way that damages their femininity, whereas men can resolve it in a way that reaffirms their gender identity. After she feels deserted by her father, the girl suffers from the frustration of her "feminine love attachment," from feelings of anger and cravings for revenge directed against her father, and from feelings of guilt produced by her incestuous fantasies (50). The male who identifies with the mother and the girl who identifies with the father both repudiate their sexual roles, but powerful forces work against the male's identification with the mother and in favor of the girl's identification with the father. The male's identification with the mother is "at variance with his conscious narcissism" and implies the realization of his fears of castration, but the girl's identification with the father "is confirmed by old wishes" for a penis and is a defense against oedipal guilt (53). Females want to be like the opposite sex because "being a woman is in itself felt to be culpable" (53).

As Zenia Odes Fleigel (1973) has observed, Freud's "Some Psychological Consequences of the Anatomical Distinction Between the Sexes" (1925) seems to have been a response to Horney's "On the Genesis of the Castration Complex in Women," and Horney's "Flight from Womanhood" was a reply to Freud's essay. Freud accepted part of Horney's argument in "Genesis," for he agreed that "if the girl's attachment to her father comes to grief later on and has to be abandoned, it may give place to an identification with him and the girl may thus return to her masculinity complex and perhaps remain fixated in it" (1925, 195). But he maintained the primacy of penis envy in the girl's development by insisting that her wish for a child is a response to her disappointment at not having a penis and leads her to take her father as a love object. For Freud, as for Abraham, women are castrated creatures whose development is determined by their need to compensate for their lack of a penis.

In "The Flight from Womanhood," Horney argued that psychoanalysis reflects a male bias and does not accurately present women's real nature (1926a, 57). Men stress the difference between the male and female genitals, but they ignore "the other great biological difference," namely, the different roles played by men and women in reproduction (59). Women have in the capacity for motherhood "a quite indisputable and by no means negligible physiologi-cal superiority," and men have a corresponding "envy of pregnancy, child-birth, and motherhood, as well as of the breasts and of the act of suckling" (60–61). The male envy of motherhood gives rise to an unconscious tendency to depreciate women that is reflected in psychoanalytic theory. Men assuage their sense of inferiority by believing that the desire to have a child is really a desire for the penis and that motherhood is a burden they should be thankful they do not have to bear. As long as it is assumed that women are actually defective, it is impossible to see that "the dogma of the inferiority of women had its origin in an unconscious male tendency" (62).

As she had done in her preceding essay, Horney contended that the desire to be a man has very little to do with early penis envy but is "a secondary forma-tion embodying all that has miscarried in the development toward woman-hood" (64). Girls recoil from the feminine role at the oedipal stage when they renounce the father as a sexual object, and the strength of primary penis envy is then reinforced "by retrogression from the Oedipus complex" (68). Horney developed this idea somewhat differently here than in "Genesis," however.

Because of its association with incestuous desires, "female genital anxiety, like the castration dread of boys," bears "the impress of feelings of guilt"; but whereas the boy can inspect his genitals to see whether the dreaded damage has occurred, the girl remains uncertain on this point (66). To escape her anxiety, the girl "takes refuge in a fictitious male role" (66). Fantasies of being a man se-cure the girl "against libidinal wishes in connection with the father" and enable her "to escape from the female role now burdened with guilt" (67). Women have castration fantasies because when they adopt a male role their "feminine genital anxiety is . . . translated into male terms—the fear of vaginal injury becomes a fantasy of castration" (69). They wish for the restoration of the penis they imagine themselves to have lost, "as a proof of guiltlessness" (69).

Horney traced the female sense of inferiority to the girl's flight from oedipal guilt and genital anxiety into the masculine role. The girl is bound to feel inadequate when she judges herself by "values that are foreign to her specific biological nature" (67). Although her "sense of inferiority is very tormenting," it is more tolerable "than the sense of guilt associated with the feminine atti-tude, and hence it is undoubtedly a gain for the ego when the girl flees from the Scylla of the sense of guilt to the Charybdis of the sense of inferiority" (67).

Culture exacerbates the difficulties produced by the oedipal stage, especially the girl's sense of inferiority. The relation between the sexes is that of master and slave. Horney quotes Georg Simmel's observation that it is " 'one of the privileges of the master that he has not constantly to think that he is master, while the position of the slave is such that he can never forget it'" (69). The "disadvantage under which women labor in social life" is ignored in male-dominated psychoanalytic theory, but "a girl is exposed from birth onward to the suggestion — inevitable, whether conveyed brutally or delicately — of her inferiority, an experience that constantly stimulates her masculinity complex" (69).

Horney saw women as victims of both biology and culture. Their "unconscious motives for the flight from womanhood are reinforced" by their "social subordination" (70). They are bound to have a masculinity complex because of their need to escape the guilt and anxiety that result from their oedipal situation, and they are bound to be alienated from their essential feminine natures because of the overwhelming power of their male-dominated culture.

In her next essay, "Inhibited Femininity: Psychoanalytic Contributions to the Problem of Frigidity," Horney argued that by inducing frigidity, the masculinity complex compounds the woman's feeling of inferiority, for "at a deeper level" frigidity "unerringly is experienced as an incapacity for love" (1926b, 76). The woman therefore feels deficient in relation to the feminine ideal of lovingness as well as in relation to masculine standards of mastery and achievement.

In her account of the origin of the masculinity complex, Horney cited penis envy, disappointment in the father, and favoritism toward a brother, but she also observed that the girl may "shrink back from her female role" because she perceives the mother as "being raped, injured, wounded, or made ill" by sexual intercourse (78–79). "Real brutality on the part of the father and sickness of the mother" may give the child the idea "that the woman's position is precarious and one of danger" (79). A favored brother, a brutal father, and a mother made ill by her marital unhappiness were all prominent features of Horney's own history (see Paris 1994).

"Inhibited Femininity" was followed closely by "The Masculinity Complex in Women" (1927), the first essay in this collection. Although this essay had much in common with its predecessors, it introduced new nuances and details, and it differed from them in emphasizing the girl's fear of the father as her major reason for giving him up as a love object and seeking to escape from her female role. Her oedipal fantasies induce an unconscious fear of the father's sexual aggression, which threatens her with genital injury. Boys also develop anxieties as a result of child-parent conflicts, but with the girl an "element of 'real danger'" exists, given that "in a purely physical sense the little girl is more threatened by possible sexual aggression than the boy because of the way her genitals are made" (throughout this book, unattributed quotations can be assumed to come from the essay or lecture under discussion). In "Genesis," Horney had posited primal fantasies of sexual possession by the father and resulting castration, but her emphasis was on the girl's sense of desertion and betrayal. In "The Masculinity Complex" she incorporated into her theory not only a longing for and disappointment in the father but also a fear of him.

Despite her increasing emphasis on cultural factors, Horney continued to argue that the masculinity complex is independent of culture and hence is "a piece of specifically feminine psychology." We might have expected her to be sympathetic toward Adler's position that the masculinity complex (which he called the "masculine protest") is the result of a social situation in which "we instinctively equate male with superior and female with inferior," but she dismissed Adler by saying that it was not possible to understand "the actual driving force" behind the masculinity complex on a social basis. Rather, the driving force is "the fear of female sexual experience" that arises "from early emotional relationships." It is striking, however, that she cited factors in the family situation, such as the preference given to a brother, which are influenced by the higher value that her society placed upon males.

Despite her dismissal of Adler, Horney acknowledged that social factors reinforce women's "rejection of their feminine role by providing a real basis for their unconscious masculinity fantasies." She felt it to be "quite plausible that if the sexes were fully equal in status, many outward forms of the complex would be different." It might become more deeply unconscious because the conscious ego would have no reason to prefer the male role. Equality would provide "better opportunities for sublimation," so that much of the envy that currently takes a pathological course could be "put to better use in ego-appropriate cultural work." This is Horney's most hopeful conclusion so far. Since social factors are subject to melioration, whereas biological ones are not, Horney became more optimistic as she gave them more weight.

In subsequent discussions Horney continued to attribute the masculinity complex to disappointments at the hands of a father or brother, but she increasingly emphasized disturbances in the girl's relationship with her mother. In "Psychogenic Factors in Functional Female Disorders," she spoke of an "infantile hatred" of the mother for forbidding "sex life and sex pleasure" through her prohibition of masturbation (1933b, 169). Horney's next essay, "Maternal Conflicts," developed the role of the mother more fully. Competition between mother and daughter may begin in the daughter's infancy and take "grotesque forms" if "the mother's own Oedipus situation has caused an excessively strong sense of rivalry" (1933c, 179). Her rivalry with her own mother for the attention of her father is transferred to her daughter, whom she seeks to outshine in the competition for men. The mother may then "ridicule and belittle" the child, "prevent her from looking attractive or meeting boys, and so on, always with the secret aim of thwarting the daughter in her female development" (179). Mothers who are themselves fleeing from womanhood induce masculinity complexes in their daughters by communicating their dislike of the female role. They teach their daughters "that men are brutes and women are suffering creatures, that the female role is distasteful and pitiable, that menstruation is a disease ('curse') and sexual intercourse a sacrifice to the lusts of the husband" (180).

Horney also explored the masculinity complex, and especially its relation to female homosexuality, in lectures she gave in Berlin in 1932 and Chicago in 1933. I have found what appear to be stenographic transcriptions of some of these lectures in Harold Kelman's papers, and they are published here in edited form for the first time. The reader should keep in mind that these are lectures and not finished essays. They often ramble and fail to develop the ideas they introduce in a full and satisfying way. But they give us a sense of the kinds of patients Horney was seeing and of the problems with which she was grappling. They show that although Horney disagreed with Freud about some of the details of feminine psychology (her major break with him was but a few years away), in the early 1930s she was still very much under the influence of orthodox thought. Many of her ideas now seem dated, such as her attitudes toward female homosexuality, but they are of considerable interest as a reflection of the thinking of the time.

In the first of her 1932 lectures, which were probably given as a course at the Berlin Psychoanalytic Institute, Horney asked her audience to be patient because, as far as she knew, this was "the first attempt to describe female homosexuality in some depth." She was familiar with the work of Helene Deutsch, Jeanne Lampl-de Groot, Ernest Jones, and Otto Fenichel; and she made special mention of Freud's "wonderful essay" on "The Psychogenesis of a Case of Homosexuality in a Woman," published in 1920. But she found her predecessors' treatment of female homosexuality extremely limited and announced that she would try "to throw light on the diversity and range of manifestations" of the phenomenon. Her treatment was also quite fragmentary, but we should keep in mind that we have only two lectures from what may have been a substantial series in Berlin and that the first two lectures of the seven she gave in Chicago are missing.

In the first Berlin lecture, "Manifestations of Repressed Female Homosexuality," Horney laid out the questions she wished to explore: "What are the manifestations of repressed homosexuality? What are the relations of repressed homosexual women like toward men? How does homosexuality generally express itself in character? And what psychological conflicts take place?" She was also interested in the genesis of repressed homosexuality in the girl's relations with the female members of her family and in the masculinity complex.

Horney began the lecture indirectly, with descriptions of four patients who had seen a male analyst and had then come to her, two because they had moved to Berlin and two because their male analysts were threatened by their sexual aggressiveness and thought they had better see a woman. In all these patients the transference to the male analyst at first seemed to be a manifestation of their old passionate attachment to the father, but Horney came to feel that this was only part of the story, for unreal elements were also manifest in their relationship with their male analyst, fantastic beliefs that the analyst loved them or would marry them, even if he already had a wife. Horney initially thought that the analysts had mishandled the transference, especially in the case of Anna, the first patient she describes, but she came to see that these women could not separate imagination and reality in their relationships with other men as well and that they carried their propensity for fantasizing into the transference. Horney proposed that their behavior toward their analysts, and toward men in general, could be understood as a manifestation of their homosexuality. They did not really love any man but covered up their homosexuality by developing a "fantastic superstructure" and playing a role. In some cases a relationship aimed at a woman was acted out with a man and in others the women escaped into relationships with men because they were afraid of their homosexual tendencies.

According to Horney, the most prominent manifestations of repressed homosexuality in women are ambivalence and identification with the male role. Horney recognized that not all homosexual women are aggressively masculine in their approach to other females, but she argued that a masculine attitude is present even when their behavior is submissive and masochistic. Horney attributed such behavior to "a great fear, conscious or unconscious, of either the mother or the sister and immensely strong but repressed sadistic tendencies that are also feared by the patient." The dread of mother or sister generates rage and sadistic impulses that must be repressed because of a fear of retaliation. The desire to behave in a masculine, aggressive way toward other females is likewise repressed because these women fear the intensity and consequences of their sadistic impulses and become masochistic instead. Horney cited the case of one very masculine-looking woman who allowed other women to abuse or ignore her but who "strangled and maimed" them in her dreams.

In her lecture "Behavioral Patterns of Repressed Homosexual Women," Horney elaborated the case of Anna, the first of the patients she had described in "Manifestations." Anna had had a positive oedipal attitude toward her father, but it was disrupted when he disappointed her and when her older sister, who saw her as a rival, tormented, humiliated, and seduced her. She developed a libidinal attachment to women, partly because her disappointment in her father had led to an identification with him, and partly because of her experience with her sister, which she sought to repeat with other women. She also sought revenge against her sister by doing to other women what her sister had done to her, and this led her to develop a masochistic attitude as a defense against her sadistic impulses. She was defensive with men and afraid of success in her profession because she feared that something terrible would happen if she competed with her sister. She was also afraid of her mother, who she felt begrudged her her relationships with men. She herself begrudged other women everything and threw tantrums when her friends became engaged.

In this lecture, Horney's primary interest was in the transference behavior of repressed homosexual women with a female analyst. Anna displayed fear and distrust toward Horney that had originated in her experiences with her mother and sister. She developed the paranoid idea that "the analyst wanted to keep her from becoming involved with a man" and took Horney's urging her not to give up her profession as an effort "to *prevent* her from getting married." She saw the analysis as "a duel in which one of the two participants had to succumb," just as she had felt that her mother would have to die before Anna would be free to look for a husband. Her death wishes toward her mother were reflected in her desire to murder her analyst. Horney observed that some repressed homosexual patients court the female analyst in a demonstrative, masculine manner, sending her gifts such as flowers, while others are aggressive in a different way, making demands, throwing tantrums, or fantasizing violence. One patient "refused to pay because she felt that having to pay was synonymous with being a weak woman."

Another patient did not court the analyst in an overt way but was very reserved. She had tried to make her male analyst fall in love with her, but when she began working with Horney, she suddenly fell in love with a man and started pursuing him: "This love represented a clear escape from the transference, a fact which became apparent in her dreams, in which men turned into women and in which she had tea with the analyst, danced with her, and made obvious advances toward her." The patient's reserve toward the analyst was self-protective. She was afraid of her libidinous desires because she hated her mother's sexuality and feared that if she herself were sexual she would suffer the same things she wished upon her mother. Moreover, she equated her analyst with her mother, whom she saw as a cold, unfeeling witch who denied her sexual pleasure. She could enjoy herself only when her analyst became ill: "During this time, she was very relaxed and active with her boyfriend and kept cheering, 'I'm on Horney-holiday.'"

Horney discussed the masculinity complex and its relation to homosexuality again in the lecture "Common Deviations in Instinct Development," delivered in Chicago on 2 May 1933. All deviations from normal female development involve withdrawing from the female role and wanting to be a man. Women with a masculinity complex often resent giving in to authority and convention and dislike being in a subordinate role. They do not want to become emotionally attached to anyone because this means being dependent. When males are attracted to them, they try to maintain a superior position by being aloof and indifferent. All this sounds very much like Karen Horney herself, a woman who did not submit to the authority of Freud or Abraham, whose sexual behavior was quite unconventional, and who seems to have needed to attach men to herself while preserving her own independence (see Paris 1994).

The mother is now the central figure in the history of women with a masculinity complex. Either these women are afraid that their mother will do "something horrible" to them, or they have a "terrific hatred" of her, which may manifest itself in their being overanxious, afraid that the mother will meet with an accident. This overprotective attitude disguises a repressed death wish against the mother. There is a connection between the fear and the hatred. When the child is threatened or thwarted by her mother, she reacts with hostility, and her hostility makes her fear her mother's retaliation. A vicious circle is set in motion: the child's fear makes her resent the mother even more "as an enemy"; her increased resentment intensifies her fear, which intensifies her resentment, and so on. Only in this way can we explain the intensity of the hostility that emerges in the course of analysis. The girl's fear and hatred of her mother lead her to flee the feminine role. Because she hates the mother, she does not want to be like her; and because she fears her, she shrinks from being her rival.

Horney argued that it is not only because of the mother but also because of the father that some women are driven to adopt a masculine homosexual attitude. Initially the girl appears to have had no emotional tie whatever to the father, the weaker partner in the marriage; but eventually "it comes out that there had originally been a very strong, even passionate attraction to the father" and that the girl "had suffered some disappointment from his side." This may have been an injustice, such as preference for an older brother, an unexpected punishment, or an inconsistent attitude. The disappointment that the girl has experienced from her father or brother colors her attitude toward all males and drives her away from a love life. Horney herself was not driven away from a love life, but she seems to have been afraid to become too dependent on a man, perhaps because of her early disappointments.

Horney's description of the girls whose masculinity complex leads them to become boy-crazy rather than homosexual also seems autobiographical. These girls crave relationships with men but never succeed in them. They either quarrel with their partners or drop them when they show serious interest. Even when they are successful in attracting men, they feel inadequate as women, convinced that they are unattractive, that no man could like them, and that if a man does, it is in spite of their undesirability. They feel that they are not normal, that something is wrong with them, but they cannot say what it is. Perhaps they have injured themselves through masturbation or through early sexual experiences (a recurring motif in Horney's essays). They are delighted to have children because this reassures them that they have not been damaged permanently.

Horney felt that boy-crazy girls have many things in common with homosexual ones. They do not develop homosexual attitudes but instead have a strong fear of them, which they counteract through their relations with men. They have to have men around them in order to prove that they are "normal." Boy craziness and homosexuality are both manifestations of the masculinity complex, and women who display them may have similar backgrounds.

The relationship with the mother again plays the central role in "The Overvaluation of Love" (1934), one of Horney's finest essays, in which she developed many of the ideas she had introduced in the Chicago lectures, but with much less emphasis on libidinal forces and much more on social factors and family dynamics. Horney emphasized the role of the mother again in "Personality Changes in Female Adolescents," an essay in which she discussed four types, instead of the two she had described in "Common Deviations." In addition to developing homosexual or boy-crazy tendencies in adolescence, girls may become "absorbed in sublimated activities" or be "emotionally detached" (1935b, 234–35). What the four types have in common is their discomfort with the feminine role, which they "dodge" altogether, reject, or exaggerate (237). Such girls have an antagonistic attitude toward men but an even more intense hostility toward women, which derives from their life history: "Certain reproaches against the mother come up: lack of warmth, protection, understanding, preference for a brother, over-strict demands as to sexual purity" (237).

Let us return for a moment to Horney's Chicago lectures on feminine psychology, for I have not yet commented on all of them. She apparently delivered a total of seven lectures, to an audience that consisted largely of gynecologists. The first two are missing. The third lecture was on homosexual women and boy-crazy girls. The fourth lecture was on frigidity, which Horney connected here, as she had done in "Inhibited Femininity," with the masculinity complex. This lecture overlaps with the earlier essay to some extent, but it reveals new facets in Horney's thinking on the subject and contains numerous case studies that give us a vivid picture of her clinical experience.

The remaining lectures in the series were addressed specifically to the physicians in the audience, with the object of helping them understand the psychological aspects of problems they encountered in their medical practice. Horney had given a paper on "Psychogenic Factors in Functional Female Disorders" to the Chicago Gynecological Society on 18 November 1932, shortly after she arrived in the United States, and had had it published in the *American Journal of Obstetrics and Gynecology* (1933b). Her 1933 lectures expanded on that paper and provided a rich array of clinical examples. Although I doubt that they have much to say to gynecologists today, the lectures are of great historical interest, representing as they do the experience of women in the 1920s and early 1930s, the thinking of the day about their problems, and the final expression of Horney's Freudian phase. They are surprisingly orthodox, given that Horney was about to launch her critique of the psychoanalytic emphasis on biology and infantile origins. This was the last time she described analysis as the process of "uncovering infantile conflicts and fears that are still operating in the patient's life and recognizing the connections between these infantile sources and present difficulties" ("Uses and Limitations").

As we have seen, Horney gradually moved away from her initial position that the masculinity complex is a distinctively feminine piece of psychology, biological in origin, and increasingly recognized the importance of cultural influences and of particular kinds of experiences in the family. After initially proposing father-centered explanations that invoked the Oedipus complex, she came more and more to emphasize problems in the girl's relationship with female members of the family, especially the mother. As she paid less attention to biology and more to culture and family dynamics, her explanations became less universal and she began to doubt the possibility of making generalizations about specifically female trends and attitudes. In the mid-1930s, she stopped writing on this topic and never returned to it. Her loss of interest in feminine psychology has led some critics to question whether she was ever a true feminist, despite her trenchant critique of the patriarchal ideology of her culture and the phallocentricity of psychoanalysis.

Among the material in Harold Kelman's papers was the typescript of a talk Horney gave to the National Federation of Professional and Business Women's Clubs in July 1935, entitled "Woman's Fear of Action." This talk best explains why Horney stopped "bothering about what is feminine." She had reached the conclusion that all "we definitely know at present about sex differences is that we do not know what they are." Why we do not know had already been spelled out in several of her essays, especially "The Flight from Womanhood" (1926) and "The Problem of Feminine Masochism" (1935), which emphasized the role of culture in shaping the feminine psyche.

Even though she had recognized the impact of culture as far back as the early 1920s, Horney had difficulty integrating it into her thinking. She was increasingly impressed by the writings of sociologists, anthropologists, and ethnologists concerning cultural variations and the role of social forces in the formation of gender identity, but it was not until "The Problem of Feminine Masochism" that she consistently employed a social-psychological perspective. A brief look at this essay will help us appreciate "Woman's Fear of Action."

In "The Overvaluation of Love," Horney had asked whether the patriarchal ideal of woman "as one whose only longing is to love a man and be loved by him" corresponds to her "inherent character" (1934a, 182). The fact that women so often behave in accordance with this ideal has led many to infer "an innate instinctual disposition," but Horney pointed out that "biological factors never manifest themselves in pure and undisguised form, but always as modified by tradition and environment" (182–83). This line of thought was central to her argument in "The Problem of Feminine Masochism," which challenged the idea that "masochistic trends are inherent in, or akin to, the very essence of female nature" (1935a, 214). Because of the frequent occurrence of masochism in patients, psychoanalysis had supported "the theory of a given kinship between masochism and female biology" (214), but Horney felt that it had made "an unwarranted generalization from limited data" (222). Freud had argued that "pathologic phenomena merely show more distinctly as through a magnifying glass the processes going on in all human beings" (223). Because analysts have regularly found the Oedipus complex in patients, they have inferred that it is a ubiquitous phenomenon. This has not been confirmed by the study of "normal" people or by ethnological studies, which "have shown that the peculiar configuration denoted by the term Oedipus complex is probably nonexistent under widely different cultural conditions." We are led to conclude "that this peculiar emotional pattern in the relations between parents and children arises only under certain cultural conditions" (223). The same considerations apply to feminine masochism: it is a pathological condition that is not necessarily part of normal femininity, and the frequency of its occurrence is probably the result of social and cultural factors. It has not been established as a universal phenomenon belonging to woman's essential nature.

Horney identified a number of social and cultural conditions that tend to make women more masochistic than men, but comparative studies show that these conditions have not been universal and that some societies have been more unfavorable to women's development than others. In cultures in which the conditions conducive to feminine masochism are present, ideologies develop "concerning the 'nature' of women; such as the doctrines that woman is innately weak, emotional, enjoys dependence, is limited in capacities for independent work and autonomous thinking." Horney included among these ideologies "the psychoanalytic belief that woman is masochistic by nature." These ideologies "reconcile women to their subordinate role" by presenting it as unalterable and lead them to seek fulfillment in the expected ways. In our society, "it is hard to see how any woman can escape becoming masochistic in some degree, from the effects of the culture alone" (231). Horney did not deny that there are physiological factors "that may prepare the soil for the growth of masochistic phenomena" in women (232), but she argued that these are secondary and reinforcing rather than determinative. The ways in which women experience their physiology are profoundly affected by culture.

In "Woman's Fear of Action," Horney reported that after all the speculation of psychologists, we have not gone much "beyond the biological differences." She believed that important differences certainly exist between the sexes but contended that "we shall never be able to discover what they are until we have first developed our potentialities as human beings." We cannot know what women are capable of becoming until they have been freed from the conceptions of femininity fostered by male-dominated cultures.

Horney was opposed to a continued emphasis on what is distinctively feminine because she *was* a feminist and wanted to promote the emancipation of women. She argued that an interest in sexual differences "must be regarded as a danger signal for women, particularly in a patriarchal society where men find it advantageous to prove on biologic premises that women should not take part in shaping the economy and the political order." When jobs are scarce, as they were in the mid-1930s, men contend "that it is in absolute accord with woman's 'nature' that she keep out of competitive fields of work and remain restricted to emotional fields of life, concerning herself with charity, sexuality, and child bearing."

Most of "Woman's Fear of Action" is devoted to the effects that these views of woman's nature have on women themselves. They become "leaning and dependent" and "often regard professional pursuits as secondary to love and marriage." Such behavior tends to confirm the male ideology, but Horney pointed out that individuals in any group that has been suppressed for a long time undergo "a psychic adaptation which brings them to accept the limitations which the dominant group finds it advantageous to impose." Despite great changes in recent years, "psychic effects of the long history of restriction linger." These psychic effects include the overvaluation of home, children, sexuality, and love; the cult of beauty and charm; and the fear of losing erotic attractiveness through age.

The central point of the essay is that these effects of cultural attitudes keep women "from becoming genuinely and actively concerned with the great economic and political questions of our time, even when these broader interests concern woman's own position in the world and should be of vital interest to her." Women need to cooperate, to join together in a common cause.

In addition to her essays on feminine psychology, in the 1920s and early 1930s Horney wrote a series of essays on the relations between the sexes. The first of these were the three essays she contributed to *Die Ehe: Ihre Physiologie, Psychologie, Hygiene, und Eugenik — Ein Biologisches Ehebuch* (Marriage: Its physiology, psychology, hygiene, and eugenics — A biological marriage book), edited by Max Marcuse and published in 1927. These essays — "Psychological Fitness and Unfitness for Marriage," "On the Psychological Determinants of the Choice of a Marriage Partner," and "On the Psychological Roots of Some Typical Marriage Problems" — are published here in English translation for the first time. They were followed by "The Problem of the Monogamous Ideal" (1928), "The Distrust Between the Sexes" (1931), "Problems of Marriage" (1932), and "The Dread of Woman" (1932). Horney continued to examine the relations between the sexes in her books, as part of her analysis of strategies of defense and disturbances in human relations. I have included here some previously unpublished contributions from the 1940s: "Sadistic Love," "Overemphasis on Love," "Enslavement in Marriage," and three lectures from her course "Pride and Self-Hatred in Neuroses."

In *Karen Horney: A Psychoanalyst's Search for Self-Understanding* (1994), I argued that Horney's essays on feminine psychology and the relations between the sexes are often highly autobiographical and that in writing them she was trying to understand herself and to gain relief from her own emotional problems. In her essays in the *Ehebuch,* she seems to be trying not only to understand why her relations with men have worked out so poorly but also to protect her pride by universalizing those failures. After an unhappy marriage, with many affairs on both sides, she and Oskar Horney had separated in 1926. There is a consolatory pessimism in these essays and also in "The Problem of the Monogamous Ideal," which was published the following year. In the essays published in the 1930s, Horney displayed a growing awareness of the ways in which the psychology of the individual contributes to relational difficulties, and she held out some hope for melioration.

In the three essays in the *Ehebuch,* Horney described marriage as having a "basic tragic nature" ("Roots"). It requires positive sexual and emotional attitudes toward the partner and, if the union is to be "lasting and exclusive," the ability "to enter into a longer relationship with one and the same love object" ("Fitness"). In many men, however, a split between the tender and sensual impulses causes sexual inhibition toward their wives; women are subject to the masculinity complex, which makes them feel resentment and rivalry toward their husbands; the libido may be cathected onto the self, in which case the partner is valued only for his or her ability to gratify narcissistic needs; or conscious or unconscious homosexual trends may interfere with the relationship. It is "absolutely normal," moreover, for new love objects to appear in the course of a relationship because people are not attracted to just one person, because they develop in different ways after marriage, and because marriage itself "inevitably leads to disappointments and conflicts that drive [them] toward other love objects" ("Fitness"). As a result of these conditions, normal people are unfit for marriage, and neurotics are much worse. The human aptitude for marriage may not have been greater in the past, but this was disguised by the fact that women were more dependent and hence willing to make greater allowances.

Marriage has a tragic character not only because of the contradiction between what it requires and the psychology of the partners but also because of expectations that people carry into it, which are bound to be disappointed. The partners are looking for someone like their "ideal image" (*Idealbildung*) of mother or father, and of course no such person exists ("Determinants"). Either they do not marry at all, because "no one is perceived as measuring up," or they project the desired characteristics onto the partner and engage in a "sexual overestimation" that cannot last ("Determinants"). They are looking for fulfillment of their oedipal desires, moreover, and are bound to be disappointed, because the partner can be only an imperfect substitute for the parent. This may lead to Don Juanism, the continuing search for the perfect love object.

The oedipal character of the marriage relationship is another source of insoluble problems. The danger exists not only of too little sexual fulfillment but also of too much, which will result in feelings of guilt. We carry the incest taboo into marriage, along with our oedipal desires, and it either inhibits us toward the partner or punishes us if we find satisfaction. In either case, we withdraw our sexual desires from the forbidden object, as we did in childhood, sublimating our libido, directing it toward other objects, or suppressing it. All these solutions cause problems. If we throw our energies into our work, we may neglect our partner and avoid facing the problems of marriage. A polygamous disposition can mobilize jealousy and a desire for revenge on the part of the injured party. The unfaithful partner may also become vindictive in response to the irritating behavior of the jealous mate. In the faithful spouse, suppressed desires can lead to hatred of the frustrating partner, a projection of desires for unfaithfulness onto him or her, a regression to oral or anal satisfactions (eating, money, housekeeping), or a revival of homosexual tendencies in the form of same-sex friendships.

In a striking reversal of her condemnation of marriages of convenience in her diaries, Horney argued that arranged marriages may work out better than love matches, which are always fed by dangerous instinctual sources: "If the marriage has to a great extent been brought about by factors *other than personal,* as by family arrangement, social considerations, economic factors, it is held together by these elements" ("Roots"; see also Horney 1928a, 87). There will be less passion but fewer conflicts. Only "impaired people," however, consent to such marriages ("Determinants").

In "The Problem of the Monogamous Ideal," Horney again tried to normalize her marital problems and her promiscuous behavior by invoking psychoanalytic theory. Her object in the essay is to demythify the monogamous ideal by showing it to be both primitive and unjustifiable. The wish to monopolize one's partner is a derivative of the oral, anal, and oedipal phases of development. Even though it is an ideal supported by law, the "claim to permanent monopoly" is "unjustifiable," for "it represents the fulfillment of narcissistic and sadistic impulses far more than . . . the wishes of a genuine love" (1928a, 94). The monogamous ideal is greedy, sadistic, and unworkable. Those who live up to it are genitally inhibited, obsessional, or given to magic gestures.

In "The Distrust Between the Sexes," Horney again depersonalized disturbances in love relations by presenting them as "entirely comprehensible, unmitigable, and, as it were, normal" phenomena. But she also discussed the ways in which particular childhood conflicts affect later relations with the opposite sex, and she emphasized that childhood conflicts "can vary greatly in intensity, and will leave behind traces of variable depth." Their destructive effects can be meliorated by psychoanalysis, which "can also attempt to improve the psychological conditions of childhood and forestall excessive conflicts" (1931a, 118).

In "Problems of Marriage," Horney began by asking whether the failure of marriage is "an unavoidable law" or whether we are "subject to forces within us, variable in content and impact, and perhaps recognizable and even avoidable" (1932b, 119). Although she continued to present inevitable conflicts between the demands of marriage and human nature, her emphasis here was on "the unresolved conflicts we bring into the marriage from our own development," and she wanted to know which "factors that lead to dislike of the marriage partner can be avoided," which can be "alleviated," and which can be "overcome" (131).

By the time she wrote "Problems of Marriage," Horney had come a long way from seeing marriage as basically tragic in nature. The dominant theme of this essay is that the "chances of marriage are dependent on the degree of emotional stability acquired by both partners before marriage" (131). As Horney moved away from orthodox analytic generalizations and toward ideas rooted in the particularities of individual experience, she evinced a concomitant shift from the resigned, self-exculpating pessimism that was characteristic of her Freudian phase toward the hopefulness of her later theory. If our difficulties are the result of our personal development rather than the inevitable product of human nature and the human condition, maybe we can do something about them, especially if we own them as ours.

Thus far, I have been concerned mostly with the first phase of Horney's thought, in which she was trying to modify orthodox ideas but was still essentially a Freudian, and the early stages of the second phase, in which she broke away from Freud and developed a psychoanalytic paradigm in which culture and disturbed human relationships replaced biology as the most important causes of neurotic development. The remaining essays in Part 1 must be understood in the context of her mature theory, of which I can only give a brief account here. (For a more detailed account, see Paris 1994.)

The second phase of Horney's thought is most fully represented by *The Neurotic Personality of Our Time* (1937) and *New Ways in Psychoanalysis* (1939). In these books, Horney proposed a model for the structure of neurosis in which adverse conditions in the environment as a whole, and especially in the family, create a "basic anxiety" against which the child defends itself by developing strategies of defense that are self-alienating, self-defeating, and in conflict with each other. In a striking departure from Freud, she dismissed libido theory and the Oedipus complex (at least as a universal phenomenon) and advocated starting with the current constellation of defenses and inner conflicts rather than with early experience. Our problems are the result of past experiences, to be sure, but these produce a character structure with an inner logic of its own that can be understood without reference to infantile origins. Our character problems are not the result but the cause of difficulties in our sexual lives.

In her mature theory, developed in *Our Inner Conflicts* (1945) and *Neurosis and Human Growth* (1950), Horney retained the emphasis on the present and the basic conception of the structure of neurosis developed in earlier works, but she described the defenses and the relations among them much more systematically. She argued that people respond to feeling unsafe, unloved, and unvalued by developing both interpersonal and intrapsychic strategies of defense. The interpersonal strategies involve moving toward, against, or away from other people and adopting a self-effacing, expansive, or resigned solution. Each of these solutions entails a constellation of personality traits, behaviors, and beliefs, and a bargain with fate in which obedience to the dictates of that solution is supposed to be rewarded. People tend to employ more than one of these strategies and are consequently beset by inner conflicts. In order to avoid being torn apart or paralyzed, they give priority to the strategy that best accords with their culture, temperament, and circumstances; but the repressed tendencies persist, generating inconsistencies and rising to the surface if the predominant solution fails.

In the self-effacing solution, individuals try to gain safety, love, and esteem through dependency, humility, and self-sacrificing "goodness." Their bargain is that if they are helpful, submissive people who do not seek their own gain or glory, they will be well treated by fate and other people. There are three expansive solutions: the narcissistic, the perfectionistic, and the arrogant-vindictive. Narcissists are full of self-admiration, have an unquestioning belief in their own greatness, and often display unusual charm and buoyancy. Their magic bargain is that if they hold on to their exaggerated claims for themselves, life is bound to give them what they want. Perfectionists take great pride in their rectitude and strive for excellence in every detail of their lives. They make a legalistic bargain in which correctness of conduct ensures fair treatment by fate and their fellows. Arrogant-vindictive people have a need to retaliate for injuries received in childhood and to achieve mastery by manipulating others. They do not count on life to give them anything but are convinced that they can reach their ambitious goals if they remain true to their vision of the world as a jungle and do not allow themselves to be influenced by their softer feelings or the traditional morality. Resigned people worship freedom, peace, and self-sufficiency. Their bargain is that if they ask nothing of others, they will not be bothered; that if they try for nothing, they will not fail; and that if they expect little of life, they will not be disappointed.

The intrapsychic strategies of defense are linked to the interpersonal. To compensate for feelings of weakness, inadequacy, and low self-esteem, people develop an idealized image of themselves that they seek to actualize by embarking on a search for glory. The idealized image generates a pride system, which consists of neurotic pride, neurotic claims, and tyrannical "shoulds." People take pride in the imaginary attributes of their idealized selves, they demand that the world treat them in accordance with their grandiose conception of themselves, and they drive themselves to live up to the dictates of their solution. The pride system tends to intensify the self-hatred against which it is supposed to be a defense, for any failure to live up to one's shoulds or of the world to honor one's claims leads to feelings of worthlessness. The content of the idealized image is most strongly determined by the predominant interpersonal strategy, but given that subordinate strategies are also at work, the idealized image is full of inner divisions. As a result, people are often caught in what Horney calls a crossfire of conflicting shoulds. Since obeying the dictates of one solution means violating those of another, they are bound to hate themselves, whatever they do.

From the mid-1930s on, Horney saw the relations between the sexes in a way that differed greatly from the perspective of her earlier essays, especially from that of the essays in the *Ehebuch*. She was no longer concerned with the vicissitudes of instinctual development, with fixation, regression, and the conflict between desire and the forces of repression. Instead, she tried to understand relationships and the problems that beset them as products of the interaction between people with inner conflicts who have differing character structures and predominant defensive strategies. In *The Neurotic Personality of Our Time,* she focused on people with neurotic needs for affection or for power and explored the ways in which these two kinds of people, who tend to be attracted to each other, play out their neurotic needs in their relationships.

In *Self-Analysis* (1942), Horney presented her most extended case history, that of a patient named Clare, who was trying to free herself from her "morbid dependency" on Peter, her lover. Since Peter was predominantly detached, Horney explored here the dynamics of a relationship between a woman with a neurotic need for love and a man with a neurotic need for freedom and independence. I have argued in *Karen Horney* that the Clare case is highly autobiographical and that in the account of the relationship of Clare and Peter, Horney was depicting the vicissitudes and ultimate breakdown of her own relationship with Erich Fromm.

As she had done since "Problems of Marriage," in "Sadistic Love" Horney attributed disturbances in sexual or love relationships not to universal psychological laws but to the "personal difficulties" of the partners. She focused here on the sadistic personality and "its tendency to find conscious or unconscious gratification or thrill in criticizing, degrading, humiliating, enslaving, or exploiting the partner." Instead of using case histories as illustrations, she drew on three works of literature: Ibsen's *Hedda Gabler,* Shaw's *Pygmalion,* and Kierkegaard's *Diary of a Seducer.* This is her fullest discussion of Hedda Gabler, a character she alluded to repeatedly in her writings, beginning with her diaries. In "Sadistic Love," she presented Hedda as an essentially hopeless person who feels her life to be empty and useless and seeks to assuage her own unhappiness by making others equally miserable. (For a more extended and somewhat different analysis of Hedda that employs a Horneyan approach, see Paris 1997). Henry Higgins is an emotionally dead person who has no regard for Eliza Doolittle "as a human being with rights of her own" but arrogantly turns her "into a creature who responds to his demands and fulfills his wishes and ambitions." The seducer in Kierkegaard's work is a man who enjoys having the power "to attract and reject, to arouse and disappoint another human being" and shows no concern about the damage he is doing. Although Horney did not develop the point, she observed that the success of the sadist depends in part on the psychology of the victim.

"Sadistic Love" was first presented as a talk in 1943, when Horney was beginning to work on *Our Inner Conflicts* (1945), and some of its ideas found their way into her chapter on "Sadistic Trends." In 1946, Horney revised "Sadistic Love" to include the typology she had developed in her book. She observed that "the dynamics of sadism will vary, depending on the structure of the individual's neurosis." Subtle manifestations of sadism appear in compliant and detached people, but it is most prominent in the aggressive (later called the arrogant-vindictive) personality. People are not born sadistic; they become that way because they have not received love and respect and have suffered humiliations in childhood. As a result, they want "to get even, and to enjoy a vindictive triumph." Because they also have a side that "wants to be decent and fair," they are subject to inner conflicts. The sadistic person "regains his lost pride by crushing the pride of others; he recaptures a feeling of strength by the sense of power he acquires in enslaving and controlling others; he rids himself of some measure of guilt by accusing other people and making them feel to blame."

"Overemphasis on Love" was a lecture Horney gave on 16 October 1945. Its topic was one to which she returned again and again. She addressed it in "The Overvaluation of Love" (1934) and in "The Neurotic Need for Love" (1937), a lecture based on *The Neurotic Personality of Our Time* (1937). She devoted four chapters of *Neurotic Personality* to the compulsive need for affection and dealt with this topic again in her chapter on "Masochistic Phenomena" in *New Ways in Psychoanalysis*. The long chapter on the Clare case in *Self-Analysis* is titled "Systematic Self-Analysis of a Morbid Dependency," and the discussion of the "compliant" or "moving toward" solution in *Our Inner Conflicts* deals with excessive dependency on a partner. Two chapters on the topic appear in *Neurosis and Human Growth:* "The Self-Effacing Solution: The Appeal of Love" and "Morbid Dependency."

Whereas in "Sadistic Love" Horney addressed the kinds of problems an aggressive person brings into a relationship, in "Overemphasis on Love" she focused on the compliant personality. While acknowledging that love is one of the most important things in life, she observed that some people need it too desperately and have unrealistic expectations of what it can provide. These are the people with whom sadists can succeed. We are overemphasizing love "when all of our interests, wishes, plans and fears revolve around the other person," when "an extreme dependency on the partner" leads to "a fear of desertion or a clinging that is actually degrading." Many people overemphasize love because they feel themselves to be defenseless, and love seems to offer an ally in coping with a hostile world. Aggressive partners are particularly appealing because they provide protection and a vicarious sense of accomplishment and glory.

This lecture is especially interesting for Horney's discussion of the role of imagination in the overestimation of love. Dependent people believe that love "has magic qualities and can bring them a fantastically wonderful life." It is a "ticket to Paradise." Like Madame Bovary, they envision love as a "great bliss descending on them that will bring them out of the humdrum into a world of glamour and delight." (See Paris 1997 for a Horneyan analysis of *Madame Bovary*.) Because such people "live so much in imagination," they "do not take into account the reality of either their partner or themselves." Returning to a topic she had taken up in her lectures in Berlin, Horney now explained the desire of women for the love of their analysts not as a defense against homosexuality but as an expression of "their dependency needs and their unrealistic belief in the power of love to give them a sense of fulfillment. Off in a world of their own, they refuse to consider whether the analyst is married or might be inclined to love them. In their imaginary realm, such things do not matter at all."

"Enslavement in Marriage" is the abstract of a talk in which Horney traced feelings of enslavement not to conditions inherent in marriage but to the defense systems of the partners. Some people feel enslaved because they are married to aggressive partners who want to control their thoughts, feelings, friendships, and activities. Such behavior does not necessarily make for an unhappy marriage, however, for compliant people may be comfortable with a certain amount of domination. They, too, can be highly controlling, as they make demands for attention and love through their helplessness and suffering. Detached people may feel enslaved not because of the behavior of their partners but because they have "an extreme need for unlimited freedom." As a result, "every tie, every legitimate obligation, every suggestion made, every expectation or wish is felt as an intolerable coercion." They do not recognize that the problem is within themselves but feel that they are being strangled by their mates.

The final items in Part 1 are three lectures from a course Horney gave, "Pride and Self-Hatred in Neuroses," at the New School for Social Research in 1947 and 1948. A full set of typewritten notes has survived from this course, which was clearly a prelude to the writing of *Neurosis and Human Growth*. The course consisted of fourteen lectures, the first seven of which correspond to the first six chapters of that book. These deal with the search for glory, neurotic claims, the tyranny of the should, neurotic pride, self-hate and self-contempt, and alienation from self. The lectures on human relations and work also correspond to parts of *Neurosis and Human Growth*, as do the lectures on Freud (see Part 2) and on therapy (see *The Therapeutic Process*, Paris 1999). Although the titles are similar, some of the chapters vary considerably from the lectures, and the second half of the course only faintly resembles that of the book. What we have, moreover, are merely the notes from which Horney spoke; she no doubt elaborated her ideas in the lectures themselves. Readers should go to *Neurosis and Human Growth* for the fullest articulation of Horney's mature theory, but the lectures show her thought in the process of evolving, and they contain some material that does not appear in the book. Here I have included the lectures that pertain to the relations between the sexes: Lecture 8, "Influence [of Pride and Self-Hatred] on Human Relations"; Lecture 9, "Influence on Love Life"; and Lecture 11, "Influence on Sex Life."

Whereas *Our Inner Conflicts* had focused on conflicts between the interpersonal strategies of compliance, aggression, and detachment, in her lectures on "pride and self-hatred in neuroses," Horney concentrated on an intrapsychic conflict that became one of the major foci of *Neurosis and Human Growth*. In Lecture 6, "The Dilemma Between Pride and Self-Hatred," Horney introduced the motif of the devil's pact, the Faustian bargain that people make when they sacrifice their souls (their real selves) in an effort to actualize an idealized image of themselves that they have developed to compensate for feelings of weakness, worthlessness, and unlovability. They try to restore their pride through self-idealization, but the strategy fails—for according to an inexorable psychological law, attempts to achieve an impossible glory succeed only in intensifying feelings of worthlessness.

In Lecture 8, "Influence on Human Relations," Horney emphasized the ways in which intrapsychic problems affect people's relations with others. People beset by inner conflicts are preoccupied with themselves, and their egocentricity "results in emotional isolation." To ease their inner tensions, they engage in externalization and experience what is going on inside them as though it were outside. In externalizing their shoulds and self-hatred, they may relate to other people in ways that have nothing to do with reality. Their feeling of inner weakness makes them afraid of others, with whom they compare themselves unfavorably. Their fear also stems from their neurotic pride, which makes them "extremely vulnerable to anything that seems like criticism, rejection, or neglect." A person whose neurotic pride is hurt "is easily thrown into an abyss of self-contempt. Because of his insecurity, he protects his pride by anticipating rejection" and showing others he does not care. If they react negatively, he "feels rejected, not knowing that he originally caused" their response. Hurt pride also disturbs human relations by engendering hostility and a need for vindictive triumphs. Compensatory self-idealization gives rise not only to neurotic pride but also to neurotic claims, and the world's failure to honor these claims is another source of hostility.

To compound the problem, disturbances of the self make people "feel weak, helpless, and lost" and thereby intensify the need for other people. Need for others' approval stems from self-condemnation and need for their protection from the inability to fend for oneself. This puts needy people in the uncomfortable position of being dependent on the very objects of their hostility, fear, and dislike.

In Lecture 9, "Influence on Love Life," Horney observed that "since every love relationship is a human relationship," all the difficulties described in the preceding lecture were still pertinent. It is especially characteristic of love relationships that people are often caught between feeling unlovable, on the one hand, and having "a particularly great need of love on the other." If they hate themselves, they cannot believe that anyone else can love them. They will disregard signs of affection, assume that other people are attracted to them only because of the needs they fulfill, and "need endless reassurances that never suffice." At the same time, they have a particularly great need of love to counteract their self-contempt, enable them to escape their isolation, and give meaning to their lives.

People try to deal with the conflict between their need for love and their feeling of unlovability either by renouncing love altogether or by trying to prove that they are indeed lovable. Those who renounce love may regard it as an impediment and cut it out of their lives; feeling that "love in reality is something poor," they may prefer to fantasize about it; or they may reject it as a temptation that threatens their independence. Those who pursue love may become Don Juans who constantly need to prove their irresistibility, or they may believe that by acting self-effacing and living to "love, serve, and adore," they will earn love.

At the end of this lecture, Horney briefly returned to the topic of how individual psychology affects one's choice of a marriage partner. She treated it this time in light of the particular neurotic needs of aggressive and of self-effacing people. She observed that relationships based on neuroses need not end in disaster for those whose neurotic trends complement each other, but she warned against blaming marital difficulties on having the wrong partner: "When difficulties arise, we must start with ourselves, with the attitudes, expectations, and vulnerabilities we carry into a relationship."

In Lecture 11, "Influence on Sex Life," Horney rejected Freud's assertion that character disorders derive from disturbances in sexual development and affirmed the reverse: "Sex does not determine character but character determines the sex life. The whole determines the part, not the part the whole (Gestalt)." Our sexual problems "are not the source but the effect of our difficulties." Sexual problems will vary according to a person's character structure and conflicts, as will the neurotic needs sex is employed to satisfy. Sex is important for mental health and happiness, but in neurosis it assumes undue importance, serving "functions that should not really belong to it, such as allaying anxiety, . . . escaping isolation, or being a source of pride and triumph."

Horney returned to the issue of splitting, which Freud explained as originating "in an ambiguous image of the mother as both an idealized asexual being and a whore." She argued that this explanation was untenable because splitting occurs in women as well as men (it was a problem that she experienced personally). She explained splitting partly in cultural terms, as a result of the Puritan attitude that sex is "a thing apart, something crude and degraded that has nothing to do with our finer feelings and our sense of who we really are." Those who regard sex as degraded "feel comfortable seeking it only with a degraded partner." The degradation of sex may also be the result of psychological factors: "In the healthy person, sex is the physical expression of love. In the neurotic person, sex is degraded because it . . . becomes a means to such ends as control, domination, prestige, etc. The partner, too, becomes a means to an end, an object one uses to serve one's own needs." Self-alienation also plays a role, for "when a person loses touch with his own identity," he "engages in pretenses and becomes emotionally insincere. Sex becomes impersonal and degraded because he engages in it without really being there."

Comparing Horney's views on the relations between the sexes as expressed in her unpublished writings in the 1940s with those developed in essays and lectures from her Freudian phase gives us a vivid sense of how radically her thought had changed in the intervening years. She remained interested in many of the same problems, but her explanations were quite different. The selections in Part 2 will contribute to our picture of the later phases of her thought. (For an extended treatment of the relation between Horney's mature thought and modern feminist theory, see Westkott 1986, 1989.)

The Masculinity Complex in Women (1927)

This essay, originally entitled "Der Männlichkeitskomplex der Frau," was published in *Archiv für Frauenkunde* 13: 141–54. It was translated by Andrea Dlaska and revised by Christa Zorn. The final version, in which I have made a few editorial changes, is by Marian Price. As I indicated in the introduction to Part 1, Horney discussed the masculinity complex in a number of other essays, including "On the Genesis of the Castration Complex in Women" (1923), "The Flight from Womanhood" (1926), "Inhibited Femininity" (1926), "Psychogenic Factors in Functional Female Disorders" (1933), "Maternal Conflicts" (1933), and "Personality Changes in Female Adolescents" (1935), all of which can be found in *Feminine Psychology* (1967). She also discussed the masculinity complex in lectures that are published here for the first time: "On the Manifestations of Repressed Female Homosexuality" (1932), "Behavioral Patterns of Repressed Homosexual Women" (1932), and "Common Deviations in Instinct Development: Homosexual Women and Boy-Crazy Girls"

(1933). She provided an account of Helene Deutsch's views on the topic, with some comments of her own, in her review of Deutsch's *On the Psychology of Female Sexual Functioning* (1925). "The Masculinity Complex in Women" most closely resembles "Inhibited Femininity," which immediately preceded it in composition and which it occasionally repeats.

I imagine that people unfamiliar with the psychoanalytical term "the masculinity complex in women" will at first think of the recent phenomenon that is generally called the masculinization of women, encompassing everything from a boyish haircut and figure to independence and the claim to sexual freedom, which up to now have been reserved for men.

The question has been raised — justly, it seems to me — whether the term "masculinization" is really applicable to these changes — that is, whether such manifestations really are of a specifically masculine nature or merely seem to be so. That is indeed a very difficult question, for if we are honest, we must admit that we know very little about what traits are actually specifically masculine and specifically feminine — that is, which traits exist independent of the pressure of social relations and social values.

However, the fact that these traits do appear masculine to us when adopted by women is the path to a psychological understanding of these manifestations. It leads us to ask whether perhaps this idea of masculinization contains a kernel of psychological truth if not of objective fact — that is, whether in the end the element in the woman's instinctive life that leads her to adopt such a reorientation is really a wish to be masculine.

In order to avoid misunderstandings, I must emphasize that what we understand as a woman's masculinity complex is fundamentally different from the social manifestations associated with masculinization. It is a purely psychological phenomenon which encompasses certain aspects of a woman's psychosexual development. Although it may shed some light on the modern alterations in the feminine attitude, it is not the explanation for these alterations, which are anchored in social and economic change.

Let us begin with what we know. In women who are suffering from some kind of neurotic symptom — in effect, in most women of educated circles — but also in many who are considered psychologically sound, we encounter a number of disorders in female sexual functions: dysmenorrhea, amenorrhea, depression or irritability before and during menstruation, and, most frequently of all, frigidity. These symptoms occur so often that scientists could very well ask whether they do not actually represent the normal sexual adjustment of the "decent" woman. Other neurotic disorders are related to problems with motherhood, ranging from psychological difficulties in conceiving — which undoubtedly exist, even if one does not go so far as Kehrer, who links them to frigidity — to complaints during pregnancy, functional disorders while giving birth, and impairment of lactation and of mothering in general.

We should also include such symptoms as flux, pain, and hemorrhage — insofar as they have no underlying organic cause — which may well make up the bulk of cases in day-to-day gynecological practice. We should finally consider the possibility that psychogenesis can have its part even in rarer organic disorders such as myoma and oorphorilida. This brief enumeration indicates the breadth of the field I would like to approach psychologically. This list is by no means exhaustive, for the field also includes a great number of psychic disorders, from character disorders and problems in love life to pronounced neurological symptoms.

Functional organic disorders are usually treated in isolation, first one, then another; but the psychologically oriented physician can recognize the connection between physical symptoms and certain recent conflicts — for instance, between flux and masturbation or the hypochondriacal fears which follow masturbation; or between hemorrhages and a woman's wish to withdraw from sexual relations with her husband. This knowledge, which we largely owe to psychoanalysis, is certainly of great importance for general medical practice and especially for gynecological practice because it helps avoid unnecessary and harmful operations. However, it does not allow insight into the larger connections at work here.

These connections can be approached only by a method that considers the whole person, as psychoanalysis does. The mere possibility of linking all these disparate phenomena makes our psychoanalytical approach valuable, no matter how one thinks about it otherwise, and offers a definite inducement to involve oneself with it.

Without our precise knowledge of unconscious sex life, we would hardly be able to get beyond certain general assumptions, such as realizing that something is wrong in the overall adjustment to sexuality. But the slightest attempt to describe what is wrong in more detail often fails. Sexual disinclination, for instance, is by no means a common denominator for all symptoms mentioned above. If we think about frigidity, we know that it is not always connected with a negative attitude toward sexual experience. Even if — in spite of all the apparent contradictions — we accepted the hypothesis that frigidity always involves some secret rejection of sex, it would not get us very far. We would still be perplexed by the details of the individual case; for instance, we would not know why one woman has hemorrhages and the other a fear of cancer.

As a matter of fact, in analysis of these women we find that they do not always reject sex in general; many see sexuality as something positive. What they do reject is the individual role they have to play, and specifically their feminine role. This is not immediately obvious. First we hear, despite the patient's conscious emphasis on her femininity, that as a child she would rather have been a boy and that in her judgment men have it better than women in social relationships and in general. Or we get a strange contradictory picture, with the patient showing hostile, derogatory tendencies toward men but at the same time elevating men above women and equating the feminine with inferiority. All sorts of complaints come up, such as: I do not like myself the way I am — not my body, not my personality, not my intellect. Only a closer look reveals that all of these attitudes originate in extensive desires and fantasies of masculinity, which are bound up with an intense envy of men.

What the nonanalyst may find odd and hard to accept is that these fantasies of masculinity are not general in nature, but at their deeper unconscious levels are quite concretely and unambiguously directed at the possession of the male genital organ. Analysts can understand the astonishment about this all the more, as we ourselves were surprised about ten years ago by the relatively late discovery of penis envy. There are two sources of evidence for penis envy. First, there are the wishes revealed in analysis that stem from early childhood, a stage at which thinking is very concrete, as everyone can recall. The little girl sees that the little boy has something she lacks, and she wants it, too. Second, there is ethnological material that may persuade those not convinced by analysis. For instance, phallic cults show us the naive admiration paid by primitive, unrepressed thinking to the male genital organ.

The effects of women's secret envy are manifold. On the one hand, it leads women to overestimate everything male and to feel contempt for their own sex. It often blinds women to their own advantages and merits. They measure their lot against that of males — that is, by a measure that is alien to their nature — and find it wanting. Many women even depreciate motherhood. On the other hand, their envy creates a pronounced resentment toward men as the privileged sex, and it can turn into inward bitterness, such as a worker feels toward an employer. It can grow into secret hostility, lying in wait to defeat the man or to lame him psychically with a thousand weapons in the everyday warfare that we see at first glance in countless marriages. Because women are envious, questions of prestige, power, and superiority gain special importance for them. The feeling of being fundamentally disadvantaged by fate can also lead them to make unconscious demands of life, and of men in particular, for compensation. The fact that an excellent observer such as Adler made envy the pivotal point of his whole psychology shows that we are dealing with a widespread phenomenon, one which has far-reaching cultural consequences. There is envy on the man's side as well, which I shall briefly come back to later.

In many women, dreams and symptoms very clearly show that they have not really accepted their femininity, but that in their unconscious fantasies they uphold the fiction that nature created them male but that they were injured or maimed. Thus a recurrent image in analysis is the idea that the female genital organ is really a wound. A girl's early observations of traces of her mother's blood and later her own menstruation nourish these fantasies. When these ideas make an appearance in analysis, we see that they are charged with strong emotions — not only with a fear of sexual intercourse, which appears understandable under these circumstances, but also with intense feelings of guilt and shame, which are not as easily accounted for.

In some patients we encounter the feeling that their supposed sex change is something so shameful that nobody must know about it, that anyone who discovered it would scorn them. This fear of discovery can become so great that it holds women back from marriage or any contact at all with men. It also explains much of the fear women have of medical examinations; however, it can also give rise to a wish to be examined again and again, in order finally to get rid of the unconscious doubt as to whether one is built normally.

Usually the existence of this sense of shame is established early in analysis; it surfaces simultaneously with the masturbation theme, and we hear — often directly, often indirectly — about fears that these assumed sex changes have come about through masturbation or other forms of sex play. At this stage in analysis, we often find disturbances in physical functions with a strongly hypochondriacal component — such as pain or fear of cancer in either the genitals or other organs. These complaints are connected remarkably often with the wish for an operation.

One patient was in psychoanalysis because of her compulsion neurosis and her overwhelming desire to be male. Her first symptom was the compulsion to look at the genitals of men on the street. In this phase she was suffering from a heart complaint. I sent her to a colleague for an examination and was told that no organic causes for the heart complaint could be found, apart from an occasional insignificant murmur. When he told the patient the same news, she reacted with absolute despair as if it were the end of everything. But before her anxiety could be analyzed, she felt acute pain in her right side, again with no organic cause. At this time, there was an interruption in the analysis. She finally found a surgeon who was willing to operate on her duodenum because of a shadow on an x-ray. This shadow was later more accurately interpreted as a muscle contraction. As she lay in the hospital, she suddenly realized: "Maybe I want to be operated on." With the dawning of this insight all her pains vanished as with a single stroke. A later analysis—about a stubbornly recurrent idea that she had swallowed a needle which was now wandering about in her body and needed to be removed—plainly revealed the unconscious fantasy that the penis was somewhere inside her body and had to be taken out.

This case sheds light on the many women who go from one doctor to another with the demand to be operated on. One patient with a strong masculinity complex, for instance, had five laparotomies before her analysis, three of them due to complaints which later turned out to be clearly of psychogenic origin.

All the functional disturbances listed at the beginning of this study are essentially rooted in women's fantasies that they are injured or maimed males. Because of the central importance of their fantasies, they have given the entire complex its original name, the feminine castration complex.

Boys also have hypochondriacal anxieties accompanying masturbation, but it appears that the anatomical differences are disadvantageous for girls, since the female genital apparatus is not as accessible and, therefore, does not allow for an immediate check with reality. It appears that women more often than men are driven by their anxieties into uncontrollable fantasies. To avoid misunderstanding, I would like to stress very clearly once more that these fantasies as well as their connection with psychic and physical symptoms are deeply rooted in the unconscious, and that it will never be possible to diagnose them in an ordinary medical consultation.

One may find the psychoanalytic perspective interesting but still have difficulty believing that so many psychic and physical symptoms all have their origin in penis envy. One may grant the existence of the little girl's desire for a penis—one can hear it confirmed in direct statements by children—but it sounds unbelievable and indeed unbiological that penis envy could not only affect the entire life of an individual woman but also cause widespread characteristic problems among cultivated women as a group.

On the issue of biological validity, our conscience can always be eased by the fact of bisexuality, whose great importance was first recognized by Fliess. Bisexuality means not only that everyone has traits of both sexes, but also that it is not possible to content ourselves with one sex role. We need only look at the ancient images of gods with breasts and phalluses, which give a form to these bisexual desires—desires which are by no means limited to women. We can find equally intense wishes in the unconscious fantasies of men concerning motherhood; their "birthing envy" not only manifests itself in neurotic symptoms but also gives rise to their obviously very powerful drive for cultural achievement.

But even if a man unconsciously believes his inability to give birth to be a hidden flaw and thus feels the impulse to create other works instead, this creativity does not impair his masculinity. Rather, it becomes so much a part of it that creativity has been considered a typically male activity. In women, on the other hand, the masculinity complex is supposed to cause a rejection of the female role. The difference is not so very marked, however, because we diagnose a masculinity complex only in cases where the desire to be male remains unreconciled and interferes with normal development. To understand why such interference occurs more often in women than in men, we first have to explain how these wishes are assimilated during normal development.

Our experience has taught us that sexuality does not have its onset at puberty, but that we are born with our sex drive. The sex life of a child does not differ in intensity from that of an adolescent or adult — that is, we don't begin with a smaller quantity that gradually increases until it breaks through in puberty, but rather the early sex life is of a different quality. A child can feel as passionately as an adult and can suffer from conflicts that correspond to those of an adult. We have seen that the principle of attraction to the opposite sex, which is at work everywhere in nature, makes itself felt from the first years on; therefore, on a purely instinctual basis, a girl feels more strongly drawn to her father and a boy to his mother. Furthermore, these instinctive impulses, in a way comparable to genuine passion, lead to a conflict called the Oedipus complex, which for a girl includes rivalry with her mother. This whole complex of feelings is by its very nature bound to perish, as it comes up against not only actual denial by the parents but also the deeply rooted prohibition of the conscience known as the incest taboo. In primitive peoples this taboo has led to countless rules of avoidance and punishment. The theologian and linguist Joseph ben Gorion has recently demonstrated in his paper "Sinai and Gorizim" that this taboo must have formed the basis of the fourth commandment, "Honor your father and your mother," in a legislation older than the Mosaic.

The further development of the child ideally takes the following course: the sensual part of the incestuous impulse is repressed — that is, it becomes unconscious — while the purely affectionate feelings remain partly directed toward the parents. At the same time, a process of detachment begins that will be completed during puberty, so that the adolescent will be able to transfer these feelings entirely to a new object, one that corresponds to the conscious desires and is therefore ego-appropriate.

In a girl's development, the desire to possess a penis normally evolves into the desire for sexual union with a man and the wish to have a child. If the development takes this positive course, the remnants of the masculinity desires can be sublimated. This knowledge is in agreement with the observation that women who are at ease with their femininity show no significant traces of the masculinity complex as described here.

Psychoanalysis has shown, however, that many conditions have to be fulfilled to guarantee such a normal development and that many inhibitions and developmental disorders are possible. Several factors — some of them accidental — can make a girl recoil from her female role. The often blatant preference given to a brother can contribute much to increasing the masculinity desires in little girls at an early stage. Just as frequently, a strong masculinity complex in the mother can be projected onto the girl, making her reject the female role. An even more lasting fear of female experience may come from witnessing her parents' lovemaking at an early age; if the home is one where sexual matters as a rule are kept secret from the children, these impressions take on the character of the forbidden and uncanny. In our experience, such sexual observations are without exception interpreted as violence against the mother. The mother's menstruation, illnesses, and childbirth then seem to confirm that being a woman is dangerous.

These accidental factors easily give rise to the anxieties that are typical of the oedipal fantasies themselves; only in these cases the fears are experienced more intensely than usual. In analysis of such cases, we hear over and over that there was a fear of the father, and dreams most clearly show the sexual basis of this fear.

In dreams the father may appear as a dog or lion that wants to bite the child, with the dreamer wondering why her mother so casually lets him run around loose. In one case of agoraphobia, the girl dreamed that her father was Death pursuing her and trying to get hold of her. Here, as often happens, death and man, dying and the sex act are unconsciously equated. In this case, the girl had an intense relationship with her father; she was his favorite, and even as a grown girl she was very jealous of her mother and of any girlfriend who gave her father a friendly look. At the same time, she felt fearful and embarrassed about being alone with her father. Her agoraphobia clearly had the meaning, Mother must not leave me alone with my father.

It may be instructive to sketch the further development. A pretty girl with exquisite feminine traits, she fell ill during her first menstruation, and she showed hostility and fear toward men who tried to approach her. She once said herself, "If someone doesn't look like my father, I don't like him, and if he does look like him, pretty soon he becomes disgusting." She volunteered this without any prompting. This patient was very mistrustful and not at all suggestible. Her dreams revealed her genital anxiety in a transparent symbolism. For instance, burglars break into the house, threaten her, and steal or destroy something. She took refuge in masculinity fantasies and clung to them pathologically. These fantasies were unconscious, but the change in sex roles clearly manifested itself in her way of life. She went into her father's firm and took over when he became ill and was unable to work, thus taking her father's place in reality.

This patient's development contains something typical. Generally speaking, one might put it like this: the little girl, caught in the spell of oedipal fantasies and of an anxiety which at its unconscious core is the fear of sexual aggression, easily comes to fear her father and, under the pressure of this fear, is apt not only to give up her father as a love object but also to flee altogether from her female role.

A brief remark may help explain such fear and its frequency. Boys also develop anxieties under the pressure of parent-child conflicts, which are aggravated by feelings of guilt as well as by possible threats of being punished for masturbation. All these factors affect girls in the same way. But with girls, something else interferes, something I would like to call the element of "real danger." First, in a purely physical sense the little girl is more threatened by possible sexual aggression than the boy because of the way her genitals are made. We can observe everywhere in nature that the fact of endangerment is mirrored on a psychic level by instinctive fear. We need only think of the flight instinct which animals have in the face of specific dangers.

There is also the hypothesis that little girls' fear reflects a piece of phylogenetic experience from a time when they were actually exposed early to older men's aggression — something we still find among primitive tribes, according to Ploss-Bartels, and which is not so rare with us in proletarian circles.

So if we encounter in little girls a great many fantasies about sexual aggression, I would like to interpret these primal female fantasies in part as fallout from phylogenetic experience. This may help explain an aspect that continually amazes me — namely, that these fantasies so often are taken for real experiences.

The real driving force behind the masculinity complex is a fear of female experience, which is increased by an intense relationship with the father. Under the pressure of this fear, the girl takes refuge in a fictitious male role. When this happens, the penis envy of early childhood, which might have been well on the way to being overcome, is intensified and can develop the far-reaching effects I have outlined above.

To understand the full implications of this process, we have to ask ourselves what the girl gains from this exchange of sex roles. Certain analytical observations can help our understanding. It is not so very difficult in analysis to uncover masculinity fantasies, but even after they are discovered and accepted by the patient, they are stubbornly held on to until we succeed in breaking down the underlying female fears. In accordance with analytical principles, this experience forces us to conclude that even in earlier times masculinity fantasies functioned as bulwarks, as safeguards, against female desires and fears, and that they had to be maintained for this very purpose as long as these wishes were felt to be a danger.

Another benefit for the girl grows out of her simultaneous identification with her father. The normal process, after all, is for her to identify with her mother: she wants to have a husband and children, like her mother. If instead she accepts her father as a model and measure for herself, she will succeed in loosening the actual object relation with him. It is comparable to the situation in later life in which a woman loves a man who is unattainable as a love object, maybe because he is committed already, and so she puts aside her desire for love and contents herself with sharing his interests.

Keeping in mind that the actual pathogenic agent of the masculinity complex is a fear of female experience, we can understand why symptoms of disease break out in such women at the very moment some incident inescapably reminds them of their female role. This happens mainly during menstruation, during sexual intercourse, especially defloration, and during pregnancy and childbirth; but it can also occur through sex education or any other sexual impression, or with the first stirrings of love. In this regard I have already repeatedly referred to the classic portrayal in Schiller's *Die Jungfrau von Orleans,* a play about Joan of Arc. In the prologue, we find a pronounced ban on female experience: "The love of a man must not touch your heart," and so on. This is followed in the plot by Joan's complete and successful switch to the masculine role, and finally by a breakdown under the most oppressive feelings of guilt at her first female stirrings of love. What poetic intuition shows us here on a large scale, we see often enough in a smaller version during a consultation. Just as the literary work shows us a conscious motivation for Joan's breakdown — namely, her love for an enemy of her country — so also the patients give us various conscious reasons for their breakdowns, above all disappointment in love. Of course, one must not underestimate these later events, but our analytic experience reminds us that these later misfortunes in love life can in fact be a consequence of the attitude acquired in childhood.

The most frequent and thus the most important consequence of this developmental disorder is frigidity. How much the woman's sexual functioning is obstructed depends on the degree of her resistance to her feminine role. We can follow a seamless continuum from those women who recoil from the mere thought of sex on down to those whose inhibitions come through only in the organ-language of frigidity. In cases of comparatively little resistance, frigidity need not be a fixed and unchangeable reaction but can be given up under certain, usually unconscious, conditions. For one woman the condition of the forbidden must be fulfilled; for another the condition of being violently over-powered; for a third the condition of a relationship between kindred spirits; for the fourth the condition that there is no such relationship, and so on.

Because of the variable occurrence of frigidity, it has been rightly concluded to be of psychological origin. Analytical insight into its development tells us, furthermore, that its appearance and disappearance in specific psychological situations is strictly determined by the developmental history of the individual. Thus, the much debated phenomenon of frigidity must be seen in a larger context. The question of whether frigidity in itself has the status of an illness has no general answer. Certainly it is a serious symptom, for not many women can easily tolerate the damming up of the libido through a lack of genuine arousal. In any case, frigidity signifies that something in the psychosexual development is not in order.

Once frigidity is entrenched alongside the masculinity fantasies, the woman is trapped in a vicious circle. If she originally fled from her female role into the fiction of a male role, her frigidity heightens her rejection of everything female, adding an overtone of contempt.

The elements that drive a woman away from her female role at a deep instinctual level are paralleled by elements on a conscious level which attract her to the male role. For we live, as Georg Simmel has expressed it, in a masculine culture — that is, government, economic life, the arts and sciences are creations of the male and are therefore filled with his spirit. At least until recently, there has been an almost purely masculine influence on value judg-ments concerning the relative worth of man and woman. The result was that women were measured predominantly according to those traits that made them valuable to men, such as their capacities as wives and lovers, whereas achievements in various fields, worthiness of character, or intellectual abilities have been seen as specifically masculine. Delius declares, "Woman's psychol-ogy is the deposit of man's wishes and disappointments." Let me remind you of the Jewish morning prayer, in which the man thanks God that he was born male, while the woman simply thanks God that she was born human.

I should like to point out just three major effects of these attitudes on women:

1. Even in cases where the parents are not especially male-biased, the sense of being "only a girl" is inescapable in the nursery, through the more impres-sive status of the father or the greater freedom of the boys.
2. The possibility of adequate sublimation has been given almost exclusively to boys.

3. Males have far fewer limitations in their love life. For psychologically understandable reasons — understandable because of the complex described here — this point initially got little attention in the women's movement, although it is perhaps the most important.

Insights of this kind have led Adler to say that because of this social situation we instinctively equate male with superior and female with inferior. Since he presupposes a primary need for validation, he takes it for granted that a protest should be raised against this hierarchy — he calls it "the masculine protest" — and that this protest, in countless disguises, lies at the bottom of all kinds of neurotic symptoms and character disorders.

Adler's explanation of the masculinity complex from a social standpoint is received with great approval because the journey into the depths is so arduous. I don't mean to begin a discussion of Adler and Freud here; I only want to say that I see no possibility of understanding on a purely social basis what has been revealed as the actual driving force in each of the cases discussed here — namely, the fear of female sexual experience in connection with the early emotional relationships that condition this fear. However, it cannot be denied that the social factors reinforce women's rejection of their feminine role by providing a real basis for their unconscious masculinity fantasies. I consider it quite plausible that if the sexes were fully equal in status, many outward forms of the complex would be different. For example, the complex might disappear more deeply into the unconscious, because for the conscious ego there would be no grounds to adopt the masculine role; furthermore, with better opportunities for sublimation many of the currents that today take a pathological course would be put to better use in ego-appropriate cultural work. However, in all its essential elements the complex itself would remain untouched by social equality, and we would still have the original problem before us, a piece of specifically feminine psychology.

2

Psychological Fitness and Unfitness for Marriage (1927)

In 1927, Horney contributed three essays to *Die Ehe: Ihre Physiologie, Psychologie, Hygiene, und Eugenik — Ein Biologisches Ehebuch,* edited by Max Marcuse: "Psychological Fitness and Unfitness for Marriage," "On the Psychological Determinants of the Choice of a Marriage Partner," and "On the Psychological Roots of Some Typical Marriage Problems." This essay is published here in English translation for the first time. It was originally translated by Andrea Dlaska and was then revised by Christa Zorn. The final version of the translation is by Marian Price. I have made some editorial changes to reduce Horney's wordiness and to speed the flow of ideas. In some cases, I have incorporated material that was originally in footnotes into the text. These three essays have most in common with "The Problem of the Monogamous Ideal," which was originally published in 1928 and later included in *Feminine Psychology* (1967).

In one of the previous essays in this volume, the question of fitness for marriage was discussed from a medical-eugenic viewpoint, with a focus on the health of husband and wife and the potential for healthy offspring. While the importance of physical health cannot be overestimated, we need to go beyond the tradition of somatically oriented medical science, for it neglects the question of psychological fitness. A purely somatic approach seems particularly inadequate in the case of marriage, since marital success or failure depends largely on psychological factors.

If you doubt whether personal happiness is a subject worthy of scholarly research, bear in mind that it is the foundation for our development as human beings and our worth to society. How children thrive depends to a significant degree on the psychological atmosphere of the marriage. Considering how marital conflicts sap the partners' vitality and breed neuroses in their children, we need to ask whether it is possible, by establishing psychological criteria of fitness for marriage, to anticipate and prevent such detrimental effects, just as we try to anticipate and guard against a possible syphilitic infection.

I dare to tackle this problem because of the insight gained from my clinical experience with couples, with whom I have observed that marital conflicts inevitably grow out of previous emotional problems. If we can trace the causes of marital failure in a fairly straight line to early disorders in the psychosexual development of the partners, then — given enough information — we can hope to see in advance how the makeup of an individual might put the marriage at risk.

Two different starting points for this approach are possible. One is to proceed from established constitutional types or, in a more naive way, from certain human traits.[1] Then you ask how well suited for marriage this or that type is, and what kind of problems will foreseeably arise from the traits associated with this type. In actual practice, however, it becomes apparent that the types established so far are either too physiologically oriented or too general to tell us anything about a person's ability to cope with the specific tasks of marriage.

A second method for understanding fitness or unfitness for marriage is to proceed from the emotional demands a marriage makes on the partners. What conditions are necessary for each individual to meet those demands? How can we tell whether those conditions are present? This is the route we shall pursue here. All these conditions could be summed up as "the ability to love," but this would not get us very far. Not only would it grieve us to see such a basic and obvious ability called into question, but as a practical matter the origins of this ability are complex and hard to trace.

We must therefore try to break down the psychological demands marriage makes on the partners into their individual components, which leaves us with the following three conditions:

1. As a sexual relationship, marriage requires a positive sexual adjustment to the partner.
2. As an attempt to form a community with another person beyond the merely sexual, marriage requires a positive psychological attitude to that person.
3. If this community is not meant to be temporary but lasting and exclusive, it demands the ability to form long-lasting ties to one and the same love object.

The first of these conditions is easily defined: quite obviously, an absolute rejection of sexual activity is just as bad for the marriage as a lack of sexual restraint. Since marriage both gratifies and restricts sexual desires, it presupposes a degree of inward sexual freedom that is equally distant from complete disinclination and from unchecked instincts.

Both extremes can as a rule be recognized through simple observation. A lack of self-control would go unnoticed only if external pressure had rendered premarital experiences impossible. Otherwise the nature of these experiences (such as promiscuity) will reveal it. Similarly, extreme sexual avoidance is obvious to the practiced eye; it reveals itself in various traits — in a general ignorance of sexual matters, in the show of emotion with which sexual incidents are pronounced immoral, or in aversion or awkwardness regarding indirect expressions of the erotic in social life.

These deliberations yield relatively clear and simple criteria in regard to the first — and crudest — of the proposed conditions, but little is gained by them. While they enable us to identify a small number of people as unsuited for marriage, they shed little light on the cases that lie on the broad spectrum between these extremes. Moreover, sexual feelings depend to a high degree on one's psychological adjustment to one's partner.

My concern here is not with the ways in which psychological adjustment within the marriage is adversely affected by the partner's behavior, but with negative attitudes toward the opposite sex that are already present before marriage, that is, irrespective of the particular spouse. The capacity for object-love, which is a confluence of affectionate and sensual impulses, is the result of a child's psychosexual development, during which a variety of disorders can occur.

For instance, both currents may be well developed but unable to converge on one object. Such a splitting in the love life was described by Freud and has since become well known. This splitting, which is particularly characteristic of today's male, manifests itself in the fact that he feels no desire for the woman he loves affectionately and may be impotent with her, while he degrades other women to mere sex objects. The man so split achieves at least a modus vivendi if not a complete fulfillment in love, but his love object of the moment gets the short end of the stick, either spiritually or sensually.

Although such splitting can greatly jeopardize the principle of monogamy, the marriage relationship itself may not be in much danger, since the outside relationships that may exist are only partial ones. Moreover, splitting does not necessarily make a person totally unfit for marriage; how much damage it will cause depends far less on the severity of the split than on the partner's reaction. If a man with a splitting in his love life marries a woman with a pronounced disinclination for sex, it is conceivable that no difficulties will arise. But if the man is matched with a woman of full feeling, the relationship is headed for catastrophe, for the man will expect the wife whom he tenderly adores to represent an inaccessible and untouchable ideal, which also implies that she is barred from having other relationships.

How such a disorder will actually work itself out in a marriage cannot be predicted. It is not difficult to recognize the disorder beforehand — at least in its pronounced form — even in cases where no previous experiences have betrayed such a division. For the splitting manifests itself just as plainly in a man's attitudes toward women as in his actual experiences. As a rule, such a man cultivates friendly but distant feelings toward women who remind him of mother or sister with regard to race, genealogy, or social status, while displaying a general contempt toward other females.

The love life can also be split in another respect, namely by a strong attraction to members of the same sex. When discussing homosexuality, I shall be considering only cases in which the libido has a bisexual orientation. Given the solid structure of exclusively or predominantly homosexual orientations, it is clear that such persons are not suited for marriage.[2]

It is difficult to pronounce on the fitness of those whose homosexual proclivities, conscious or unconscious, are strong but not predominant. Compatibility is not necessarily threatened when only part of the libido flows to the partner, while another part is aimed at the same sex. A man with homosexual tendencies might sublimate them in male friendships, membership in all-male organizations, or professional relationships with other men, with no harm to the marriage so long as the woman has other intimate ties and her demands for love are minimal. If such a relationship is not complicated by neurotic mechanisms, it can even be relatively harmonious and good-natured, since the potential for conflict is less when libidinal involvement is weaker. Indeed, observation of everyday life often shows — even more than in medical practice, since healthy people are being studied — that precisely those men who exhibit to the trained eye a considerable measure of unconscious, well-sublimated homosexuality make comparatively good husbands. They stick to their choice once they have made it, enter into no serious relationships with other women, take good care of their families, and are generally wrapped up in their work, which incidentally brings them into closer contact with other men.

Let us take a moment to consider how these seemingly auspicious cases might develop. We are dealing here with men who certainly have a strong unconscious homosexual bent, but who sense unconsciously that this homosexuality is a danger to themselves and who therefore seek refuge from these powerful urges in marriage. While such men lack a deep loving feeling for their own wives, they have in its place a pronounced feeling of gratitude, which not only serves as a counterfeit for the love they lack but apparently provides a good basis for married life. Or we may see a special emphasis on their commitment to their wives, or an exaggerated potency on the physical level. These are all overcompensations for repressed homosexual impulses.

However, in cases where the reaction patterns are not so successful, repressed unconscious homosexuality asserts itself in a roundabout and secret way. Out of the abundant possibilities I will select only some of the most striking. A man may project his homosexual desires, of which he may not even be aware, onto the woman: it is not I who love this or that man, it is my wife who loves him; or, it is not I who am homosexual, but my wife (Strindberg). The husband may take a detour through his wife in search of indirect relationships with men; thus he is attracted to the kind of woman who has had or could have relationships with other men. For this reason, he may tolerate or even encourage his wife's relationships with other males. His homosexual proclivity may be the very reason for his seeking extramarital relationships, especially those, as with prostitutes or married women, which make it possible to establish indirect relationships with men.[3]

If a man's inner defenses against his own homosexuality are strong, a completely different picture emerges, for he will be especially touchy regarding even indirect relationships with other men. Even the slightest advances by other men toward his wife then seem unbearable. His own inward revolt against homosexuality can manifest itself as sharp aggression against his wife. These disparate possibilities can also exist side by side. For instance, the man may at first approve of his wife's relationships with other men and later persecute her with violent jealousy. Or he may suspiciously want his wife to avoid contact with men while using other women as a route to indirect relationships with males. The marital conflicts that can arise from a heightened degree of unconscious homosexuality will be intensified when the homosexuality is not simply a withdrawal of the libido from the opposite sex, but a flight from and a hostile rejection of it.

Putting everything together, we have to admit that while we can recognize strong unconscious homosexual orientations beforehand, even on the basis of a relatively brief analysis, we usually cannot make a prognosis for a marriage. Certain unfavorable outcomes have early warning signs — for example, we can judge a man as relatively unfit if his secret hostility to women is deep-seated, or if his hidden homosexuality attempts to assert itself neurotically by having relationships with other men through women.

We now come to consider the second of the three conditions required by marriage — namely, a positive attitude, beyond the sexual, toward the partner. To be sure, the emotional relationship in marriage is adversely affected by an unfavorable sexual adjustment, but the capacity for object-love can be further reduced when too much libido is bound to one's own ego. Such egocentricity can take the primitive form of masturbation and direct self-love, but it can also appear in a highly sublimated form such as we see in creative people, whose essential qualities include intense centering on the ego, or in hobbyists and businessmen, who are totally wrapped up in their activities. In determining psychological fitness for marriage, all these limitations boil down to one all-important criterion: how much object-friendliness can be mustered in spite of these deficiencies. In all these cases we are dealing with a restricted fitness, and the sustainability of the marriage depends largely on how willing and able the partner is to put up with the mate's limited ability to love.

One might think that everything we tend to summarize under the rather sensational term "gender hatred" will destroy the marital relationship, but, again, the outcome is difficult to predict in cases that do not show this phenomenon in a crass or overbearing form. No psychologist would dare to imagine that a Schopenhauer or a Weininger would have made a good husband if the "right woman" had come along. Our experiences show that even if it is disguised, such "hatred" can be strong enough to threaten the companionship between husband and wife in a serious way. Again, we are not discussing a kind of hatred that grows out of the disappointments and conflicts within marriage, but a preexisting disposition. If we trace this predisposition for gender hatred back to its development in childhood, we encounter two emotions above all: envy and fear of the opposite sex, with envy being more conscious than fear. In its deepest roots, gender envy is connected with the bisexuality of human beings and springs from the fact that we cannot really be content with our own gender role.[4]

This biological envy, as we might call it, evidently affects men no less than women,[5] although it has been better researched in women under the name "masculinity complex."[6] Biological envy brings in its wake all the emotions we usually encounter in envy — above all rivalry, resentment, and belittling. All things being equal, it appears that the less secure and at home one feels with one's own gender role, the greater one's biological envy. This kind of insecurity can be constitutionally determined, as in the case of a feminine man or a masculine woman; but it can also originate in purely psychological factors, such as impressions from early childhood that have created a lasting fear and horror of sexuality.

Depending on the origins of her masculinity complex, the resulting marital difficulties for a woman may manifest themselves in a rejection of the female role, in frigidity and menstrual disorders as well as an aversion to all functions that are considered female, or in a wish to be male. The latter leads to the adoption of masculine traits in outward appearance as well as in ways of thinking and feeling, and to an emphasis on everything that is considered specifically masculine, especially the will to lead and dominate. Questions of prestige and recognition will play a special role in the marriages of such women, which is a graphic illustration of Adler's theory of the importance of the need for validation. With respect to motherhood, women with a masculinity complex either reject it as too feminine or overemphasize it because they unconsciously equate it with masculinity. In the latter case, they may be able to love the husband because he fathers the child.[7]

In extreme cases of the masculinity complex, women are unfit for marriage and will often reject it of their own accord. However, a well sublimated masculinity complex that is not too severe seems not unfavorable for marriage, insofar as it can form the basis for good companionship. But even cases that are not extreme can be regarded as only partially suited for marriage because of the many serious possibilities for conflict.

In view of the preceding discussion, we must ask ourselves how many civilized people are actually well suited for marriage. Some degree of splitting in love life seems to be characteristic of people these days. The masculinity complex of women and the corresponding insecurity of men are certainly typical products of civilization, at least in educated circles; and it is clear to anyone who has at all comprehended these phenomena how tremendous a role is played in marital success or failure not only by conscious homosexuality but even more by its various unconscious manifestations. It seems that we cannot avoid the conclusion that today's cultivated human being has only a limited aptitude for marriage, a conclusion which the actual course of most marriages confirms.

It is possible, however, that this "aptitude" was never greater than it is today, and that in the past unfitness for marriage manifested itself less openly because the urge to get free was more strongly repressed by society. Here we must recall the difficulties created for contemporary marriage by women's increased self-reliance. We have seen that in many cases where the ability to love is stunted, a partnership is nevertheless conceivable if the partner adjusts to the limitation. When women were more dependent, they used to accept such limitations more easily. But they are less likely to do so today when they are asserting their own wishes and demands.

If we include the vast army of neurotics, the impression that aptitude for marriage is limited — at least among civilized people — is intensified. Our previous reflections did not apply to actual neurotics, but only to people with deviations in development who may not live up to a fictitious ideal but nevertheless represent variations within the range of normal psychology.

The question of the degree to which a neurosis renders a person unfit for marriage cannot be answered uniformly. Although it seems doubtful that marriage can cure a serious neurosis, we must consider, as Freud[8] and Sachs[9] have already emphasized, that marriage is the only sanctioned form of sexual gratification, and that it may after all bring about healing in cases of neurotic disorders that stem from insufficient sexual gratification or abstinence brought on by external causes. With regard to fitness for marriage, the prognosis is also good for neuroses that are reactions to recent traumatic experiences, as long as they are cleared up before marriage.

Experience tells us, however, that in the case of those who have more serious neuroses or a neurotic character resulting from disorders in their psychosexual development, the inevitable disturbances in their social and sexual adjustment will show up most agonizingly in marriage. As Freud has observed, one has to be quite healthy to be able to "digest" marriage. Experience has often shown that a person who was sane before marriage can contract a neurosis — or, more accurately, that marriage can make a hitherto latent neurosis manifest.

We now come to our third point: the ability to maintain a lasting commitment in marriage. Understand, to begin with, that no new problems are waiting to be introduced; rather, everything that diminishes the capacity to love or increases the potential for conflict also endangers the commitment. But, as we shall see, this is true only to a certain degree. Even with psychologically healthy people, the duration of a relationship cannot be predicted, for it is absolutely normal in the course of a marriage for new love objects to appear and exert an attraction. This happens not only because we do not limit our choice of love objects unambiguously to one person, and not only because old commitments can naturally loosen as further psychological development takes place, but also because marriage itself inevitably leads to disappointments and conflicts that drive us toward other objects.

In psychologically unstable people the divisive forces are certainly greater; living together is more difficult, and conflicts are less bearable. Yet we see again and again that such marriages can prove extremely resistant to a definitive break-up. The forces that produce commitment may spring from the same unconscious forces that cause the conflicts. As new relationships develop, the same deeply ingrained sense of restriction that makes the marriage difficult will prove effective at reducing the threat to the marital bond. Furthermore, we often see that people with neurotic tendencies in their love life instinctively choose partners with corresponding peculiarities. Such an interplay of complexes in no way guarantees a happy married life, yet it may well establish a tight structure. In the end, the inimical, escape-seeking tendencies may spark overcompensating reactions that forge an especially strong commitment to the partner. The interplay of such forces in marriage can no more be predicted than an equation with too many unknowns can be solved.

Some of the binding forces are more conscious than unconscious. They may take the form of an identification with the partner that grows out of some common interests within the marriage, such as children, household affairs, social and economic concerns, or similar spiritual attitudes. We must not overestimate the importance of these factors in and of themselves, for they are of value only as a foundation from which, in the most favorable cases, an identification can develop.

Since Freud's study of mass psychology[10] we have been well aware of the importance of identification for any kind of group formation, including that of two people in marriage. We know that identification reduces aggression against the person who is felt to be part of the group. But again, we cannot foretell under what circumstances and to what extent the identification will develop.

Summing up the few positive results of this analysis, we arrive at the following: in order to be able to judge psychological fitness for marriage, it is necessary to understand the psychosexual adjustment of the people in question. Such knowledge allows us to foresee the possibility — and only that — of this or that difficulty by looking at the nature and extent of certain deviations from the norm. This leads us to the conclusion that even the profound psychological insight we gain through psychoanalysis allows us only to guess, and to a very limited extent, the outlines of a future development. Even the growth of a single person cannot be foreseen, for while we can recognize existing instinctual tendencies, we cannot assess their quantitative proportions.[11] In addition, marriage involves the development of two individuals and their likely influence on each other.

This study represents only a first and rather incomplete attempt to achieve clarity with regard to psychological criteria of fitness for marriage, but when we consider the fundamental limits of prediction, we find little reason to hope that deeper and more exact insights into these correlations will enable us to foresee the fates of marriages.

Notes

1. Kretschmer, *Körperbau und Charakter.* Jung, *Psychologische Charaktertypen.*

2. On this subject, see Magnus Hirschfeld, *Die Homosexualität des Mannes und des Weibes,* Verlag Louis Marcus, 1914, and "Sind sexuelle Zwischenstufen zur Ehe geeignet?" *Jahrbuch für sexuelle Zwischenstufen* 3.

3. Cf. Boehm, "Beiträge zur Psychologie der Homosexualität." *Internationale Zeitschrift für Psychoanalyse,* 1920/21.

4. One thinks of the god images from the most diverse ancient cultures, which as visual expression of these longings bear the identifying traits of both sexes, and also of the old Greek myth of the human being as uniting both masculine and feminine from the beginning. See in this regard F. Giese, "Androgynenproblem," in *Handwörterbuch der Sexualwissenschaft,* 2d ed. (Bonn: Max Marcuse, 1926).

5. It is difficult to compare psychological quantities with one another, for they are more obviously subjective than is customary in science. But it seems to me that this secret envy is no slighter in males than in females, and that its appearance in females is stronger and more pronounced only because they have another envy on top of it, arising out of their factual disadvantages in real life (curtailed erotic freedom, narrowed possibilities for sublimation, and so forth).

6. Abraham, "Äußerungsformen des weiblichen Kastrationskomplexes," *Internationale Zeitschrift für Psychoanalyse,* 1921; Horney, "Zur Genese des weiblichen Kastrationskomplexes," *Internationale Zeitschrift für Psychoanalyse,* 1923.

7. See the representation of this situation in the volume of novellas by Unamuno, *Der Spiegel des Todes,* especially the novella "Zwei Mütter," Meyer & Jessen Verlag, Munich.

8. Sigmund Freud, "Die kulturelle Sexualmoral und die moderne Nervosität," *Gesammelte Schriften,* vol. 5.

9. Sachs, "Psychoanalytisches über den Umgang mit Menschen," lecture, 1925.

10. Freud, "Massenpsychologie und Ich-Analyse," *Gesammelte Schriften,* vol. 6.

11. "In other words, we wouldn't be able to predict the nature of the outcome from our knowledge of the preconditions" (Freud, "Über die Psychogenese eines Falls von weiblicher Homosexualität," *Gesammelte Schriften,* vol. 5).

3

On the Psychological Determinants of the Choice of a Marriage Partner (1927)

One of three essays that Horney contributed to *Die Ehe: Ihre Physiologie, Psychologie, Hygiene, und Eugenik — Ein Biologisches Ehebuch,* edited by Max Marcuse, this essay is published here in English translation for the first time. It was originally translated by Andrea Dlaska and was then revised by Christa Zorn. The final version of the translation is by Marian Price. I have made some editorial changes to reduce Horney's wordiness and to speed the flow of ideas. In some cases, I have incorporated material that was originally in footnotes into the text.

Even those who do not place much credence in the working of unconscious forces must recognize that without a knowledge of their unconscious motivations, we cannot understand why two people without the least thing in common have chosen each other. Indeed, no object choice is entirely the result of the partner's conscious decisions, not even when a marriage is based predominantly on social or economic motives.

As always when we pursue unconscious motivation diligently, we can trace the unconscious determinants of the choice of a certain partner all the way back to childhood, to those objects which were available to our earliest need for love—that is, to relationships with parents, brothers and sisters, playmates, and other people in our earliest environment.

Psychoanalytic experience has shown that sexuality does not have its onset at puberty but that signs of it appear in the first years of life. The sex life of a child does not differ in intensity from that of an adolescent or adult—that is, we do not begin with a smaller quantity that gradually increases until it breaks through in puberty. Rather, the early sex life is of a different quality.[1] A child can love and hate as passionately as an adult; we are just not used to taking the expressions of children's emotions seriously.

The principle of attraction to the opposite sex can be seen at work everywhere in nature, even when an actual physical union is out of the question. Therefore, a boy instinctively feels more strongly attracted to his mother, and a girl to her father. Because these first feelings of love include a desire for exclusiveness similar to the one we know from later love life, they give rise to a conflict which psychoanalysis calls the Oedipus complex. The term signifies above all a rivalry with the parent of the opposite sex. This whole complex of feelings is by its very nature doomed to failure, as it faces not only denial by the parents but also the deeply rooted prohibition of the conscience known as the incest taboo. In primitive peoples this prohibition is maintained by countless taboos and penalties.[2]

The normal outcome of the Oedipus complex is that the sensual side of the child's feeling is suppressed, so that it becomes unconscious, while the emotional side continues to be directed toward the desired parent in the form of trust, attachment, and affection. During puberty, these bonds should gradually be loosened until the adolescent's entire devotion can be transferred to another object outside the family—someone who fulfills the demands of the conscious ego and is therefore "ego-appropriate."

The mere fact that there is a developmental connection between early childhood experiences and later object choices might seem of little interest now that certain fundamentals of Freud's discoveries are becoming common knowledge; but the pathways leading from childhood attachment to the adult's love choice are so diverse and so obscure that a mapping of the main routes is needed in order to comprehend the forces at work here.

Only in comparatively few cases is the connection between childhood attachment and object choice plainly visible. Take, for instance, a young girl who used to hang on her father with infatuation and now marries a man thirty years older who is strikingly similar to her father in body and character, right down to his courtesy and wit. If her marriage never progresses far beyond father-daughter affection, it is quite obvious that the husband has directly taken the father's place. Much more disconcerting are those cases in which the father was feared rather than loved — perhaps he was an inconsiderate, brutal drunkard — but the girl still chooses a husband after his image. Although the unconscious compulsion is more starkly visible in this second case, the underlying pathway is the same in both instances.

What is essential about these cases is that the psychological work of inward detachment from family bonds, which should be completed in puberty, has been only superficially accomplished. The unconscious libidinous attachment to either father or mother remains and is transferred almost unmodified — and usually with the same limitations that underlie a parent-child relationship — to an object of the greatest possible similarity. Often, much later, when either death or the person's own development forces a letting go of the partner chosen in this way, a sexual crisis occurs which can only be interpreted as a kind of belated puberty. Up to this point, such persons take pains to be absolutely faithful to their partners; the fixation is so strong that they lack even the impulse to be unfaithful.

Slight shifts in the intensity of the oedipal attachment can create completely different outcomes in later love life. If, for instance, the attachment to father or mother is only a little stronger, it may be virtually impossible to transfer the love to another object. The result is a general reserve toward the opposite sex, and marriage is hardly within the realm of possibility. If, on the other hand, the bond to the opposite-sex parent is a little weaker, the feelings can be transferred to another person, but they will not last. Rather, they will cool off easily and jump to other objects, with whom the same game is then repeated. The fact that the inability to be faithful or the inability to be unfaithful both originate in the same stage of psychosexual development indicates that they are not innate but acquired characteristics.

In the majority of cases, the connection between childhood attachment and object choice is less plainly visible, but it exists nonetheless. From the child's point of view, there are two main factors that are characteristic of father and mother: the age difference and the bond between the two parents which renders them unattainable. It does not come as a surprise that the unconscious motives that enter into object choice are often related to these factors. We become aware of the secret inner compulsion that determines the choice of a partner only if it seems to work against the chooser's happiness and if it repeats itself, as when a man repeatedly falls in love with much older women or a woman with men who are already married. We habitually hold "fate" responsible for our falling in love, but from a psychological perspective, "fate" is a projection of unconscious forces within ourselves. As Wallerstein says, "In your breast are your fate's stars." If we think we are in love in spite of a powerful reason for which we should not be, that very reason is the decisive unconscious motive in service of which we are compelled to desire the other person.

A theoretical knowledge of the connection between early parent-child relations and later object choices does not guarantee an understanding of the individual case. For one thing, the unconscious forces that condition our choices in love hardly ever work in isolation, and it is often difficult to determine which force is at work. If a man falls in love with a woman who is already committed to another, it may be because of his rivalry with the man. This motive can be peripheral, or it can be so powerful that the personality of the woman is of only secondary importance. The lover may even lose interest in her altogether once the aim of defeating his rival has been attained. Freud called this precondition for love that of the "injured third party" and attributed it to a particularly strong rivalry toward the father.

Another complication is that unconscious impulses do not necessarily take a direct route to fulfillment; repression can cause all kinds of bends in the road. Some people have such a strong taboo against competing for love that they give up at the mere thought that the person in whom they are interested may have a relation with someone else. One patient even told me that she did not want to attach a man to herself because she might thereby deprive some other woman of the possibility of marrying him. In cases like this, every move toward a person of the opposite sex, however innocuous, is experienced as the initiation of a forbidden rivalry. This makes a real, active "choice" of a partner virtually impossible. Understandably, passive people with such inhibitions hardly ever marry, and then mainly when they are chosen by someone who is determined to have them. A retreat from rivalry is frequently conditioned by a person's relations with siblings, those first rivals for the parents' love. The retreat can often be traced to a pronounced jealousy of a particular brother or sister.

Like rivalry, other impulses for choosing a partner that originate in childhood can turn into their opposites and thus become unrecognizable. For instance, one might choose a partner who is in no way reminiscent of the parents but, on the contrary, represents their exact opposite in race, character, social standing, or intellectual level. To avoid the two most typical qualities of parents, a man may consider only very young, never-attached girls as object choices. As so frequently happens, if the male loves an older woman early in life but later behaves just the opposite and marries a very young girl, this change of preference is not to be understood by rational considerations alone;

rather, it corresponds to a gradually increasing repression of his original bond with his mother — or even, in some instances, an untying of that original bond.

The preference for the virgo intacta can be seen as a product of what we call ideal formation [*Idealbildung*]. The male is seeking not the likeness of his real mother, but rather — to use Spitteler's brilliant coinage — that of her "imago," which he has created in his imagination in an effort at wish-fulfillment. We see this process of idealizing the parents already at work in childhood, when out of an apparently deeply rooted need all kinds of perfections are attributed to them. Most typical of these perfections is the idea of their sexual "purity," to which children often cling in spite of personal observations to the contrary. Even when children accept the facts of life in general, they often insist that their parents are exceptions to the rule. When we consider the great cultural importance that the ideal of the virgin mother has for men (the cult of the Madonna!), we can understand its significance for their choice of a partner, especially since this ideal is reinforced and supported by conscious social attitudes.

The requirement of sexual purity is only a special instance of the idealization of infantile love objects, for the process of idealization is integral to the partner choices of "normal" people. Indeed, fortunate object choices will always prove to be determined by a mixing of the real and idealized features of the first love objects. The process of ideal formation is as strictly determined as are all psychological events. Ideal formation addresses above all those qualities of the parents that have caused the child suffering or deprivation. These qualities are reformed according to the child's wishes, and in this way the path is opened for the old objects to be made acceptable to the conscious ego.

If the old ideal expectations remain alive and unchanged, the resulting exaggerated demands can become a serious obstacle to any choice of partner, for it will be impossible to find any real partner who can live up to the fantasy image. Dynamically, such inflated expectations can become a means of actually holding on to the old attachments. If the person does marry, however, the marriage can be the result only of an enormous sexual overestimation, by means of which the desired characteristics are projected onto the object. In extreme cases, the true nature of the object plays no role at all; the object needs only the ability to become the momentary carrier of certain illusions.

The lines which lead from childhood to a choice of partner are obscured, then, by the mechanisms of repression, conversion into their opposites, and ideal formation. They can be complicated even further by any deviations from a "normal" psychosexual development. To understand these aberrations, we have to bear in mind that the parent-child relationship, insofar as it is rooted in the instinctual life, represents a conflict which — like any other conflict — can lead to different outcomes. There are three main possibilities for abnormal development: limitations on the ability to transfer the feelings originally attached to the parent, a relaxation of the pull toward the opposite sex, and a withdrawal of love from all objects other than the self.

In the first outcome, the original object can be retained, but the later transfer of feelings to other persons is subject to limitations, the most important of which is a splitting in the love life, an inability to concentrate all one's feelings of love on one person. In my essay "Psychological Fitness and Unfitness for Marriage," I explained that a man with a split love life usually chooses a wife who matches the idealized image of his mother and then looks for physical sexual gratification outside the marriage. Here I must make an additional point. Many times a man marries a woman with whom he originally had a merely sexual relationship or who has a markedly bad reputation, or at least the hint of one. The agent at work here is an impulse that also originates in childhood, namely, the desire to "save" the woman[3]—an impulse which is usually so deeply rooted in the imagination that the man cannot see the woman as she actually is. Most marriages entered into on this basis quickly end in catastrophe.

A second limitation on the ability to transfer love for the parent to other persons consists in holding on to the conditions that love be secret and that it be forbidden. When these conditions are met, love may well be transferred to a later object, but there is an often insurmountable fear of legitimacy in a relationship. Indeed, if legitimacy is forced, the relationship will scarcely be tolerable. Frequently, when a man who requires secrecy and prohibition marries, his wife loses her allure as soon as the vows are spoken. To our conscious thinking, the certainty of possession might seem to be responsible for his abrupt loss of interest after marriage, but this does not explain why the sudden drastic reversal from attraction to indifference takes place only in some cases.

When we trace the unconscious processes in such cases, we see that the love life of these people is subject to a certain extent to the incest taboo, which is not very strictly administered, inasmuch as it grants one permit—the Secret and Not-Official License. This circumvention of the incest taboo finds a parallel in the way the state tacitly tolerates illegal arrangements, such as prostitution, as long as they do not come to the fore and claim to be publicly sanctioned. The need for secrecy as a way of avoiding the incest taboo helps us understand why many people fear marriage and why their rational explanations for avoiding marriage, such as fear of responsibility or fear of being hindered in their careers, are so unshakable.

A second abnormal development resulting from conflicts in infantile love life is even more serious in its effects, because it does not stop at limiting the choice of a partner but leads to a fundamental weakening of the relationship to the opposite sex. In normal development, a girl grows into the role of the mother, at first in play and then in a more serious desire to have a child and a husband herself. In cases where her sexuality has reoriented itself, however, we can observe that from early in life the little girl fervently wishes to be a boy. Such wishes are frequently expressed and do not signify much in themselves, since they can in part be explained by the real disadvantages of girls by comparison with boys. Insofar as these desires represent true instinctual demands, they can be worked out later on by means of sublimation. But they can also signify the onset of an inner conversion, the meaning of which is that the girl no longer simply loves the father but also wants to be like him. Given her identification with the male role, she will later be looking primarily for a comrade whose interests she shares.

Turning away from her own differently constructed being toward a masculine model has serious consequences for the girl's further love life, for it creates an uncertainty about herself and her gender role. Her inner insecurity can decisively affect object choice by creating, as a reaction, a heightened need for admiration, superiority, recognition, or confirmation of her sexual attractiveness. Thus, she will look for a partner who is inferior in some respects — economically dependent, intellectually inferior, less energetic, or in greater need of nurturing — or who has other qualities that will strengthen her self-confidence, such as being important, highly respected, or much sought after. The significance of sex-role uncertainty is confirmed by the fact that as accurate an observer as Alfred Adler made insecurity and the consequent craving for admiration the key issue in his psychological system. However, he went astray in regarding insecurity as something elemental, rather than as something that needed to be further analyzed.

Another symptom resulting from the reorientation sketched above may be the girl's identification with the male's object choice as well as with the male, a change that results in homosexuality. Sometimes a person so reoriented continues to choose persons of the opposite sex as objects of love, but because of powerful unconscious homosexual tendencies a woman seeks a man with the features of the mother-imago, as a man with homosexual tendencies may seek a woman with the traits of the father-imago. The details of these choices are determined, of course, by the individual circumstances.

The object choices I have been describing all occur under the pressure of partial tendencies, that is, tendencies that are contradicted by the overall ego or at any rate are not supported by it. We often say that such choices lack the proper "certainty of instinct," and we are inclined to view certainty of instinct as a special talent that a person is either given or not given by nature. On the basis of the interrelations outlined above between early love relationships, sexual orientation, and object choice, we can try to formulate a more accurate definition of instinctual certainty. Such a definition must include the ability to make a choice with the type of unerringness that is unique to the unconscious — a choice that reflects the essence of our being, that not only gratifies most of our conscious and unconscious instinctual demands but can also be affirmed by our conscious thinking and our ideal conceptions. Certainty of instinct must be missing when specific fixations during psychosexual development give rise to isolated, rigid conditions for love, and to desires and inhibitions that are detrimental to the whole personality.

Finally, a third result of infantile conflicts may be the withdrawal of feelings of love from objects altogether and the constitution of one's own ego as the center of attraction. It is beyond the scope of this essay to discuss the theoretical foundations of this development and its various possibilities in detail, but I should observe that in these cases, as in the preceding ones, choice of partner is determined by infantile object attachments and what becomes of them, and that more than one factor is involved. The main determinants are not to be found in the nature of the partner but in how well the partner is suited to serve the person's egoistic tendencies. To a man whose ego has become the center of his love feelings, a woman's social status, her connections, her managerial skills, or her wealth are more decisive than her human or erotic qualities.

It is easily assumed that "marriages of convenience," of which I have just given one example, are built on too slight a foundation to sustain so complicated and personal a relationship, yet such marriages often prove to be stronger than real love matches. We need to keep in mind that the two kinds of marriages are not such absolute opposites as they appear, since in marriages of convenience there is also a transfer of old emotional attitudes to the partner. In these cases, the transfer follows rather than precedes the object choice. While there may be less passion, there is also less acrimony, so that the marriages are actually less vulnerable to the most serious blows. But it must be acknowledged that people who marry for convenience by their own choice are severely handicapped in their capacity for object love. As a result, the personal relationship to the spouse simply is not as overwhelmingly important for them as it is for people whose love life has developed more harmoniously.

In reviewing the psychological factors that determine partner choice, we may be left with the impression that too much weight has been given to the unconscious transfer of emotions and not enough to accidental influences and needs. How else can we explain, for instance, that a man can successively or simultaneously love women of totally opposite characters? For an accurate evaluation of the problem of multiple love choice, we have to distinguish between the various possibilities.

First of all, we have the Don Juan type who is unconsciously fixated on a specific childhood object and is basically looking for this one object. It is easy to understand that during his search he comes across all kinds of women, none of whom is the one he is actually looking for.

Furthermore, there are people who hold on to rigid, isolated conditions for love, such as the need to be controlled or the wish to rescue. In all such cases, entirely different objects can serve, as long as they fulfill the one main condition.[4] Finally, we have that large group whose relationship to the opposite sex is uncertain at best. Decisive for their choice are factors like the injured third party, prestige, or an increase in power or possessions. Here, too, none of the demands are tied to the unique character of one person.

All these categories have one thing in common—namely, that the choice registers only certain qualities of the partner, which are either so narrowly formulated or of such a general nature (the most general being simply the partner's gender identity) that they completely bypass what is essential in the other person. In these cases, there is no inner necessity to hold on to one particular object; on the contrary, one partner can easily be exchanged for another.

People with a less inhibited development can concentrate their total libido on one object and, therefore, can appreciate to a larger extent— consciously or instinctively—the uniqueness of the other personality. The chance for a lasting relationship with the partner is much greater in such cases, although even here it is doubtful that just one choice is possible. Analysis seems to suggest a psychological determination of partner choice, but it does not show that a person's psychosexual development has necessarily to lead to a particular partner or to one very similar to him. This could be owing to the fact that even the deepest analysis cannot give us total insight into the dynamics of the forces at work. But our imperfect insight may be less to blame than the polymorphic nature of early impressions and the later conversions through which they are diffused, like a ray by a prism.

The multiplicity of factors involved makes possible different paths of fulfillment in love life—especially for those who are not rigidly bound to specific conditions. That is why Goethe was able to love two women as different as Charlotte von Stein and Christina Vulpius, choices that can both be readily explained by reference to his childhood development. But the concept of two people being "made for each other" may prove to be an illusion that we refuse to have destroyed because of its practical value.

Notes

1. Freud, "Drei Abhandlungen zur Sexualtheorie," *Gesammelte Schriften,* vol. 5.

2. Freud, "Totem und Tabu," *Gesammelte Schriften,* vol. 10.

3. Freud, "Zur Psychologie des Liebeslebens," *Gesammelte Schriften,* vol. 5.

4. Especially among neurotics, one encounters the strangest qualities functioning as the main condition — such as, for example, physical defects, a certain posture, and so forth. See Freud, "Geschichte einer infantilen Neurose," *Gesammelte Schriften,* vol. 6.

4

On the Psychological Roots of
Some Typical Conflicts in Marriage (1927)

One of three essays that Horney contributed to *Die Ehe: Ihre Physiologie, Psychologie, Hygiene, und Eugenik — Ein Biologisches Ehebuch,* edited by Max Marcuse, this essay is published here in English translation for the first time. It was originally translated by Andrea Dlaska and was then revised by Christa Zorn. The final version of the translation is by Marian Price. I have made some editorial changes to reduce Horney's wordiness and to speed the flow of ideas. In some cases, I have incorporated material that was originally in footnotes into the text.

Marriage forges bonds which have always led to conflicts between the personalities so bound. If the intensity and extent of the conflicts make married life unbearable, one tends to say that the two people are "incompatible." This expression originates in the belief that the individual characteristics of two people have to "harmonize" or "complement each other." Studies of marital conflict that proceed from this premise are bound to be unprofitable, for it can be easily observed that people of like character can have either happy or unhappy marriages and that a contrast in natures is neither a good nor a bad predictor of marital success. Even the qualities of tolerance and adaptability, which in other group situations help guarantee cohesiveness, cannot prevent failure in marriage. In this study, therefore, we shall set aside differences in disposition, as well as cultural or economic causes of marital conflict. Instead, we shall investigate those aspects of marital relations which can be established in all cases and for all times.

There is only one feature that all kinds of marriage have in common: namely, the sexual component of the partnership. This is where we must begin our investigation into the origin of typical conflicts, although we must remember that, as Georg Simmel has pointed out, sexuality is never the sole factor determining the nature of a marriage.[1]

The psychological factors that cause sexual problems in marriage include those which lead to the rejection of the partner, such as disappointments or antagonistic feelings of any origin, and those which cause attraction to other objects, such as curiosity about other people's sexual behavior or the narcissistic need to confirm one's own sex appeal. In addition, we must remember Freud's premise that direct sexual desires sooner or later take second place to aim-inhibited feelings.[2] Moreover, fulfillment of physical (genital) sexual desire—above all, easily available, constant fulfillment—diminishes sexual excitement.

Although easy availability is such a handy, seemingly self-evident reason for the decrease in sexual excitement, several considerations warn us not to take it as the only one. Masturbation, for instance, offers the same regular and easily available genital gratification, yet people don't tire of it. Furthermore, decrease in excitement is dependent on so many diverse psychological influences that it is difficult to assess just how important the factor of easy fulfillment is.

Direct sexual desire can metamorphose into aim-inhibited eroticism in the forms of tenderness, nurturance, and clinging devotion. How much of the libido continues to be directed toward the partner in these forms is of decisive importance to the fate of the marriage. The transformed libido can also be sublimated into some kind of work, directed toward other love objects, or repressed in some way. Although I have separated these three kinds of transformation here, they occur in all imaginable combinations and can provide the foundation for a variety of conflicts.

The sublimation of libido in work or a hobby does not produce conflicts by itself, but its tendency to drain energy from the marriage can provide a theater for the play of other conflicts, which may be more or less unconscious rather than overt. Let us consider, for example, the husband who lives in a "happy marriage" but who harms or destroys his wife through a failure at work, or who devotes far more time than necessary to his work in order to avoid his wife and the problems of marriage. As a result, the problems are not confronted but are merely covered up. This process may lessen their destructive effects in some cases, however.

As we know, the ability to sublimate has its individually determined and usually very narrow boundaries; the amount of libido not tied up in this way will involuntarily and automatically strive for direct physical satisfaction by turning to other objects. In the face of this simple fact it seems unnecessary to raise the old debate about a "polygamous disposition," especially as we can be even less sure about dispositions than about developments that play themselves out before our eyes.[3]

Is it better for the continued existence and happiness of the marriage if polygamous desires are suppressed, or if they are yielded to? This question would leave a philosopher of ethics less at a loss than it does the unbiased psychological observer, who sees its fatal resemblance to the choice between Scylla and Charybdis. Like the related question of the value of asceticism, this question can be answered only for the individual case and only with reservations. Our task is limited to showing what conflicts may actually arise from various kinds of behavior.

If one partner turns to a new object, there is the danger not only that the greater intensity of the new attachment will wreck the marriage but also that it will mobilize in the partner the most dangerous and inexhaustible well of hatred: jealousy. Originating in the depths of our dark archaic instincts but often legitimized and sanctioned by law and custom, jealousy can make an already difficult situation unbearable. Being the object of jealousy can drive the straying partner further out of the marriage and waken vengeful impulses to reveal the new relationship with the secret or open intention of wounding the jealous partner. Although such impulses readily hide behind the duty to be truthful and aboveboard, they are no less hurtful than open revenge.

The same basic danger, the activation of hatred, also exists when extramarital desires are suppressed. In his most recent work, Sadger has demonstrated that even as the first feelings of love in a child arise in conjunction with the gratifications received while being cared for, so also the first feelings of hatred are directed at the caregivers, for they can thwart the child's wishes.[4] In a similar way, the marriage partner can also awaken feelings of hatred because, although he provides a certain amount of satisfaction, he stands in the way of other possibilities of gratification, by demanding fidelity, for example. Hatred will be directed against the partner, even if the demand for fidelity comes not from him but from one's own personal ideals. Feelings of hatred need not be directly expressed through irascibility or accusations; they can also take roundabout forms — such as mistrust, for instance, if a suppressed desire to be unfaithful is projected onto the partner.

If suppressed desire is the underlying cause of hatred, it is often hard to detect, because as a rule it remains unconscious and comes to light only in the actual pain it inflicts on the spouse. Matters become even more complicated because the repressed libido is easily forced into regressive paths, that is, into areas of interest appropriate to an earlier stage of sexual development, such as the oral or anal stage. These are then charged with new meaning, not only in the direct form of overemphasis on eating and digestion, but also in the subli- mated form of overemphasis on household or money matters. Often enough the secret enmity takes a detour; the husband will berate the wife about money while she will nag him about household chores. Such hostility readily asserts itself since regression of the libido lessens the ability to love, thus unleashing destructive forces that are otherwise restrained.[5] These regressive tendencies can easily lead to the formation of neurotic symptoms which are often pointed like a weapon against the partner and can wound more deeply than any open expression of hostility ever could.[6]

Just as frequently as it leads to regressions, the repression of heterosexual drives results in the revival of homosexual tendencies. As Freud rightly ob- serves, everyone's libido oscillates throughout life between heterosexual and homosexual objects. With married people, the intensification of same-sex friendships, which in and of itself is a normal and culturally meaningful course of events, can be placed in the service of antagonistic feelings, as Strindberg has so strikingly described.

The only form of libido transformation that has a positive value for mar- riage is the conversion into affection, which guarantees the stability and happi- ness of the relationship. The extent to which this can happen is dependent on a person's total psychosexual development. It is restricted, moreover, by all of the hostile impulses that arise in marriage.

In addition to the sources of sexual disinclination already enumerated, an- other one originates in the feeling of obligation that accompanies marriage. Many people, observing that human nature does not tolerate constraint very well, have invoked this feeling as an explanation for marital conflict. But this generalization is not very satisfying, for we see that in many situations people not only tolerate the feeling of being obliged but actively seek it, as long as they do not consider themselves to be the victims of despotism and tyranny.

What has seduced people, in spite of their knowledge that feelings cannot be forced, into believing that the situation is different in marriage? I have found that the commandment to love your partner is experienced in the unconscious as a repetition of the Fourth Commandment, which is to honor your father and mother. We know that this commandment is the only one the lawgiver found it necessary to connect with a reward, obviously aware that he was requiring something with which it was hard to comply.[7] We also know that in early childhood everyone inevitably gets into a secret or open conflict with this commandment and that long after the conflict has disappeared from consciousness, it leaves its imprint on the character. Analyses of married couples show us with great regularity that when the old commandment is remobilized, so is the old resistance against it. As if under a compulsion to repeat, the partners transfer to each other, along with love, the old demands, reproaches, jealousy, and mistrust that they felt toward their parents.

It seems, then, that there are forces at work within marriage that cannot be explained by either the behavior of the partners or any of the details of their current situation. We see persistent jealousy, for whose intensity we find no explanation in the behavior of the other; or reproaches and accusations whose actual basis is incommensurate with their severity; or antagonism and desires for revenge that do not seem to have been produced by the conflicts we can observe. In short, we find emotions that are not entirely produced within the marriage itself but which obviously have their origins elsewhere.

It is not only the duty to love, with its overtones of the Fourth Commandment, that puts the partner into a parental role as far as the unconscious is concerned. We also see extraordinarily often how the parents' relationship is reenacted in the children's marriage, not merely as a good or bad example on a conscious level, but much more strongly as an unconscious identification. Thus, the wife may inadvertently adopt and turn upon her husband certain reactions of her mother that she had severely criticized as a child. Convinced that her image of her husband is realistic, she may project onto him traits of her father that she cherished, dreaded, or hated. There may be a double distortion of reality, insofar as these traits are not necessarily characteristics of the real father but belong to a memory-picture (imago) that has been idealized or debased by fantasy. Jung has presented us with several especially instructive examples of the way in which, as if under a magic spell, children faithfully reexperience their parents' conflicts in their own marriages.[8]

However, such a high degree of aftereffect occurs only in people who still have a strong bond with their parents at the time of their marriage. The more a person succeeds in breaking free of parents, the less compelling and disturbing are the old impressions, which are then worked through in a more ego-adequate way—that is, they become better adapted to the demands of the conscious ego and of reality. Neurotic marriages are distinguished from so-called normal ones by the power and extent of the influence of childhood impressions. But there are aftereffects of childhood in all marriages; indeed, the choice of a partner is decisively conditioned by the father or mother imago, as I have attempted to show elsewhere ["On the Psychological Determinants of the Choice of a Marriage Partner"].

Not only does the choice of a partner have obvious origins in the depths of infantile wishes, so does the inner impetus to marry — that "natural desire" for a wife (or husband) and child. By the same token, the dread of marriage springs far more from an inhibition regarding these infantile desires than is suggested by the rational explanations given for it. Presumably marriage owes its imperviousness to all historical vicissitudes to the anchoring of the desire to wed in these instinctive depths. This insight should make us skeptical of any prophesies about the imminent dissolution of marriage owing to impending social upheavals.

We can now better answer the question that Keyserling has recently raised anew: What is it that prompts people to get married in spite of the frequency of marital unhappiness through the ages and of the bondage rather than satisfaction it brings to the individual from the standpoint of self-interest? Apparently the deepest driving forces are not at all conscious but are rather unconscious, unreal, and as it were irrational expectations of happiness. They assert themselves in spite of all experience and reflection, not only because they are fed by the strongest instinctual forces, but also for the very simple reason that they — like all truly unconscious wishes — are not open to correction by experience and reflection.

Because of their unreal nature, these wishes cannot be fulfilled and therefore unavoidably carry within them the germ of disappointment. One may object here that not every marriage ends in disappointment. No, but it invariably begins with it. Indeed, disappointments of some sort arise in the best marriages at the outset, even if they crop up only briefly and are soon overcome. To the conscious mind they are linked to certain characteristics or behaviors of the partner or to difficulties in the outward situation (household, personnel, lodgings, and so forth). Their irrational origins become obvious when reactions are far out of proportion to the perceived cause or when the disappointments are stubbornly denied, while an ideal image of the partner is retained in consciousness. Cases of the latter kind, which are not infrequent and are obviously within the range of what is considered "normal," show quite clearly that we are dealing not simply with the disillusionment that comes after being in love but with the unfulfilled instinctual demands of the unconscious.

These demands cannot be fulfilled for two reasons: first, our expectations of happiness originate in an early childhood fantasy of our parents' happiness in love. Even if that happiness was practically nonexistent, it still appears fantastically magnified in the unconscious memory, in part because the thinking of this early time was not subject to a reality check and in part because the pleasures from which we are excluded are always exaggerated in our imagination. The second reason these infantile desires cannot be fulfilled is that they are attached to very specific persons. Although a healthy detachment from the parents makes it possible to transfer these desires to other people, there still remains — and probably always will — a certain noticeable difference between the actual object and the sought-after imago modeled upon a parent. The tension resulting from this discrepancy can work in favor of the partner, but it can also create a strong impulse to look for other love objects, either out of a deceptive hope of finding the ideal imago after all (via serial affairs in the manner of Don Juan) or because different people may embody different traits of the imago and therefore exert an attraction. One of the reasons second marriages are often more solid than first ones is that infantile expectations are not carried into them with untamed force but have faded through contact with reality, thereby lessening the possibilities for disappointment.

The stability of monogamous relationships is threatened from another side as well. Insofar as the partner plays the role of the parent for the unconscious, the incest taboo with all its feelings of guilt and fears of punishment may act as a moral authority, blocking the way to the partner. So in many cases what we see is not a simple lack of interest in having sex with the spouse, which could be explained as just a natural drop in sexual excitement, but pronounced inhibitions. These inhibitions manifest themselves as frigidity in the wife, especially toward her husband, and as a split in the husband's love life, which makes it impossible for him to feel desire for his lawful partner.

The resulting picture is a strange one: in marriage individuals with their need for love get caught in a crossfire between the disappointment of too little and the guilt of too much fulfillment. To understand this conflict, we must recognize that we are dealing with two currents, both unconscious, but stemming from very different levels of the psyche. On one side are the demands of the elementary infantile instincts that crave a union with the parent of the opposite sex, and on the other side is a moral authority forbidding the fulfillment of these very demands. The forbidding forces are the same that lead to the incest taboo, both in the childhood of the individual and the history of mankind.

As the old conflicts repeat themselves automatically, so do the old attempts to solve them. Different as they may be in detail, the solutions have one thing in common: sexual desire is withdrawn from the forbidden object. The transformation of sexuality in marriage into an affectionate relationship, as well as sublimation and repression, obviously correspond to the processes that led the way out of the oedipal complex in childhood. These processes repeat themselves in all their details. We have also observed how the less favorable outcomes of the complex, such as homosexual tendencies or uncertain gender roles in later love life, can lead to specific problems, such as the struggle between the sexes for validation and power. It is beyond the bounds of this study to describe these problems in detail. In spite of their frequency, they are determined by individual circumstances and cannot claim the same universality as the basic processes I have described.

We can sum up by saying that the fact of diminishing sexual desire in marriage seems first of all a direct and immediate result of satisfaction and the release of sexual tension. However, the extent and rapidity of this process depend on the degree to which infantile conflicts repeat themselves in regard to the partner — in other words, they depend on the degree of detachment from those first love bonds.

If one wants to speak of the "fundamental tragedy"[9] of marriage, one can see that, in its deep unconscious foundations, the strongest impulses to marry flow from the very same sources that give rise to the conflicts that are capable of destroying the relationship. Here also are the roots of the strange phenomenon that love matches are such a poor guarantee of a long and happy marriage, for passion and falling in love are always fed by these instinctual sources. The greater their share in a marriage, the more it is subject to the conflicts I have described. A marriage that is based mainly on other than personal factors, such as arrangement by the families, social duties, or economic considerations, is also held together by these factors. Although basic conflicts cannot be avoided altogether, these binding forces can exert an ameliorating influence. In conclusion, the seemingly unsolvable problems in modern marriage are probably no greater than those in marriages of former times. They merely attract more attention in an era of increasing individualism in which first men and then women have been trying to free themselves from the shackles of family and society.

Notes

1. "Whatever marriage may be, it is always and everywhere more than sexual intercourse; however divergent the directions might be in which the marriage moves outward from the sexual relation, the fact that marriage does go beyond the sexual is what makes it marriage in the first place. Sociologically, this is an almost unique phenomenon: the very point which alone is common to all forms of marriage is at the same time exactly the point beyond which marriage must go, in order to produce a marriage."

2. [Sigmund Freud], "Massenpsychologie und Ich-Analyse," *Gesammelte Schriften,* vol. 6.

3. The impossibility of proving the hypothesis that males are more polygamous by nature leaves the impression that such hypotheses are less a striving after scientific clarity than an attempt to assure the male a special right to be polygamous and to create a justification for such behavior.

4. [Sadger], "Sadomasochismus," *Internationale Zeitschrift für Psychoanalyse* 3 (1926).

5. See Freud, "Jenseits des Lustprinzips," *Gesammelte Schriften,* vol. 6.

6. This is only one of the many ways in which marital conflicts can lead to neurosis. To analyze them all in detail would require a separate study.

7. [Sandor] Rado, "Das vierte Gebot," *Imago* no. 1 (1923).

8. C. G. Jung, "Die Bedeutung des Vaters für das Schicksal des Einzelnen," *Jahrbücher für Psychoanalyse* 1.

9. Keyserling, *Ehebuch.*

5

Berlin Lectures on Feminine Psychology (1932)

Among Harold Kelman's papers at the Postgraduate Center for Mental Health were two lectures in German, headed "Weitre Fragen der Weiblichen Psychologie" ("Further Questions of Feminine Psychology") and "3. Kursstunde" ("3d Lesson"). "Weitre Fragen" included the information that it was a lecture given on 24 February 1932 at the Berlin Psychoanalytic Institute. I have renamed them "On the Manifestations of Repressed Female Homosexuality" and "Behavioral Patterns of Repressed Homosexual Women," respectively, titles that more clearly describe the topics of the lectures. "Manifestations" was apparently the first lecture in a course and "Behavioral Patterns" the third. We have no record of the second lecture, nor any way of knowing how many there were altogether. The two lectures were evidently part of the same series, for "Behavioral Patterns" develops the case of "Anna," which was introduced in "Manifestations."

These lectures may well have been from the last course Horney taught at the

Berlin Psychoanalytic Institute, because she left for the United States in September of 1932. They are the first in a series of discussions of female homosexuality in which Horney engaged between 1932 and 1934. She dealt with the topic again in her lectures in Chicago in 1933, in "The Denial of the Vagina" (1933), and in "Personality Changes in Female Adolescents" (1935), which had first been delivered as a paper in 1934.

Both lectures have been translated by Andrea Dlaska and revised by Christa Zorn. They seem to be stenographic transcriptions, for they display numerous characteristics that would not have been present had Horney written them in advance: loose organization, some irrelevant material, and often incomplete expression or development of Horney's ideas. I have tried to improve the readability of the lectures through judicious editing, but their extemporaneous character will still be evident.

On the Manifestations of Repressed Female Homosexuality

I should like to begin by saying that for this lecture I take for granted a profound knowledge of Freud's work, for I believe that only those who are familiar with the fundamentals can profit from my presentations. Those of you who meet this criterion have probably read Freud's latest work on female sexuality [Freud 1931]. To my mind, this work is extremely valuable because here for the first time Freud emphasizes the immense importance of the mother for female psychology. Although my conclusion is quite different from Freud's, I believe that female psychology cannot be understood without a detailed analysis of the mother-daughter relationship.

I return today to the topic of my last lesson in the summer, when I spoke on the subject of "female homosexuality and its effects." Since my limited experience with manifest female homosexuality does not allow me to say much about it, the best title for this lecture might be "On the Manifestations of Repressed Female Homosexuality." I believe that my observations will have practical value, for such manifestations are easily overlooked in analysis.

I should like to begin with a few perhaps indiscrete revelations. Male colleagues have often asked for my advice when they got stuck with female analysands, and sometimes I have taken over the analysis of a woman patient from a male colleague. These cases have given me insight into the typical difficulties male analysts have with female patients, since certain patterns have kept repeating themselves, especially with respect to the transference. I also saw that particular aspects of the transference situation had been overlooked or slightly misinterpreted.

Quite often, the transference toward the male analyst had the symptoms of a passionate father-transference, including all the signs of strong desire, such as vehement longing for proofs of love or excessive manifestations of jealousy toward real and imaginary women, who were sometimes simply ignored as obstacles. There were also extreme hate reactions in cases in which the attachment to the analyst was being denied. Although these reactions could take various forms, the ones most often encountered were prostitution fantasies and, in one case, a real attempt at prostitution.

When I consulted the history of these patients, it became obvious that most of them had indeed had a pronounced love for the father, which was often connected with certain conflicts. I was ready to conclude that in the transference, this old relationship recurred basically unchanged, but, as I am going to show, my conclusion was only partially correct. Sometimes the analysis got caught up in transference struggles that took up the whole time. Although I found the real problem to lie elsewhere, some of the patients seemed to be like the women Freud described who had such an intense and passionate temperament that they could be contented only with real gratification. Naturally, my male colleagues felt uneasy in these situations, and many of them thought that these patients had better be sent to a female analyst.

This thinking was not entirely wrong, but I think that a man could have battled out the conflicts with these patients. However, the analysts were wrong in thinking that these patients had either no relationships with men or only very unhappy ones, although this was certainly true for a number of them. The analysts further thought that the unconstrained discussion of sexual matters, which revealed and relaxed certain reactions of denial with respect to the relationship with the father, had loosened up something in every one of the patients. Their repressed sexuality now emerged and impetuously demanded to be satisfied by the analyst. It is understandable that the analysts' desire for an honorable retreat played a part in their sending these patients to a female analyst.

As I worked with these patients, certain features of their behavior both in life and in the transference situation struck me. To begin with, these women who had been unable to relate to men successfully, if at all, became so free after only a little analysis that they could openly experience a vehement father-transference. I also noticed that their relationships with men, or with their analyst, contained a great many unreal elements. Even granting that every amorousness contains unreal elements and that people in love have the right to be a little silly, the excessive number of unreal elements in these cases was striking.

There was, for instance, a patient I shall call Anna, whose analysis I had taken over because she had moved to Berlin from another city. At first, her reports gave me the impression that her previous analyst must have been unusually careless about his transference attitude. Certain imprudences had indeed occurred. The analyst had played tennis and had gone to the theater with her, and he had even told her that when he went on a journey they might be able to meet and do a bit of analysis. This behavior awoke strong hopes in the patient. I was at first inclined to put the whole blame on the analyst and told myself it was no wonder that this patient had fantasies about his marrying her one day. I should mention that he was already married.

She told me other things about the analyst that gave me the impression that he must have liked her very much but that there was no trace of love. Besides, I saw after a while that the things he had mishandled were actually rather minor. But my patient indulged in elaborate fantasies of marriage, even ignoring the existence of his wife. This surprised me because, as I soon found out, the patient was a very astute judge of people.

When a curious situation soon arose that made it clear to me that she had carried the unreal character of her relationships with men into the transference and would probably have done so even without the analyst's carelessness, I found myself, in my mind, asking the analyst for forgiveness. The patient went on a trip with a man with whom she believed herself to be in love, but, to her great disappointment, he also took along a female friend she had not expected to come along — indeed, of whose existence she had not even known. He slept with the girlfriend at night and told the patient that she was expecting his child. The situation could not have been more obvious. Still, the patient, who was otherwise a sensible person, imagined that she was the one the man really loved. She considered the girlfriend's pregnancy an illusion on his part. She did not register the actual circumstances but maintained the belief that the man loved only her and was going to marry her one day. Thanks to this fiction, she did not feel too unhappy in this unfortunate situation.

We discussed the unreal elements in all these fantasies at the time, but we did not analyze them completely. Then the situation repeated itself, only on a smaller scale. When she met a man at a ball who flirted with her in a way not unusual in a ballroom situation, she immediately developed elaborate marriage fantasies, down to the last piece of furniture.

The wish to get married was like a compulsion neurosis in this patient. Her analyst had written to me that she had become so feminized through analysis that she did not even want to work in her profession (arts and crafts) any longer but was thinking only of marriage. I became concerned about that right away. Marriage is fine, but to discard one's profession for it completely seemed a little too much.

The next patient, whom, following the alphabet, I shall call Bertha, believed from the beginning that her analyst loved her, even though this belief was not inspired by any real circumstances or justified by any behavior on his part. Indeed, her aggressiveness must have made her repulsive, for there were vehement scenes of jealousy and of hostility toward his wife. Bertha also had other unrealistic relationships. For instance, she would fall in love with men on the basis of some mutual intellectual interests, but when the men withdrew, frightened perhaps by her aggressiveness, she still followed them around constantly and never really accepted her failure.

"Cecilie" is another patient I took over from a male colleague because she had moved. She also had marriage fantasies about the analyst, or at least the illusion that she was loved by him, although there had been no major transference blunders on his part. She fantasized that he had promised to buy her a fur coat—which was nonsense, and she knew it—and that he did not really love his wife, but only her. The source of this strange, unreal, and very fixed attitude became apparent when she told me with great conviction that she could have any man she wanted. There was no reason for her to be so sure, and on one occasion I told her that I doubted that her conviction was entirely genuine. When I saw her out of the room afterwards, a little scene occurred that was quite illuminating. My dog barked and I whistled for him to be quiet. Strangely enough, he was quiet immediately. Cecilie reacted to this with an incredible tantrum directed at me, which she explained in the next session: "My father always pretended he loved me; but if my mother only wanted something or whistled, he went to her." It turned out that her fantasy that she could have any man she wanted was a way of avoiding—or, rather, of denying—disappointment.

I was told that another patient, whom I shall call Dora, was a borderline schizophrenic who had become extremely attached to her analyst. She loved him dearly and constantly gave him all kinds of strange presents, to which he never reacted, in order to make him marry her. The analyst felt helpless because she pressed him vehemently and could not be appeased. There were unreal elements in this relationship as well. For instance, Dora forced her analyst to promise that he would write to her while he was on vacation. He complied by having his secretary type a note saying, "Dear Miss So and So, I am fine. I send my regards. Yours sincerely, etc." He had these letters posted from his hometown every week, although Dora knew very well that he had gone somewhere else. Yet she was happy with this ridiculous arrangement, which somehow satisfied her need to fantasize about their relationship. Earlier, this patient had invested a relationship with a man who did not care much about her with certain fantasies that were quite real to her.

In all these patients there were strong homosexual elements. Anna had had a number of aim-inhibited erotic relationships with women. All the struggles in Bertha's life were struggles with her mother. She had street anxiety [agoraphobia], which meant that her mother had to accompany and protect her. One of her earliest memories was of having been sexually aroused by the sight of her mother's legs while lying under a table. For Cecilie, the friendliest relationship of her life had been with a woman. When she struck up a relationship with the brother of her friend, nothing came of it. Dora moved mainly among women, with whom she had very good friendships, none of which, however, were consciously or manifestly erotic. These homosexual elements had not been transferred as such, nor had they even been correctly classified by the women's prior analysts.

I wish to suggest an explanation for the strange behavior of these women. They do not really love their analyst or any other man. Their love for a man is a cover-up, a fantastic superstructure, a role they are playing. These women are actually homosexual, which is to say that their libidinal energy and conflicts are focused on their relations with women. This is a very general hypothesis, and, in reality, things are certainly less simple. It is quite striking, for instance, that despite their strong homosexual tendencies, these women put their relationships with men in the foreground.

The underlying mechanisms are quite complex and, in my experience, differ from case to case. It is possible that a relationship that was aimed at a woman was acted out with a man or, as Freud puts it, was simply overwritten [*überschrieben*]. There are also cases in which women escaped into relationships with men because they were afraid of their own homosexuality. In most cases, my explanations were strikingly successful, and the analysis progressed because the patients now realized what was actually going on.

Before I continue, let me list some significant questions. What are the manifestations of repressed homosexuality? What are the relations of repressed homosexual women like with men? How do these women behave toward women? How does homosexuality generally express itself in character? And what psychological conflicts take place?

I must ask your patience with the following discussion, since, as far as I know, this is the first attempt to describe female homosexuality in some depth. There are, of course, a number of works on female homosexuality, above all, the wonderful work by Freud on the genesis of female homosexuality [Freud

1920]. But whereas he exemplifies his observations with only one case, I shall attempt to throw light on the diversity and range of manifestations.

What first struck me about female homosexuality was its very pronounced ambivalence. This was to be expected, for repressed homosexuality cannot express itself directly in either its desires or its antagonisms. However, in repressed homosexual relationships, the tendency toward hatred and rage lies under a much thinner veneer and can be aroused and break out more easily than in aim-inhibited relationships between men and women. Furthermore, repressed homosexual relationships are haunted by a tremendous amount of fear, which cannot be overestimated.

In general terms we can say that the commonest tendency in repressed female homosexuality is a masculine attitude, an identification with the male role. I have never seen a case in which the homosexual attitude was not based on a more or less conscious, but in origin always unconscious, male identification. However, there are cases in which the manifest or actual attitude toward women, female friends as well as the analyst, is one of devotion and even masochism. But even in this kind of behavior, the masculine attitude operates as a dynamic agent.

Masochistic tendencies may manifest themselves in various ways. A woman may have a fantasy of being beaten by a woman, or she may imagine a girl being beaten by a woman. In other cases, we may observe a kind of adoring idolization of the female partner or the desire for a friend's shoulder to lean on. There are women who dare not express or insist on their opinions. In one case, a woman was led to do some not altogether harmless mischief under the influence of a friend whom she did not dare to contradict. These women are all dominated, used, or betrayed by other women, such as maids or landladies, whom they idolize at the same time.

As is usually the case, women with masochistic tendencies find partners who give them what they are looking for, women who are less inhibited in their aggressiveness, in their sadism. They allow these dominating women to maltreat them, or arrange to be maltreated by them. I am thinking of a case in which the woman in question did not dare to assert herself against her maids. Not only was she afraid to criticize them, but she even arranged for them to steal from her by not checking the books, the kitchen, or the storage room for several weeks. A maid has to have a fabulous superego not to start stealing in such a situation. The woman managed to overlook the stealing for a long time, until somebody pointed it out to her. This will give you an idea of what I mean when I say that such women "arrange to be maltreated."

In the transference, these women do not dare say "we" if they refer to the analyst and themselves. They constantly feel neglected, maltreated, disadvantaged, cheated, abused; and they are offended by any interpretation as though it were an infamous assault by the analyst.

In the genesis of these cases, an older and often sexually more active sister or an actively homosexual mother frequently play an important role. The influence of the older sister often seems more important than that of the mother, at least in explaining the origin of the disease. A long analysis often reveals that the sister seduced and abused the patient. There are practically always severe homosexual conflicts with the sister. One's first impression is that later, in the transference, a repetition of the early experiences of gratification with the sister is sought under the pressure of a repetition compulsion. Such an explanation appears plausible. If a woman who has experienced such a relationship fails to find access to men, it seems understandable that she would try to repeat her relationship with the sister in the same masochistic way.

Although this explanation applies to many cases and has been therapeutically effective, I have become skeptical about its importance. One of my patients exhibited the behavior described above, but she had neither such a sister nor an especially sadistic mother. And I have not found masochistic traits in women whose history would have made it likely. We must not accept our explanations too easily, even if they seem quite plausible. But the necessary caution can come only from a range of experience that makes it possible to compare cases and to realize that the same causes do not always lead to the same effects. We must try to understand the dynamics that generate particular manifestations in each patient.

There are things, however, that I have found in all my cases of masochistic behavior — namely, a great fear, conscious or unconscious, of either the mother or the sister, and immensely strong but repressed sadistic tendencies that are also feared by the patient. I have found that the driving agent behind openly masochistic tendencies is often a repressed masculine-aggressive attitude.

Let me begin with a case that is not entirely appropriate here, since the woman in question was a manifest homosexual. She was aware of her exclusively homosexual tendencies but never had any sexual relationships with women. There could be no doubt about her masculine tendencies, for she stomped into the room dressed like a man. She was straddle-legged and heavy and was rather like a man in disguise. She told me of a dream about a witch who persecuted her and whom she thought capable of all kinds of evil. I do not remember the dream entirely, but I was shocked by the tremendous fear of the mother it revealed, a fear that I later discovered was actually founded in the patient's life.

This woman showed an exquisitely masochistic attitude toward the women she loved. In a series of relationships, she allowed them to abuse or ignore her without being put off by this treatment. Several things showed that an immensely strong but repressed sadism lay behind this behavior. She had twice turned this sadism against herself when the relationship came to an end by attempting suicide. One of these attempts was incredibly violent, for she had tried to cut her throat with a knife. Her dreams confirmed her sadistic tendencies: in one of them she strangled and maimed the women she loved. Her actual behavior toward women was either openly or covertly masochistic because she was afraid of her own aggression. She rationalized not having sexual relations with them on the grounds that she was afraid that she would hurt them some day, and her dreams seemed to support this fear.

We have to stop now, but I shall proceed from this point next time.

Behavioral Patterns of Repressed Homosexual Women

I shall present the case I introduced in the last lesson in more detail. The patient remembers a relationship with her father during her second and third years in which the father was clearly responsive to her, and she was often teased because she developed a kind of coquettish "little woman" behavior. This behavior was disrupted by her older sister, who tormented the patient, humiliated her, and seduced her sexually. Her first analysis revealed a clear father-transference of an unrealistic nature. At the end of this phase, the patient refused to hear anything about a profession but was preoccupied with marriage plans. The second analysis, with a female analyst, proved these marriage plans to be of a compulsive nature; they were not an expression of a genuine feminine need of the patient.

This patient showered the woman analyst with complaints, often in the form of accusations, and showed a marked distrust of everything connected with the analysis. She resented having to pay for the analysis, the length of the analysis, and the interest the analyst had in her. Above all, she suspected that the analyst wanted to keep her from becoming involved with a man, and she developed paranoid ideas. The patient believed, for instance, that the analyst had secretly gotten in contact with a man with whom [the patient] had a date but who did not show up. Even in later stages of the analysis, the patient still threw veritable tantrums with the analyst whenever a man did not call. She was afraid of the analyst, and her fear took different forms, such as the fear of remaining homosexual, of being released without having finished, or of being kept in analysis forever. When the analyst recommended that she not give up her profession, the patient again believed that the analyst wanted to *prevent* her from getting married. Having a profession was synonymous to her with renouncing marriage.

The patient's dreams revealed that she saw analysis as a duel in which one of the two participants had to succumb. The same held true for her relationship with her mother. She thought that only after her mother's death would she be free to find a husband. Her death wish against her mother obviously originated in her fear of her mother, whose death would eliminate all obstacles.

The patient was also afraid of men and of her own success. She became defensive when a man approached her, she sabotaged her own achievements, and she did not want to admit any improvement during analysis. Deep down she seemed to fear, "If I do not avoid all rivalry, something terrible will happen." In a dream, she was constantly chased around the room by her sister.

In her behavior toward women, she wanted to do to them what her sister had done to her. She threw tantrums at failures in analysis or at the engagements of her girlfriends. She begrudged other women everything. In this context, her fear became more understandable: it seemed to originate in the fear of revenge and in a belief that other women felt the envy and vindictiveness toward her that she felt toward them.

The patient constantly failed with men and avoided success in other areas of her life because of her fear of triumphing over the sister and thus arousing her desire for revenge. The patient's fear of men led her to develop a vaginismus which meant: "I want to castrate the man in order to get his penis. With it, I will hurt my sister, destroy her. I want to do to the man what my sister did to me."

Even at the end of analysis, the patient rejected feelings of gratitude toward the analyst. She wanted to be the stronger one and wished the analyst to succumb. This originally surfaced in the wish to murder the analyst, but later this wish turned into something more productive, the desire to find her own way, not to let anybody dictate to her what to do.

Stratification: At the bottom we have the positive oedipal attitude. The patient departed from this attitude because of disappointments experienced with her father, and the result was an identification with the father. In the second phase there was a libidinal attachment to women. This was partly a repetition of her experience with her sister, but it was also the product of a desire for revenge against her sister, a doing to other women of what her sister had done to her. This resulted in an increased fear of the sister, because of the talion principle, and in a masochistic attitude that was a defense against her sadistic impulses: "I am terribly afraid of your revenge, but if I don't arouse your hostility, you won't harm me." Superimposed on all of this was the attempt to find a man.

Freud believes that for girls the bonding with the mother is primary, while the father is an annoying rival. Only conflicts with the mother bring about a loosening of this bond and a transference of it to the father. These conflicts are partly of an unspecific nature, resulting, for example, from the prohibitions and threats connected with the education of children. But they are also partly of a specific nature, for the girl blames the mother for her lack of a penis. In the case we are examining, however, the bond with the father seems primary. Hence, the question arises: "If the bond with the father is not the result of a turning away from the mother, how did the bonding with the father come about at all?" The answer is that we are dealing with the law of heterosexual attraction, such as we find throughout the animal kingdom. At the same time, however, observers of animals repeatedly report that they find homosexual relations.

I shall now discuss some of the behavioral patterns of repressed homosexual women. The courtship of these patients is often of a distinctly demonstrative character and represents an emphasis on their masculinity. Their courtship of the female analyst's love often finds expression in gifts such as flowers. They may put great demands on the analyst (for example, by changing appointments). One patient refused to pay because she felt that having to pay was synonymous with being a weak woman. Another patient fantasized about serving the analyst by being her maid, with the object, it turned out, of having a better chance to poison her food. What appeared to be a loving gesture was really a means to murder. Some of these women use sexuality to make other people dependent on them and try to arouse the love of men for this purpose. In one case there was an obvious conflict between a resentment against men because they are able to woo and a fear of being too aggressive and imposing on others.

I had one patient whose courtship did not surface in an overt way, because she was one of those women who keep up an anxious reserve. This was a woman who began to live only after 8 p.m. Her life meant going out, playing cards, drinking wine, and doing other trivial things that were a waste of time. She showed a feeling of resignation toward men. The only manifestation of her homosexuality was a relationship with a younger woman friend. Otherwise, she vehemently rejected homosexuality. She tolerated men, whom she treated like pretty little dogs. Of course, she was entirely frigid. The kinds of men she tolerated were all very devoted to her.

Part of her rejection of homosexuality derived from her fear of going to sleep, which expressed itself in an avoidance of going to bed and could be traced back to old memories of crawling into her mother's bed. She was touchy about even indirect relations with women. For instance, she could not bear it when the men she was with mentioned women from their past.

Her transference led her to try to make the male analyst in her first analysis fall in love with her. With the female analyst, she remained reserved, while at the same time she fell suddenly and passionately in love with a man and courted him. This love represented a clear escape from the transference, a fact that became apparent in her dreams, in which men turned into women and in which she had tea with the analyst, danced with her, and made obvious advances toward her.

Her reserve toward the female analyst can be explained as the rejection of libidinous desires. The reason for her rejection lay in her sadistic attitudes toward her mother. Her dreams, for instance, featured tortures of women, such as maiming of the genitals. Reports of abortions or sexual murder scenarios aroused her — for example, the scene in *Pandora's Box* (she identified with the killer, her mother with the prostitute). She rejected libidinous desires because of her fears: "If I engage in sexual activity, I will have to suffer the same things that I wish on my mother for her sexuality." She was afraid that her mother might hear of her journey with a man. Her deep-rooted fear of the mother emerged especially clearly when I fell ill. During this time, she was very relaxed and active with her boyfriend and kept exclaiming, "I'm on Horneyholiday." Later, this event became subject to absolute amnesia.

In this case, the analyst is perceived as a superior force, like life: cold, unfeeling, destructive. Such perceptions can repeatedly be traced back to the mother, as can fear of witches. Thus the patient's reserve is self-protective. It is also the expression of a fear of being rejected, which is related to the desire for masculinity, since courting is equated with the masculine. The fear of being rejected corresponds to the fear of the impotent man and points to a disorder in self-esteem, to feelings of inadequacy.

The tragic problem of homosexuality lies in the absence of something for which no substitute can be found: the penis.

6

Chicago Lectures on Feminine Psychology (1933)

In April and May of 1933, Horney delivered a series of seven lectures which was titled "Female Psychology." Stenographic transcriptions of the last five of these lectures were in Harold Kelman's papers at the Postgraduate Center for Mental Health. Internal evidence indicates that the lectures were delivered to an audience consisting largely of gynecologists. Perhaps this series was a sequel to the paper Horney had read at the Chicago Gynecological Society on 18 November 1932, "Psychogenic Factors in Functional Female Disorders." The paper was subsequently published in the *American Journal of Obstetrics and Gynecology* (Horney 1933b). The lectures cover some of the same ground and use some of the same examples, but they are fuller and present much more case material.

In some cases, I have retitled the lectures and divided them in a different way than they were divided in the originals. I have added a subtitle to "Common Deviations in Instinct Development." "The Problem of Frigidity" was originally entitled "Conflicts in Relations with Men (The Problem of Frigidity)." I have incorporated into this lecture the continuation of the discussion of frigidity with which Horney began her next lecture, "Psychogenic Factors in Menstrual Disorders." When Horney had not finished with a topic in the lecture assigned to it, she completed her discussion in the following session. Her discussion of psychogenic factors in menstrual disorders began in the second half of the lecture so titled and concluded in the first half of the one that followed, which had the same title. I have combined the two halves to create one lecture on this topic. In the second half of the second lecture on menstrual disorders, Horney began a discussion of problems relating to pregnancy, and she concluded this discussion in the first half of her final lecture, which was originally titled "Possibilities and Limitations of Psychotherapy." I have combined these two halves into a lecture I have called "Psychogenic Factors in Problems Relating to Pregnancy," and I have titled the remainder of the final lecture "The Uses and Limitations of Analytic Knowledge in Gynecological Practice."

As editor, I have done much more than reorganize and retitle these lectures. The stenographic transcripts frequently present garbled ideas in a fractured English, and they are very difficult to follow. It is impossible to say whether the fault was Horney's or the stenographer's. The many gaps in the text indicate that the stenographer was having difficulty recording what Horney was saying, but we must remember that Horney had not had much experience lecturing in English and may have been struggling to express her ideas. To make these lectures intelligible, I have had to act as Horney's co-writer. I have pondered the texts, decided what I thought Horney was trying to say, and then said it, using her words when possible. I have deleted stray thoughts, fragmentary ideas, and passages that did not make sense to me. I believe that I have accurately conveyed the substance of these lectures, but the reader should be aware that the wording is a combination of Horney's language and mine.

Common Deviations in Instinct Development:
Homosexual Women and Boy-Crazy Girls

Last time, I talked about girls' early fears and observed that we never find them present overtly at the beginning of analysis. Now we must ask the question, "Why are they not present?" I shall explain this by using an example that is based on material from a series of analyses.

Consider a girl who has originally had a strong fear of the consequences of masturbation. She will have gone through a conflict between her sexual desires on the one hand and her fear of being damaged on the other. There are two possibilities: either she will continue to masturbate, fighting a constant battle between guilt and fear on the one hand and desire on the other, or she will stop masturbating if fear is stronger than desire. If her analyst talks about masturbation, she will probably not remember ever having masturbated as a child. She will say it has never played a role with her, that she has felt that only men did such things; or perhaps she will say that she attempted masturbation in puberty after hearing about it from other girls but that it never had any meaning for her.

Yet since the sexual impulses or desires are the strongest, she will not have been able to eliminate them altogether. Her history will show that she inevitably tried to substitute some other activity for the original masturbation. Perhaps she started to pick her nose or ear or play with her hair, or perhaps she found a substitute gratification in certain fantasies. Because the fantasies approach her infantile situation too closely and arouse feelings of guilt, she represses them in their turn and starts reading books indiscriminately. She has less guilt at the beginning because she is not the one who has produced the fantasies but is only their consumer. But as she swallows books indiscriminately, her feelings of guilt are activated again, and she gives up reading and turns to an interest in something like mathematics.

Such a girl would seem to be someone who has no interest in sex whatever, who is rather poor in her fantasy life, who has no particular interest in any fields of knowledge that are concerned with human relations but only in fields that are abstract, such as mathematics.

Now let such a girl come in contact with a sexual problem. Let a friend of hers marry and let her come into a milieu in which there is a freer indulgence in sex. Then the old conflict may be stirred up again. Or let her have a failure in her professional life, let us say in her mathematical career. Upon being disappointed in this one field that was spared from repression, she may begin to have an obsessional neurosis — perhaps an obsession with washing her hands, which repeats her old struggle about masturbation — or she may develop some neurasthenic symptoms. If, guided by a knowledge that an obsessional neurosis, such as washing herself, may in many cases be an expression of the struggle against masturbation, her analyst told the girl that possibly some sort of sexual conflicts lay behind her troubles, she would very likely feel neither fear nor disgust in response to this interpretation but would simply feel that her analyst was speaking Chinese. She would not understand.

At the same time, she might consciously have very reasonable views on sex with regard to others. If her analyst has had no great experience with such psychological difficulties, he might doubt whether the findings of analysis were right at all, whether he was not on the wrong path, and, at a loss to explain the situation, he might conclude that the girl had overworked herself.

A person who has had a conflict in childhood that was connected with great fears will tend to find some solution for it. She will try one solution, leave it, find another solution, leave it, and so on until she has stabilized her conflict in some way. A great superstructure will have been built up over the original conflict, and it may take months or years to reveal what is beneath it and to enable the patient to find a better solution than she was able to do on her own. This is what must be done if therapy is to be efficacious.

Perhaps the most common result of being in a situation that generates fear is losing pleasure in the situation and withdrawing from it. One thing which is common to all deviations from normal female development is disliking the female role and withdrawing from it. Such a withdrawal may show itself overtly in manifestly homosexual women — who think that feminine trends are incompatible with their personality, though they may be fond of them in other women — or in girls between six and twelve years of age, who may openly declare that they would rather be boys and play a tomboyish role. Apart from such overt manifestations, a dislike of the feminine role can take many forms. It may show itself in an aversion to what is regarded as feminine in work, character, or interest. Or it may be expressed in an antagonism toward female biological functions.

A distaste for the female role may show itself in puberty in a feeling of shame about the breasts or pubic hair or in a dislike of the female genitals. It is manifested in the widespread practice of describing menstruation as "the curse." It can be found in the general attitude of women these days that they have to be slender. As an analyst, I have found that for those patients who passionately wanted to be thin, being full-figured in any way meant something sexual, meant being a woman and, on a more unconscious level, being pregnant. Without knowing that they are feeling an aversion to the feminine role, many women develop a disgust toward sex, which they regard as dirty, and toward everything connected with it.

Antagonism may be directed against housekeeping, or sewing, or dressing nicely, and especially against anything that means giving in. For instance, women may rebel against any regulation of their time: they may resent having to meet a train, be at the theater at a certain time, or keep an appointment they have made earlier. This may make them feel that they are being imposed on and forced to give in. They resent submitting to convention or authority or being in a dependent position. They may resent getting attached emotionally because being attached to anyone means in a way being dependent on him. In the therapeutic situation, they revolt against free association or feel it extremely humiliating if they accede to the analyst's demand that they say everything that is going through their minds.

Not always but very often the behaviors I have described are antifeminine in nature and are a signal to the analyst that he must seek for deep resentments against the feminine role. Withdrawal from the feminine role combined with the desire to be a man is what we call the masculinity complex.

Penis envy is part of this picture. Little girls who have the opportunity to observe that a brother is built differently from them want to grow a penis so that they can urinate like a boy. They will at least try to climb trees like boys do and will say openly that they want to be a male. One of my patients who wanted to be a boy came into the bathroom where two of her brothers were bathing when she was six years old. She saw that they had penises, became very desperate, and started wetting her bed. Since she could not urinate like a boy in reality, she started doing it in her dreams. Later on, the effort to be like a male will take other forms, such as driving a car when driving was considered a masculine activity. Nowadays it may take the form of the wish to be a pilot and to fly.

Women with a masculinity complex adopt the aggressive attitude of men and have a wish to be superior. This is often an unconscious wish that has no reasonable limits; it is a wish to be superior at any price and in every way. This helps to explain the behavior of domineering women and of women with intense ambition. In the analytical situation, such women either try to do all the work themselves, showing the analyst to be superfluous, or they blame the analyst for their problems. If they experience improvement, they maintain the superior role by insisting that the analyst had nothing to do with it. Or they may resist changing for the better because that would mean that the analyst had succeeded, and being superior is more important to them than making progress. In their relations with men, they maintain their superior position by being aloof and indifferent, by refusing to become attached to men who are attached to them. Or they may develop a pseudomaternal attitude in which they care for men, but in a superficial, condescending way.

When you get to know these patients better, you often find that the secret infantile expectation that they will get a penis is still alive in them. One patient remembered having the fantasy as a small child that if she grew, she would become a boy. Another made a study of internal secretions in the expectation that if she knew a great deal about them, she could change from a woman into a man. The same patient felt very unhappy about waking up in the morning, until she remembered that as a child she had had to learn Latin, hadn't liked it, and had hoped that she would know all about it when she awoke. She was hoping that when she awoke she would be a boy.

Masculinity wishes are particularly expressed in dreams. For instance, a girl concerned about birth control may dream that she goes into a drug store to buy a pessary and buys a condom instead. A woman's masculinity wishes may be expressed in waking life by the carrying of a sword or stick, the usual phallic symbols, or in a disguised form through dreams of burglars. A woman having such dreams will usually have fears of being attacked and overwhelmed by a man, but she may also want to be the burglar herself and to attack other women.

I suppose that masculinity wishes will be found in every woman, partly because of the bisexuality we are supposed to have and partly because women's fears lead them to withdraw from the feminine role and prefer to be a man. For similar reasons, there are also feminine trends and desires to be a woman buried in every man. One patient remembered wondering in boyhood whether it would be more dangerous to be a woman or a man. A woman has to have children, but a man has to go to war. The question is, Which is the less dangerous? How can I avoid fears? Fears of the dangers of womanhood lead women to want to be men, and fears of the dangers of manhood lead men to want to be women.

I want to talk about two frequent deviations in instinct development in women in more detail, in order to give you a sense of how such attitudes may develop. They are the homosexual woman and the boy-crazy girl.

Homosexual women may have either manifest relations with other women or conscious but inhibited desires for amorous relations with them. They may feel more attraction to other women than to men or have relations with women that are much more highly charged emotionally than their relations with men. Homosexual women most closely follow the pattern I have been discussing: "I have a fear of the female role. I do not want to be a woman. I prefer to be a man."

The outstanding fear in this type of woman is of the mother. In the typical history that is unrolled in the initial session, the father seems to have played no role. In some cases you get the impression that the father was a nice gentleman who lived in the house, while in others there is a more or less open contempt for the father. As the analysis proceeds, the conflict with the mother emerges. Either these patients tell of their fear of the mother, or they reveal a terrific hatred of the mother, or they show some overcompensation for this hatred in the form of being overanxious about the mother, being afraid that she will meet with an accident while crossing the street, that something will happen to her. Beneath this overprotective attitude is a repressed death wish against the mother. These patients demand that the mother do everything that they want and become enraged if she does not submit to their demands.

There is an inevitable relationship between the fear and the hatred that emerge in relation to the mother. Suppose a child is thwarted by the mother in something she wants to do, in masturbation, for instance, or asking for sexual information. The child will feel obstructed in something she thinks is both justified and vitally interesting, and she will react with some degree of hostility. Because of the talion principle, her antagonism necessarily generates a fear of the mother: "Since I am hostile toward you, I am afraid that you will want to harm me in return." This fear will lead the child to resent the mother as an enemy and will generate a stronger antagonism toward her, a process that helps to explain the intensity of the hostility which emerges. We cannot understand this intensity unless we keep in mind the vicious circle in which fear increases hostility, hostility increases fear, and so on.

One question that arises here is, What is the content of the girl's fear of the mother? It seems to be a very general fear of something horrible the mother might do to her. In one patient named Clara, her old fears of the mother came up at a time when there was a very strong "transference" in which her feelings toward her mother were felt in relation to me. She regarded me as a ruthless power who in a cold and devilish way wanted to destroy her, especially her feelings.

A second question is, Are there any specific conditions that prompt the fear of the mother? The patients have an uncomfortable feeling about the mother and realize that they are still haunted by a fear of her, but they cannot give us a clear explanation of its source. We must guess the source of the fear from their reactions in real life, as well as from their reactions in the transference and from their dreams. In Clara, for instance, there appeared a very striking fear that the mother would get to know something about her relations with men and would feel that these relations were queer. In fact, the men in her life meant nothing to her; she felt no emotional ties and was frigid. The precautions she took to prevent her mother from knowing about her relations with men were absolutely ridiculous because Clara was an independent woman who lived on her own. Moreover, she had managed to intimidate her mother, who would not have dared to express any opinion about her relationships, even if she had known about them. Yet Clara was still afraid. We must be clear on this point: the fear did not originate in the present but was a remnant of Clara's infantile fear of letting her mother know that she had sexual feelings or experiences.

Another patient — I shall call her Elise — was an intellectual who realized perfectly well that I was interested in helping her find some relationship with men that was more complete. She realized that she was a failure in her relations with men and that her only emotional relationships were with women. Although she knew that I wanted to help her when she failed with men, as she always did, she always strongly reproached me as though I were the one who had inhibited her in her relationships. She was transferring to me the feelings she had toward an older sister who had wanted to remain the beloved only daughter that she had been until Elise's arrival. Instead of ridiculing Elise or tying her to herself in a homosexual way, her sister had frightened her away from her female role and thwarted her in her female development.

Over and over again in the analysis of these types of women, I have found that there was a mother or sister who did not want them to be feminine, to enjoy a sexual life, to have relations with men. They have dreams which express the feeling that they can get married or be with a man only if the mother or sister dies. Their fear of their mother or sister originates in the extreme jealousy these females felt toward them. I have already given an example, and I could have given more, in which a sister showed an extreme jealousy toward her younger rival from the beginning and managed to disable her as a competitor; but I have also found a pathological jealousy on the part of some mothers, not only toward growing daughters, as is more understandable, but from the beginning; and these mothers have often succeeded in thwarting their daughter's feminine development. In some cases, there were mothers who themselves had strong masculinity complexes and who reacted with disgust to any manifestations of femininity in their daughters.

In the later stages of analysis, patients often come to realize that the father was more important than they had thought, that they were not as indifferent to their fathers as they had at first imagined themselves to be. Gradually it comes out that they had originally felt a very strong, even passionate, attraction to the father and that they had suffered some disappointment from his side. The disappointment may have consisted in an unjust and unexpected punishment, or it may have been the result of an inconsistent attitude on the father's part. There may also have been a disappointing older brother.

I remember a case in which the father had really displayed very intense signs of attachment toward the girl, showing how much he liked her and making her his confidant. He would tell her how impossible the mother was, how much he disliked her and wished her dead. When he subsequently had a breakdown and was hospitalized, the girl became enraged as she saw him walking around the sanitarium rather peacefully with the mother. She had been the one he had loved and taken into his confidence, but then he had turned to the mother.

Or take Freud's "The Psychogenesis of a Case of Homosexuality in a Woman." The girl in this case develops a homosexual attitude at around the age of sixteen when her mother has another child. Until then, the girl was very much attached to the father, and this attachment put her in conflict with her mother, who was coquettish and selfish and obviously regarded the girl as a competitor. The girl had shown signs of avoiding competition with the mother in the female line by having no erotic interest in men but displaying instead a maternal attitude. She had evidently given up competing for males with her mother and other women and had confined herself to other aspects of femininity.

Her maternal attitude must go back to the typical early fantasies of girls about having a child by their father. Just at the time of puberty, when oedipal conflicts flare up, this girl's mother has a child by the father, and the girl's reaction is to turn away from the father abruptly and to display obvious signs of a homosexual attitude. In response, her father becomes quite upset, but her mother does not. The responses of the parents mirror the girl's double motive. She is relinquishing further competition with her mother and expressing spite toward her father: "I don't want anything to do with you." The mother is pleased by her daughter's withdrawal from feminine rivalry, while her father resents her rejection of men.

In relation to the mother, the homosexual girl develops a very deep fear, which culminates in the avoidance of rivalry: "I don't want to compete with you or any other woman. I shall avoid competition on the female line. I withdraw there." A strong hatred toward the mother results in the feeling: "I don't want to be like her at all." The girl may consciously resent having any of her mother's traits, such as her attitude toward children or her way of dressing, but what she basically resents is being female. She doesn't want to be like her mother because that means being a woman.

Some women are driven to a masculine homosexual attitude by their relationship not only with their mother but with their father as well. As far as the father is concerned, a disappointment that they have suffered from him or from a brother is expressed over the whole male sex and drives them away from a love life. As I have explained before, they give up the father as a love object and identify with him. This process needs explanation. Freud describes the way in which a child who lost a kitten did not show any particular signs of mourning but rather crept around and acted as though she were a kitten herself. This shows the process I have in mind: the loss of a love object may result in a partial identification with the lost object. We make up for the loss of the object by incorporating it, by playing the same role ourselves. Women who have been frustrated in their relationships with several men will sometimes incorporate attitudes of each man, taking on the political interests of one, the behavior of another, and so on.

Women who have homosexual tendencies do not all present the same picture. Some have a masculine physical habitus, and some have feminine traits. Some are aggressive toward other women and play the masculine role, while others behave in a passive, masochistic way. Masculine behavior does not necessarily correlate with physical masculinity, since we find such behavior also in women who have an absolutely feminine appearance. It is important to note that although the manifest attitude toward women friends may be very different, at bottom there are invariably unconscious fantasies of being in the masculine role.

How can we account for the differences in appearance and behavior when underneath we always find the same masculine trends? Why are some women aggressive and some passive toward their female friends? The explanation lies in the origin of the homosexual attitude in conflict with the mother. There is both a hatred of the mother and a fear of expressing this hatred that results in its repression. Often homosexual women consciously want to have relations with other women but refrain because they have a fear of damaging them. Their dreams show that this fear is justified because in them they may tear these women to pieces, suffocate them, or do them other kinds of severe physical harm. Some women act out through masculine, domineering behavior the aggressive impulses toward other women that originated in their relationship with their mother, while others defend themselves against these impulses by going to the opposite extreme and being masochistic.

One meets with boy-crazy girls frequently today. It may seem rather normal that as children they play with lots of boys and later focus all their energy on getting married; but the fact is that although they want relationships with men very badly, they never succeed in them. Either they are unable to find such relationships, or, if they do, they quarrel with their partners or drop them as soon as they show a serious interest. There are other problems as well. In spite of being gifted and intelligent, these girls lack interest in their work or their mental development. In their relations with men, moreover, they show no discrimination: one boy can be exchanged for another. They are not interested in the boys as individuals; rather, they like those who are preferred by other girls, who have made themselves conspicuous in some way, or who flatter their narcissism. They may pretend to love the boys, but when you get to know them, you will see that they have no emotional bond whatever to males.

A deeper knowledge of these girls reveals that they have profound feelings of inferiority about their feminine capacities. Some girls who are actually very beautiful may be afraid to look in the mirror because they are convinced that they are unattractive and that no man could like their appearance. If a man does like them, they will never be convinced that it is because of their attractiveness but will attribute it to something else. These girls have a fear that they are not normal, that something is wrong with them, although they cannot say what it is. They try to appear normal, like the girl who in her first consultation with me said that she had these little fits now and then but nothing was the matter with her. There are girls who resent analysis because it means admitting that something is wrong. They resent physical illness because it indicates that they are not perfectly "normal." Often these girls have a fear of having damaged themselves by early masturbation or other early sexual experiences, and they are afraid that they can never recover. They need to attract men and to have children in order to prove that no lasting harm has been done.

Boy-crazy girls have much in common with homosexual women as far as their discomfort with their femininity is concerned, but they have a strong fear of homosexual tendencies, because these would confirm their sense of defectiveness. Having relations with men is so important to them partly because it is a way of proving their normality in this respect.

The Problem of Frigidity

As with all problems that concern the relations between the two sexes, it is difficult to be objective about frigidity. Our judgment is influenced not only by our personal attitudes but also by the prevailing climate of thought. The current ideal that a woman should be chaste, pure, and asexual has led women to be sexually repressed, and this repression has seemed to confirm the asexual nature of women.

Since many of you come from the natural sciences, you might expect experimental proof of what I have to say about frigidity, but I must make it clear from the beginning that we have not been able to develop such proofs so far. Indeed, I doubt that they will ever be possible. For one thing, we cannot experiment with a sexual situation. Even sexual experiments with animals probably will not lead very far. They may give us some knowledge about reactions, but only to a very limited extent. We have devised experiments for some emotional situations, as when we give people an insoluble problem and then observe their reactions, but even if we could do this in a sexual situation, we would not learn very much. Sexual responses are the product of tendencies that have developed over a lifetime and cannot be understood without a knowledge of the whole life situation of the individual in question. Certainly, we shall not be able to understand a woman's frigidity without understanding her attitude toward men in general. There may be frigid women who show no particular neurotic symptoms, but there will always be an observable disturbance in their attitude toward men. What I shall give you here is not experimental situations but case histories, perhaps thereby confirming in your minds the reputation of psychoanalysis as nonscientific.

I want first to present a case which may show the mechanisms that are present in vaginismus. A patient came to me some time after her marriage had gone to pieces. Although she had often sent her husband away, she had a severe breakdown when he really left her. She sought help partly because there were people in her surroundings who knew about psychoanalysis and had diagnosed her as suffering from a masculinity complex, perhaps because she displayed masculine tendencies in a rather demonstrative way.

Her basic attitude toward men was that she wanted to defeat them. She liked to attract men and then to drop them when she felt she had some power over them. She especially liked situations in which she could triumph over a competing woman, and she thus revealed a destructive rivalry toward women as well. Her competitiveness toward men was clearly revealed in a story she told about her behavior after she became engaged. Her fiancé and some of his friends had built a little shack in the woods and were very enthusiastic about it. Then she came and, finding fault with everything, told them how she could make it better. This defeated them by showing them the inadequacy of their efforts. Her husband was an engineer, and after her marriage she had the fantasy of inventing a machine that would be better than any other and that would make all of her husband's machines useless.

Her dreams showed that the instinctive basis of her need to defeat men was her desire to castrate them. In one dream she had a fight with a man, similar to those she had had with her husband, and he jumped out the window and was injured. There was a cripple in this dream who proved to be the man who had jumped out the window, and she was able to feel great affection toward him. In addition to having dreams about castrating, she displayed many overt castrative attitudes toward men.

Her masculine aggressiveness and competitiveness also came up in the transference situation. She had a fantasy, for example, of establishing herself as an analyst across the street from my office, on which she would post the sign: "Across the street is a really good analyst." As a result of her aggressiveness, she had deep feelings of guilt, which she tried to overcome by provoking me to injure her. She dealt with her guilt, in effect, by becoming masochistic. She had behaved this way with her husband, whom she loved very much but drove away, suffering greatly afterward. After I came to know her well, I immediately reacted to aggressive behavior at the beginning of an hour by asking, "What do you feel guilty about?" I knew that when she felt guilty she wanted to provoke me into treating her badly.

Two brothers play a dominant role in her history. A brother who was some years older than she had aroused her sexually when she was five, and she had started to masturbate. Since she lived in an environment that was strict about sexual matters, she had very deep feelings of guilt and fear because of her masturbation, and these feelings had persisted into her later years. They had made her turn away from the female role and develop strong wishes to be a boy, particularly a boy like her beloved brother.

An important turning point occurred when she dashed into the bathroom one day, saw her two brothers bathing, and realized that they were built differently than she, that they had penises. Already fearful of the consequences of masturbation, she concluded: "I have spoiled myself by masturbation," or "My brother has spoiled me." She felt that she was a castrated boy who was spoiled forever. One of the immediate consequences of this event was that she began wetting her bed, while dreaming that she was urinating like a boy.

Another traumatic event occurred when her older brother developed a preference for an older sister. My patient became terribly jealous of this sister, a jealousy that was still in full bloom even though she was now more than thirty years old. This led to a deep craving for revenge against her sister, and all other women, and against her brother as well. She wanted to defeat all women by taking men away from them and to defeat men by making them dependent on her love. In the transference situation, she brought me presents and stopped only when I interpreted her behavior as an effort to make me dependent on her. She acknowledged that this was correct and came out with the idea that love was a means of killing another person.

Her vengeful attitude toward men manifested itself in a desire to castrate them and in her tendency to drop them in the same way that she had been dropped. The first instance of this was her seduction of the brother who was one year younger than she, by playing with him sexually when he was eleven. When this brother later died of the grippe, she had deep feelings of guilt, which lasted into adulthood. She felt that she was to blame for his death because he had begun masturbating as a result of her seduction, and she believed that his death was caused by his masturbation. This guilt feeling was rather fantastic, considering that she was an intelligent woman. It can be accounted for by the fact that her seduction of her brother had not been dictated simply by sexual wishes but by the desire to damage him as she had been damaged.

When she married, this patient had a marked vaginismus that prevented her husband from penetrating her, even though he was potent. She would not allow her husband to deflower her but insisted that a physician do it, after which she reacted to the physician with immense rage. This reminds me of Freud's discussion in "The Taboo of Virginity" of the practice in primitive tribes of having a man other than the husband deflower the bride because of women's destructive rage against the men who take their virginity. An experienced gynecologist I know has told me of his amazement that many women do not want to marry the man who has deflowered them but prefer another man. My patient with vaginismus experienced intense castrative impulses toward men and a corresponding fear of retaliation: "Because I have such aggressive impulses, I am afraid that something similarly horrible will happen to me." In other cases of vaginismus, I have always found strong castrative impulses, often conscious and easily detected.

After being deflowered, my patient was frigid in her married life. She experienced some sensation but had no orgasm. As soon as intercourse was finished, she dashed into the bathroom to relieve herself of this dirt, as she felt it to be. This is not surprising when one considers her aggressiveness and her feeling that sexuality was dirty.

An interesting aspect of her history is that after her separation from her husband she had two affairs in which she was not frigid. What are we to make of this psychologically? She was fond of the first man and had a serious love affair with him. A married man, he was tied to his wife not by bonds of love but by feelings of obligation. My patient reacted with rage toward this situation, but it also excited her. I often wondered whether it was love for the man that kept her in this situation or the contest with his wife. She was not frigid, because having sexual relations enabled her both to win the man and to damage the other woman. Being only the mistress satisfied her masochistic need to be punished for her aggression.

When she became angry with this man for not sticking with her, she found an outlet by throwing herself away on another man, for whom she felt contempt, although she appreciated his technique in dealing with women. Although she did not love this man, she was not frigid with him either. There were several reasons for this. Her relationship with this man was a means of taking revenge on her previous lover, on whom it gratified her to inflict damage. At the same time, throwing herself away satisfied her masochistic tendencies, for she could say to herself, "I am not the one who has behaved sadistically but the one who is being humiliated." This relieved her of the guilt she felt about her aggressive behavior.

In my experience, we seldom find a frigid woman who has never experienced excitement or gratification. We must therefore ask what the specific conditions are under which excitement or gratification is possible. I have had a patient who experienced vaginismus in her first sexual relationship and was later frigid in the sense of having no orgasm. She had one castrative dream after another. There was one situation, however, in which she had had a full orgasm, and that was when she had masturbated in a particular way. She had a ring that had been given to her by her father and that seemed to her to be part of him. She had masturbated vaginally to orgasm with this ring, and then it had slipped away and she was afraid that she would have to go to a doctor to find it. The feeling that she had incorporated part of her father fulfilled her secret fantasies and gave her orgasmic feelings.

We discovered why the father played such an important part for this woman through an early memory of having been sexually aroused by his erect penis and an odor that seemed to have been given off by his excitement. She had reacted with vaginal discharges that frightened her very much and led to a desire for revenge on the father. Her early sexual arousal led to particularly passionate feelings toward the father, but a sister won out in the competition for his affection, driving her away from the whole field of female rivalry. So, in addition to the fear she experienced because of her aggression toward men, she had a fear of an older sister that also contributed to her frigidity. After her first attempt at intercourse, she had a dream in which her sister chased her around.

In another case of frigidity, the patient had a very childlike appearance. Although she was thirty, they did not want to admit her when she went to the movies because they thought she was under eighteen. Her husband was a tough fellow who had left her, and she felt rather unhappy about it because she was fond of him in a way. Her chief complaint about her married life had to do with her frigidity. She got the idea into her head that she was built too narrowly to have a normal sex life, and she would not give up this idea, even when I pointed out to her that she had given birth to a child. She had no secretion at all during intercourse and therefore had to use lubricants. She insisted on having a bath before and after intercourse because she felt that it was dirty.

As often occurs with patients who complain of frigidity, other symptoms were present. Although her legs seemed fine to me, this patient was convinced that she had bowlegs and often thought of seeking a corrective operation. Her conviction that she had bowlegs had led her to leave the stage, on which she had played for a number of years, because she thought that performing enabled people to see her bowlegs. Another symptom was that she would get dizzy and faint and as a consequence was always very careful in choosing her underwear in case she had to be examined at an emergency clinic.

These symptoms were easily removed because they had to do with what we might call prostitution fantasies. The fainting was confined to streets frequented by prostitutes, where people engaged in flirtatious promenades and women were liable to be talked to. Her concern with her legs went back to an inflammation she had when she was twelve and a girl had told her that women with bowlegs were bad women because they got that way from putting their legs around men. This childish idea had taken root and had come out in numerous ways in her dreams about having casual affairs with men.

Although she suffered from frigidity, there were certain conditions under which this patient could become passionately aroused and have an orgasm. There had to be an element of fantasy or unreality. She was aroused by prostitution fantasies in which she had casual or forbidden relations with men. She could feel passionate, and even have an orgasm, on stage, since this was not reality but a kind of game. Before her marriage, she was able to have a full orgasm by masturbating vaginally, but this was partly because masturbation — like fantasies, dreams, and acting — involved no real relationship with a man.

Her prostitution fantasies could be traced to her relationships with her father and mother. Her father left her mother when she was three and then philandered with other women. Her mother, who was very repressed in sexual matters, often disciplined the child and made deprecating remarks about the father's running around. The girl became attached to her father because her mother was so strict and, whenever he saw her, he was brilliant and scintillating. Her love life was concentrated on him. To her, being a loose woman originally meant being loved by the father. At the same time, her prostitution fantasies were also a protest against her strict mother. She mentioned again and again in analysis that her mother had a female cat that she prevented from mating. She resented her mother's repressive attitude, and her resentment was deepened because she sided with her father and blamed her mother for his departure.

Her resentment toward her mother was held in check by two factors. One was that her infantile fear of the mother had caused her to develop a superego that was just as strict as the mother was. The other was a feeling of obligation because her mother had worked very hard to bring her up in a decent way and to educate her. She felt an irrational guilt for having things any better than her mother did. She felt guilty about marrying because her mother had no husband, and she hesitated quite awhile before having a baby because she thought her mother might resent being a grandmother.

Her feeling of obligation toward her mother was mainly responsible for her need to have sexual pleasure in a clandestine way. Her mother must not know about it. Because marriage did not meet this condition, it conflicted with what she felt that she owed her mother. Her sex life was full of discrepancies, since she had strict superego demands on the one hand, while on the other she could obtain satisfaction through fantasies of prostitution and degradation. She did not deal with her conflicts by withdrawing from the feminine role and assuming a masculine one but by imagining herself to be narrowly built. The meaning of this was, "I am too small to have intercourse. I am still too much of an innocent little child."

Although it is difficult to discover the nature and origin of the conditions under which gratification can and cannot be obtained, this is the only way to bring about a change. In a case I have already mentioned, fear of the mother was an important factor. This patient could achieve some satisfaction, although not an orgasm, by assuming the masculine position and being on top during intercourse. In all her relations with men, they had to be submissive, while she played the dominant role. She treated them kindly, but they had to obey. The first time that she had a truly satisfactory intercourse with full orgasm was after an analysis of her fears of her mother and when I, who represented the mother, was absent because of an illness. With the easing of her fear, she no longer had to play the masculine role but could give in and be a real woman.

Masculinity wishes can work in various ways. Usually they result in inhibitions in intercourse and in a more or less marked frigidity. I had one patient who was too passive in intercourse, although she was otherwise a very vivacious and active woman. What caused her passivity was a very intense fear of being too aggressive. She had castrative wishes that kept her from being active in intercourse and that manifested themselves in other areas of her life as well. Although very intelligent and capable, she was inhibited in her work and in earning money.

I can give only a few details about her history. There was one situation in which she was able to have a full orgasm. While she was reading a vivid description of a murder, all her sexual repressions suddenly disappeared, and she had a full orgasm through masturbation. This was a much more intense sexual experience than any she had had through intercourse. This was not a masochistic response for her but a breaking through of all her sadistic impulses toward other women.

This patient had a background of extreme conflict with her mother. When she was nineteen, she got a lover of her mother's to fall in love with her and was about to take him away. Her competition with her mother aroused feelings of guilt that troubled her for years. In her first two marriages, she always yielded when her husband started flirting with another woman. Her marriages would not have broken up if she had not yielded so easily. Another time, she took a married man away from his wife. She drew a picture, which she later destroyed, of a hatchet hanging over a blonde head. Her rival was a blonde, and this picture expressed all the destructive impulses she felt toward her competitor. At the same time, having conceived this picture filled her with guilt and fear.

I have tried to show that frigidity arises from conflicts originating in childhood that cause a fear of intercourse. If we are afraid of something, we lose the ability to take pleasure in it. This is the mechanism that is at work in frigidity; fear prevents the woman from having sensations and being able to enjoy intercourse.

The sort of fear I have in mind can have many sources. It can be a lasting fear of the mother that is incorporated into the superego, which then forbids relationships with men. Or it may arise because masculine tendencies, which are unfavorable to acceptance of the feminine role, lead to an aggressive behavior toward men that makes the woman dread retaliation. Or fear may be aroused by masturbation or satisfactions that lie in the realm of fantasy.

To make matters still more complicated, frigidity may have infantile sources that will be difficult to grasp for an audience with little knowledge of analytic theory. Our experience shows us that between the ages of three and six, children go through a period that we may call a sort of infantile puberty during which they have their first real genital sensations and sexual desires. But children are born with their sexual drives, and so it should not surprise us to find expressions of sexuality in them before that time. These expressions are not specifically genital but are closely attached to such physical functions as sucking, eating, and excreting. Sucking has not only to do with the satisfaction of hunger, for, as the research of David Levy has shown, children who have not been given adequate time to suck will suck their thumbs. This indicates that they do not suck simply to gratify hunger but that there is another kind of pleasure involved. As for the connection of the excretory functions with sexual excitement, I think that observation of children will show that at a certain age they will regard excretion as a great but hidden pleasure in the same way that they will later regard their sexual activities.

When conflicts in love and sexual development arise, the child may withdraw part of his instinctual life from the genital sphere and regress to these earlier forms of pleasure-seeking. This simply means that eating and drinking, for example, may have an emotional charge that derives from the fact that these activities have a sexual tinge. Some men care more for wine and a good meal than they do for women.

Now the real aim for persons who have thus regressed is not being united physically and psychically with a person of the opposite sex but getting something from him or her. The fantasies of girls of this type will not be about being loved by or loving a man but about being married or kept by a wealthy or prominent man who will heap gifts on them. When frigidity is not deep-rooted, you may see it disappear in such women if the man gives them a present. But they will lose interest if the man loses his money or no longer bestows presents upon them. For women of this type who have very strong wishes to be a man, intercourse may mean receiving the male organ as a present.

I remember a patient who came to see me because she had a psychosomatic skin disease for which she had been treated for ten or fifteen years. She pretended not to be frigid when the topic came up but said that she felt upset if her husband showed no desire for intercourse for a number of days. I was suspicious because there was an obvious disparity between her pretended non-frigidity and her secretly hostile attitude toward this man. Apart from her skin disease, she suffered from a terrible fear of having her blood sucked by a vampire, a fear that haunted both her daydreams and her dreams at night. She would become frightened if she were alone in the room in the evening, so frightened that she did not dare to move. Analysis showed her fear of a vampire to be the product of her desire to be a vampire herself, a desire of which she discovered the origin when she recovered the memory that one of her brothers had performed a perversion on her. Her fantasy of being a vampire was an expression of her wish to be a man and to possess the male organ. For her, having intercourse represented the fulfillment of this wish: "The man is giving me his organ, which I incorporate." By uncovering all the conflicts behind her frigidity, she was able to arrive at a real sexual response on a feminine basis.

I have said that the excretory functions can also be connected with a regressive form of sexuality. It is very common for people who get excited to have to urinate. Sometimes children suddenly start wetting the bed when they stop masturbating. Some women have pathological fears because of the easy connection between excretion and sexuality. One woman whose frigidity was related to these fears was afraid of letting out gas or of having to defecate or urinate when in the society of other people. Her anxiety was so great that she did not dare go out and led a very isolated life. In other cases, women have a fear that if they let themselves go during intercourse, there will be an excretory accident. This leads them to restrain their emotions and makes it difficult for them to have an orgasm. Such fears may be covered up by rape fantasies, for the women feel that if they are raped they are not responsible for whatever happens.

In the past, women who refrained from intercourse because of their fear of an excretory accident were often given bad advice by their physicians. The woman I mentioned in the last paragraph suffered consciously from her abstinence and very much wanted to have sexual relations. A physician might easily have told her that she should have sex or get married, but that advice would have been futile, for she would have found reasons for staying away from men or breaking off an engagement. In cases where there is such a deep regression of the libido to infantile levels, nothing but psychoanalysis can be of help.

Finally, I want to comment on some other factors that can be responsible for frigidity: fear of pregnancy, ignorance in sexual matters, and lack of tenderness on the part of the man.

Fear of pregnancy can certainly play a role when no adequate contraceptive measures are employed. Women may have good reason to be afraid of pregnancy, but I think that this factor has been overemphasized, since many women are fully capable of giving and receiving sexual pleasure in spite of this fear.

Ignorance about sexual matters is sometimes traceable to women's childhood experience, for they may have developed inhibitions about wanting to know. They may have been intimidated when they asked questions in childhood and have turned away from the subject as a result. They will not even listen on occasions when they might get information about it, or they will not observe sexual things when they have the opportunity—with animals, for instance. They will avoid situations in which sexual matters are being discussed. The result is ignorance, when knowledge might have been of help. We should be clear, however, about what is the most efficacious factor when we give our patients information. The good result in many cases is the product not only of the knowledge we impart but of the spirit in which we convey it. The doctor can play the role of an authoritative parent who, when talking about sex, lets the patient know that it is not bad but something she is allowed to do, thus relieving her conscience.

Lack of tenderness on the part of the man can certainly be an important factor in frigidity, for tenderness and affection are more closely linked to sexual arousal in women than in men. I wish to leave it an open question whether the reason for this connection is that intercourse has a much greater biological significance for women, given that it can result in pregnancy, or whether the closer connection with tender feelings is the product of social factors. In any event, since men can usually respond to a woman even when there is no tenderness in the relationship, frigidity in women is much more common than impotence in men. Whereas conflicts in their feelings toward the opposite sex tend to make women frigid, such conflicts lead to rudeness in sexual behavior or a lack of tenderness in men. Although psychic disturbances in relations with the opposite sex occur with approximately equal frequency in women and men, women's physiologic responses are more easily impaired than those of men. Hence, frigidity is much more common than impotence.

Where no deep conflicts are present and frigidity is due to the man's lack of tenderness, a cure may be effected by a change of partner or a change in the attitude of the man. When a frigidity that arises from a woman's own conflicts is responsible for the sexual behavior of the man, his withdrawal of tenderness will increase her frigidity, which will further antagonize him, and so on, in a vicious circle.

Psychogenic Factors in Menstrual Disorders

In gynecological literature there is not much disagreement about two extreme groups of menstrual irregularities: (1) cases where local or general lesions are obviously responsible for menstrual irregularity, and (2) cases in which the disturbance is not physical but psychological in origin. Some people have wondered whether the psychic problems are themselves the product of physical disturbances, but my experience as a psychiatrist indicates that the psychic problems existed long before the functional symptoms appeared.

Among students of menstrual disorders there are, of course, differences in the amount of emphasis placed on physical and psychological causes, and it would be desirable to have cooperative research into the relationship between these two factors. Deviations in the position of the uterus often seem to be responsible for a dysmenorrhea, but how do we account for the fact that in many cases of such deviations there is no menstrual irregularity? The existence of glandular conditions does not rule out psychic factors, since glandular problems can sometimes be improved through psychological treatment. Here again, cooperative research into the interactions between the physical and the psychological would be very desirable. Sometimes menstrual disorders are attributed to masturbation, which is seen as a physical consequence of pelvic congestion. This point of view is certainly false, since patients with dysmenorrhea are often those who do not masturbate but who have repressed their sexual impulses. Moreover, masturbation is too widespread a practice to make it responsible for menstrual disorders. Because many patients are afraid of the consequences of masturbation, it is often they who suggest to physicians that their physical problems are the result of their having masturbated.

Although distinct physical changes take place around the time of menstruation that affect blood pressure, metabolism, and sexual excitability, it is my experience that women who are balanced in their psychosexual life are not much disturbed by these changes, whereas those who have disturbances in their psychosexual life are likely to react adversely to the increase in libidinal tension. They may have been able to maintain a certain balance but now are unable to do so. They can be thrown out of balance by other stresses as well.

The fact that menstruation is dangerous for the psychic stability of neurotic women accounts for the analyst's seeing a great many menstrual disturbances, though women rarely come to us because of these problems alone. It is important to note that menstrual disorders usually disappear with a successful treatment of the neurosis, as is the case with other conversion symptoms. Indeed, they often disappear more rapidly than other symptoms, such as hysterical convulsions, which involve character difficulties and social adjustment, or frigidity, which is an expression of the disturbance in their entire attitude toward men. Whereas a dysmenorrhea may go away quickly, the whole neurosis may have to be resolved before these other problems can be cured.

As you no doubt already know, the physical problem of amenorrhea may have a psychological source in either the fear of becoming pregnant or the wish for a child. I have never encountered an amenorrhea without one of these factors being present. I'm sure you have frequently seen girls develop problems with amenorrhea when they start having, or thinking of having, sexual relations. They will have a conscious fear of becoming pregnant even when there is scarcely a possibility that they have conceived. When we get to know these patients better, we often discover that although they speak of being afraid, a conflict is really going on. Consciously, they do not want a child and may feel disgust at the thought of bearing one, but at the same time they have a deeply repressed wish for a child and unconsciously want to conceive.

In some cases, there is a conscious wish for a child as a means of bringing about marriage, but the same thing may happen at an unconscious level. For instance, I had a patient who did not have periods for two or three months after she started a relationship with a married man. At the time, she had not the least idea of wanting to marry him, but the wish was nonetheless present, and it came out distinctly in dreams. Eventually she married this man. Although she did not want to get pregnant, she forgot about birth control. It often happens that women become pregnant not because they lack methods of birth control but because of unconscious errors. This patient's carelessness about birth control was the first thing that indicated her wish for a child. She said, "I thought the man would take care of it"; but this was nonsense because he was younger and it was her responsibility. She was in conflict between consciously not wanting a child because of the whole social situation and unconsciously wanting a child as a way of securing the man. Her amenorrhea was related to this conflict.

Amenorrhea sometimes represents a premature menopause. I have analyzed three cases of this sort, and of course I cannot swear that this menopause would not have occurred if no conflict had been present. In one case, the patient lived with her brother, to whom she had a very strong emotional tie, and was quite jealous of the women with whom he associated. Behind this fixation on the brother was a fixation on the father. At the time of her premature menopause, when she was thirty-five or thirty-six, she had started a sexual relationship with an older man who clearly represented the father to her. Although she loved the man, she had conscientious qualms about this relationship and was uncomfortable with it. She wanted to be finished with her sexual life and to get rid of her conflicts. At this point, her amenorrhea set in.

In some cases, women have an opposite set of feelings and are disturbed by the arrival of menopause. They don't want to be finished with sex and feel they are no longer women when they stop menstruating. I suppose that these are women who have always worried about their genital integrity, about being normal, and that the cessation of the menses is like the dropping of a sword they have felt hanging over them.

In certain circumstances, menstruation is a welcome event. This was true in the case of a girl who had a strong phobia about going alone into the street. Her symptoms improved when she was menstruating because she was no longer afraid of being raped. Every practitioner has seen cases in which menstruation is welcomed as an excuse for not having intercourse, even within marriage.

Some women ignore menstruation altogether. These women have strong masculine tendencies, and for them menstruation, like child-bearing, reminds them of their womanhood. They will insist on going swimming and climbing mountains, with a total disregard for their condition when they are menstruating or pregnant.

The fact that the incidence of dysmenorrhea has declined with the growth of more reasonable attitudes toward menstruation shows, better than any scientific study, the importance of psychic factors in menstrual disorders. As Dr. Yarrows has pointed out in *Sex and the Modern Woman,* in the past decent women were supposed to be frigid, whereas now women feel inferior if they are not sexually responsive, and the incidence of frigidity has declined with this change of attitude.

There is often a connection between menstrual disorders and frigidity because mothers who tell their daughters that menstruation is a disease also convey that sex is a sin and suffering the lot of woman. Indeed, menstrual pains may be experienced as punishment for sexual activity. One patient told me that she thought her pains had to do with having gotten mixed up with boys and having sexual desires. Such ideas are not uncommon in young girls. They often feel that sex is forbidden and that they are being punished for indulging in it by menstrual bleeding and pain.

I imagine that there are many cases in which telling the patient that sexual relations have nothing to do with menstrual pain may be sufficient. But, once again, it is important to convey the information in an emotionally supportive way. The doctor can play the role of an absolving priest by telling his patients that what they are doing is not wrong and they need not be afraid of punishment.

I have spoken earlier about some of the early fears of the female child. These include fears of being physically damaged as a result of masturbation or fantasies of intercourse. Because the process of bleeding may make a woman feel that she has been wounded, it can revive those early fears. In patients with menstrual disorders one tends to find intense worries about genital integrity, fears that something has been destroyed and that they are responsible for it. Despite being very prudish, a patient named Mary asked one of her older sisters to look at her genitals and tell her if she was normal. She had a fear of being catheterized, again because she was afraid it would reveal that something was wrong with her. Another patient who also suffered from dysmenorrhea was averse to the idea of marriage because she feared that her future husband would find her genitals to be abnormal. Some women are afraid of gynecological examinations for similar reasons. The fear of being genitally damaged also shows up in dreams. One patient dreamed that there was suddenly a hole in the piece she was embroidering. Her associations to this dream revealed her fantasy that she had made a hole in herself by masturbation, that the vagina was originally something biologically different that she had destroyed.

Women's fears of being damaged or abnormal are not always connected with the genitals but may center on some other part of the body. One patient who had a severe menorrhagia was afraid that there was something wrong with her feet. She would ask other people if her feet were normally built and would go to art galleries to compare her feet with those of statues. She asked me if I would commit suicide if my feet were not perfectly normal. Her disproportionate emotion sheds light on women's demands for beautifying operations and their disappointments in them.

Some women with dysmenorrhea develop hypochondriacal fears, such as anxieties that they have cancer because of a slight discharge. Then they may go from one physician to another in order to obtain reassurance or to find someone who will operate on them. The patient I have called Mary had undergone five operations. Two could not be avoided, but she had the other three because she thought that her severe pains were due to adhesions, whereas in reality they were of psychogenic origin. An operation will provide such women only temporary relief because the underlying fears have not changed, and soon they will be seeking additional surgery. Psychotherapy is the only solution in these cases. Even if gynecologists give them reassurance about their sexual and genital integrity, this will not have a lasting effect because the deeper causes of their fears have not been removed.

For some women menstrual bleeding awakens an undefined sense of guilt because it seems to be a proof that something has gone wrong. It is a common human reaction to displace such feelings onto someone else, and we often find that these patients become extremely aggressive and reproach their husbands for all sorts of things. Anna was the only patient who came to me specifically because of her dysmenorrhea and her subsequent irritation about menstruation. She was very critical of her husband and kept talking about his failures and her disappointments and feelings of not being understood. This kind of reproachful behavior is not uncommon and is very much feared by the husbands. Women who are otherwise quite peaceful and pleasant become infuriated by the slightest annoyance during menstruation and are inaccessible to reason. Their irritability subsides when their menstrual period ends. Statistics show an increased suicide rate for women at the time of menstruation.

Ethnological studies help us understand the more severe cases by showing us how much fear there is of menstruation. I need only remind you of the taboos surrounding menstruation that we find in so many cultures. In some cultures it is believed that animals will die in the woods or fish in the sea or that crops will wither if a menstruating woman touches them. Her touch can even kill a man. There will be all sorts of regulations to prevent such things from happening. Menstruation itself, especially the first menstruation, is in some places conceived as intercourse with a demon, and the girl is considered the bride of a snake or a spirit. The first child is often considered to be the offspring of a spirit. I mention these widespread beliefs because they can help us to understand the similar conceptions that we find in the fantasy life of women.

I shall give you some examples of extreme menstrual disturbances because extreme cases show more clearly what is going on. Mary came to me because of an obsessional neurosis and numerous phobias. In addition to vague pains in her abdomen, she had severe dysmenorrhea. She was in her mid-forties when she started analysis and had never had any sex life. She had stopped masturbating at the time of puberty after she read that masturbation was a substitute for intercourse. Her entire sexual life consisted of fantasies, particularly fantasies of rape. Although she was by no means psychotic, her fantasies were so vivid that she often could not tell whether they were real or not. She took her pain to be a proof that something had actually happened to her. She would often say to me, "Dr. Horney, I have these pains and so something must have happened there."

Mary's pains were so severe that a nurse had said to her, "This is just like other women in childbirth." The nurse had guessed a psychological truth.

Mary's fantasies of rape were particularly intense at the time of menstruation. She regarded every man as a bloody monster who was waiting to rape a woman, while women who married were martyrs. Intercourse for her was the same sadistic act she had thought it to be as a child. She had slept in her parents' bedroom and had observed their intercourse, and in the dreams that were prompted by these early observations, her mother was being attacked by a snake or other wild animal, while she was defending her. Her whole sexual life consisted of infantile fantasies of being raped and having children. Her painful menstruation was the realization of these fantasies of rape and child-birth. At the same time, she felt her suffering to be a punishment for these guilty fantasies.

Another patient, Anna, who had dysmenorrhea, had very deep guilt feel-ings, partly because of masturbation but chiefly because of a strong incestuous tie to her father. She remembered, after puberty, that her father had paid her attentions of a distinctly sexual character that had frightened and embarrassed her and had also aroused fantasies. In childhood she, too, had thought of intercourse as something bloody. She remembered seeing on the side of her mother's bed a bloody piece of meat, which was probably a bloody pad. The flow of blood in menstruation revived her infantile incestuous fantasies, and these aroused a guilt of which she tried to rid herself by turning her reproaches on her husband. The aggressiveness that comes out during menstruation may be not only a defense against guilt but also the expression of a bottled up aggressiveness toward the father or mother. In the case of Anna, with her strong incestuous fantasies, there was naturally an intense jealousy of the mother and fantasies of taking the father away from her. Statistics show an increase of criminality in women at the time of menstruation.

Another patient, Margaret, had a severe menorrhagia that made her feel that she was drowning in blood and guilt. She was quite an attractive girl who could easily have had sexual relations with men; but she had very distinct fears of intercourse, while consciously wanting it, and always managed to break off a relationship when intercourse seemed imminent. The greater part of her sex life lay in fantasies of an incestuous character. She had a deep fixation on the father, which was shown by her attachment to an older man who had been her singing teacher and who was consciously a father substitute. She was the oldest of eight children, all of whom were born at home. She remembered being frightened when her mother gave birth and having seen bowls of blood carried out of her mother's room. For this patient, too, intercourse was con-nected with the idea of something horribly bloody going on. When her mother had a hemorrhage of the lungs, Margaret attributed it to her marital relations. She had an Oedipus complex in the pure form of a deep attachment to the father and a deep jealousy of the mother. She thought of her mother as a whore and felt guilty for doing so.

The mechanism underlying Margaret's menstrual disturbances was something like this: "I cannot take the place of my mother, not only because I cannot have relations with my father but also because I experience too much guilt and fear even with a father substitute. I can take her place only in fantasies, but even there I can only do so by assuming the suffering role that she played." Her severe bleeding during menstruation symbolized the bleeding inflicted on her mother by her father and was the condition that allowed her to engage in her guilty fantasies. The most important part of her sexual life was lived out in her menstrual disturbances.

Psychogenic Factors in Problems Relating to Pregnancy

Whether women have a primary instinctive drive to have a child is still an open question both in analytic circles and elsewhere. Observations of animal behavior certainly favor such an assumption, for we regularly see the female animal refuse intercourse after having been fertilized. Moreover, animals such as dogs and goats that have not been fertilized when in heat still experience an enlargement of the mammary glands and a secretion of milk at the time when they might have given birth. They also prepare a place to give birth, just as they would if they had actually been impregnated. They seem to be acting under a genuine instinctive compulsion.

Yet we cannot automatically draw parallels between animals and humans. The primary instincts of hunger and sex are much the same in both, but in humans they are greatly modified by tradition and other social factors, especially because our brains mature over a much longer period of time and are subject to many influences. I personally favor the assumption that women have a genuine biological drive to have a child, because otherwise it seems incomprehensible to me how the wish for a child could play such an enormous role in female psychology. I do not offer this as a proof, however, but as an impression.

Perhaps we should stick to the factors that may either inhibit or reinforce the wish for a child, for we can see these more clearly. Children are intensely curious about pregnancy long before they are physically able to have a child. They want to know how the child gets into the mother and how it comes out. Such curiosity in children never has a merely intellectual origin but is always motivated by wishes and fears. To some extent, these wishes and fears may be independent of the mother's becoming pregnant, but the mother's pregnancy always has a great influence, and in my experience later disturbances in the attitude toward motherhood all have to do with cases in which the mother did become pregnant. We must keep in mind, however, that the attitude toward pregnancy is dependent on the whole emotional situation of the child.

We must differentiate between the child's reaction to a newborn sibling and her reactions to the mother. Up to the age of six, a child invariably reacts to a new sibling with jealousy. A girl of eight, nine, or ten may identify with the mother, however, and be motherly toward the infant. The jealousy toward the new sibling may be reinforced by two factors. If the child has received too much attention and tenderness, she may be afraid that the new baby will take some of the parents' affection from her. This is particularly so if she has been an only child up until then. Something similar will happen when a child has had too little love from the parents, for then the child will be afraid of the sibling's taking away the little she has received. The second factor that reinforces jealousy is the parents' making too much of a fuss about the new-comer, as is the case when there have been only girls and the long-awaited boy has arrived.

The child is not only jealous of the new sibling but may also feel resentment toward the mother and father. In children of three to five years, there may be an intense hostile reaction to the mother because they are jealous of the atten-tion she is giving to the infant, and this can result in feeding problems that force the mother to give a great deal of her time to the older child. A girl of this age may have another reaction that is more repressed and therefore much less accessible to observation, and that is an envy of the motherhood of the mother. The girl's hostile reactions may be reinforced by the oedipal situation, especially if there has been an overly affectionate father, a cold and unloving mother, or an early sexual arousal of the child. When the mother gives birth, the girl may have the envious, resentful feeling that "my mother gets the child, not I."

With one of my patients, such envy found expression in her response to the birth of a brother when she was three-and-a-half. Her mother had the nice idea of giving her a wonderfully dressed baby doll, which was lying in a cradle. My patient contemptuously ignored this doll as a way of saying, "That is no substitute. I want to have a real baby." Later on, the doll played an immense role in her fantasies.

The hostile reaction to the mother because of envy of her being pregnant or having given birth may be very intense. This often comes out clearly in the transference situation, when patients get the idea that I am getting fatter and fatter and react with sudden hatred and disgust. It turns out that they are reacting so violently because they imagine that I am pregnant and expecting a child. This is a repetition of what they experienced when their mothers became pregnant. Their disgust with their mothers, and in the transference situation with me, is an expression of their envy and jealousy.

From the time that a child realizes in an infantile, distorted way the role of the father in pregnancy (usually by the age of five), a jealousy of the new sibling may also be a jealousy of the mother's possession of the father. The existence of the infant is a definite proof that something sexual has gone on between the parents, and I have found that for many patients oedipal wishes toward the father culminate in a desire to have a child from him.

The children's jealousy and rage manifest themselves in their symptoms, in their fantasies, in their attitudes, and in their impulse to kick the mother in the womb, an impulse that some of my adult patients still have when they see a pregnant woman on the street. Some children react to the birth of a sibling with bed-wetting or feeding difficulties or irritability or frightening fantasies about childbirth. I have had adult patients who still remember fantasies in which the womb bursts during childbirth or is cut up in some sadistic way. The origin of these fantasies is not so much fear as a desire for the mother's death in childbirth, a desire that frequently produces the fear that she will indeed die. Often there are fantasies of taking the child away from the mother. The mothering role that some older children play toward a newborn may be motivated by a competitive desire to say: "I am the real mother, not you." What comes out in this milder form in older children may take the cruder form in younger ones of fantasies of robbing the mother of the child and destroying her womb.

I suppose that all of this sounds bizarre to you, but although you may distrust the findings of analysis, I urge you to consider that in this case they have something like experimental confirmation. David Levy has conducted experiments in which he presented children of different ages a mother doll who had a baby doll in her arms. He did not give them any suggestions but encouraged them to do what they liked with the dolls. Invariably the children tore the baby doll to pieces with a certain amount of rage and then tore the mother doll to pieces as well, ripping off first her breasts and then her head, arms, and legs. If we dismiss the early emotions connected with pregnancy and the wish for a child as just the fantasies of psychoanalysts, we will be at a loss to explain the severe disturbances that we find in these areas later on. Many women have conflicts about pregnancy because it is associated with their early hostility toward the mother and with incestuous wishes toward the father. The fact that having a child means the realization of their old oedipal wishes at once reinforces their desires to become pregnant and triggers extreme feelings of guilt and fear.

I should like to return to the case of Anna, for whom, you recall, menstruation aroused guilt feelings connected with her incestuous fantasies about her father. She tried to rid herself of these guilt feelings by reproaching her husband. Her attachment to her father resulted in both an intensified desire for children and increased fears about having them. Her desires found expression in fantasies and poems in which she was a goddess of fertility who had many offspring. Her fears were not so much of dying in childbirth as of being desolate, poor, and deserted after having children. She had these fears long before there was the possibility of becoming pregnant. Given her intense and conscious desire for her father, it is not surprising that she repeated the oedipal situation by beginning a sexual relationship with her eventual husband at a time when he was married to another woman with whom he had had children. He certainly represented the father for her. After he divorced his first wife, Anna became pregnant by him and suffered because she was not married as yet and had little money. She might have avoided this situation, but she had a need for self-punishment. She felt that if she committed so horrible a crime as having a child by a father-substitute, then she had to pay with suffering. That she felt guilty in relation to her mother as well was shown by a dream in which she was in a church and had to give back her child to a threatening mother-goddess.

It is unusual for wishes for children and guilt feelings about these wishes to be as conscious as they were with Anna. More often guilt and fear lead women to repress their wishes for a child. One young woman who came to be analyzed had the idea that pregnancy and babies were disgusting and did not want to have a child. She felt that it was a piece of malice on the part of men to force women to have babies. This had not always been her attitude toward pregnancy, for I discovered later that she had wanted to have a child when she was a very little girl. But her mother became pregnant when she was five, and she reacted with a disgust that came out toward me in the transference. Shortly before puberty, sex play occurred between her and her father, and she became intensely worried about having a child, even though they had not had intercourse. Unconsciously, she wanted a child, but consciously she was in dread of becoming pregnant. When one of her brothers teased her about getting fat at this time, she nearly starved herself to become thin, because to her being fat meant being pregnant. She eventually reached the conclusion that she really had no objection to having a child but was afraid she could not conceive because she had damaged herself by masturbation. She explained her aversion to pregnancy as a kind of sour grapes; she defended herself against frustration by not wanting what she was afraid she could not have.

Although this reasoning sounds convincing, and I have received similar explanations from other young girls, it is not sufficient, because many women masturbate, even vaginally, without being afraid of not being able to conceive.

Her attitude toward pregnancy was produced less by a fear of having been physically damaged than by masturbation fantasies in which she imagined herself destroying the pregnant mother and child. I learned of these fantasies from her dreams and from fits of rage during which she destroyed her clothes, cutting them into small pieces. These fits were followed by intense guilt because she felt as if she had committed murder. She did not destroy all her clothes but only those that made her look fat — that is, pregnant. By cutting up her clothes, she was really destroying the pregnant mother and baby. The real meaning of her masturbation fears was this: "My fantasies show that I want to tear mother and baby to pieces, and I am afraid that the same thing will be done to me if I become pregnant." Her disgust at the idea of pregnancy vanished after we analyzed her masturbation fantasies and her compulsion to destroy her clothes.

For women, then, the idea of having a child can be surrounded by all sorts of conflicts. Unconscious emotions may reinforce the natural wish for a child. For instance, if sexual desires are repressed altogether, the wish for a child may replace these desires and be charged with the emotions that belong to them. Or, although pregnancy is an exquisitely female function, it may be a means by which women who are alienated from their feminine role can fulfill certain masculine fantasies. Having a child may seem to be an achievement that is equal to masculine accomplishments, or it may be an unconscious substitute for possessing a penis. At the same time, very intense fears may be connected with the idea of pregnancy, such as the fear of dying in childbirth or being destroyed by the child with which one is pregnant. These fears can usually be traced back to old conflicts with the mother, particularly when she was pregnant. The result may be a disgust with pregnancy and an unwillingness to bear children.

A related problem is that of sterility, which sometimes has no organic basis in either the man or the woman. These cases have remained a mystery to gynecologists. Insofar as they have tackled it, they have considered a connection to frigidity. In both Germany and America, some gynecologists have proposed that sterility may be a direct consequence of frigidity. This seems improbable to me, for in a great many cases of frigidity pregnancy occurs. The idea that there may be psychogenic causes is not as fantastic as it may at first appear, given that fertilization is dependent on a great many functional processes — such as internal secretions, reflex movements of the vaginal canal, and so on — that can be disturbed by psychic influences. Sterility may be the result not of frigidity per se but of psychological conflicts of the sort I have mentioned that may also be responsible for frigidity.

Premenstrual disturbances may be related to attitudes about pregnancy.

These disturbances involve feeling depressed, irritated, apprehensive, and moody in various degrees. They may be so serious that they give rise to suicidal impulses, which sometimes result in self-destruction. They are sometimes responsible for kleptomania. So far, premenstrual disturbances have not been much studied by psychoanalysts, largely, I think, because they have nothing to do with the process of bleeding, which lends itself so readily to interpretation. Nor can they be explained by the increase in libidinal tension that precedes menstruation, because although it is doubtful that this tension decreases when menstruation starts, menstruation brings great relief. I suggest that premenstrual tension may be related to the fact that all kinds of changes have been going on in the ovaries and uterus to prepare the organism for pregnancy. The onset of menstruation may bring relief because it means that conception has not taken place.

I have in mind a particular case. This patient had typical depressive moods before menstruation and the typical relief when the bleeding started. Without being influenced by my analytic approach, she told me that before her period began she often had dreams about having children, and she described herself as feeling guilty, sensuous, and full. When menstruation began, she spontaneously felt, "Now the child is here." This seems to contradict the idea that she was experiencing relief, but only if we do not understand how the unconscious works. Two things were going on at once. In her unconscious fantasies, menstruation represented a sort of childbirth, while she was consciously aware that it meant that she would not have a child.

This patient had a typical history of a very deep father fixation, which resulted in her marrying a man of the same age and habitus as her father. For a long time, she felt a conscious disgust at the idea of having children, but I could guess from her intense maternal attitude that her wishes for children must be particularly strong. Her sexual feelings for her father were repressed so deeply that she had never felt a strong erotic attraction to any man. At a very early age, the wish to have a child by her father had taken the place of all her original sexual desires. Eventually, her wish to have children emerged in a very direct way.

This and similar cases in which there is a striking correlation between premenstrual disturbances and conflicting attitudes about having a child lead me to hypothesize that the physiological processes that are preparing the woman for pregnancy give rise to increased wishes for a child at this time. Such wishes are not conscious but they do appear in dreams before menstruation begins, and the conflicts which they arouse result in depression and irritation. If this is so, it is understandable that menstruation gives these patients relief. I should like to see this hypothesis investigated further along analytical lines, for it not only could help relieve disturbances that are sometimes very severe but also could be of great theoretical interest. It could illuminate the connection between physiological processes and their psychic representation, and it could help to establish that the desire for a child has a biological basis and is not simply a wish that is secondarily acquired.

There may be psychogenic factors also in two disturbances of pregnancy: *Hyperemesis gravidarum* [pernicious vomiting] and spontaneous abortion. I speak of these disturbances together because psychologically they might both be attributed to the wish to get rid of the child. A well-known therapeutic measure for hyperemesis is removing the patient from the family and placing her somewhere else. Spontaneous abortions are of psychological interest when there is no organic reason for them. Zilboorg has recently presented an interesting paper about a patient of his who had seven such abortions. When he uncovered her conflicts about having a child, she was able to have a successful pregnancy. One case is not convincing of itself, but observations that I and other analysts have made show a correlation between spontaneous abortions that have no organic basis and very strong conflicts connected with having children. These observations lead me to think that psychological factors may be strong enough to initiate such abortions. The woman seems to perceive the fetus as something threatening, an enemy, some sort of dangerous growth that she must get rid of. Hyperemesis may not have such a deep foundation but may mean, "I don't want a child from this particular man."

In the absence of organic explanations, psychogenic factors may be at work in otherwise puzzling cases of deficiencies in labor. There may be a vague or unconscious but nevertheless intense fear of dying in childbirth, in which case having vigorous contractions would be tantamount to hastening one's own death. In other cases, the state of pregnancy itself may constitute a wish fulfillment, and the woman is reluctant to have it come to an end.

The Uses and Limitations of Analytic Knowledge in Gynecological Practice

A well-known gynecologist in Berlin acknowledged the influence that psychological factors may have on all sorts of female disturbances but argued that although it is good to know about such things, a gynecologist should nevertheless refrain from doing any kind of therapeutic work. His motto was, "Psychotherapy for the psychotherapist." Such clear-cut formulations are attractive, but I think that the situation is more complicated than that.

You may not have believed three-quarters of what I have said in these lectures, but the fact remains that there are a great many instances of pain, bleeding, and discharge, and of difficulties in conception, pregnancy, childbirth, and nursing for which you have no adequate organic explanations. In the case of glandular disturbances, we know more at this time about psychological factors than we do about physical ones, and many physicians are disposed to attribute indeterminate cases to the psychic side.

The question is: How can a knowledge of psychological conflicts and their relation to physical symptoms be profitably utilized in gynecological practice? We are often confronted with a similar question by educators when we tell them that conflicts experienced in childhood may result in a severe neurosis in later life. They want us to give them a prescription for avoiding these difficulties and to tell them how to educate. We feel embarrassed because all we can do at this point is to indicate certain attitudes on the part of educators that we regard as mistakes. In the same way, a knowledge of psychological factors can prevent a physician from making mistakes.

One thing that can be prevented is unnecessary operations, something that gynecologists themselves recognize as a serious problem. Gynecologists are often confronted with situations in which no organic problems can be found but in which patients demand an operation. The obvious thing to do here is to look for psychological explanations for their behavior. Much more difficult are cases in which patients demand an operation not in words but with symptoms. They may have such severe pains or bleeding that their symptoms will compel you to seek a surgical remedy. The psychological point of view is important here, too, for if a doctor is firmly convinced that excessive pain and bleeding do not necessarily have an organic basis, he will be less ready to perform an operation without a clear indication that it is called for. A physician who is convinced that such suffering *must* have a physical origin will be likely to try an operation even if he cannot find an organic basis for the symptoms. If he has this attitude, he will always find some justification for surgery, because there is no functional disorder for which an operation has not been recommended and reported to have been successful. Besides, a physician may have the feeling in these borderline cases that "if I don't perform an operation, somebody else will!" My main point is that it can make a big difference in physicians' attitudes toward surgery if they know that even the most alarming symptoms can be initiated by psychological factors.

To be sure, it is often difficult to decide between surgery and psychological treatment. Dr. A. A. Brill has recently told me of the case of a woman with a bleeding stomach who was referred to him. The patient was hysterical because of her severe hemorrhaging, and Brill refused to treat her, sending her to an internist instead. After she went from one doctor to another, she finally had to be fed rectally, and plans were being made for surgery. But one of her doctors suspected that her symptoms were psychogenic in origin, and he sent her back to Brill, who then agreed to treat her and cured her through psychoanalysis.

Some doctors feel that as long as it does no harm, an operation may provide relief to the patient even when no organic cause is present. Although this may happen sometimes, I cannot endorse such a procedure. One of my patients was convinced that something was wrong with her, because she felt guilty about masturbation and was afraid she had damaged herself. Before she began working with me, she had had an operation on her cervix that had provided temporary relief. But as a result of her operation, her menstrual flow was reduced, and this convinced her all the more that something was wrong with her. Her guilt and fear were revived, and she became depressed because she now had a definite physical basis for feeling abnormal. Such possible outcomes must be considered before proceeding with surgery.

There are many psychological reasons for which a woman might want an operation. It may be her way of realizing an infantile conception of being raped, especially if she has repressed her sexuality and it has no other outlet. Or it may be a form of self-punishment or a manifestation of suicidal ideas.

Psychological factors should always be taken into account before advising an abortion for other than compelling organic reasons, for the consequences might be devastating. The patient might be depressed and want the abortion very badly at the time, but later she may suffer from deep self-reproaches for having murdered the child. Sometimes these self-reproaches continue for years and are easily triggered by an accident that results in the death of a child. Leaving aside the legal issues, experience shows that we must pay close attention to psychological factors when determining whether an abortion would really be beneficial to the patient.

Gynecologists often make the mistake of ignoring the suggestive element in treatment. Sometimes a confidential talk with the physician will have a beneficial effect, even though no organic changes have taken place. Much depends on the emotional atmosphere of the relation between doctor and patient. The patient may improve if the relationship is good or get worse if it is not.

The emotional relation between doctor and patient is crucial in psychotherapy, of course, but all physicians will recognize that confidence on the part of the patient and a caring but detached attitude on the part of the physician are essential to a positive result. This is true even with functional diseases. Every physician will also have experienced violent reactions on the part of patients, who may fall passionately in love with him or feel resentful without any apparent reason. In the analytic situation we study these reactions very carefully, and instead of allowing them to disrupt the therapy, we make use of them in our treatment. Irrational reactions on the part of the patient may include being suspicious of the doctor, spitefully misleading him, and wanting to be mistreated.

All these reactions represent an awakening of old emotional patterns as they developed in relation to parents and siblings in childhood and a transference of them to the doctor. How do we deal with such transferences in analysis? In the first place, we recognize that the patient's irrational attitudes derive from his early experiences and that they have little to do with us. They belong to the patient and could just as easily have been evoked by someone else. The rule we try to follow is never to take them personally. The love and admiration the patient bestows on us are not due to our personal qualities, nor are his spite and suspicion. We must try to understand these reactions, which are probably typical of the way he responds to other people and to life in general. By analyzing his transference behavior, we can help the patient gain insight into his difficulties in human relationships.

The possibilities of working in this way with transference outside analysis are naturally very limited. Other physicians do not get to know the patient as well as we do and cannot work with him in the same way. They might need some help from those with more experience in psychological matters, perhaps in the form of seminars in which transference reactions can be discussed. But even a general knowledge of the way transference operates might help them to deal with difficult outbreaks. It is useful to know that a worsening of symptoms may be an expression of the patient's resentment and that he is seeking to punish the physician in this way. It is better to have some idea of what is going on than to have a naive, emotional reaction to it.

I have tried to suggest how analytic knowledge can help physicians avoid certain pitfalls in medical practice. It can also be used in a positive way. Sometimes a simple explanation can be of great help to the patient. I have already spoken of cases in which patients experience severe menstrual pain because they feel that they should be punished for their sexual desires and activities. They may not be aware of this connection themselves, but if the physician is aware of it, he can bring them considerable relief by calling it to their attention and assuring them that there is no need to feel guilty. A knowledge of the possible psychogenic factors in other disturbances of menstruation, pregnancy, and childbirth can have a similar beneficial effect.

In many cases, of course, such simple explanations are not of much help. In addition to lacking knowledge, patients often have a deep emotional resistance to uncovering the conflicts that lie behind their symptoms. A patient may have protracted menorrhagias because of her sexual fears and inhibitions, but her symptoms are valuable to her precisely because they protect her against sexual dangers, and she will not want to understand them or give them up. The physician must be sensitive to resistances and not try to force a patient to see something she is not ready to confront. As I have said, analysis involves uncovering infantile conflicts and fears that are still operating in the patient's life and recognizing the connections between these infantile sources and present difficulties. This is a lengthy and arduous process, and I do not expect gynecologists to undertake it, any more than I am ready to do surgery in addition to psychoanalysis.

But not all symptoms have origins in the distant past. For instance, menstrual disturbances may reflect conflicts in the marriage or inner struggles about whether to have an affair. The spectacle of a friend beating a child may produce hyperemesis or some other difficulty in pregnancy. Sometimes just pointing out the connections can bring the patient considerable relief.

It is impossible to tell from a cough alone whether the patient has a cold or tuberculosis. The same is true of functional female disorders, especially in borderline cases. The physician must determine whether they require physical or psychological treatment, or some combination of the two. As I have suggested, this can be a very difficult diagnosis. If the patient's problems are psychological, in whole or in part, the physician must further decide whether his help will suffice or whether psychoanalytic therapy is called for.

7

Woman's Fear of Action (1935)

The following talk was in Harold Kelman's papers at the Postgraduate Center for Mental Health. It was given to National Federation of Professional and Business Women's Clubs in July 1935. It is a remarkable statement for its time and helps to explain why Horney stopped focusing on feminine psychology. It has been published before as an appendix in *Karen Horney: A Psychoanalyst's Search for Self-Understanding* (Paris 1994). The version presented here has been more highly edited.

When I look back on the history of woman's position in the last centuries, a striking fact appears: in times when women were seriously granted all opportunities for the development of human values, such as the time before the French Revolution, the so-called period of enlightenment, there was no interest in special features of feminine psychology. The ideal was that all human beings should develop their full potentialities regardless of sex. In politically reactionary periods, such as the time after the French Revolution, called the period of romanticism, and also in periods of economic crisis such as we are going through today, there appears a consuming interest in woman's "nature."

For some time I took this interest in feminine psychology at its face value. I have done some work in the field of feminine psychopathology and am frequently asked what, to my knowledge, are the specific trends in female psychology. The only answer I can make is that I hope to know at some future time, for after all the speculation of psychologists concerning the possible differences between men and women, we do not appear to have gone far beyond the old discussions in the Talmud, namely, that we do not know much beyond the biological distinctions. Then, it occurred to me that it was not so important to try to answer the question about differences as to understand the real significance of the keen interest in feminine nature nowadays.

Why are people so very interested in woman's nature? There are economic reasons based on the highly competitive nature of society. Although many individuals do not realize it, they are not honestly searching for valid answers to the question of differences. What they really want to do is to prove that it is in absolute accord with woman's "nature" that she keep out of competitive fields of work and restrict herself to charity, sexuality, and child bearing. Whether their reasoning is based on the sin of Eve, as in the Catholic Church, or on the rules laid down by German philosophy with respect to sexual relations or on Freud's statements of differences in anatomy, the result is the same. . . . When jobs are scarce, it becomes necessary to prove in any way possible that woman's "nature" forbids her free admittance to the market.

Any sudden increase in interest over sex differences, therefore, must be regarded as a danger signal for women, particularly in a patriarchal society, where men find it advantageous to prove on biologic premises that women should not take part in shaping the economy and the political order. Elaborate arguments serving the interests of masculine ideologies become strategical means of preserving male superiority in the economic and political world by convincing woman that innately she is glad to keep out of it.

Frequently women themselves strengthen the masculine ideologies. They often regard professional pursuits as secondary to love and marriage. They become so preoccupied with the emotional side of life that they are little concerned with the great problems that are moving and shaking our time. They become leaning and dependent and develop a need to be taken care of. All these attitudes help to support the theories men wish to establish as a means of eliminating women from competition.

So far this is fairly transparent, but we have not always recognized that any group which is restricted in its activities for a long period of time undergoes certain psychic changes; that within individuals of the suppressed group a psychic adaptation occurs that brings them to accept the limitations which the dominant group finds it advantageous to impose. Thus women have come to regard love and devotion as specifically feminine ideals and virtues; homemaking and rearing of children, the one possibility for happiness, security, and prestige. Although great changes have come about in recent years, psychic effects of the long history of restriction linger.

Some of the psychic consequences of woman's own attitudes that we can expect to find, and do find, still in existence are the following:

1. Since woman's happiness, security, and prestige depended on her relations to home and children, she came to regard them as the only real values in life. The boy-crazy girl and the woman who is lost and miserable if she is not being continually sought by men represent the extreme outcome of such an overvaluation of love and sexuality. These types supply evidence for the psychologists who like to believe that "the essence of woman's being is love" or "sexuality is for women something central, for men peripheral," and so on. As a matter of fact, it would be difficult to explain how, with conditions as they are, woman could avoid overrating sexuality and love. The most serious outcome of this emphasis on her part is that she comes to expect far too much from these relations with men and children and is often doomed to bitter disappointment. The woman who concentrates her expectations on relations with husband and children, whether to satisfy her ambition or to secure their gratitude and attachment, handicaps husband and children as well as herself and is all too likely, in the end, to render the emotional relationship upon which she relies so heavily completely unsatisfactory.

Another disastrous result of the overrating of love is that it is bound to degrade any pursuits outside this sphere. Thus we see the neurotic attitude of the woman who regards other pursuits as unsatisfactory substitutes that she views with secret resentment. Her inner attitude is expressed by such phrases as "because I am not attractive to men I have to be a teacher" or "I wasn't the feminine type, had no sex appeal, and so I had to go into business." Lacking respect for these other pursuits, which are to her only poor substitutes for woman's "normal" preoccupations, she cannot devote all her energies to them. An undercurrent of resistance, which interferes with whole-hearted devotion, mars her satisfaction and success and gives rise to a belief that she is inferior and incapable. There are many other sources of woman's conviction of inferiority, of course, but this is an important one, because it so often keeps her from becoming genuinely and actively concerned with the great economic and political questions of our time, even when they concern woman's own position in the world and should be of vital interest to her. This is one of the reasons why woman has not been more active in improving conditions for herself; such action was outside the magic circle within which her existence was confined.

2. As fulfillment for woman came to mean love, sex, home, children, all depending on her relations to man, it became of paramount importance to please man. Thus came about the cult of beauty and charm. And thus came the fear of being "unfeminine." The unfeminine included any attitude or belief which stood in opposition to masculine ideas about the divine order of things. To be "feminine" was to be submissive and devoted regardless of how one was treated. Any struggle for improvement in the position of women was, therefore, "unfeminine," a denial of what had come to be accepted as women's "nature." The residue today of this fear, as seen in the lack of interest, in the don't-care attitude, is the outward expression of a subterranean fear which can be best explained by an illustration with which we are all familiar. Here is a girl who does not care for parties. She cannot be persuaded to go to parties because, she says, she prefers reading alone at home. She is quite honest; her lack of interest is genuine; she is interested in other pursuits, but usually this lack of interest is rooted in fear. She is afraid of being neglected or of meeting criticism, but she does not know that she is afraid. She does not know that when she says she doesn't care for parties, she is really expressing her unconscious fear. This attitude has created an undercurrent of fear that prevents women from taking action in economic and social spheres which concern them most vitally. It is important that we recognize this subconscious fear, because if we would change attitudes, it is necessary to understand the sources of the energy which sustains them.

3. Fear of displeasing men is not the only anxiety created through restriction [to an emotional sphere]. The fear of losing erotic attractiveness through age is a very real and acute anxiety due to the same overvaluation of love life. Except in times when unemployment is widespread, we would consider it definitely neurotic if a man became frightened and depressed as he approached middle age; in a woman it is regarded as natural, and in a way it is natural, because physical attractiveness has come to represent the supreme value for women. This age-phobia is pathetic enough in itself, but it has two aspects that are more serious than is generally recognized and which help to account for the inactivity of women in the world's work. The fear of age is not limited to the period when a woman is no longer in her bloom. It throws its shadow over most of the years after twenty and creates a feeling of insecurity that thwarts the life-rhythm. A woman of thirty-five or forty will say: "Still five years ahead then my life will be declining." She feels that she must crowd a great deal into the short time left. The resultant anxiety and half-despair accounts for the jealousy between mothers and adolescent daughters and frequently spoils their relations. It may also create hostility toward all other women.

Age is a problem for everyone, of course, men as well as women, but it becomes a desperate one if youth and erotic attractiveness are the chief values of life. Their overvaluation of youth makes it difficult for women to recognize the worth of the qualities of maturity, such as poise, independence, autonomy of judgment, wisdom — qualities that have great value for the entire culture. Our mature personality should be more secure and stronger than our youthful one, for it has the advantage of experience, but how can the maturing woman develop this security and strength if she believes that her very nature demands that love be the center and sole purpose of her being and at the same time regards her mature years as ones of decline in this sphere? The emphasis on erotic values results in a great waste of human values for women. The young woman feels a temporary security because of her ability to attract men, but mature women can hardly hope to escape being devalued even in their own eyes. And their feeling of inferiority robs them of the strength for action which rightly belongs to maturity.

Inferiority feelings are the most common evil of our time and our culture. To be sure we do not die of them, but I think they are more inimical to happiness and progress than cancer or tuberculosis. When the subject of inferiority feelings comes up, someone usually remarks, "But, men too have inferiority feelings." True, but there is an important difference: men do not, as a rule, feel inferior just because they are men, but a woman frequently feels inferior because she is a woman. The restriction of woman to a private emotional sphere leads to inferiority feelings because a sound and secure self-confidence must draw on a broad basis of human qualities — such as initiative, courage, independence, capacity for mastering situations, talents — as well as erotic values. As long as homemaking was a big task with plenty of responsibilities, as long as the number of children was not restricted because children added to the wealth of the nation, woman knew that she was a constructive factor in the economic process. This conviction gave her a sound basis for self-esteem. With the change in social conditions, woman has lost one important foundation for feeling herself valuable.

As far as the purely sexual side is concerned, puritanical influences, however one may evaluate them, certainly have added to the debasement of woman by giving sexuality the connotation of something sinful and low. In a matriarchal society, this attitude toward sexuality would have led to disregarding men as animal-like beings. In a patriarchal society, it was bound to make woman the symbol of sin, which is the way she is depicted in early Christian literature. As a rule, woman does not herself know that the shadow she feels on her self-esteem comes, to some extent, from sexual attitudes that are deeply rooted in Christian culture.

Self-confidence built on success in giving and receiving love is built on a foundation too shaky and small. It is too small because it leaves out many personality values, and it is too shaky because it is too dependent on such accidents as finding adequate partners, marriage possibilities, and so forth. Basing self-confidence on erotic success very frequently leads to dependence on the other person's affection and appreciation and produces a deep feeling of unworthiness if one is not loved and appreciated. This emotional dependence also involves fear of criticism and ridicule, which turns us back to the original point; that every woman who fights for the opportunity to realize her potentialities as a person exposes herself to all kinds of insinuations and ridicule. She must recognize this as a repressive technique and be prepared to face it.

I have sometimes been told that, although the picture I have drawn may be accurate for European women, conditions are quite different in this country. To the extent that the American woman has succeeded in important achievements outside of home, that is a valid distinction. She is a great factor in social and cultural life, and artistic pursuits are regarded as a domain wide open to women here. But although opportunities for women are certainly wider than in Europe, we must not be blinded by the surface. For the principle is the same here as there. That general self-confidence which is the psychic capital for achievement is not won, because a few women have succeeded in competition with men. There are too many neglected tasks that require initiative, creative imagination, courage, planning experience, capacity to stand on one's own feet which can be accomplished only by women endowed with this self-confidence.

Since it is impossible to fight successfully without feeling justified, where are we to find justification for the struggle of women for self-confidence? In this thought: As long as women are thwarted in their personalities, men and children are afflicted too. If we fight for the chance to develop our human values, we certainly shall be happier ourselves, and men and children will benefit as well. Ultimately the fight is a joint enterprise, for the well-being of everyone depends on success in the battle against men's prejudices and fears.

Once it was believed that something innate in women made it impossible for them to cooperate with one another. It is true that women's long restriction to the emotional sphere has made action in solidarity more difficult for them and has created a stronger rivalry among women than among men. Their competition for men has generated a great deal of anxiety and insecurity, and the resulting hostility has made it difficult for women to work together. This has given rise, even among the greatest psychologists, to the belief that women are biologically disposed to be more jealous than men.

Until recently men, and men only, were forced by their own interests to form cooperative groups for economic or political action. This education in solidarity has taught them to develop the discipline that is necessary for united action.

Solidarity is necessary for any great action, and it is particularly important for women because of all the inner insecurity they feel. The more insecure the individual, the greater is her need for support from a cooperative group.

It is not sufficient to say, as women do these days, that we must overcome the delusion of inferiority. It is more than a delusion, for the handicaps we have faced have created real deficiencies. But we need to understand that there are no unalterable qualities of inferiority of our sex due to laws of God or of nature. Our limitations are, for the most part, culturally and socially conditioned. Men who have lived under the same conditions for a long time have developed similar shortcomings.

Once and for all, we should stop bothering about what is feminine and what is not. Such concerns only undermine our energies. Standards of masculinity and femininity are artificial standards. All that we definitely know at present about sex differences is that we do not know what they are. Differences between the two sexes certainly exist, but we shall never be able to discover what they are until we have first developed our potentialities as human beings. Paradoxical as it may sound, we shall find out about these differences only if we forget about them.

In the meantime what we can do is to work together to promote the full development of the human personalities of all for the sake of general welfare.

8

Sadistic Love (1943/1946)

There are two versions of this lecture. The first bears the heading "The summary of a lecture by Dr. Karen Horney, before the Auxiliary Council to the Association for the Advancement of Psychoanalysis [AAP], given October 14, 1943." The second was copyrighted in 1946. Both versions were printed by the Auxiliary Council — the lay arm of the AAP, founded in 1941, which was the umbrella organization for the American Institute for Psychoanalysis, the *American Journal of Psychoanalysis,* and later the Karen Horney Clinic. The Auxiliary Council made copies of this and other lectures by Horney and her colleagues available for ten cents each, as part of its effort "to aid in broadening the public understanding of Psychoanalysis." Many of the lectures were based on chapters of Horney's books. All were aimed at a lay audience.

Although "Sadistic Love" is described as the summary of a lecture, I believe that it is the entire lecture in Horney's own words. The 1943 version is neither as full nor as well written as the one from 1946. Horney seems to have revised the lecture after the publication of *Our Inner Conflicts* in order to incorporate some of her latest ideas. There is no evidence that she delivered the revised version, although it is possible that she did. She used some of the material from the original version in the chapter "Sadistic Trends" in *Our Inner Conflicts,* but the discussions of *Hedda Gabler, Pygmalion,* and *The Diary of a Seducer* are much fuller here than in the book. Horney made many references to literature in her writings and frequently taught a course on literature and psychoanalysis at the New School for Social Research. She may have developed some of the interpretations that appear in this lecture in that course. I have made a few editorial changes in the wording, punctuation, and paragraphing of the 1946 version of "Sadistic Love."

Our love life should and could be a source of the greatest happiness in our lives and help to offset the sources of distress in our daily struggle for existence — the competition, fears of failure, subversive and open hostilities. With a friend, a lover, a husband, or a wife, we want and need to find peace, understanding, affection, support, sympathy, mutual faith, and respect. Yet all too often a relationship which apparently begins auspiciously, with falling in love, and even with a will to build something good, becomes a source of misery. Two people enter a relationship happily and hopefully, but after a while find themselves disappointed and disillusioned. When that happens, it is almost always the "other fellow" who is blamed.

In my consultations with married couples, I find, for example, that a wife will complain of her husband's staying out late and neglecting her, or whatever the grievance may be. She feels sure that he should be analyzed. Then when the husband is interviewed, he insists that he is all right, but that his wife is very demanding, nagging, an impossible person to live with.

We observe that many love relationships end in a loss of happiness, and we should like to find a simple answer to this problem, along with a simple remedy. In order not to arouse hopes and later disappoint them, we may say at once that there is no simple answer, and there is certainly no simple remedy. A sexual or love relationship cannot be better than the two people entering into it; each brings his personal difficulties into the mutual situation and these difficulties operate to disturb the relation. This evening we are going to discuss one such difficulty: the sadistic tendencies that may enter into a love relation.

The word "sadistic" will call forth associations with sexual perversions, conditions in which people can find sexual satisfaction only when the partner is tied, beaten, or otherwise mistreated. While such tendencies form an interesting aspect of the general problem of sadism, it is not the aspect we shall talk of this evening, and for two reasons: perversions are comparatively rare occurrences, and they are only one among many more important manifestations of the sadistic character. We shall speak instead of the sadistic character, and in particular of its tendency to find conscious or unconscious gratification or thrill in criticizing, degrading, humiliating, enslaving, or exploiting the partner.

The sadistic person may be driven by a compulsive desire and need to enslave others, especially a love partner. In consequence, his "victim" will be reduced to the status of a superman's slave, deprived not only of independent wishes and feelings but of making any claims whatsoever on the "superman." Sometimes this compulsive drive expresses itself in the impulse to mold or educate the victim. In its most benign state, it may have some constructive aspects, as in the case of parents with children or teachers with pupils. More frequently, however, this desire to shape and mold another personality is activated by purely selfish motives.

This desire is occasionally evident in sexual relations, especially on the part of the maturer partner. It appears in homosexual relationships involving a younger and an older man. Frequently, though not invariably, the sadistic partner in a sexual relationship is haunted by a possessive jealousy and exercises it to inflict torture. Since keeping a bulldog grip on the victim is of such vital interest to the sadist, he may be inclined to neglect his career and even to forgo the pleasures and advantages of meeting other people rather than permit his partner any degree of independence.

The sadist uses various devices to enslave a love partner. These devices vary only within a comparatively limited range, depending upon the neurotic structure of both persons involved. Thus, the enslaved recipient will be given just enough to make the relationship appear worthwhile. And although the sadistic person will fulfill certain of the partner's needs in a tantalizing, inadequate sort of way, he will at the same time impress upon him the unique quality of what he does give. Through brow-beating and intimidation, he will succeed in convincing his partner that nobody else would be capable of giving him such understanding, such powerful support, so much sexual satisfaction, so many varied interests. In fact, who else would tolerate him? All these tactics achieve the desired goal — effectively isolating the partner from all other contacts. And when, through the combined pressures of possessiveness and disparagement the partner is reduced to a state of complete dependency, that is often the moment selected by the sadist to threaten to leave him.

We can use as illustrative material three pieces of literature: Henrik Ibsen's *Hedda Gabler,* Bernard Shaw's *Pygmalion,* and Søren Kierkegaard's *Diary of a Seducer.* You have probably read them, but if not, you can read them later, or reread them if you already know them. Points escaping you this evening may then become understandable or more vivid.

From *Hedda Gabler* we can learn almost all there is to be learned about sadistic tendencies. Hedda feels bitter resentment toward life because it has not fulfilled her expectations, and her resentment is actively turned back onto life. She has all that should make for happiness: security, a home, a devoted husband; but for inner reasons she can enjoy nothing. She is intelligent, attractive, but she cannot love. Her life is actually empty and useless. Her permanent attitude is one of boredom, and beneath her boredom we sense a profound hopelessness. She is like a person who is tied to a tree at the fringe of a beautiful garden full of fruit, food, and water; she can look into the garden, but starves within sight of its abundance. Although Hedda is unable to get anything out of life, she is by no means resigned. Her desire to participate takes distorted forms.

We must understand the despair of a person who feels forever excluded from all life has to offer, and who, because of the shriveling of his emotional capacity, is completely cut off. It is important to realize the pervasiveness of his sense of deprivation, bitterness, and despair, because it is the soil in which sadistic trends grow. A desperate suffering turns a person sour and venomous toward others. The attitude becomes: "If I can get nothing from life, why should you? I'll make you pay for my unhappiness."

In Hedda's case the attempt to extract such payment from the people around her takes several characteristic forms. She makes endless demands. She must have parties, a new piano, a butler; not because she really wants these things, but in order to make her husband feel guilty for not having supplied them. Everything has been prepared for her welcome, but in return she offers only criticism.

She uses every opportunity to humiliate others, and is clever at finding people's weak spots so that she can wound them more effectively. In the second act there is a telling example of this attitude. Her husband's old aunt has bought a hat to honor Hedda's arrival, and has left it in the living room. Hedda knows whose hat it is, but picks it up with the remark, "Look there! the servant has left her old bonnet lying about on a chair."

She tries also to enslave others, to have them constantly at her beck and call. She shows possessive jealousy, not only toward her husband, but toward an old friend, Eilert Lövborg. Because another woman has helped him, Hedda drives Lövborg to suicide, then with savage glee burns the manuscript that was his life's work. Everyone around her is intimidated, and constantly in fear of not doing what she expects. She finds fault with everything.

Hedda shows an uncanny capacity to sense other people's wishes, but only to frustrate them. She leads people on skillfully and drops them at the moment when they will be apt to feel the disappointment most. She goads a man into wanting her, then turns frigid and tries to make him feel guilty. She is invariably right; others must be made to feel the blame for any failure or disaster.

Certain sadistic trends can to some extent be attributed to bitter envy, a tendency to devaluate, and a consequently pervasive discontent. Although we understand why the sadist is driven to make greedy demands on others, to find fault, to frustrate, and even to inflict suffering, we cannot appreciate the degree of his arrogant self-righteousness nor the extent of his destructiveness unless we realize what his hopelessness does to his relation to himself.

At the same time that he disregards the most elementary dictates of human decency, he cherishes an idealized image of himself, involving especially high and rigid moral standards. Because he feels woefully unable to live up to such standards, he determines to be as "bad" as possible. This compulsive resolution may even drive him to engage in his badness with a kind of frantic, feverish delight. Having pursued this course, he has succeeded merely in immeasurably widening the gap between his idealized image of himself and his actual self. Consequently, he is imbued with a sense of irretrievable loss and of hopelessness, and plunges into recklessness with fanatical vigor.

Such a person, it is easy to understand, would be driven to disparage others. Also, the inner logic of his compulsive fanaticism in wishing to reform others — especially his partner — becomes clear. Because he cannot measure up to his own idealized image, he is determined that his partner shall do so; and the merciless rage that he feels over his own inadequacy he will vent on his partner for any failure in this direction.

To perpetuate these aggressions, and to feel that other people are upset, hurt, agonized, crushed, affords the sadistic person a special kind of satisfaction that, more often than not, is unconscious. In a diabolical way he will sometimes use the "victim's" reactions as means for further injury. He may, for example, scold him for being all too easily hurt. The satisfaction derived from this pernicious game is a thrill, comparable to the excitement of the hunter or gambler. While these satisfactions do not bring happiness, they do provide a temporary feeling of being alive, which, owing to the sadist's emotional barrenness, he otherwise lacks.

In Hedda Gabler we see nothing of real love. She is a cold person, with seemingly no other side to her nature. The artist presents only the essentials, and Ibsen has simplified the picture. If we translate his account into everyday experience, we find many Hedda Gablers, both male and female, but either they are not so far gone in sadism as Hedda, or their natures show more conflict. They will generally feel more need to deceive themselves and others into accepting them as fair, generous, sacrificing, and decent. They will show the same tendency to irritate those around them with endless demands, reproaches, humiliations, and exhibitions of possessive jealousy; but they will not be in the least aware of such attitudes, and will probably feel misunderstood, neglected, and abused. They do show that they possess at least a vision of charity, warmth, and love in exactly the same way that Hedda does. When the picture of sadism is not so stark, the victim may be even more helpless and will often feel more guilty if he does not fulfill any of the exaggerated demands made upon him.

In Bernard Shaw's *Pygmalion,* Professor Higgins exemplifies sadistic tendencies very similar to those of Hedda Gabler. He is an elusive, ascetic man, emotionally dead. He is a person whom we could not possibly associate with the enjoyment of a good show, or a good joke, or a beautiful sunset. We cannot imagine him showing affection. He is absorbed in his own ambition, and even his ambition has a negative and cynical goal: to fool society. Emotionally he is a sort of Zombie, entirely cut off from life — for we live only insofar as we feel, not more, not less.

He tries to turn Eliza Doolittle, an ignorant flower-girl from the London slums, into a lady; and in his behavior toward this girl we find a repetition of many of Hedda's attitudes. We see his complete disregard for the girl as a human being with rights of her own; we see the arrogance with which he dominates her and makes her into a creature who responds to his demands and fulfills his wishes and ambitions; and we see the cutting impatience of his criticism wherever she does not meet his exactions.

We could round out this picture, too, and bring it nearer to the experience of everyday life. Then we should have someone who has another side to him, who is at least able to fall in love, and be at times charming and affectionate. Again we should see that there are many Professor Higginses. Such individuals are apt to find themselves attracted to people from lower economic levels, with little education, or to people who are simply in trouble. To these unfortunates they offer help, support, and advice and may actually be helpful to a certain extent; but the help is usually given for the purpose of gaining a thrill in the power to rescue, educate, or mold another human being. They are immediately mortified when the creature they create shows signs of independence, or of attempts to enter into a real relationship with them, on terms of equality.

The Diary of a Seducer, by Søren Kierkegaard, tells the story of a sophisticated man who succeeds in seducing a girl who is a virgin. All his plans and thoughts are directed toward persuading the girl to yield to him. Every move he makes is carefully schemed to the last detail, and considered in the light of its possible effect on her: he may decide to keep her waiting five minutes, to see her, not to see her—it is all minutely mapped out. In this "seducer" we see another example of a man who lives in his reason, a man for whom even physical desire is bare, meager, and intellectual. What he enjoys is the power he has to attract and reject, to arouse and disappoint another human being. He shows a completely callous disregard of what his attitude may mean to the girl. He is absorbed in the thrill of stimulating her sexually and then frustrating her, building her hopes and then crushing them, keeping her apprehensive of a break, and withdrawing at the exact point to cause the greatest suffering.

In translating this third case into actual life, I am reminded of a patient of mine who believed himself madly in love with a girl, and who spent most of his time and thoughts in attempts to possess her. One side of his nature was unfeeling and calculating, yet he seemed very much in love. The girl on her part was obviously playing cat-and-mouse with him. I told him that there was nothing of love in his attitude, though he did feel sexual desire. He later accepted and confirmed my interpretation. He confessed that though he finally proposed to the girl—and was refused—he had not given a thought to the possible development of such a relationship, to how it would work out. He had thought no further than to the moment when he would possess the girl. He pictured how he would enjoy tying and beating her.

There you have the sadist! Attracting, rejecting; arousing, disappointing. By such means he is able to gain absolute power, and to feel the thrill that is so necessary to him because he cannot really love or enjoy anything. A happy person does not have this need for thrills and excitement.

What kind of people are these sadists? Very egotistical, you would probably say, and I should agree. But it is an egotism of its own kind. It differs from the egotism we find in the wonderful study of a neurotic, *What Makes Sammy Run?* Sammy has simply no feeling for human relations. No moral values exist for him. All he wants is to make a career. Though he does step over people, it does not bother him, it does not interest him, nor does it thrill him. The only thing that can excite him is to go a step ahead in his career. The egotism of the sadist differs also from that of a pleasure-loving person who wants only a good cigar, good food, good wine, and who does not mean to be bothered with anything else. Such a person is egotistical, but he can enjoy something of life.

Or one could say that sadistic people are hostile. That is true. They no doubt have a great deal of hostility, but it, too, is of a special kind. We are all hostile at times. If someone hurts us or attempts to interfere with our work or purposes or commits an injustice, we react with hostility. This is reactive hostility. But sadistic people are fascinated by their power to hurt, exploit, enslave, and humiliate. Their attitude is quite different from reactive hostility. André Maurois describes their uncanny intuition for discovering exactly where others are most vulnerable as a kind of X-ray vision that reveals "the straw that breaks the beam's stability" and enables them to make unerringly for the other's vulnerable spots.

Why don't we call these people simply mean? Well, they are mean, or have mean streaks; but they are not born mean, and I think no one is. They have become mean through crushing experiences in their childhood. They have suffered not only too little respect and love but too many humiliations. Their experiences have left them determined to get even with the world. For most of them there is also another side — a side which wants to be decent and fair — opposed to the desire for revenge. It is like the problem of Dr. Jekyll and Mr. Hyde. They have become so entangled in the conflict that they feel completely shut off from life. They go empty-handed. And that is why they want to get even with those who have humiliated them.

So, we might call them vindictive people. Yes, if any one term can describe the special quality of the sadistic tendency, that term comes nearest. They need to avenge themselves on two scores: on the one hand, for what they have gone through in childhood, experiences that have greatly undermined their pride and self-respect; on the other hand, for what these experiences have done to them. What sustains the sadist's attitude and makes it poignant is his further development, the distant end result of the early humiliations, the stifling and shriveling of his emotional life, the inner despair about himself. In spite of any surface bravado, he has given himself up as a bad and hopeless job. He does not expect, and in many cases, defiantly, does not even want, what life has to offer.

From this basis of bitter envy, resentment, and despair, he has come to want only two things: to get even, and to enjoy a vindictive triumph. He cannot enjoy; he will ruin others' enjoyment. He cannot feel pleasurable anticipation; he will mar the hopes of others. He has lost his pride and self-respect; he will humiliate other people, degrading them into mere creatures whom he dominates and exploits. In spite of an aura of righteousness, he feels guilty; he will make others feel guilty. His desire for vindictive triumph shows itself in a determination to gain a victory over all who have frustrated him, and also in a restless drive to excel. The fairy tale of "Cinderella" — her early humiliations at the hands of her step-sisters and her final triumph over them — illustrates this craving for a vindictive triumph.

However, the sadist's desire for revenge is not merely an expression of his bitterness and resentment. It is also his way of solving his problems, and this is what makes it so strong. He regains his lost pride by crushing the pride of others; he recaptures a feeling of strength through the sense of power he acquires in enslaving and controlling others; he rids himself of some measure of guilt by accusing other people and making them feel to blame.

It is really amazing how much sadistic behavior can be manifested over a period of time without the individual's realizing it himself or recognizing it for what it is. He is merely sporadically aware of occasional inclinations to mistreat a weaker person, of being stimulated when he reads about sadistic acts, or of having some obviously sadistic fantasies. For the most part, he is unconscious of the significance of his daily behavior toward others. Until this numbness of feeling for himself and others is dispelled, he will not emotionally comprehend what he does. Unfortunately, the self-justifications that camouflage the sadistic tendencies are often clever enough to deceive not only the afflicted person but even his victims.

The dynamics of sadism will vary, depending on the structure of the individual's neurosis. The compliant type, for instance, will enslave the partner under the unconscious pretense of love. His demands will be attributed to his special needs for attention, due to frailty or timidity. The aggressive type, although expressing sadistic tendencies quite openly, is not necessarily more aware of them. The detached person is characteristically unobtrusive in manifesting sadistic tendencies. Quietly frustrating others, making them feel insecure by his readiness to withdraw, and subtly conveying the impression that they are cramping him, he takes secret delight in letting them make fools of themselves.

From this exposition it becomes clear that a person is not sadistic by nature. His attitudes are part and parcel of a neurosis, and need to be treated as such. Only a person who despairs of himself and life *can* be sadistic. A happy, strong person could not be so.

There is one other factor to be considered in regard to the problem of sadism: the victim. Brickner — in the chapter "The Paranoid and His Victim" in his book *Is Germany Incurable?* — holds that the more decent and fair a person is in his attitude toward a sadist, the more readily he will be victimized. I think that that is not always so. It is my experience that there is generally also something the matter with the person who becomes helplessly involved with a sadist. One of the two will seem the more openly and obviously sadistic; the other may be very dependent, but will also possess somewhat more hidden sadistic trends.

The best way to protect oneself from a sadist is to analyze one's own sadistic inclinations; that will make the whole problem easier. For only a person who is pretty healthy, and who is capable of love, can deal effectively with a sadist.

Love has been badly treated here this evening. The capacity to love is in a way the direct opposite of everything involved in sadistic tendencies. The sadist is unhappy and makes other people unhappy. Love, on the other hand, is the capacity to be happy and make others happy. The power to love is not like the ability to eat, sleep, or walk, something of which we are all capable. Rather, it is a goal for which we must strive.

9

Overemphasis on Love (1945)

The typescript of this lecture was in Harold Kelman's papers at the Postgraduate Center for Mental Health. The top of the first page bears the notation "Lecture given October 16, 1945." Since this seems to have been an unrevised draft, I have made some editorial changes to improve its readability.

As I observed in the introduction to Part 1, the topic of the lecture is one to which Horney returned many times. Among Kelman's papers were three pages handwritten in German on crumbling yellow paper that were entitled "Gedanken über die Liebe" [Thoughts on love] and that dwelt on the idealization of love and its consequences. I cannot date these pages, but I assume that they were written before Horney left Germany in 1932. There is nothing quite like them in her writings in German, but they have a good deal in common with "Overemphasis on Love," and they indicate how close to Horney's heart this topic was. They seem to be a personal effusion, possibly written while her marriage was breaking up. This seems like the best place to reproduce Horney's "Thoughts on Love." The translation is by Andrea Dlaska.

Have we not made love something divine and thus deprived it of its actual human value? Have we not turned it into a phantom, which we chase, which eludes us, if we are trying to grasp it?

Look at love, said the man with drunken eyes — look how she hovers with divine levity. Look how she gives with queenly extravagance. Yes, this is what love is: with dancing feet she hovers above everything of earthen heaviness; with seeming carelessness and playfulness she gives from the plenty of her abundance to those who approach her. She never makes strict demands. What should she demand, she, the dancer of exuberant life! I will be like her.

All the gifts of heaven and earth I will bring to my beloved. Unfathomable surprise will be in her eyes. Never will anything like that have happened to her. Never will anything like that happen to her again.

Look at love, said the woman, her eyes heavy with dreams and desire. She will still all my cravings. She will soothe the pain of my loneliness. She will hold me in her arms. And I will be like a child who has found its way home.

They found each other in their dreams and were happy in their delusion. He was the giving god, she was the receiving child. But no delusion can last forever. Very slowly it vanished, so slowly that they did not even notice. With the ardor of their faith they held on to it when it had long disappeared. They insisted that they were happy when they had long been unhappy.

And thus it happened that disappointment set in suddenly, abruptly, like a catastrophe. But even then they refused to see that their belief had been wrong and insisted, both of them, that their expectations and hopes were justified, that they could be fulfilled, if only one looked hard enough.

And then they became angry at each other. Each felt betrayed by the other. He was a fool who had let himself be exploited. She had been maliciously deprived of her right to happiness.

This is how hatred emerged. He wanted to leave. But she did not want to let him go, for she wanted to extort her share of love. After all, it had been promised her. Why did he not give it to her? But this made him feel enslaved, and he only hated her the more.

And so everything broke into pieces. And they both accused fate! How could something end so miserably that had started so beautifully! They still did not recognize that the love they had looked for and believed they had found was nothing but an illusion.

Will they ever understand that love wears work clothes, and that she is wearing them because she has to perform so many, so infinitely many tasks?

When speaking of *love,* I do not mean sexual infatuation but love in the broader sense — when it involves friendship, affection, closeness. Sex may or may not be part of the relationship. Everyone longs for *love* in this sense, even the so-called hard-boiled. Such love not only brings happiness but is of unique value for our growth as human beings. In fact, love is so important that some of you may be surprised at the title of this lecture and ask: "Can love be 'overemphasized'? Is there not a greater danger that we will underrate its importance? Wouldn't the world be better off if people loved *more?* Couldn't we thus avoid or eliminate wars? Can children have too much love? Don't they grow much better if they get *more* love? Aren't we completely right in feeling that a life without love of some kind is unfulfilled?" I wholeheartedly agree. Love is one of the most important things in life, if not the most important.

Nevertheless, if we expect from love what it cannot give, or expect its benefits under the wrong conditions, it will not grow. When we plant strawberry seeds, for example, we do not expect apples to grow — nor do we expect the plants to lay eggs, give shade, or provide wood for the fireplace! To get strawberries, we must plant the seeds properly, in the right kind of soil, supplying moisture, sun, and shade as needed by this particular plant. Also, the young shoots should be replanted when at the right stage of growth and the plants continuously cultivated. Similarly, we must have appropriate expectations of love and nurture it carefully.

How can one discover whether he or someone else is overemphasizing love? It is not easy. It is difficult to say where the normal stops and the pathological begins. Similarly, how does one differentiate between "being economical" and "being stingy" or between "taking responsibility" for others and dominating them? Many will ask, Is it not natural, particularly for a woman, to be desperate if a fiancé does not call or write, or to go to pieces if a husband goes out with other women, or to want all his time, even begrudging his interest in his business?

There is a neurotic overemphasis on love when all of our interests, wishes, plans, and fears revolve around the other person: *Why doesn't he write oftener? Will he come home early this evening? Why doesn't he call? How much does he love me?* When we are obsessed with these questions, everything else in life is meaningless, and we have no interest in work or friends. We are living for the moment when the partner will come or call.

If a woman does not have a man, she might become neurotically preoccupied with obtaining love. All her hopes, longings, and plans will be directed toward this objective. She will feel excluded from life, which seems empty to her, for everything else is meaningless. She will be desperate most of the time and will envy other women who have husbands or "boyfriends."

There is an overemphasis on love when frustration brings a reaction of deep despair and depression, when we find it a strain to be without our partner and are apt to feel humiliated if he doesn't get in touch with us when expected. Many women in this condition feel it a disgrace to go to the movies alone. Sometimes they can stand being alone, but often they are very upset or feel quite resourceless when they are on their own.

An overemphasis on love is often manifested in an extreme dependency on the partner, in a fear of desertion or a clinging that is actually degrading. Any relationship is troublesome for an overly dependent person, but there are particular difficulties when the partner is a detached person who has a compulsive need for freedom and independence. There may be even more serious trouble with a sadistic partner who ruthlessly exploits his dependency.

Some of the features that characterize a neurotic overemphasis on love may be found in a normal relationship, but if many are present, the effects are crippling and bring real suffering.

There is a considerable variation in the degree to which people are aware of their overemphasis on love. Some feel that their behavior is entirely natural. Others say to themselves, "If I only could find the right partner, I would be all right." And there are some who have a clear realization of their state of dependency and want to get out of it. They know it is having a damaging effect on their character.

An extreme dependency on love may be due to a need to allay the fear of hostility from others. This was manifested by one patient with a neurotic need for affection in a picture she made showing herself as a small baby in the midst of menacing animals and insects — a bull, a bee, and a cat — all threatening her existence. Patients like this have a general fear of people, who seem strange and menacing to them. They overemphasize love because they feel so defenseless, and love seems to offer reassurance. The partner is regarded as an ally against the "hostile" world. A woman may rely on her husband to speak to the landlord when something needs attention or to take charge of dealing with the maid. She expects him to defend her against others, and often against relatives.

Such dependent people seem to be afraid to be aggressive and act as if they had no fight in them. They bend over backwards in order to be agreeable and are frequently apologetic, as well as too yielding or too appeasing. At the same time, however, they are actually smarting underneath because of the subordinate role in which they have placed themselves, and they show a certain amount of aggression indirectly. Without being aware of it, they may oppress the partner by their clinging, by showing how disappointed and miserable they are.

A woman who is overdependent on love will expect her husband to take over her care and support almost entirely. She will expect him to cope with life for her, to assert himself on her behalf and make all decisions for her. He should always take charge of the baggage when they travel, for instance, or change the flat tire, no matter what the circumstances. She may even expect him to know her wishes without her having to express them.

An aggressive partner is appealing to a person of this type because she feels so inhibited about her own assertiveness. She likes a resourceful person because she is at a loss herself most of the time. She feels that if she has a strong protector, it is safe for her to be weak. Unfortunately, this leads to a perpetuation of her weakness.

Some people expect that their partner, through his love and admiration, will supply them with the self-confidence they need. A woman of this type will feel that life is worthwhile only when she is wanted and needed, loved and admired. She has a sense of being only what others think she is. Without their confirmation of her worth, she feels that she is insignificant and that life holds nothing of value for her. For some, the needed self-confidence is acquired through reflected glory, pride in their partner's accomplishments. They live a vicarious existence.

The dependent people I have been describing have no sense of their own value, no measure of themselves. They get a feeling of worthiness only through others. Their moods change violently. They feel on top when they are admired and quite crushed if they are not.

Then there are those who are emotionally dead and expect that love will instill life in them. They are unable to tap their own resources and need other people to stimulate their feelings. These people remind one of the myths about the old men or old women who felt more alive after sleeping with a young person. Actually, these emotionally dead people do feel more alive when someone loves them, but they are still unable to call on their own resources.

Those who overemphasize love believe that it has magic qualities and can bring them a fantastically wonderful life, as it did Cinderella in the fairy tale. Thoughts of love arouse high hopes of delight, as they did for Madame Bovary in Flaubert's famous novel. Love is like a ticket to paradise, where they will be entitled to everything, and nothing will be expected from them. It will be a great bliss descending on them that will bring them out of the humdrum into a world of glamour and delight. Such are their imaginings.

People who are alienated from themselves, full of neurotic fears, shut off from their own resources, must live through another person. They look for a solution that will not require them to change in any way or to exert any effort on their own behalf. Because they cannot cope with life as it is, they escape into a glamorous imaginary world that they think they can enter by finding love.

But like strawberries, love must be cultivated if it is to grow and bear fruit. We must consider what we must be or do if we are to have the benefits of love. We must realize that we can find fulfillment in love only if *we* can love or if *we* can be a good friend. People who are looking for love never ask whether they are capable of it themselves but take their own qualifications for granted. I think that we all have capacities for love, if they are developed. However, all our fears, weakness, and pretenses, and the excessive demands that we make on love prevent us from actualizing our potential. We can see the inherent ability to love in analysis, for when people get rid of fears and inhibitions and become more realistic, their capacity to love becomes evident. They must have had this capacity to begin with, since we can only liberate something that is already there.

Why is the question of our capacity to love never raised? One reason is that in our culture we have the habit of taking it for granted that everybody can be a good mother or lover, just as everybody can be a good democratic citizen. More important, many of us have an interest in not raising that question, because asking whether we are capable of love threatens to confront us with reality. Instead, we cherish the illusion that we are unusually loving.

Because the thought of being in love has such a magical, appealing quality, many people try to develop characteristics, such as friendliness and consideration, that will make them lovable; but they are too hemmed in, too afraid, too self-centered to do so in a genuine way. Instead, they become appeasing, ingratiating, charming, overly modest and bend over backwards in their efforts to please. Since their belief in being lovable is so vitally important to them, they mistake their unconscious strategies for the real thing. They confuse dependency with loyalty, and appeasement with genuine consideration of the other person's feelings. Because of their illusion that they have an unusual capacity to love, they have unrealistically high expectations of their partner.

Many factors interfere with neurotic people's capacity to love, and doom them to failure in any close relationship. Absorbed as they are by their fears, they are bound to be self-centered, and this leads them to see the partner not as he really is but as they need him to be. They live so much in imagination that they do not take into account the reality of either their partner or themselves. Their illusions about themselves foster an exaggerated sense of dignity that prevents them from giving themselves to others, while making them highly vulnerable to hurt and humiliation. They are also made vulnerable by their excessive expectations. They do not realize that they are demanding the impossible. They feel entitled to have everything they want without having to work for it. Because they expect so much and are able to give so little, they glorify "unconditional love," which really means unconditional surrender. No matter how they behave, the partner should always be devoted to them.

In the analytical situation, we can see the overemphasis on love very clearly in the cases of women who tell their male analysts that they do not want to be analyzed but to be loved. "If you would love me," they say, "all my problems would be solved." Freud thought that such women are driven by a biological need for sexual gratification, but I feel that they are motivated by their dependency needs and their unrealistic belief in the power of love to give them a sense of fulfillment. Off in a world of their own, they refuse to consider whether the analyst is married or might be inclined to love them. In their imaginary realm, such things do not matter at all.

The sad truth is that when all one's hopes and energies are focused on love, frustration is inevitable. An overemphasis on love transforms that which can be a source of happiness and growth into something that makes us miserable and thwarts our human development.

Enslavement in Marriage (1946?)

This undated abstract of a talk was in Harold Kelman's papers at the Post-graduate Center for Mental Health. Horney was in great demand as a speaker, and she gave many talks to both professional associations and lay groups. This talk was probably not delivered at a meeting of the Association for the Advancement of Psychoanalysis, because summaries of talks that Horney gave to the association were usually published in the *American Journal of Psychoanalysis*. I assume that the talk was given after the publication of *Our Inner Conflicts*, for it draws on the conceptual scheme developed in that book. In the abstract, section I B does not seem to be on its ostensible topic, "domination through emphasis on duty." Perhaps that section was more pertinent in its developed form.

Abstract

The title may give rise to two opposite reactions: those who hold marriage in high regard may have misgivings about another psychological attack launched against established beliefs. Those who have suffered from marriage or are afraid of it may feel a gleeful expectation that it will be divested of its halo.

I have to reassure the first group and disappoint the second. Marriage requires certain adaptations and imposes certain restrictions on both partners, but in itself it certainly does not constitute an enslavement.

Yet marriage is frequently felt as an enslavement, sometimes consciously, more often unconsciously. Since such a feeling not only jeopardizes harmony in marriage but may actually destroy its constructive value, it may be helpful to know its sources and its consequences. Roughly, there are two main reasons marriage may feel like an enslavement: tendencies to dominate and hypersensitivity to semblances of constraint and coercion.

I. *Tendencies to dominate*
   Tendencies to dominate may be obvious — at least to others — but they may also be disguised to such an extent that neither partner is aware of them. They are mainly disguised as "love" and as "duty."
   A. *Domination through "love"*
      a) Jealousy. Jealousy may spring from love and then is a warranted fear of losing the partner. Jealousy born of a drive to power is recognizable by its appearing without any or without adequate provocation. Examples: It will transcend the erotic sphere and extend to any feelings, thoughts, friendships, or occupations that are beyond control. The absence of a loving attitude in general (affirmation of the partner, tolerance, encouragement, concern, considerateness) gives the lie to the claim of love as the source of jealousy.
      b) An apparent wish for a close community of interests. This wish would be an ideal basis for marriage if it were based on affection and reciprocity. But it often is the egocentric demand of one partner that the other should share his interests. In this instance, there is often but little capacity to understand and feel the other's needs and wishes.
      c) Emphasis on helplessness and suffering with explicit demands for attention and exclusive "love" put on that basis.
   B. *Domination through emphasis on duty*
      Tendencies of this kind are engendered not only by repressed drives to control others, but also by unconscious endeavors of persons harboring great anxiety toward the dangers of life to eliminate all risks by foreseeing all possible emergencies. Since this type usually is con-

vinced of always being right and of knowing everything better, he feels it as his responsibility to guide others.

Which means are used to exert control depend on the personality structure of the partner. But if the zest for power is present, no matter in which form, marriage will approximate a kind of enslavement.

II. *Feeling enslaved because of a hypersensitivity to coercion*

For various reasons, a detached person may have developed an extreme need for unlimited freedom. Then, every tie, every legitimate obligation, every suggestion made, every expectation or wish is felt as an intolerable coercion.

The capacity of this type for initiative of his own, for knowing what he himself wants or appreciates, is impaired because all his life his feelings, thoughts, and actions have been determined by others, because of either his compliance or his defiance. Hence, the integrity of his personality is actually constantly endangered. Therefore, he feels any wish, expectation, or obligation as a kind of hostile attack made upon him.

Consequences

Dominating tendencies of a partner are not necessarily conducive to an unhappy marriage. The other partner may feel at ease in a dependent relationship. If, however, the other partner has a strong sense of independence, or if the tendencies to control are vicious in nature, then an intense resentment may ensue. The hypersensitivity to coercion always breeds resentment because the person as a rule does not recognize that the problem is within himself. All he feels is that the other strangles him. This resentment may be repressed for various reasons, but it is bound to manifest itself in one or another form: irritability at slight provocations, inconsiderateness about the partner's needs and wishes, extramarital affairs, and so forth, interfering with the happiness that otherwise might be derived from marriage.

Feeling enslaved in marriage jeopardizes not only happiness but also the development of the best human potentialities in the partners. The criterion of a good marriage lies in whether or not it furthers the development of the partners, whether or not it inspires more self-confidence, liberates energies, increases spontaneity and productivity.

Pride and Self-Hatred in Neuroses (1947)

In the files of the American Institute for Psychoanalysis was a fifty-two-page, single-spaced typescript, titled "Pride and Self-Hatred in Neuroses by Karen Horney, M.D.," and dated 1947. The typescript consists of an elaborate set of notes for fourteen lectures that Horney gave in her course on this topic at the New School for Social Research in 1947 and 1948. When the course was announced under the title "At War with Ourselves: Self-Contempt and Self-Acceptance," Horney immediately received an enquiry from Storer B. Lunt, then head of W. W. Norton, whether this might be "the groundwork of another possible Karen Horney book" (Horney-Norton correspondence, 9 October 1946). Horney replied that as a matter of fact it might, and the lectures clearly prefigure *Neurosis and Human Growth*.

The table of contents for the typescript is as follows:

1. Search for Glory
2. Claim for Special Prerogative

The first seven lectures correspond to the first six chapters of *Neurosis and Human Growth,* and the eighth and tenth lectures correspond to its chapters on human relations and work. The chapters "Theoretical Considerations" and "The Road of Psychoanalytic Therapy" in that book are anticipated to some extent by lectures twelve and fourteen. Lecture 14 has been published in *The Therapeutic Process* (Horney 1999), and lectures 12 and 13 are included in Part 2 of this book.

Despite some correspondences between the lectures and the book, Horney's ideas had evolved considerably by the time she wrote *Neurosis and Human Growth.* The important chapters "The Expansive Solutions," "The Self-Effacing Solution," "Morbid Dependency," and "Resignation" have no counterpart in the lectures, although they do in the chapters on moving against, toward, and away from people in *Our Inner Conflicts.* In the lectures, Horney focused entirely on intrapsychic processes, whereas in *Neurosis and Human Growth* she tried to integrate the interpersonal and the intrapsychic.

I have edited Horney's detailed but somewhat fragmentary lecture notes to make them more readable, and I have deleted portions that I found unintelligible. I have modified the wording in some places, completed half-expressed ideas, turned phrases into sentences, supplied some definite and indefinite articles, and changed the punctuation. Whereas Horney separated each thought with an ellipsis (. . .), I have supplied commas, semicolons, and periods.

Lecture 8: Influence on Human Relations

INTRODUCTION

Neurosis is a disturbance in relations with others and also in relation to self. Disturbance in relation to self starts early in childhood. The child who is ill treated or pampered develops certain strategies for relating to others, but changes also take place in the child's confidence and attitude to self. In early years, disturbances in the child's relation to self and others can be remedied by putting him in a healthy environment. In later years, a change in the environment, such as marriage or new relationships, may have some beneficial influence, but it is limited, for it produces no real change in the person himself and in his neurotic tendencies. This is because our disturbed relationships in childhood lead us to develop compulsive trends that are carried into all relationships, no matter what kind of people we are dealing with. It is true, however, that some people may fit our neurosis better than others and that we relate more successfully to them. Analysis of disturbances in relations with others too often neglects disturbances in the relation to self and ignores the fact that both areas must be explored.

INFLUENCE OF DISTURBANCES IN SELF ON HUMAN RELATIONS

When the personality structure is full of tensions, a person can barely maintain his equilibrium. The structure has a core of weakness, which is the impairment in the function of the "real me." A person who is full of explosive forces is like a country in which a civil war is raging. It may be able to survive if not disturbed by other countries, but it will have little interest in what is going on outside itself. In a person, this is called being egocentric. By egocentricity we mean seeing and reacting to others in terms of our own needs and fears and being preoccupied with our own equilibrium. Egocentricity leads us to shy away from other people and from many areas of life. It results in emotional isolation and prevents us from relating to others with mutuality and enjoyment.

In addition to being egocentric, the neurotic is fearful of other people, whom he feels to be a danger. Even if he is hostile, aggressive, and self-righteous himself, he is still afraid of others and on guard against them. He may deal with his fear in a variety of ways — by being compliant or detached, for example. The root of his fear is his feeling of inner weakness, his sense that others are stronger than he. He constantly compares himself with other people, asking if they are cleverer and more attractive. This leads him to see others as rivals and prevents him from enjoying them as they are. As a result, he often withdraws from groups, friendships, and even marriage. His fear also stems from his neurotic pride, which makes him extremely vulnerable to anything that seems like criticism, rejection, or neglect. When his pride is hurt, he is easily thrown into an abyss of self-contempt. Because of his insecurity, he protects his pride by anticipating rejection and taking an offhand attitude to show others he doesn't care. When others have a negative reaction to this attitude, the neurotic feels rejected, not knowing that he originally caused their reaction.

The neurotic's relationships are often disturbed by the hostile attitude he carries into them. His hostility may be covered up by compliance, a pseudo-liking of everyone, a conviction of being objective, or suffering. Indeed, suffering may have great subjective value as a means of expressing unconscious reproach: "See how badly the world treats me. It is bad but I am good." Whether open or covert, hostility is caused by hurt pride and the need for vindictive triumphs. Hostility is often a product of the search for glory, which involves putting oneself above other people, and of the world's failure to honor our neurotic claims.

Finally, disturbances in the self affect our human relations because they make us feel weak, helpless, and lost, and therefore very much in need of other people. Because he does not like himself, the neurotic needs to be liked by others. Because he condemns himself, he needs others to approve of him. Since he feels he has no rights, he depends on others to look out for him. Except for the detached person, he usually dislikes his own company and cannot stand to be alone.

In short, then, the neurotic is an egocentric person with an impaired capacity to love. Full of hostility himself, he feels endangered by other people, whom he perceives as potential enemies. At the same time, because of his sense of helplessness he needs others to take care of him. He is in the uncomfortable position of being dependent on others toward whom he feels hostility, fear, and dislike.

EXTERNALIZATION

Since he projects his own inner tendencies onto others, the neurotic may relate to other people in a way that has nothing to do with their individuality. He is not aware of what is going on within himself but experiences it as if it were going on outside him. This may ease his inner tensions, but it impairs his human relations, for no matter how others behave, he perceives and reacts to them in terms of his externalizations.

KINDS OF EXTERNALIZATIONS

1. Externalization of self-hatred, self-contempt, self-dislike. The person no longer feels that he hates himself but that others do not like him. Since he feels unlikable, he cannot believe that anyone else can like him as he is. As a result of this unconscious conviction, he may give up and not bother to be nice, or he may hope against hope and try to win affection for what he offers in the way of friendliness, advice, service, and so on.
2. Externalization of "shoulds." The neurotic does not experience his own shoulds but believes that it is others who are making demands on him. It is others who are applying pressure and who are discontented with him. He may make every effort to please those onto whom he has externalized his shoulds, feeling that "others will like me only if I am perfect." Since he can approve of himself only if he is perfect, he can't believe that others will like him if they know of any imperfections. Or he may rebel against his externalized shoulds by developing a sensitivity to coercion which is expressed by refusing to do anything that other people expect of him.
3. Externalization of everything that I dislike in myself. We project our own faults onto others and see them more easily there. We may become enraged with others for having these faults and want to reform them. Unless we are very detached, we shall be unable to see others objectively and as whole persons.

We must ask ourselves: 1) What do I carry into relationships that influences my reactions to others, and 2) Am I externalizing something inside me? Are my suspicions of other people justified, or am I reacting to hurt pride or being pathologically jealous?

BASIC ANXIETY

Factors in basic anxiety are isolation, fear, hostility, and helplessness. A child growing up under adverse conditions feels isolated and helpless in a hostile world, and this feeling leads to anxiety. In an effort to allay the anxiety and to find a way to relate himself to others, the child chooses one of three major paths: compliance, aggression, or detachment. Any exacerbation of the anxiety reinforces the solution the child has chosen.

The method an adult uses to deal with his inner difficulties — that is, be-numbing resignation, feeling superior, identifying with his despised image, and so forth — is similar to the original path the child took. The *alcoholic* is unable to find a feasible solution to his conflicts and oscillates between extreme aggression, extreme compliance, and withdrawal. In *resignation* there is a giving up of the struggle, a moving away from others, with the adoption of a detached attitude. In *superiority and militant rightness* there is a reinforcement of aggression, movement against others, who are perceived to be dishonest, and an abandonment of the effort to be liked. In this most blatant use of externalization, vindictiveness becomes a virtue. The person who has *identified with his despised image* has given up ambition and glory, accepted his worthlessness, and stopped feeling that he has any rights. He moves toward people, makes efforts to please, and hopes that others will like him for what he can do for them.

Love, fame, recognition, and so forth, cannot solve the problems that arise from basic anxiety, for there is no substitute for the security that comes from inner self-confidence. In analysis, we must work on the individual's relationship both to himself and to others in order to help him function properly as a human being. He cannot be a good friend to others unless he is a good friend to himself.

Lecture 9: Influence on Love Life

BASIC ANXIETY IN CHILD AND ADULT

The original basic anxiety felt by the child is a response to a factual situation. The child is really isolated and helpless and cannot do much about it. The anxiety of the adult may also be a response to the environment, but often it is a reaction to what is going on inside himself. As a rule, the environment is less of a causal factor than it was for the child, and inner troubles are more important. The adult feels helpless because he is weakened by his inner conflicts and isolated because he is so consumed by his inner difficulties that he cannot relate himself to others. He feels that he lives in a hostile world partly because of his own vulnerability and partly because he carries so much hostility into his human relationships. A change in the environment holds limited benefit for the adult because his troubles stem from within. Since despite evidence to the contrary, every neurotic has the illusion that he is easy to get along with, he cannot see how he contributes to his difficulties but places all the responsibility on others: "Others are hostile and I am helpless and isolated and must defend myself against them." This is a not a productive attitude, given that we cannot change others but only ourselves.

INFLUENCE ON LOVE LIFE

Since every love relationship is a human relationship, all the difficulties presented in the last lecture appear here also. People are suspicious, make silent claims, feel abused if their claims are not fulfilled, and become vindictive when their pride is injured. They alternate between being enraged with their partner for not honoring their claims and with themselves for not living up to their shoulds. While the difficulties that occur in all relationships will also appear in love life, one problem is especially characteristic of it: namely, that the person feels unlovable on the one hand and has a particularly great need of love on the other.

FEELING UNLOVABLE

What does it really mean to feel unlovable? If a person can't dance, he can make up for this deficiency through other accomplishments, but there is no way to compensate for being unlovable. Feeling unlovable means feeling excluded from happiness forever; it means that there is something in me that makes me unlovable not just to one person or another but to *everybody*. As long as we regard ourselves with hatred and self-contempt, we can't believe that *anyone* can like us.

SIGNS OF AN UNCONSCIOUS CONVICTION OF BEING UNLOVABLE

1. Even though another gives us indubitable signs of affection, it means little. We think: "He likes me for my looks, talents, the help I can give, and so on, but he doesn't love me for what I am, with my good and bad qualities." This makes the other person's affection meaningless. We may feel the same way about children: "They love me for what I did for them."
2. Because we cannot really believe that another person can love us, we are too ready to discard signs of affection. "This person loves me because he is seeking a mother substitute, or he is lonely or dependent, or if he knew me as I am, he wouldn't love me. Maybe I am a phony or he is a fool."
3. We may have easily aroused suspicions. We may feel loved at first and then begin to wonder whether our partner has fallen out of love. Or if our partner asks a favor, we may interpret that to mean that he doesn't really love us but is out for something. Or if the proof of love is absolute surrender, then anything less means the partner does not love us. We make insatiable demands and need endless reassurances that never suffice.

NEUROTIC NEED FOR LOVE

We all need and want love, but whereas the normal person wants it because it makes life richer and happier, the neurotic needs it for different reasons:

1. Love is a source of affirmation that makes him believe for a while that he is not as contemptible a person as he thinks.

2. Because he cannot stand himself, he has a bitter need of human contact, which frees him from his tormenting isolation and helps him escape his self-hatred.

3. Love gives him a feeling that life has meaning. This can be a healthy feeling, for life can have sufficient meaning only with others, but the neurotic feels that his existence is useless in itself and that he must be important to somebody else if life is to have any significance. He may try to gain this sense of importance by doing things for others.

The dilemma of the neurotic is that he has both an unconscious conviction of being unlovable and a terrific need to be loved. The story of Julien Sorel in Stendhal's *Red and the Black* illustrates this dilemma very well. It also shows how neurotic pride can mar a love relationship, for in order to satisfy his pride, Julien must be the one to love less, a position that permits him to dominate and control the partner. For him, being loved is not enough.

HOW PEOPLE TRY TO RESOLVE THEIR DILEMMA

Among the many efforts at solution, there are two extreme ones:

I. People may renounce love altogether and thus not have to confront their feeling of unlovability. This renunciation takes various forms.
   A. Militantly righteous people feel love to be an impediment and deliberately cut it out of their human relationships. They squelch in themselves any desire to please others. Since the desire to improve human relationships generates a desire to grow, the renunciation of love deprives us of that incentive.
   B. Those who live in imagination feel that they cannot deal with life or love. They fantasize about love, instead. This approach can be elevated to a philosophy: love in reality is something poor; the perfect experience can be found only in imagination.
   C. Resigned people who have given up all ambition want nothing to do with love, because it represents a temptation that threatens their detachment. They may feel that they are too old for love or that there is no point in bothering with it. Those who have renounced love may or may not have given up sex. Detached people often use sex as a bridge to other people.
II. Instead of renouncing love altogether, people may embark on a determined search for love, thus trying to prove that they are indeed lovable. The quest for a glorified romantic love becomes the most powerful motivating force in their lives. Passionate love becomes *the* achievement; everything else is of minor importance. Love is the great redemption, the excuse for every-

thing, the remedy for self-hatred. "If I love and am loved, I am worth-while." Love gives meaning to life and takes one out of oneself. People hope to cure their neuroses by finding love. Freud believed that when the patient falls in love with the analyst, it means that he is unable to sublimate and must have an actual sexual experience. In my view, what is behind this is the hope that love is the cure for everything, the solution to all problems.

A. People who identify with their idealized image and feel superior may imagine themselves to be great lovers and pursue glory by trying to be conquering Don Juans. They must prove their irresistibility. If they are resisted, then doubts arise, and this cannot be permitted. They want to triumph by overcoming and controlling other people, by gaining their unconditional surrender. They can be very calculating and withdraw their interest at the point of conquest, after which they feel contempt for the defeated person. Only the unattainable appeals to people of this type. Available people excite no desire, even if they would be better partners than those who are unattainable. Don Juan types cannot be faithful, for they constantly need new proofs of their irresistibility. They may get stuck with one person if that person makes some concessions, but they maintain their reservations. Don Juan types are searching for the perfect partner and perfect love, and since these things do not exist, they are always disappointed. This often makes them cruel to their partners.

B. Self-effacing people, who identify with their despised images, yearn for strong partners who will give them everything they feel too weak to obtain for themselves. They want partners who will protect, stimulate, and care for them. In return, they will give their adoration. The motto of these morbidly dependent people is: "If I subordinate myself, love, serve, and adore, then I'll be loved." They are haunted by a fear of desertion, which makes them feel helpless, worthless, and isolated.

INFLUENCE OF PRIDE ON CHOICE AND FUNCTION OF PARTNER

1. Aggressive people may put love in the service of glory and use the partner as a tool to further their own ambitions. Whether their ambitions are realistic or fantastic, they feel that they cannot attain them on their own and are looking for a partner to give them support. Their love is elicited by the hope that the partner will facilitate their search for glory, either by being wealthy, glamorous, or prominent or by being willing to serve as a helper.

2. Self-effacing people have given up the hope of attaining great things on their own and have transferred their ambitions to their partner. They may

promote the partner and push him on to glory or put themselves in his service and so help him on toward imaginary grandeur.

As in Pearl Buck's *This Proud Heart,* there are cases in which people want the partner to help them attain their ambitions and want to help the partner attain his ambitions, both at the same time.

FUTURE OF THESE RELATIONSHIPS

Must these relationships based on neuroses end in disaster? Not necessarily, because things may work out fairly well for people whose neurotic trends complement each other. Even so, there will be many difficulties, given that our neuroses are not really conducive to happiness in love.

When difficulties arise, we may ask: "Is this the right person for me? Do I really love my partner? Is he so neurotic that I cannot live with him?" These questions are futile. Differences between people create tensions, but problems tend to arise less because of such differences than because of the individuals' neurotic difficulties. The question is less really whether one can love this particular partner than whether, and under what conditions, one is capable of loving anyone. And focusing on the partner's neurosis tends to leave out one's own psychological problems.

When difficulties arise, we must start with ourselves, with the attitudes, expectations, and vulnerabilities we carry into a relationship.

Lecture 11: *Influence on Sex Life*

INTRODUCTION

Freud believed that sex is the all-important dynamic factor in life, that everything we do is determined by sex. Sadism, for example, is due to sadistic sexual impulses. I believe the reverse: sex does not determine character, but character determines the sex life. The whole determines the part, not the part the whole (Gestalt). The way people relate to others will be reflected in their sex lives. Compliant people will be compliant in sexual as in other relationships, and the same holds true for aggressive and detached people.

FUNCTIONS OF SEX

The functions of sex will vary according to a person's character structure and conflicts. Sex may serve as a means of allaying anxiety, or it may be a bridge to another person, as it often is for detached people. All I have said in these lectures regarding the search for glory applies to the sex life. A compulsive need for triumph may be expressed in the pursuit of sexual conquests.

People may idealize themselves as great lovers or seek the perfect sexual experience, just as they strive for perfection in other areas of life.

Self-destructive tendencies also operate in the sexual sphere. If a person does not permit himself any pleasure, his capacity for sexual enjoyment will be impaired. If he has a sense of unworthiness, then sex will simply mean being "used." Excessive self-consciousness can also impair sexual performance and pleasure.

My fundamental idea is that the problems we have in our relations with ourselves and with others will manifest themselves in our sex lives and that our sexual problems are not the source but the effect of our difficulties.

INHIBITIONS IN SEX LIFE

1. Desire. If a person experiences sex only as something he is doing for another, or as a duty, this detracts from desire. If the partner is sadistic or self-degrading, this detracts from desire also, unless one has a neurotic preference for such behavior.
2. Performance. If a man regards sex as a testing ground where he proves his virility, his pride will be very vulnerable, and so much anxiety may be connected with the sex act that the anxiety will interfere with his performance. Or if a person must always be perfect, his performance may be adversely affected by self-consciousness and lack of spontaneity.
3. Enjoyment. Enjoyment is limited if there is a prohibition on pleasure because of self-hatred or detachment, or if enjoyment depends on special neurotic conditions, such as danger, the violation of social mores, the masterfulness or inaccessibility of the partner, and so on.

IMPORTANCE OF SEX

Sex *is* important for reproduction, enjoyment, mental health, happiness, and so on; but in the neurotic use of sex it acquires *undue* importance. In neurosis, sex has functions that should not really belong to it, such as allaying anxiety, serving as a means of escaping isolation, or being a source of pride and triumph. If sex serves these functions, then it acquires an *undue* importance.

The neurotic person tends both to debase and to glorify sex, although he is usually conscious of only one of these moves. He glorifies sex because through it he hopes to prove his lovability, feed his pride, or experience a sense of triumph. At the same time, he regards sex as low and filthy, a debased activity, either because it is a means of showing contempt for others or because he has contempt for himself. In the latter case, he believes that sex is the only thing he has to offer and feels degraded by his sexual relationships.

In the healthy person, sex is the physical expression of love. In the neurotic person, sex is degraded because it is not an expression of love but becomes a means to such ends as control, domination, prestige, and so forth. The partner, too, becomes a means to an end, an object one uses to serve one's own needs.

DEGRADATION OF SEX

Freud saw that there may be a split in the love life, in which an individual can have sexual relations only with a degraded person and fine personal relations only with someone to whom he is not sexually attracted. He felt that this split originated in an ambiguous image of the mother as both an idealized asexual being and a whore. This explanation is untenable for several reasons. For one thing, the splitting Freud describes occurs in women as well as men and cannot be easily attributed to their image of their fathers. And it persists even though sex is not as taboo as it was in Freud's time. I do not believe, moreover, that we can explain adult difficulties only in terms of childhood experiences.

As I see it, in persons in whom such splitting occurs, sex is degraded for some reason, and therefore they feel comfortable seeking it only with a degraded partner. The degradation of sex may be partly the result of the Puritan attitude that a person should govern all emotions by will and reason, thus making desire and passion a source of evil. This has the effect of separating sex from the rest of the personality, making it a thing apart, something crude and degraded that has nothing to do with our finer feelings and our sense of who we really are.

This depersonalization of sex has a great deal to do with the phenomenon of splitting, in which our love relationships are personal, while our sexual relationships are not. Some people enter into the marriage relationship with their whole personalities but have little sexual desire. Or there may be a fairly normal sex life, but some intensity of enjoyment is lacking. A man may feel a great urge to go to a prostitute, because with her he can really "let go." Or he may have a fleeting affair, which is still an impersonal relationship. Or he can have thrilling sexual experiences in fantasy but be unable to have such experiences with a real partner. People whose love life is split may be able to have satisfactory sexual experiences only when neither their own personality nor that of their partner enters into the relationship. They can be remarkably ghostlike and alienated from themselves in the sexual relationship.

Indeed, such people are often suffering from a loss of contact with their real selves. They hate themselves, feel unworthy, and lose interest in themselves as human beings. This may lead to an overemphasis on the sexual organs. Normally, people are human beings first and men or women secondarily. But if they do not feel like human beings to begin with, they may put their primary emphasis on being a man or a woman and on proving it through their sex organs.

SEX AS A THING APART

When a person loses touch with his own identity, he is no longer aware of his real feelings and desires, which become distorted or repressed. He engages in pretenses and becomes emotionally insincere. Sex becomes impersonal and degraded because he engages in it without really being there.

The process of self-idealization is part of a vicious circle that degrades sex even further. People may idealize purity in order to compensate for feelings of degradation. They may want to be virginal, to have nothing to do with sex or with other physical processes, such as urination and defecation, which also become disgusting. The ideal of purity then makes sexual desires and activities all the more degraded in their minds.

A conflict arises here because even though the neurotic regards sexual activity as a form of degradation, he also overvalues it as a means of proving his lovability. Because he beats himself down, he feels that no one can love him, but, as we have seen, he has an overwhelming need for love and human contact. He feels that even though he is unlovable as a person, maybe another will love him for sex, which is all he has to offer. So sexual attractiveness is a substitute for being lovable, and the sexual partner provides the human contact the neurotic craves so desperately.

METHODS OF DEALING WITH CONFLICTS IN SEX LIFE

1. Divide sex and love between two partners, the degraded partner for sex and the admirable partner for affection. As in Dr. Jekyll and Mr. Hyde, constructive and destructive forces are separated.
2. Accept the degradation of sex. Sometimes the need to be loved is so great that a person embraces the degradation of sex and is able to enjoy it only when it feels low and dirty, either in actuality or in fantasy.
3. Try to combine sex and love. Since the degradation of sex is due to the exclusion of love, a person may try to bring these two forces together. Even though he is not able to love, he persuades himself that he has found his great romance. Then he can feel that sex is allowed and legitimate as part of a grand passion. This idealization of his relationship enables him to avoid reproaching himself for his sexual desires. Again, it is important to remember that the neurotic person is not really able to love another person and that he is deceiving himself.

APPROACHING THE IDEAL

As John Macmurray has observed in *Reason and Emotion,* a relationship is healthy when sex is the physical expression of mutual love and psychic closeness. Then sex is not primarily an appetite but a means of communion, simple and natural. Real love is the communion of two people meeting in the full integrity of their personalities.

THERAPY

We cannot deal with sexual difficulties in an isolated fashion. Rather, we must deal with the underlying neurosis. To have a healthy sex life, one must be a real person with a capacity to love and be loved.

PART **II**

Writings, Talks, and Lectures, 1931–1952

Introduction

Whereas the items in Part 1 can be grouped into those focused on feminine psychology and those dealing with the relations between the sexes, the material in Part 2 is more miscellaneous. It is, at the same time, more of a piece, because it represents Karen Horney speaking in her distinctive voice and developing her own theory.

By the time she wrote "Culture and Aggression," which contains her critique of *Civilization and Its Discontents,* Horney was emerging from her Freudian phase and laying down one of the central tenets of her thought: that destructive aggression is reactive rather than innate. In the remaining pieces from the 1930s, she tried to define her relation to Freud and to develop her view of neurosis as a product of family dynamics and culture. In "Can You Take a Stand?" a little-known essay from 1939, Horney offered one of her most vivid pictures of the self-alienation that results from the child's not feeling "wanted or appreciated for his own sake," and she began to speak of the "real self."

The material from the 1940s and 1950s shows us the mature Karen Horney. We can see her developing the ideas that received their most systematic expression in *Neurosis and Human Growth* and also dealing with some topics that did not make their way into her books. Of particular importance are three classic essays—"The Value of Vindictiveness," "On Feeling Abused," and

"The Paucity of Inner Experiences" — the last two of which appeared after the publication of her final book. "Human Nature Can Change," almost our last word from Horney, is a defense of the measured optimism that she had announced in "Culture and Aggression" and that informed her post-Freudian thought.

I have included some of the items in Part 2 mainly for their historical interest. Among them are Horney's letter of resignation from the New York Psychoanalytic Society (signed also by four others), two essays dealing with issues raised by the Second World War, and abstracts of papers and contributions to symposia that were published in the *American Journal of Psychoanalysis*. Even though many of the ideas in them were developed more fully elsewhere, these abstracts help us trace the evolution of Horney's thought and envision the level of her activity in the last seven years of her life. I shall comment separately on some of the shorter pieces in the headnotes.

"Culture and Aggression" marks the beginning of the second phase of Karen Horney's thought, in which she broke away from Freud and developed a new psychoanalytic paradigm. In the late 1920s and early 1930s, Horney oscillated between sounding quite orthodox, as in her lectures in Berlin and Chicago, and criticizing Freud, as in "Culture and Aggression," where she took issue with his ideas about the sources of human destructiveness. Although it was written in 1931, this essay anticipated her later thought in a number of ways.

Horney felt that *Civilization and Its Discontents* was important for its recognition of the role of nonerotic aggression. Earlier, Freud had attributed hostile-aggressive impulses to sadism, which he saw as a partial drive appearing during the development of infantile sexuality. Sadism was directly expressed in infantile cruelty, and later destructive behavior was a regression to this libidinal phase. In *Civilization and Its Discontents,* Freud relinquished the effort to explain everything in terms of sexuality and posited two basic instincts, Eros and Thanatos, the death instinct. When turned outward, the death instinct is the source of human beings' primary hostility toward one another.

What Horney questioned was Freud's attribution of nonerotic aggression to a death instinct. Her first step was to insist on a distinction, which she felt Freud had obscured, between aggressive and destructive impulses. Freud regarded "the drives to rule, to exert power, to master nature as 'modified and controlled, quasi–aim-inhibited expressions of [the] drive to destruction' "; but Horney saw such drives as "constructive," as the expression of a desire "to preserve life" and improve its conditions. Freud argued that "man possesses an innate tendency to evil, aggression, destruction and ultimately to inhumanity." Horney felt that it was possible to speak of aggressive drives as innate, if by that we mean the "impulses to touch, grasp, seize, take hold of, and possess." We see such impulses in infants, and they manifest themselves later in the form "of making demands, making claims, wanting to win out, wanting to conquer people and things, and wield power over them." But where, she asked, are the destructive forces in this? Are not these impulses, rather, "exquisitely life-affirming," "varied expressions of a vital urge for expansion"? They are not expressions of "hostility, destructiveness, or desires to annihilate" but "residuals of phylogenetically acquired tendencies necessary to man in his efforts to acquire and defend his foodstuffs, his love objects, and his family."

Horney acknowledged that there is a great deal of destructiveness in human beings, as attested by history and what we uncover in the course of analysis. This does not mean, however, that human beings have, as Freud postulates, "an unalterable, innate, constitutional, instinctual drive to destruction." When we examine the history both of nations and of individuals, "we find thoroughly adequate grounds for overt and covert hostility." In analysis we see that patients' "inordinate fury and destructive impulses" have "a real basis in [their] experiences with insults, with frustrations, and above all with anxiety." When their anxiety is reduced, so is their hostility. What emerges then are "life-affirming forces" that must have been there to begin with. We see here an early form of what would become a central tenet of Horney's thought: that we have inherent tendencies to grow, to expand, to realize our human potentialities; that we become destructive to ourselves and others when those tendencies are thwarted; and that we become constructive when the obstacles to growth are removed—through fortunate life experiences, social change, or psychotherapy.

In this essay, Horney agreed with Freud that there is bound to be conflict between culture and desire. "More helpless than the beast," we need culture in order to survive, but culture entails "a variety of restrictions" to which we do not respond favorably, especially in childhood. We perceive these restrictions as threats and react to them "with anxiety and a hidden capacity for hostility." Because this is so, it is impossible to have a "rosy, happy-ending optimism," but we need not be as pessimistic as Freud. Horney questioned the existence of a death instinct, which she regarded as a highly speculative concept, and she felt that the conflict between culture and desire did not have to be as severe as Freud had depicted it, given that it "contains some factors amenable to change."

Horney believed that much of our unhappiness and destructiveness is not inescapable but is the product of the specific conditions under which we are raised: "Is the child being exposed to realistic discipline, and are the necessary limitations conveyed to him without his being intimidated or spoiled? Or is he growing up in an atmosphere rife with orders, prohibitions, threats, and anxiety?" Children become destructive when they are "burdened by the superimposed pressures connected with the emotional problems of the parents." The solution is to provide children "with more contented and less pressured parents." One means to this end is social change that would "mitigate the tragic struggle for existence to which the masses are exposed" and provide "a better opportunity for uninterrupted development of their vital forces." Another is to improve the lot of women, the mothers of our children, whose "vital life-affirming forces" have been and are being suppressed: "If the woman possesses greater inner security and is more self-fulfilled, she can become the strongest force in promoting the healthy growth of the younger generation."

Horney recognized that her hopes for the future might be utopian, but she felt that if destructive drives are not innate but "have been acquired under specific conditions," we might be able to reduce "their intensity and extensiveness" by using our psychoanalytic knowledge to identify and change those conditions.

One of the leading features of the new psychoanalytic paradigm Horney developed in the 1930s was her emphasis on the role of culture in the formation of neurotic defenses and conflicts. This was in part a continuation of the sociological orientation that first appeared in her work during the mid-1920s and in part a result of her encounter with different social conditions and patients after she moved to the United States in 1932. It also reflected her receptivity to the work being done in the social sciences. While still in Germany, she had begun to cite ethnographic and anthropological studies, as well as the writings of the philosopher and sociologist Georg Simmel, with whom she developed a friendship. As the associate director of the Chicago Psychoanalytic Institute from 1932 to 1934, she met the social scientists Harold Lasswell and John Dollard, and in New York she exchanged ideas with the anthropologists Margaret Mead and Ruth Benedict. The most powerful influence on her was Erich Fromm, whom she had known in Berlin and saw again in Chicago. She began a close relationship with Fromm, probably when they both moved to New York in 1934, that was to last for many years. One of their mutual friends observed that Horney "learned sociology from Fromm and he psychoanalysis from her" (Rubins 1978, 195).

In the fall of 1935, Horney began teaching at the New School for Social Research, and she continued to do so for the rest of her life. Her first course was entitled "Culture and Neurosis." Invited by W. W. Norton to expand her ideas into a book, she submitted a draft of *The Neurotic Personality of Our*

Time in June of 1936. Her first publication on the topic was the essay "Culture and Neurosis," reprinted here from the April 1936 issue of the *American Sociological Review*. In this piece she argued that instead of focusing on symptoms, we should try to understand the "conflicting character traits" that produce them and the ways in which these traits are "molded by cultural processes."

According to Horney, people in our culture tend to be driven by insatiable neurotic ambition on the one hand and a boundless craving for affection on the other. They compulsively seek success, but the prospect of achieving it makes them afraid of alienating others, and this fear checks their aggressive impulses. "This conflict between ambition and affection," she proclaimed, "is one of the gravest and most typical dilemmas of the neurotics of our time."

People pursue both success and love as means of allaying anxiety. They never feel successful, because every achievement is bound to fall short of their "grandiose ambitions," and their sense of failure results in hypersensitivity to criticism, depression, and a defensive aversion to effort. They may then turn to love in an effort to gain reassurance, but love has its own pitfalls, especially in a competitive culture, and people just as often turn to the pursuit of success in order to compensate for disappointments in their human relationships. Their need for success is combined with a fear of succeeding, for they are afraid that people will hate them for their triumphs, just as they hate others who are more successful than they. Horney devoted much of her essay to describing the ways in which the needs for love and success "generate each other, check each other, and reinforce each other." They produce vicious circles in which every defense against anxiety tends to exacerbate it and to intensify feelings of frustration and hostility.

Horney traced the problems of individuals to conditions in the culture. We live in a competitive society in which people are struggling for supremacy not only in their economic activities but also in their families, social relationships, and love lives. We base our self-esteem on success and despise ourselves for failures, even if they are beyond our control. Our culture is full of conflicting values, moreover, and gives us contradictory messages: we are supposed to defeat our rivals in the competitive struggle, while at the same time displaying the Christian virtues. We need to be aggressive to succeed but to be "modest, unselfish, even self-sacrificing" if we are to be regarded as good and lovable people. Our "competitive life situation with the hostile tensions involved in it creates an enhanced need of security," but because the spirit of rivalry pervades love, friendship, and social relations, we are no more likely to find security there than in the pursuit of money, power, and prestige.

Horney concluded by comparing Freud's views on the relation between culture and neurosis with her own. For Freud, "neuroses are the price humanity has to pay for cultural development," because culture requires the suppression of sexual and aggressive drives, and that suppression produces neurosis. Variations in character formation in individuals and cultures depend on which drives are being suppressed and to what degree. Horney's position was that neurosis is due not to the suppression of instinctual drives but "rather to difficulties caused by the conflicting character of the demands which a culture imposes" on its members. The people who become neurotic are those who are more severely affected by culturally determined difficulties, because of the particular conditions of their childhoods.

Horney explored the relation between culture and neurosis most fully in *The Neurotic Personality of Our Time* (1937), where she expanded many of the ideas she had introduced in her essay. She developed some other aspects of the topic in a talk she gave to a group of educators in 1938, "Understanding Personality Difficulties in a Period of Social Transition." In both the book and the address, Horney was more effective in tracing personality problems to pathogenic conditions in the family than she was in relating them to culture. She attributed conditions in the family to cultural influences in ways that were often suggestive, but she did not establish precise connections.

In "Understanding Personality Difficulties," Horney made the interesting observation that although the younger generation believes in inner freedom and independence, as opposed to the dutifulness and submission to authority emphasized by the older generation, its members are unhappy and are driven by ego-alien goals instead of their spontaneous wishes. In her effort to explain why this is so, she invoked both cultural factors and childhood experiences in the family, but the latter much more effectively.

What gets in the way of spontaneity is "merciless inner demands" for "rectitude and perfection," demands Horney later described as "tyrannical shoulds." Sometimes these inner demands are the product of "families with inexorable standards" that reflect a puritanical culture, but we find them also in children whose parents are liberal and do not subject them to any harsh pressures. Horney rather lamely explained that these parents "are still under the influence of former generations" and therefore treat their children unfairly and are incapable of giving them real affection. Her examples of unfair treatment — such as preferring a brother or sister, betraying a child's confidences, or failing to keep promises and then blaming the child for being angry — seem to have little to do with cultural conditions or the influence of past generations.

The heart of the talk is Horney's explanation of how children respond to unfair treatment — and their subsequent feelings of anxiety, unworthiness, and resentment — by developing various defenses, such as feelings of superiority and compulsive needs for perfection. These defenses further impair their human relationships and damage their self-esteem, for they become "mercilessly critical" toward themselves and imagine that others are judging them just as harshly. They are incapable of loving others because they cannot love themselves.

As I have observed, one of Horney's main objectives in the 1930s was to define the relation of her emerging ideas to those of Freud. In her essays on feminine psychology, she had disagreed with Freud on such issues as penis envy, the psychosexual development of girls, feminine masochism, and woman's inherent nature; but she remained largely within the framework of orthodox theory, although she displayed a greater interest in cultural factors than did Freud. In her commentary on *Civilization and Its Discontents*, she began disagreeing with Freud's fundamental ideas, and in *The Neurotic Personality of Our Time* she developed a new psychoanalytic paradigm, in which she traced neuroses — or personality disorders, to employ a term that Horney herself used — to pathogenic conditions in the family that make the child feel unloved, unvalued, and insecure. These disturbances in human relationships generate "basic anxiety," a feeling of being helpless in a potentially hostile world, as a result of which children develop overwhelming needs for safety and reassurance. They try to satisfy these needs by adopting such defensive strategies as the pursuit of love, power, or detachment, but the strategies initiate vicious circles that intensify rather than reduce anxiety. The strategies are incompatible with each other, moreover, and create painful inner conflicts that generate new difficulties. Horney developed and refined this model of neurosis in her subsequent books but did not alter its basic features.

Although she made many references to Freud in *Neurotic Personality,* Horney did not compare her ideas with his in a systematic way. She did this in her next book, *New Ways in Psychoanalysis,* in which she engaged in the "critical review of the body of knowledge which is embraced by psychoanalysis" that she had called for in her review of Rank's *Modern Education.* She devoted separate chapters to Freud's basic premises, libido theory, the Oedipus complex, the concept of narcissism, feminine psychology, the death instinct, the emphasis on childhood, the concept of transference, culture and neuroses, the ego and the id, anxiety, the concept of the superego, neurotic guilt feelings, masochistic phenomena, and psychoanalytic therapy. Her usual procedure was to begin with an exposition and evaluation of Freud's views and then to present her own position. Although she professed great respect for Freud, she was also quite critical of his ideas, and many reviewers complained about her polemical tactics. In the *Nation,* J. F. Brown observed that "the book turns into a fourteen-round ring battle between the 'new ways' (Horney) and the 'old ways' (Freud)" (1939, 328). The publication of *New Ways* led to Horney's forced resignation from the New York Psychoanalytic Society and her excommunication from mainstream psychoanalysis.

This history lends particular interest, I think, to Horney's previously un-published talk "The Achievement of Freud." Probably dating from 1938 and addressed to a lay audience, the talk is a precursor to *New Ways* and covers much of the same ground. What is different is the tone. Although in *New Ways* Horney repeatedly acknowledged the importance of Freud's contributions, her main purpose was to indicate what was wrong with Freud's ideas and to replace them with her own. She devoted the last third of her talk to this purpose as well, but her main objective there was to give Freud credit for his amazing achievements. This talk has convinced me, more than anything else by Horney, that she really did admire Freud.

Horney's approach was to separate Freud's "imperishable contributions" from what she regarded as the debatable aspects of his theory, which included the aspects to which she devoted chapters in *New Ways in Psychoanalysis.* Freud's enduring teachings were that we have unconscious motivations, that we repress feelings of which we do not want to be aware, that we resist the unearthing of unconscious factors, and that all psychic processes are strictly determined. Freud has taught us a great deal about how unconscious processes operate — through such mechanisms as displacement, projection, and ratio-nalization — and showed us that we gain access to the unconscious through fantasies and dreams. He demonstrated that "neuroses result from inner con-flicts which are unconscious in nature" and that they are not only explicable but subject to cure. This is comparable to "the deeds of great scientists who discovered the cause of chronic bodily diseases like tuberculosis or diabetes and thus enabled us to find ways to fight them effectively." Freud provided the basic therapeutic tools with which we work, the most notable of which are transference and free association. The concept of transference enables us to work with the patient's emotional responses to the therapist instead of regard-ing them as a nuisance. Through free association, psychotherapy offers "some-thing new in the history of mankind," a "situation in which one human being confides in another without reservations and with a reasonable hope of being understood." The "understanding of human behavior that has been opened up by Freud" has not only provided a means of therapy but has "expanded our horizon in a way that is similar to the contribution of the greatest writers and philosophers, such as Shakespeare, Balzac, and Nietzsche." This is praise indeed.

Horney's chief objections, developed at length in *New Ways in Psycho-analysis,* were to Freud's emphasis on infantile origins and his instinctivistic thinking, a product, she thought, of his nineteenth-century mentality. She wanted, instead, to emphasize the current character structure and "the environmental factors responsible for creating neurotic conflicts": "It is the safety devices a child is compelled to develop in order to cope with the basic anxiety created by the environment that constitute the nucleus of neuroses." The object of therapy, then, "is not to help the patient gain mastery over his instincts but to lessen his anxiety to such an extent that he can dispense with his 'safety devices.' Beyond this aim there looms a new therapeutic goal, which is to restore the individual to himself, to help him regain his spontaneity and find his center of gravity in himself."

Horney urged her auditors not to "discard the valid with the invalid or to fling our criticism of his theory as an accusation against Freud." Although he was "a genius who was far ahead of his time," he could not help being "influenced by its mentality in many ways." It would be unreasonable to expect him to see fully and clearly all the ramifications of his great discoveries. We should "be deeply appreciative of the foundations Freud gave us" and "use them for further work."

Horney is thought of by many primarily as a member of the "cultural school," which also included Harry Stack Sullivan, Erich Fromm, Clara Thompson, and Abraham Kardiner. The fact is, however, that she focused on culture in only a few of her writings in the 1930s. Even *The Neurotic Personality of Our Time,* which began by emphasizing the importance of culture, was mostly devoted to developing her new paradigm for the structure of neurosis. Not until the end of the book did she discuss how culture produces neurotic personalities. Horney devoted a chapter to culture in *New Ways in Psychoanalysis* and published an essay on the topic — "What Is a Neurosis? — also in 1939. After that, she paid little attention in her writings to the relation between culture and neurosis.

In addition to being interested in how culture produces neurosis, Horney was concerned with the role of culture in our conceptions of what is "normal" and what is "neurotic." Is there a universal human nature and a standard of mental health that can be derived from it, or should normality be culturally defined? By *normal* do we mean what is desirable or what is typical in a given society? Horney established a culturally relativistic position in *Neurotic Personality,* but in *New Ways* and in "What Is a Neurosis?" she began to develop a conception of psychological health in light of which cultures can themselves be evaluated.

In *The Neurotic Personality of Our Time,* Horney argued that the normal is that which conforms to patterns of behavior that are usual and accepted in a given society, while the neurotic is that which deviates from these patterns.

Since what is normal in one culture may be neurotic in another, there is no such thing as a normal psychology that would hold for all people (1937a, 19). In the body of the book, Horney described a society that damages all of its members and classified the less severely impaired as normal. Neurosis is a deviation from the average, the difference being one of degree rather than of kind.

Although she has sometimes been identified with this initial position, Horney quickly moved away from cultural relativism, with its implied advocacy of adaptation to a pathogenic society and acceptance of the status quo. In *New Ways in Psychoanalysis,* she distinguished between "psychic normality and psychic health" (1939a, 182) and argued that cultures as well as individuals should be evaluated in terms of psychic health. She defined psychic health as a state of inner freedom in which our full capacities are available for use. Free of the compulsiveness and rigidity that characterize neurosis, we are able to actualize our potentialities. Self-realization is not relative to culture. Self-alienated people are neurotic even when they conform to the values of their culture, because those values may reflect the damaged state of its members. Cultures can be evaluated by the degree to which they foster or thwart self-realization, and such evaluation provides a basis for social criticism.

In "What Is a Neurosis?" Horney was more aware of the difficulties of defining psychic health, and she struggled with the question of absolute versus relative definitions. We can define neurosis in a way that is universally valid if we use basic anxiety and neurotic trends, rather than deviations from the norm, as the distinguishing characteristics. A valid standard for psychological health would be having "a good attitude toward self and others" and "the free use of one's energies." Horney recognized the subjective character of such a standard, however: even if it were acceptable as a general formulation, "we could hardly avoid making ourselves the judge as to what is a 'good' attitude toward self and others or as to what is a 'free' use of energy."

As a solution, Horney fell back on "practical criteria, such as the degree of being handicapped or the degree of suffering." This resembled her earlier relativism, but she tried to combine the two positions by agreeing that neurosis is "a deviation from the average," while insisting that the deviation concerns not manifest behavior but "the amount of basic anxiety and the quality of the defensive strategies." Horney abandoned the problem at this point and never progressed beyond this not very satisfactory definition.

In *New Ways in Psychoanalysis,* Horney began to see the central feature of neurosis as the "warping" of "the spontaneous individual self" because of parental oppression. The object of therapy is to "restore the individual to himself, to help him regain his spontaneity and find his center of gravity in himself" (1939a, 11). Horney introduced the term the "real self" in "Can You Take a Stand?" — an essay published in the *Journal of Adult Education* in 1939 — and in *Self-Analysis* she began to speak of "self-realization." In "Can You Take a Stand?" she argued that the inability to take a stand has two main sources, "fear of others and failure to take oneself seriously." This essay contains one of Horney's most vivid descriptions of the conditions in childhood that produce self-alienation and a shifting of "the center of gravity" from self to others:

> A child may feel that he is not wanted or appreciated for his own sake, but that he is acceptable only if he lives up to the expectations of others, especially those of his parents. He may feel that he is acceptable only if he obeys blindly or if he uncritically adores the one or the other parent. Or, the child may feel that he is acceptable only if he measures up to the standards that are current in the family, or fulfills the ambitions of his parents, or satisfies their desire for showing off. Again, the child may become subservient to the excessive demands of a self-sacrificing mother. Different as these situations are, they all result in the child's feeling that he, his real self, is not understood or not wanted, and that he, his real self, does not matter; that only the others and their expectations are important.
>
> People whose thoughts and feelings are determined by others are "wishy-washy," since they are constantly responding to ever-changing influences and have no center from which decisions and judgments can flow.

This state of mind has important social implications, for it makes people "enormously susceptible" to totalitarianism. In a passage that foreshadowed Erich Fromm's *Escape from Freedom* (1941), Horney analyzed the appeal of fascism to self-alienated people: "Fascist ideology promises to fulfill all their needs. The individual in a fascist state is not supposed to stand up for his own wishes, rights, judgments. Decisions and judgments of value are made for him and he has merely to follow. He can forget about his own weakness by adoring the leader. His ego is bolstered up by being submerged in the greater unity of race and nation." Horney acknowledged that adult educators can do little to correct psychological deficiencies, because they are dealing with groups and cannot be therapists. Anticipating the title of Paul Tillich's famous book, published in 1952, she concluded by urging teachers to try to give people, by precept and example, "the courage to be" themselves.

In "Children and the War," also published in 1939, Horney again explained responses to external conditions by reference to individual psychology. Even though the United States was a neutral nation and therefore in no immediate danger, some American children experienced the war in Europe "as an immediate personal threat" and felt great anxiety. According to Horney, this was the result of a fear of punishment caused by feelings of guilt "foisted on them" by their parents' "response to childish faults." Another source of anxiety was the hostility excited by the war, especially toward members of their family whose destruction they both wished and feared. It might be wise not to stimulate such children "by excessive talk of war and aggression, by stories or movies of horrors and cruelty." However, these things do not cause but rather trigger their aggressions and anxieties, the true source of which is in the family:

> It is all-important that the parents' early relation to children should be free of elements which tend to arouse fears and feelings of hate which last throughout life. Such things as unfairness, favoritism, and neglect rouse a general cranki-ness in children which in turn provokes punishment or disfavor from the parent. Worst of all, perhaps, in its results on personality development, is the child's discovery that as far as his parents are concerned, his existence means little more than a means of satisfying their personal self-importance. A child who is rejected by his parents often cannot consciously hate *them* but he ends by hating Germans, Jews, or the "enemy," in whatever guise it is presented.

Once the United States entered the war, the Association for the Advance-ment of Psychoanalysis established a War-Efforts Committee and issued a series of bulletins based in part on panel discussions held at the New School in March and November of 1942. Horney authored the bulletin on "Under-standing of Individual Panic," in which she emphasized that panic is a re-sponse less to an external danger than to the psychological threat that danger represents. She gave two examples she had observed during the first air raid alarm in New York. In one case a perfectionistic person was on an errand of his own during office hours when the alarm was sounded. This person's "un-conscious attitude toward life was that of living under a sword of Damocles which might fall at any moment" unless his behavior was "the ultimate in correctness." Since he was cheating on his employer at the time of the alarm, he felt that "the dreaded catastrophe" had arrived and reacted with panic. The second case was that of a writer who "had an insatiable and compulsive need for personal admiration" and who reacted with panic because he was afraid that if a raid really took place, he would fail to be a hero. It was this fear rather than the possible danger that made him panicky.

We can see in these three pieces how thoroughly Horney shifted, in the late 1930s and early 1940s, from accounting for individual psychology in social or cultural terms to explaining people's response to external conditions as an outgrowth of their personal histories. With this shift, she began to develop her mature theory.

The remaining selections in Part 2 are from 1947 to 1952, the years during and after the writing of *Neurosis and Human Growth*. The most important are two lectures from Horney's course "Pride and Self-Hatred in Neuroses" (1947); her essays "Inhibitions in Work" (1947), "The Value of Vindictiveness" (1948), "On Feeling Abused" (1951), and "The Paucity of Inner Experiences" (1952a), and her talk "Human Nature Can Change" (1952b).

In her lecture on "Pride and Self-Hatred in Freud," Horney compared her theory directly with Freud's, as she had done in *New Ways in Psychoanalysis*. That she referred to herself as "Horney" rather than using the first person suggests that she saw herself as a figure of historical importance whose status rivaled that of the master. The lecture is quite sketchy compared with *New Ways in Psychoanalysis* or even with the concluding chapter of *Neurosis and Human Growth*, of which it is a preliminary version; but we must remember that all we have is a set of notes on which Horney no doubt expanded as she spoke.

Horney acknowledged that Freud had seen many components of the intrapsychic structure she was describing—such as neurotic ambition, self-glorification, punitive inner dictates, and self-destructiveness; but she felt that he had missed others—such as the need for superiority, neurotic claims, and self-hatred. The main thing he had missed was the way in which these components are dynamically interrelated, such as the vicious circle in which "feelings of nothingness drive [people] to pursue lofty objectives, and their failure to achieve these objectives makes them feel even more insignificant, which compels them to seek greater glory, and so on."

Horney characterized some of the fundamental differences between her theory and Freud's in much the same way she had done in *New Ways in Psychoanalysis*: Freud explained behavior as deriving from instinct and having its genesis in childhood, whereas she saw behavior as reactive and believed it to be a product of the present structure of the psyche. What Freud called an instinct, she called a compulsive drive. Instincts can only be modified or controlled, but "compulsive drives can be *changed* because they are *acquired*."

Because of his pessimistic view of human nature, Freud failed to see the constructive forces at work in human psychology and regarded many problems as inaccessible to treatment. Horney did not believe that human beings are good by nature but contended that "if children are brought up under favorable conditions—that is, given real love, made to feel wanted, respected, and so on—they will become constructive adults." People become more and more constructive as they progress in analysis. Because of his own hopelessness, Freud did not see the hopelessness of his patients as a problem on which they needed to work. For Horney, hopelessness, like other neurotic difficulties, "is a result of the person's being caught in his conflicts and is therefore a condition that can be tackled and changed."

One of Horney's major objections was to Freud's failure to distinguish between the healthy and the neurotic, his assumption that the behavior he found in neurotics was universal. This led to his denial of authentic ideals and convictions and his inability to recognize the importance of the "real me." Neurotics, observed Horney, have "little feeling of the 'real me.' Freud generalized this as being the case with all human beings." Horney believed that "this weakness and deadness of the 'real me' is a neurotic product, the result of inner conflicts and self-alienation." We find nothing corresponding to a "real me" in Freud's theory, for in his view "the ego is a weak, undynamic part of the personality."

In Lecture 13, "Pride and Self-Hatred in Literature," Horney developed the concept of the devil's pact, which she had introduced in Lecture 6. This became one of the central motifs of *Neurosis and Human Growth,* where she described it as follows:

> There is a human being in psychic or spiritual distress. There is a temptation, presented in some symbol of an evil principle: the devil, the sorcerer, witches, the serpent (in the story of Adam and Eve), the antique dealer (in Balzac's *The Magic Skin*), the cynical Lord Henry Wotton (in Oscar Wilde's *The Picture of Dorian Gray*). Then there are the promises not only of a miraculous riddance from the distress but of the possession of infinite powers. And it is a testimony of true greatness when one person can resist the temptation, as the story of Christ's temptation shows. Finally there is the price to pay, which (presented in various forms) is the loss of the soul (Adam and Eve lose the innocence of their feelings), its surrender to the forces of evil. . . . The price may be psychic torment in this life (as in *The Magic Skin*) or the torment of hell. In *The Devil and Daniel Webster* we have the beautifully realized symbol of the shriveled souls collected by the devil. (1950a, 375–76)

Stories of the devil's pact seemed to Horney to embody one of her central ideas, that people cope with feelings of frustration or inadequacy by embarking on a search for glory in which they abandon their real selves (their souls) in favor of self-idealization. This intensifies their distress, partly because they can never achieve their unrealistic objectives and therefore feel even more worthless than they did before, and partly because their betrayal of their real selves fills them with despair and self-contempt.

Like Freud, Horney recognized that the great writers had intuitively grasped and artistically portrayed the phenomena being studied through psychoanalysis, and in her lecture "Pride and Self-Hatred in Literature" she cited a number of works that depicted the devil's pact, the search for glory, and the relation between pride and self-hatred. These included *The Devil and Daniel Webster* (Benét), *Faust* (Goethe), "The Snow Queen" (Andersen), *The Picture of Dorian Gray* (Wilde), *Peer Gynt, Hedda Gabler,* and *John Gabriel Borkman* (Ibsen), *Père Goriot* (Balzac), *Pavilion of Women* (Buck), *Madame Bovary* (Flaubert), *The Red and the Black* (Stendhal), *Don Giovanni* (Mozart), *Moby Dick* (Melville), *Hamlet* (Shakespeare), and *The Rime of the Ancient Mariner* (Coleridge). Horney's references to these works, and many more, in her writings reflected not only the breadth of her reading but her extensive preparation for the course "Literary Figures in the Light of Psychoanalysis," which she taught at the New School for Social Research.

Horney felt that great literary artists had portrayed various forms of the search for glory and many of its consequences. It can take place in the imagination or be experienced through another person. It can entail the pursuit of perfection, of love, or of vindictive triumphs. The search for glory results in a shrinking of the personality, a deadening of emotions, and impaired human relationships. It leads to a sense of futility, to self-hatred and self-ruination. Although stories portraying the search for glory usually end tragically, some depict protagonists freeing themselves from their compulsion and achieving a kind of redemption.

As I have tried to show in my literary criticism, Horney's mature theory is highly congruent with a great many fictional works (see Paris 1974, 1978, 1986, 1991a, 1991b, 1997). I have written Horneyan analyses of four of the texts to which Horney refers in this lecture: *The Red and the Black* (Paris 1974), *Hamlet* (Paris 1991a), *Hedda Gabler* (1997), and *Madame Bovary* (1997). I do not believe that Hamlet is pursuing glory by taking revenge, as Horney suggests, but her description of his dilemma is excellent: "Hamlet is caught between contradictory shoulds: he should both execute his revenge and be gentle and good." That is the best explanation, I think, of Hamlet's inability to act.

Among Horney's series of lectures "Pride and Self-Hatred in Neuroses" was one entitled "Influence on Work" (Lecture 10). Horney developed this lecture into the essay "Inhibitions in Work" (1947), included here. A comparison of the essay with my edited versions of Horney's lecture notes gives a good sense of the skeletal nature of the notes and the way in which Horney elaborated them.

Horney was concerned with the difficulties that arise in creative work, which she broadly defined as nonroutine work that requires initiative, self-reliance, and responsibility. She identified four factors that are involved in such work: gifts, consistency of interest and of effort, self-confidence, and a genuine love of and devotion to the work. She then discussed the ways in which self-idealization, with its concomitants of pride and self-hatred, affects each of these factors.

Because of a fear of the "discrepancy between superlative imagined achievement and realistic possibilities," some people deny their gifts and resign themselves to modest achievement. Others exaggerate their abilities but protect themselves from failure by equating potentialities with accomplishments.

Some people lack consistency because they take on too many projects. They cannot restrict their activities because the idea of having limitations like other human beings is intolerable. Others are motivated to sporadic efforts by "the glory of the dramatic, of the unusual," while they resent "the humble tasks of daily living." Yet others make grandiose plans but fail to carry them out, either because they feel that detail work should be done by ordinary people or because they need to protect their pride by not trying very hard. Consistent efforts constitute a "threat to the illusion of unlimited powers."

Although self-idealization is a device people employ to compensate for lack of self-confidence, it has the effect of undermining self-confidence further and thus interfering with creative work. It weakens people by alienating them from their real selves and engendering self-hatred when they fail to achieve their unrealistic objectives. Some people suppress their self-doubts and identify with their idealized selves, but then they must protect their pride by refusing to put their abilities to the test of reality. Those who try to do significant work despite their neurotic difficulties are pushed and pulled "between exacting demands for absolute perfection on the one hand and destructive self-contempt on the other." Since they are out of touch with their real selves, they have difficulty making decisions and are unsure about what they really think and feel.

Horney felt that although some people can feel a genuine interest in their work despite their neurotic difficulties, these difficulties usually interfere with such an interest. The work may become part of the search for glory, or "the tension and turmoil" that a person "feels while working may be so great that he cannot possibly love the work." In some cases, "an existing alive interest for a work is deadened by the feeling of doing it under coercion and by the concomitant resentment." This may be an unconscious process that manifests itself indirectly "in the form of listlessness, fatigue, exhaustion." There are those who "throw all their energies into a pursuit of success" because their self-hatred has led them to abandon all hope of being loved, in which case their work "is merely a means to an end." Others are inhibited in their work because they are afraid that success would make them less lovable.

Toward the end of the essay, Horney observed that we can "almost predict in a neurotic individual the kind of difficulties he is likely to have in his work—

provided we are familiar with his character structure" and that these difficulties will "disappear to the extent to which the whole personality is straightened out." These remarks prefigure Horney's treatment of "neurotic problems in work" in the chapter that bears that title, Chapter 13 of *Neurosis and Human Growth,* where she discussed the problems generated by each of the major defensive strategies — narcissism, perfectionism, arrogant-vindictiveness, self-effacement, and resignation.

"The Value of Vindictiveness" (1948) also prefigured *Neurosis and Human Growth,* in that Horney began there to formulate her conception of vindictiveness as one of the neurotic solutions. But although she made use of some of those ideas in her description of the arrogant-vindictive personality in Chapter 8 of the book, in the essay Horney dealt with the phenomenon of vindictiveness in a broader and more systematic way than she did anywhere else, calling attention not only to its aggressive forms but also to its manifestations in self-effacing and detached individuals. The title of the essay is somewhat misleading, because it gives the impression that Horney thought that vindictiveness had a positive value, whereas her argument is rather that it is highly destructive, to both self and others. She spoke of the "positive functions of vindictiveness," but by this she meant the subjective value it has in the fulfillment of neurotic needs.

Horney began by distinguishing between rational retaliation, which is under control and "proportionate to the provocation," and a "blind vindictive passion" that overrides "prudence, happiness, ambition, and even life itself." Her primary interest was in the sources of compulsive vindictiveness and the value it has for the neurotic, which is so great that "he defends it with every fibre of his being." The most important sources are hurt pride, often resulting from the frustration of irrational claims; externalization of self-hate, which turns other people into dangerous enemies; and hopelessness, which leads people to blame others for their unhappiness and want to make them just as miserable.

Their vindictiveness is "so precious" to many people because it fulfills several needs. It protects them from the hostility of those they distrust and also, by a process of externalization, from their own self-hate and self-destructiveness. By enabling them to get back at those who have hurt them, it restores their injured pride. Because it makes them feel powerful, they glorify it and scorn such qualities as friendliness, trust, and generosity. It gives them "the excitement, the thrill, the passion" of turning the tables on those by whom they feel oppressed and of experiencing vindictive triumphs. Horney pointed out that vindictive triumphs "may take fairly benign forms, where every trace of vengeance is eradicated from the conscious mind," and she offered the example of

Cinderella: "There are Cinderella's dreams of the Prince Charming who will single her out. Mother, sister, or companions, then, will realize how blind they have been toward her superior beauty and goodness. But she will not bear any grudge and in the greatness of her generous heart [will] become their benefactress." The vindictive triumph often involves a combination of revenge and self-vindication, as in the Cinderella story, which has what I call a vindication plot, of which there are numerous examples in literature (see Paris 1974, 1978, 1991a, 1991b, 1997).

One reason vindictiveness is extremely difficult to give up is that the alternatives are so unappealing. The neurotic alternative is to adopt a self-effacing attitude, a solution that is particularly frightening to an aggressive person, who would then see himself "as a helpless jellyfish, a prey to anybody who chooses to step on him and a prey also to his own self-contempt." The healthy alternative would be to relinquish his neurotic claims and become "an ordinary human being like everybody else," but this seems a terrible comedown. Horney ended her essay with advice to the therapist on how to help patients overcome their resistances and choose the healthy alternative. The most important thing is to recognize that vindictiveness is an aspect of the patient's whole character structure, which must be changed, rather than an isolated phenomenon that can be treated directly.

After she completed *Neurosis and Human Growth,* Horney focused primarily on analytic technique. She taught courses on the topic in 1950, 1951, and 1952, and it would have been the subject of her next book, had she lived (see Horney 1987 and 1999). Her focus on therapy was reflected in "Ziele der analytischen Therapie," which was published in German in 1951, translated in 1991 as "The Goals of Analytic Therapy," and reprinted in *The Therapeutic Process* (Horney 1999). In the last years of her life, "On Feeling Abused" (1951) and "The Paucity of Inner Experiences" (1952a), both of which are reprinted here, were also published. In these essays, she explored the phenomena named in the titles from the perspective of her mature theory and suggested how they might be dealt with in therapy.

By "feeling abused" Horney meant a pervasive sense "of being the victim," a feeling which "is out of proportion to actual provocations and may become a way of experiencing life." Her thoughts on this topic are very timely today, when the cultivation of feelings of victimization is widespread. Horney began by pointing out that neurotic persons often receive provocations more frequently than healthy ones, either because they are self-effacing and inadvertently invite others to take advantage of them or because they are aggressive and alienate others by their irritability and arrogance. Since they do not recognize their role in eliciting bad treatment, they feel it to be "entirely un-deserved." But the main reason they feel victimized is that their emotional responses are quite disproportionate to any actual affronts. Because of their neurotic claims, their tyrannical shoulds, and their underlying self-hatred, they feel deeply wounded by what would otherwise be minor events. Their distortion of certain situations in such a way as to cast themselves as victims suggests that they are driven by "some inner necessity" to experience life as they do.

According to Horney, feeling abused is "part and parcel" of "externalized living." Its most important function is that it makes "others, or circumstances, responsible for what is wrong in one's own life." It is a way to avoid facing one's own problems, a defense "against owning up to any neurotic drive or conflict within [oneself]." Externalized living is not merely a defense but an inevitable consequence of self-alienation, which leads people to feel that they are not an active force in their own lives. If the therapist tries to show them "the extent to which their pride, their claims, their self-accusations" are re-sponsible for their feelings of being abused, they may recognize the connec-tions in an intellectual way but will fail to register them emotionally, because they do "not experience much of anything that is going on" in themselves. They "may be consciously convinced that heaven and hell are within," but this is not how they feel and how they live. Rather, "good and evil all seem to come from outside." As long as a person "does not experience *his* feelings, *his* thoughts, *his* actions, he cannot possibly feel responsible for himself, or for his life. Whatever difficulties arise can be brought about only by others. 'They' keep him down, disregard him, take advantage of him, coerce him."

The kind of externalization involved in feeling abused presents a major obstacle to therapy, because "nobody can find himself if he keeps running away from himself." Patients will not be interested in their own difficulties as long as they make outside factors responsible for them; and they will be highly resistant to change, because they feel that it is others who are the source of their problems, not they. It is therefore essential to analyze the feeling of being abused, to help patients understand and experience it as a symptom of self-alienation and of their defensive needs. They will have better relations with others when they stop holding them responsible for things that only they themselves can change; and although owning up to their difficulties will be painful, it will give them a stronger sense of I-ness, a greater feeling of strength and vitality. When they become less preoccupied with blaming others, they will be able to use more of their energies "for constructive self-examination."

As patients progress in therapy, however, new problems are likely to arise. As their real selves emerge, they have "to defend [them] against the onslaught of the pride system," which will not give up its claims to glory without a fight. Horney elsewhere referred to this as the "central inner conflict" (Horney 1950; 1999). Moreover, when patients relinquish their externalizations and begin to *experience* their difficulties as really their own, they may turn against themselves with growing "self-condemnation, self-contempt, self-destructiveness." To defend against their self-hate, they may turn their aggression outward in an attempt to make others "appear as the evil ones." Thus, giving up their externalizations leads to greater self-hate, which leads to increased externalization and a rise in vindictiveness. Things get worse after they get better, and whether constructive or destructive forces ultimately prevail depends to a large degree on the skill of the analyst.

Horney's last essay was "The Paucity of Inner Experiences," published in 1952. Here, too, she was concerned with both understanding a phenomenon and exploring its manifestations and treatment in therapy. By a paucity of inner experiences, she was referring to a "pervasive haziness" in which people seem to have walled off their thoughts and feelings so that they have a sense of inner emptiness and are living in a fog. She emphasized that she was not just talking about alienation from the real self but a loss of touch with the "actual self," which is "everything a person is at a given time," healthy and neurotic (1950a, 158). People are out of touch not only with the alive center of their being but also with their anxieties and defenses, with their pride and self-hate, their triumphs and defeats, their hurts, angers, and frustrations.

People who are numbed to their inner experiences shift their emphasis from the inner to the outer and engage in externalized living. They experience intrapsychic processes as though they were interpersonal ones and depend on the expectations and judgments of others to give them a sense of direction. They also have a feeling of emptiness that arouses anxiety of the kind described in Kierkegaard's account of the fear of nothingness and Tillich's of the fear of nonbeing. People's sense of inner emptiness may appear not directly but in their attempts to run away from it or in "a more or less vague feeling of missing out on something, of yearning or discontentment."

People's divorce from their thoughts and feelings creates major obstacles to therapy, for they keep externalizing and intellectualizing and are unable to experience their insights: "The patient must feel his conflicts, live with his self-contempt, experience how unrelated he is to anything." The analyst cannot deal with the divorce directly but must "help the patient toward some measure of self-knowledge, toward some measure of inner relatedness to himself" by tackling "whatever is available of his neurotic structure," even if only at first on an intellectual level. Not until after he has gained some measure of self-knowledge is the patient "ready to be confronted with his feeling of inner emptiness." This is bound to be a terrifying experience: "It feels like life evapo- rating, like losing the ground under his feet, like being lost in a fog of nothing- ness." But if it comes at the right time, such an experience can "somehow" have "the power to penetrate through the wall to his alive core." The patient realizes that there is an alternative to his emptiness, that there is a part of himself "that wants to live and that reaches out for a meaning." Like Sartre, Horney stressed the importance of facing our sense of nothingness, but she was careful to distinguish her position from his. Whereas he felt that "life *is* meaningless," she saw "emptiness as the outcome of a neurotic process."

Patients dread not only their emotional deadness but also "the prospect of coming to life." Their lowered awareness is difficult to relinquish because it serves important functions. It keeps them "from recognizing contradictions, discrepancies, and pretenses" in their personalities and protects their illusions. It is a defense against all painful inner experiences, such as self-hate, their failure to live up to their unrealistic demands on themselves, and the frustra- tion of their unrealistic demands on the world. Above all, it is a way of protect- ing their idealized image, with its claims of omnipotence and omniscience.

Patients resist the therapeutic process, which fosters self-awareness and helps them get in touch with their feelings, because it is a threat to their idealized image. Coming to life would mean feeling in their "blood and bones the grip some compulsive drive" has on them, and this would mean that "far from being all-powerful," they are not even masters of themselves. Since rec- ognizing their conflicts and failures makes them feel helpless, their budding "wish to come to life will be checked by [their] dread of impotence." There is bound to be a struggle (the central inner conflict) between "the yearning for life and the fight to maintain the belief in omnipotence," with now one and now the other having the upper hand; but patients must "feelingly realize" that they have "beaten [their] head against the stone wall of the impossible" if they are to accept their human limitations and experience themselves as they are. Their defenses against pain only perpetuate their problems, for nothing can be gained "as long as we run away from an inner ordeal."

Although Horney's thought developed a great deal between 1931 and 1952, some of its basic tenets remained the same. In "Culture and Aggression" Horney had argued that destructive aggression is reactive rather than innate, and in the last year of her life, she maintained the same position at a sym- posium entitled "Human Nature Can Change." The title of the symposium was misleading: its thesis was not that human nature can change but that individuals are capable of psychological growth. Although people are often "greedy, envious, cruel, vindictive, and destructive," these characteristics are the acquired products of neurotic development rather than inherent features of human nature.

Far from believing that human nature can change, Karen Horney was an essentialist who held that human beings are inherently constructive. The object of therapy is not to change their original nature but to help them get in touch with it. Human beings also have a potential for evil. They are so constituted that they turn destructive when their desire for self-fulfillment is thwarted. What is inherent in human nature is not destructiveness per se but the tendency to become destructive under adverse conditions. When people receive what they need for healthy growth, they do not become greedy, envious, cruel, and vindictive.

Horney cited her observations of child development and her experience as a clinician as evidence for her positive view of human nature. Like other living organisms, children have an "innate urge to grow" but require certain conditions if they are to realize their potentialities. As a tree will become warped and crooked if it has too little sun, insufficient water, or poor soil, so a child will become "hostile, withdrawn, or overdependent" under unfavorable conditions. "You could not call the results of this process his essential nature," observed Horney, "any more than you would do so with" a stunted tree. She did not make the point here, but in other writings she had frequently complained that Freud made generalizations about human nature from his observation of the troubled people who came to him for analysis.

Horney's clinical experience led her to conclusions quite different from Freud's. She found that sadistic and masochistic people are "*driven* to have such attitudes by powerful unconscious forces" that are not inherent in their natures but are the product of specific kinds of unfavorable childhood experiences. Since "what is acquired can be changed," these behaviors are amenable to therapy. The change that occurs involves "not just a better control or channeling of these drives," as implied by Freud, but "the giving up of irrational destructive drives and functioning in an increasingly more self-realizing way." As the patient's compulsions lose their grip, he "starts to come home to himself. He begins to taste how it feels to be alive, and since feeling alive is the most precious thing that we have on this earth, he wants more of it. He develops an increasingly strong wish to fulfill himself and to have a meaningful life." This is the kind of change to which Horney was referring in the title of the symposium.

12

Culture and Aggression: Some Thoughts and Doubts About Freud's Theory of Instinctual Drives Toward Death and Destruction (1931)

In *New Ways in Psychoanalysis,* Horney observed that her doubts about the validity of Freud's version of psychoanalysis were first aroused by his ideas about feminine psychology and "then strengthened by his postulate of the death instinct" (1939a, 7). "Culture and Aggression" marks the beginning of her open break with the fundamentals of Freudian theory. The essay was based on her contribution to a seminar called "Das Problem der Kultur und die ärztliche Psychologie" (The problem of culture and medical psychology) that was held in the winter semester of 1930–31 at the University of Leipzig and organized by Henry E. Sigerist, professor of the history of medicine. The general topic was Freud's *Civilization and Its Discontents.* The proceedings were published in *Vorträge, Institut für Geschichte der Medizin, Univ. Leipzig* (Lectures from the Institute for History of Medicine, University of Leipzig), vol. 4 (Leipzig: Georg Thieme, 1931). Horney's essay was titled "Der Kampf in der Kultur: Einige Gedanken und Bedenken zu Freud's Todestrieb und Destruktionstrieb." The English translation, "Culture and Aggression: Some

Thoughts and Doubts About Freud's Death Drive and Destruction Drive," by Bella S. Van Bark, was published in the *American Journal of Psychoanalysis* 20 (1960): 130–38, in commemoration of the seventy-fifth anniversary of Karen Horney's birth. For a further discussion of the death instinct, see chap. 7 of *New Ways in Psychoanalysis*.

For a psychoanalyst, the problem of describing the part played by aggressive tendencies of mankind in the construction and destruction of culture is bound to be stimulating, since it leads into an almost wholly unexplored area. However, this problem is of such tremendous scope that it would require no less than a lifetime of work in the field of social psychology. I must, therefore, content myself with showing you a few aspects of the problem which resulted from psychoanalytic thinking.

Even the simpler task of working up a brief sketch of Freud's views based on his psychoanalytical thinking, as expressed in *Civilization and Its Discontents,* is not quite so easy, since precisely in this area almost everything is problematic. Precisely those ideas, recently advocated by Freud, on the innate aggressive tendencies in mankind, in contrast to other psychoanalytic concepts, have not developed from empirical observations, but are the product of speculative thinking. As such, they are open to criticism and to attack in psychoanalytic circles.

Those who have carefully followed the development of analysis in recent years realize that this statement about the purely speculative origin can be only partially correct. For out of clinical experience there has been effected a very gradual change based on increasing evidence of destructive tendencies as pathogenic factors. We could also say that *Civilization and Its Discontents* is the ultimate expression of such empirical observation.

At this point we are faced with two divergent impressions. Are Freud's ideas the product of his ingenious, although totally subjective, speculative imagination, or are they a reflection of a first, courageous affirmation of what was experienced and observed in the other? Perhaps we should not waste time on either, or on questioning, but should keep our eyes open to the boundary line separating one from the other.

Now let us see what we find on closer examination of the empirical observations. What is the nature of the change in focus to which I have previously referred? First and foremost, we must consider the changes in the concept of anxiety. Originally, anxiety was regarded as an expression of dammed-up libidinal energies, attributed to inappropriate use of sexual energies. Later, the concept of anxiety was freed from this restricting context in which anxiety was connected only with sexual factors. Then the concept was extended in the direction of regarding anxiety as an expression of the perception of all the dangers threatening us from the still-lively volcanic forces operative within. These may be strong, uncontrolled sexual forces, but much more frequently anxiety is provoked by destructive forces fused with sexual energies. Even more anxiety-provoking is the perception of destructive forces in pure culture. Even in anxiety of apparently sexual origin, as, for example, anxiety over the perception of unconscious prostitution fantasies, or over the horrible consequences of masturbation, we can at least see that the content of such anxiety is conditioned by the admixture of repressed destructive drives. The fruitfulness of such a broadened view is reflected in our understanding of the universality of masturbation anxiety.

To Freud we owe this broader perspective on the sexual problems confronting us, a perspective which has made it possible for us to start wondering about the ubiquity of masturbation-anxiety. We are not especially surprised that religious people, who turn aside from all sexual matters, would consider masturbation a heinous sin. What is even more significant is not only that we find anxieties among those who have read articles depicting every kind of terrifying consequence of masturbation, but that we also find secret anxieties in countless people who are mostly ignorant of any connection between anxiety and masturbation. The same anxieties are found, in this or that guise, in those who are not especially bothered by ethical concerns over sexual matters. Furthermore, these anxieties are not restricted to any age or cultural class. Such findings should make us thoughtful.

At first, psychoanalytic experience indicated that anxiety could be traced to threats about masturbation in childhood and that, although deeply repressed, these threats continued to operate as a residual source of anxiety. However, such threats were not elicited to any noteworthy degree in all patients. And even if they had been uncovered, it would mean only that the problem had to be shifted to the previous generation. We would then have to raise this question: What accounts for such a general parental prohibition of masturbation? Medically speaking, there is no known or rational basis for connecting masturbation with every possible illness. The tendency to make such a correlation is in itself an expression of anxiety. Educators have objected to masturbation on the ground that fostering such an easily attainable pleasure undermines character development and contributes to antisocial and egocentric behavior. They have a point, but their argument does not in the least clarify the roots of the anxiety in which masturbation is embedded.

Actually, masturbation-anxiety cannot be comprehended from those aspects which are accessible to consciousness, but can only be inferred from the guilt feelings generated by the unconscious fantasies accompanying or leading to masturbation. The content of the sexual fantasies in themselves, no matter how infantile or prohibited, cannot make understandable those specific anxieties which are found in those who unconsciously fear or consider every deprivation in life, every conceivable illness, every failure a consequence of masturbation. If there is one principle which is inviolable and operative in the unconscious, it is the ancient principle of talion (vengeance): an eye for an eye, a tooth for a tooth. If with your heart and soul you wish illness to another person, desire to eliminate him from the competitive struggle, desire his ruin or his death, you must unconsciously fear retaliation with a similar fate for yourself. In other words, only the more potent mixture of unconscious destructive elements with masturbation can make understandable the extreme ease with which anxiety is provoked.

An example may illustrate this point. An exact, detailed, psychological history of a compulsion neurosis may often show the following onset: In reaction to certain anxieties, a man has suddenly suppressed masturbation. At precisely this point, compulsive phenomena appear for the first time. What has occurred? Prior to this point, the individual has succeeded in fusing unusually large components of hostile impulses with libidinal impulses. Of course, he has had anxieties, but they have not, so to speak, threatened his very existence. As soon as the libidinal fusion is dissolved, and the hostile impulses break through and, as such, lurk naked and undisguised within the depths of the individual, he must protect himself in very different ways from the threatening danger. At this point, the compulsive phenomena arise as security measures against the unmixed destructive drives.

Now let us consider an even more common problem. We all know people who are not actually considered ill and, yet, in characteristic ways seem fated to fail in the areas of work, love, and friendship. Here, as well, we find that the particular restricting hand which appears to be fate is actually an expression of repressed aggressions. Perhaps it goes like this: for such people every competitive situation at work or in love becomes impossible and resembles life-and-death matters unconsciously. They therefore prefer to condemn themselves to failure.

Now let us take an example from an area nearer to general experience in a normal life. We might inquire as to why there are so few successful marriages. Why do we find in the most ordinary exchange between husband and wife such easily provoked undercurrents of defensiveness, anxiety, and distrust? Why must the husband belittle his wife in one way or another? The source of these reactions does not involve the sexual area, for in actuality Eros binds husband and wife. What is really involved here is this: Precisely the strongest and least controllable affects grow in the same soil as the most potent hostility; and these have been developing since childhood and are carried over to the adult in the form of a readiness to distrust.

This is not a particularly new premise. We have always realized that hostility and retaliatory drives contribute not only to the genesis of neurosis, but also to ordinary human conflicts. What has really taken place in psychoanalytic thinking is a shift from considering only the sexual factors to emphasis on the destructive forces as the true operative pathogenic factor.

And yet this shift seems to encompass more than a mere change in emphasis, at least insofar as theoretical constructs are concerned. We cannot reproach Freud for underestimating the importance of the contribution of hostile-aggressive drives in the factors affecting both the individual and society. How have we previously classified these drives directed toward destruction of the object? By and large, they were included under sadism. Sadism was commonly described as a partial drive of sexuality appearing during a particular phase in the development of infantile sexuality. Infantile cruelty appeared as its direct expression; the picture of compassion and consideration was regarded as reaction-formations against sadism. Sadism was seen as a perversion, as a regression to this phase, and residual aggressions as more or less ego-shaping transformations. Specific occupations, such as soldier and surgeon, were considered as sublimations. This mode of classification has not been satisfactory, inasmuch as there are many pathological and normal phenomena which do not in the slightest degree show any connection between the destructive drives and sexuality. We could have seen the untenability of this argument earlier when Abraham, by way of a theoretically consistent extension of this concept, raised objections to this correlation and postulated a "post-ambivalent" phase. This would mean that we could expect the following: If all the streams of sexuality were unified in the phase of genital primacy, and thus an individual had fully developed his capacity for love, then every shred of sadism, as such, would have disappeared and, therefore, the individual would no longer harbor any ambivalent emotions of love and hate towards the love-object.

In context with earlier theory, this postulate would be indisputable, but reality upsets the argument. Freud himself has often enough stressed that even under normal conditions a person does not reach this ideal state. The sharpening of our theoretical understanding of sadism has been hampered by an unsuitable broadening of the term, which grew out of a tendency to create a maximally unified concept from phenomena, in this instance from sexuality.

The newer concept of a duality of instincts seems to fit in better with the facts. I, therefore, believe that the great psychoanalytic significance of

Civilization and Its Discontents stems from the fact that here, for the first time, the important role of non-erotic aggressive tendencies is fully appreciated. This is expressed by Freud as follows: "I can no longer understand how we could have overlooked the universality of non-erotic aggression and destructiveness and how we could have failed to give it its due significance in the interpretation of life." Up to this point there is hardly anything that is problematic, and this is as far as empirical observation takes us.

What I find questionable is Freud's derivation of these destructive drives from the death instinct. The assertion of a death instinct would, grossly simplified, mean that as we find in all organic matter the biological rhythm of creation and destruction, anabolism and catabolism, and a cycle of life, growth, and death, so also we could find corresponding processes in drives which could be designated as life-and-death instincts, or as Eros and Destruction. Freud himself concedes that the arguments for such a state of affairs were not convincing. No matter how ingeniously the material derived from biology is used, it does not lend itself very well to analogies. Even the psychological arguments are not convincing as supportive evidence for the phenomena of "repetition compulsion" and "primary masochism," which could be interpreted differently and are in themselves problematic. Furthermore, the death instinct can neither be experienced, as Freud himself states, nor in any way be discovered in isolation, but "works silently within the organism toward its disintegration." Freud thinks that "the more productive idea is this one, that a component of the instinct is directed outward and then manifests itself as the drive to aggression and destruction." We must carefully examine the meaning of this sentence. Although the claim of a death instinct in itself may belong in the realm of speculation, nevertheless his idea may furnish us with a useful working hypothesis. The meaning of this statement is no more and no less than this, that "man possesses an innate tendency to evil, aggression, destruction, and ultimately to inhumanity." Freud is correct in adding that none of us cares to hear things of this nature. However, our aversion does not constitute evidence to the contrary. What should really concern us is whether this statement can or cannot be corroborated by the available psychological data. One fact stands out in the foreground: the widespread occurrences throughout history of ruthless attitudes and behavior have no bearing at all on this assertion, since the question of the innate nature of such tendencies is left open, or at least the value of such observations cannot be gauged without a careful investigation into the nature of the psychological and social pressures which might perhaps have produced them.

I believe rather that this is the more cardinal question: Can every action which appears to be directed toward destruction be considered as a derivative of a drive to destruction? Our first task is to clarify the difference between the concepts of aggression and destruction. Freud's tendency to string these two concepts together and to equate one with the other did not occur by chance or through carelessness of expression. He intentionally related them very closely and this becomes much clearer when we realize that he wants us to regard the drives to rule, to exert power, to master nature as "modified and controlled, quasi-aim-inhibited expressions of this drive to destruction."

I ask you, can the constructive in man be regarded as an aim-inhibited expression of the destructive? Isn't this a rather debatable generalization of that extraordinary, otherwise fruitful analytical thinking which assumes that the factual results of an action indicate often enough the direction in which we must search for the appropriate instinctual drive behind it? Of course, we need not be fearful of turning antiquated truths upside down — to change "man destroys in order to live" into "man lives in order to destroy"; but if we do this, we must have a more cogent basis than the merely scientific urge to embrace all living processes in one powerful, but perhaps rather overwhelmingly stretched synthesis, the synthesis of Eros and Destruction.

To be sure, every step forward in our conquest of nature also gratifies our sense of mastery. But apart from the fact that mastery gives us a heightened sense of aliveness, hunger would have driven man to conquer nature anyhow, or, to say it more succinctly, the drives to preserve life and improve the necessary conditions for life would push us in that direction. The aggressive tendencies definitely play a significant part in the drives for self-preservation. With equal certainty, we can speak of the aggressive drives as innate if we understand them in their fundamental sense as referrable to impulses to touch, grasp, seize, take hold of, and possess. We can see expressions of the *Anlage* for this drive even in the infant, and it is clear enough when we see the infant reaching for and attempting to take hold of everything. From this point onward, we can easily extend the line of development to later manifestations of making demands, making claims, wanting to win out, wanting to conquer people and things and wield power over them.

But where in all this can we identify the destructive force? Is it not possible to consider all tendencies of this order as varied expressions of a vital urge for expansion? Are not all these impulses exquisitely life-affirming? Are they not clearly residuals of phylogenetically acquired tendencies necessary to man in his efforts to acquire and defend his foodstuffs, his love-objects, and his family? The well-known lioness protecting her cubs becomes ferocious when anyone comes too close to them. However, are we dealing here with hostility, destructiveness, or desires to annihilate? Or are we actually dealing with impulses to defend and preserve life? What here leads to actual destruction of another life is unequivocally determined by a drive to life. Furthermore, under what conditions does an animal generally attack? A hungry animal attacks, as does an animal anticipating attack — again always in the service of self-preservation.

Furthermore, I see no different picture in deep analyses. Of course, we find inordinate fury and destructive impulses in the course of analysis of even the most placid and decent people. Why do we not then recoil in horror? Why is it that the better we understand the patient, the easier it becomes for us to feel with him? Probably this happens because we realize that all this fury has, or has had, a real basis in the patient's experiences with insults, with frustrations, and above all with anxiety. Clinical experience shows that when these grounds cease to operate and the intensity of unconscious anxiety has been reduced through analysis, these patients lose their tendencies to hostility. Not that these patients become particularly good, but their unconscious strivings are no longer directed toward destruction, and they become active in their own behalf, assume responsibility for their lives, are able to make requests, assert themselves, work, acquire possessions, and defend themselves. We know that we cannot be magicians, a fact which Freud was the first to emphasize. We would not be able to mobilize life-affirming forces if they were not there in the patient from the beginning; only under the stress of anxiety and damned-up libidinal drives have they turned into destructive impulses, sadism, and cruelty.

It would be ridiculous to suppose that Freud had not seen these connections, since he was the one who first taught us to use them. The inference to be drawn from his thesis is, however, that destructive drives, which are of necessity directed to the outer world, are triggered by insults, frustrations, and anxiety which bring to light an unalterable, innate, constitutional, instinctual drive to destruction. He postulates a given human tendency to be provoked to animosity, hostility, and destruction, which seizes every opportunity to discharge itself in thoughts and actions. It cannot be denied that many events in the history of nations, as well as in the history of individuals, may, at first, give this impression. However, on analytic examination, amenable to verification, we find thoroughly adequate grounds for overt and covert hostility. This hostility disappears when these grounds are removed. It was Freud who also opened the way for understanding the frequency of man's innate predisposition to hostility. He showed us unalterable factors contributing to this state. The long period of the child's dependency and helplessness presents many opportunities for clashes between the child's powerful, continuous instinctual demands and the necessary, culturally imposed demands to inhibit these drives, and accounts for a residue of anxiety and defensiveness.

It is on analytic grounds, therefore, that I feel obliged to reject the thesis of the death instinct and an innate destructive instinct, as well as the thesis of innate evil in man. I do not in the slightest wish to replace this thesis with the claim that man is basically "good." As I see it, man is born with a vital necessity for self-expanding — a necessity which drives him to grasp as much as he possibly can of life and its possibilities. Even our most frantic death wishes and our strongest drives for vengeance are dictated by this will to live and this desire to obtain as much love, success, strength, and satisfaction in living as possible. In this framework, we will regard anyone as our enemy who stands in our way or who prevents us from achieving these ends. It is not the will to destroy that drives us, but the will to life that forces us to destroy.

And now to a consideration of the will to life and the inseparable anxiety about death which leads me to another unsolved problem in psychoanalysis. What, in Freud's thesis, becomes of the anxiety about death? Freud supposes that the unconscious has no concept of death or non-being, and therefore he tends to deny the fear of death as a powerful force in our mental life. This thesis has always been unacceptable to me, as well as to many others. I would venture a conjecture that the denial of anxiety about death is accounted for by the death instinct in this way: We have no fear of death — on the contrary, something in the core of our being drives us toward death.

So much for criticism. From my remarks you will no doubt see that psychoanalysis is not a cult requiring that its adherents display blind allegiance to Freud's every word, although we have often been accused of this. To be sure, we are dealing here less with variations in the method of true scientific inquiry into facts than with differences of opinion over our emotional or, shall we say, philosophic backgrounds regarding the nature of man.

It is obvious, furthermore, that these differences extend beyond the field of theoretical problems in psychoanalysis and into the field of cultural problems. If we share Freud's viewpoint of innate destructive tendencies in man, then we must be absolutely pessimistic about the inevitability of the explosions of these instincts in crime, war, and its atrocities, as well as in vicious interclass and international struggles for power. If we do not share Freud's point of view, there is left for us a primary — and maybe the strongest — impression that man is tragically and inextricably trapped in his relationship to culture, that man, more helpless than the beast, requires certain patterns of living which bind him to the culture so that he can exist at all. This would entail a variety of restrictions, changing in quality and quantity, on the sexual and aggressive drives. Man does not respond favorably to these restrictions, especially in childhood; he perceives them as a threat and reacts with anxiety and a hidden capacity for hostility. So from this standpoint as well there is no rosy, happy-ending optimism, yet this represents a basically different point of view from that of Freud because it contains some factors amenable to change.

Of course, cultural demands for curbs on instinctual drives are unavoidable. In this process, the individual becomes subdued and to some extent forfeits happiness and possibilities for happiness. To a certain degree it becomes unavoidable in the course of this curbing process that our sexual and aggressive drives may also be transformed into destructive tendencies.

In every observation of individual fates we find that the vital point in this inhibiting process revolves around this crucial question: Is the child being exposed to realistic discipline and are the necessary limitations conveyed to him without his being intimidated or spoiled? Or, is he growing up in an atmosphere rife with orders, prohibitions, threats, and anxiety? *The basic emotional attitude of the parents is more significant than any specific method of child-rearing.* If the parents live under excessive pressures, they will in turn be forced to pressure their children. These pressures, if rooted in sexual frustration, may be manifested in excessive tenderness toward the child. Other forms of parental discontent may lead to overt or covert hostility toward the child. The less a child is burdened by superimposed pressures connected with the emotional problems of the parents, the less likelihood there is that he will suffer from destructiveness.

The next problem to be considered would be how to provide the child with more contented and less pressured parents. However, this takes us far beyond the field of psychology, and cannot be answered by focusing on a partial aspect of the problem — the institution of marriage. The problem leads us into two areas. The first is economic and political. Here we would have to investigate all the factors in the culture that could produce more favorable social conditions for the masses of humanity and would give them a greater measure of economic security. Establishing such conditions might mitigate the tragic struggle for existence to which the masses are exposed. If these goals could be achieved, psychologically speaking, we might then have conditions of decreased external pressures. Thus the masses would have a better opportunity for uninterrupted development of their vital forces. And the coming generation might grow up under less pressure.

In the second area we are concerned with woman and her specific pressures. As a mother, woman exerts such a decisive influence on the development of future generations that it is difficult to understand why there exists so little appreciation of the obvious fact that it is woman who has been, and is, living under special pressures. Here, again, we have to consider that suppression or repression of the vital life-affirming forces in general, and the sexual drives in particular, must contribute to an increase in unconscious destructive elements. Hence, if the woman possesses greater inner security and is more self-fulfilled, she can become the strongest force in promoting the healthy growth of the younger generation.

This hope for the future may be an illusion. Nevertheless, the insights we have obtained from psychoanalysis into unconscious psychological processes are of such a nature that the realization of such a hope may be very logically anticipated.

Now, to summarize the most general conclusions of these observations. Struggle, in the sense of aggression, has and will always exist. We accept that kind of aggression which is an expression of the will to live. According to Freud, aggression in the sense of various forms of mild to extreme destructiveness occurs inevitably in mankind and is as powerful as he asserts. At times this destructiveness is not overtly expressed, since the destructive drive is inhibited by civilization. However, if we adopt the view that destructive drives in man are not innate, but that they have been acquired under specific conditions, we then have to concede the existence of possibilities for reducing their intensity and extensiveness. These possibilities would have to be derived from the psychological insights which would delineate the exact influences fostering or preventing the growth of destructiveness. Such a project would be invaluable, since the future of civilization, as well as that of the individual, might depend on how effectively we can deal with the threat that arises from this destructiveness.

13

Culture and Neurosis (1936)

This essay was the first fruit of the course on culture and neurosis that Horney taught at the New School for Social Research, beginning in September 1935. It was published in April 1936, in the *American Sociological Review* 1: 221–35. At the invitation of W. W. Norton, Horney developed the ideas in her course into her first book, *The Neurotic Personality of Our Time* (1937), of which this essay is a precursor.

In his discussion of Horney's essay in the same issue, Walter Beck of Boston University (pp. 230–35) observed that Horney's interpretation of neurosis as a result of conflicting character traits was not merely a shift of emphasis, as Horney had contended, but "a fundamental departure from the psychoanalytic concept," a departure that he felt was "perfectly justified" (230–31). Although certain neuroses "can most successfully be interpreted and explained from the Freudian point of view, and perhaps only from the Freudian point of view," these "are rather special and specific types"; an inclusive theory of neurosis has to adopt "a much fuller and more complex account of personality and personal-cultural interrelations than those offered by psychoanalysis" (231). Horney's contribution is "that she demonstrates neurosis not as a one-track phenomenon growing out of the characterologically colorless individual, but as a disorder of a particularly determined personality in a particularly determined situation" (231). Horney's substitution of "'conflicting cultural demands' for the psychoanalytic suppression-sublimation mechanism" is, again, "more than a mere shift of emphasis" (232). Beck felt that Horney was offering "not mere corrections or elaborations of psychoanalytic hypotheses, but basically non-psychoanalytic formulations" that were more Adlerian than Freudian in nature (231).

Although Beck's observation was not meant as a criticism of Horney, the question of whether her theories could be called psychoanalytic was much in dispute. Her orthodox colleagues felt that they could not and drove her from the New York Psychoanalytic Society. Horney and her followers insisted that by retaining Freud's enduring contributions and eliminating debatable elements, they were enabling psychoanalysis to realize its potential (see "The Achievement of Freud").

Culture and Neurosis

In the psychoanalytic concept of neuroses a shift of emphasis has taken place: whereas originally interest was focused on the dramatic symptomatic picture, it is now being realized more and more that the real source of these psychic disorders lies in character disturbances, that the symptoms are a manifest result of conflicting character traits, and that without uncovering and straightening out the neurotic character structure, we cannot cure a neurosis. When analyzing these character traits, in a great many cases one is struck by the observation that, in marked contrast to the divergency of the symptomatic pictures, character difficulties invariably center around the same basic conflicts.

These similarities in the content of conflicts present a problem. They suggest, to minds open to the importance of cultural implications, the question of whether and to what extent neuroses are molded by cultural processes in essentially the same way as "normal" character formation is determined by these influences; and, if so, how far such a concept would necessitate certain modifications in Freud's views of the relation between culture and neurosis.

In the following remarks I shall try to outline roughly some characteristics typically recurring in all our neuroses. The limitations of time will allow us to present neither data — good case histories — nor method, but only results. I shall try to select from the extremely complex and diversified observational material the essential points.

There is another difficulty in the presentation. I wish to show how these neurotic persons are trapped in a vicious circle. Unable to present in detail the factors leading up to the vicious circle, I must start rather arbitrarily with one of the outstanding features, although this in itself is already a complex product of several interrelated, developed mental factors. I start, therefore, with the problem of competition.

The problem of competition, or rivalry, appears to be a never-failing center of neurotic conflicts. How to deal with competition presents a problem for everyone in our culture; for the neurotic, however, it assumes dimensions which generally surpass actual vicissitudes. It does so in three respects:

1. There is a constant measuring-up with others, even in situations which do not call for it. While striving to surpass others is essential for all competitive situations, the neurotic measures up even with persons who are in no way potential competitors and have no goal in common with him. The question as to who is the more intelligent, more attractive, more popular, is indiscriminately applied toward everyone.

2. The content of neurotic ambitions is not only to accomplish something worthwhile, or to be successful, but to be absolutely best of all. These ambitions, however, exist in fantasy mainly — fantasies which may or may not be conscious. The degree of awareness differs widely in different persons. The ambitions may appear in occasional flashes of fantasy only. There is never a clear realization of the powerful dramatic role these ambitions play in the neurotic's life, or of the great part they have in accounting for his behavior and mental reactions. The challenge of these ambitions is not met by adequate efforts which might lead to realization of the aims. They are in queer contrast to existing inhibitions toward work, toward assuming leadership, toward all means which would effectually secure success. There are many ways in which these fantastic ambitions influence the emotional lives of the persons concerned: by hypersensitivity to criticism, by depressions or inhibitions following failures, and so on. These failures need not necessarily be real. Everything which falls short of the realization of the grandiose ambitions is felt as failure. The success of another person is felt as one's own failure.

This competitive attitude not only exists in reference to the external world but is also internalized, and appears as a constant measuring-up to an ego-ideal. The fantastic ambitions appear on this score as excessive and rigid demands toward the self, and failure in living up to these demands produces depressions and irritations similar to those produced in competition with others.

3. The third characteristic is the amount of hostility involved in neurotic ambition. While intense competition implicitly contains elements of hostility—the defeat of a competitor meaning victory for oneself—the reactions of neurotic persons are determined by an insatiable and irrational expectation that no one in the universe other than themselves should be intelligent, influential, attractive, or popular. They become infuriated, or feel their own endeavors condemned to futility, if someone else writes a good play or a scientific paper or plays a prominent role in society. If this attitude is strongly accentuated, one may observe in the analytical situation, for example, that these patients regard any progress made as a victory on the part of the analyst, completely disregarding the fact that progress is of vital concern to their own interests. In such situations they will disparage the analyst, betraying, by the intense hostility displayed, that they feel endangered in a position of paramount importance to themselves. They are as a rule completely unaware of the existence and intensity of this "no one but me" attitude, but one may safely assume and eventually always uncover this attitude from reactions observable in the analytical situation, as indicated above.

This attitude easily leads to a fear of retaliation. It results in a fear of success and also in a fear of failure: "If I want to crush everyone who is successful, then I will automatically assume identical reactions in others, so that the way to success implies exposing me to the hostility of others. Furthermore: if I make any move toward this goal and fail, then I shall be crushed." Success thus becomes a peril and any possible failure becomes a danger which must at all costs be avoided. From the point of view of all these dangers it appears much safer to stay in the corner, be modest and inconspicuous. In other and more positive terms, this fear leads to a definite recoiling from any aim which implies competition. This safety device is assured by a constant, accurately working process of automatic self-checking.

This self-checking process results in inhibitions, particularly inhibitions toward work, but also toward all steps necessary to the pursuit of one's aims, such as seizing opportunities, or revealing to others that one has certain goals or capacities. This eventually results in an incapacity to stand up for one's own wishes. The peculiar nature of these inhibitions is best demonstrated by the fact that these persons may be quite capable of fighting for the needs of others or for an impersonal cause. They will, for instance, act like this:

When playing an instrument with a poor partner, they will instinctively play worse than he, although otherwise they may be very competent. When discussing a subject with someone less intelligent than themselves, they will compulsively descend below his level. They will prefer to be in the rank and file, not to be identified with the superiors, not even to get an increase in salary, rationalizing this attitude in some way. Even their dreams will be dictated by this need for reassurance. Instead of utilizing the liberty of a dream to imagine themselves in glorious situations, they will actually see themselves, in their dreams, in humble or even humiliating situations.

This self-checking process does not restrict itself to activities in the pursuit of some aim, but going beyond that, tends to undermine the self-confidence, which is a prerequisite for any accomplishment, by means of self-belittling. The function of self-belittling in this context is to eliminate oneself from any competition. In most cases these persons are not aware of actually disparaging themselves, but are aware of the results only as they feel themselves inferior to others and take for granted their own inadequacy.

The presence of these feelings of inferiority is one of the most common psychic disorders of our time and culture. Let me say a few more words about them. The genesis of inferiority feelings is not always in neurotic competition. They present complex phenomena and may be determined by various conditions. But that they do result from, and stand in the service of, a recoiling from competition, is a basic and ever-present implication. They result from a recoiling inasmuch as they are the expression of a discrepancy between high-pitched ideals and real accomplishment. The fact, however, that these painful feelings at the same time fulfill the important function of making secure the recoiling attitude itself, becomes evident through the vigor with which this position is defended when attacked. Not only will no evidence of competence or attractiveness ever convince these persons, but they may actually become scared or angered by any attempt to convince them of their positive qualities.

The surface pictures resulting from this situation may be widely divergent. Some persons appear thoroughly convinced of their unique importance and may be anxious to demonstrate their superiority on every occasion, but betray their insecurity in an excessive sensitivity to every criticism, to every dissenting opinion, or every lack of responsive admiration. Others are just as thoroughly convinced of their incompetence or unworthiness, or of being unwanted or unappreciated; yet they betray their actually great demands in that they react with open or concealed hostility to every frustration of their unacknowledged demands. Still others will waver constantly in their self-estimation between feeling themselves all-important and feeling, for instance, honestly amazed that anyone pays any attention to them.

If you have followed me thus far, I can now proceed to outline the particular vicious circle in which these persons are moving. It is important here, as in every complex neurotic picture, to recognize the vicious circle, because, if we overlook it and simplify the complexity of the processes going on by assuming a simple cause-effect relation, we either fail to get an understanding of the emotions involved or attribute an undue importance to some one cause. As an example of this error, I might mention regarding a highly emotion-charged rivalrous attitude as derived directly from rivalry with the father. Roughly, the vicious circle looks like this:

The failures, in conjunction with a feeling of weakness and defeat, lead to a feeling of envy toward all persons who are more successful, or merely more secure or better contented with life. This envy may be manifest or it may be repressed under the pressure of the same anxiety which led to a repression of, and a recoiling from, rivalry. It may be entirely wiped out of consciousness and represented by the substitution of a blind admiration; it may be kept from awareness by a disparaging attitude toward the person concerned. Its effect, however, is apparent in the incapacity to grant to others what one has been forced to deny oneself. At any rate, no matter to what degree the envy is repressed or expressed, it implies an increase in the existing hostility against people and consequently an increase in the anxiety, which now takes the particular form of an irrational fear of the envy of others.

The irrational nature of this fear is shown in two ways: 1) it exists regardless of the presence or absence of envy in the given situation, and 2) its intensity is out of proportion to the dangers menacing from the side of the envious competitors. This irrational side of the fear of envy always remains unconscious, at least in nonpsychotic persons; therefore it is never corrected by a reality-testing process and is all the more effective in the direction of reinforcing the existing tendencies to recoil.

Consequently, the feeling of one's own insignificance grows, the hostility against people grows, and the anxiety grows. We thus return to the beginning, because now the fantasies come up, with about this content: "I wish I were more powerful, more attractive, more intelligent than all the others, then I should be safe, and besides, I could defeat them and step on them." Thus we see an ever-increasing deviation of the ambitions toward the stringent, fantastic, and hostile.

This pyramiding process may come to a standstill under various conditions, usually at an inordinate expense in loss of expansiveness and vitality. There is often some sort of resignation as to personal ambitions, in turn permitting the diminution of anxieties as to competition, with the inferiority feelings and inhibitions continuing.

It is now time, however, to make a reservation. It is in no way self-evident that ambition of the "no-one-but-me" type must necessarily evoke anxieties. There are persons quite capable of brushing aside or crushing everyone in the way of their ruthless pursuit of personal power. The question then is: Under what special condition is anxiety evoked in neurotically competitive people?

The answer is that they at the same time want to be loved. While most persons who pursue an asocial ambition in life care little for the affection or the opinion of others, the neurotics, although possessed by the same kind of competitiveness, simultaneously have a boundless craving for affection and appreciation. Therefore, as soon as they make any move toward self-assertion, competition, or success, they begin to dread losing the affection of others and must automatically check their aggressive impulses. This conflict between ambition and affection is one of the gravest and most typical dilemmas of the neurotics of our time.

Why are these two incompatible strivings so frequently present in the same individual? They are related to each other in more than one way. The briefest formulation of this relationship would perhaps be that they both grow out of the same sources, namely, anxieties, and they both serve as a means of reassurance against the anxieties. Power and affection may both be safeguards. They generate each other, check each other, and reinforce each other. These interrelations can be observed most accurately within the analytic situation, but sometimes are obvious from only a casual knowledge of the life history.

In the life history may be found, for instance, an atmosphere in childhood lacking in warmth and reliability, but rife with frightening elements — battles between the parents, injustice, cruelty, over-solicitousness — generation of an increased need for affection — disappointments — development of an outspoken competitiveness — inhibition — attempts to get affection on the basis of weakness, helplessness, or suffering. We sometimes hear that a youngster has suddenly turned to ambition after an acute disappointment in his need for affection, and then given up the ambition on falling in love.

Particularly when the expansive and aggressive desires have been severely curbed in early life by a forbidding atmosphere, the excessive need for reassuring affection will play a major role. As a guiding principle for behavior this implies a yielding to the wishes or opinions of others rather than asserting one's own wishes or opinions; an overvaluation of the significance for one's own life of expressions of fondness from others, and a dependence on such expressions. And similarly, it implies an overvaluation of signs of rejection and a reacting to such signs with apprehension and defensive hostility. Here again a vicious circle begins easily and reinforces the single elements: In diagram it looks somewhat like this:

Anxiety plus repressed hostility
  ↘ Need for reassuring affection
    ↘ Anticipation of, sensitivity to, rejection
      ↘ Hostile reactions to feeling rejected

These reactions explain why emotional contact with others that is attained on the basis of anxiety can be at best only a very shaky and easily shattered bridge between individuals, and why it always fails to bring them out of their emotional isolation. It may, however, serve to cope with anxieties and even get one through life rather smoothly, but only at the expense of growth and personality development, and only if circumstances are quite favorable.

Let us ask now, which special features in our culture may be responsible for the frequent occurrence of the neurotic structures just described?

We live in a competitive, individualistic culture. Whether the enormous economic and technical achievements of our culture were and are possible only on the basis of the competitive principle is a question for the economist or sociologist to decide. The psychologist, however, can evaluate the personal price we have paid for it.

It must be kept in mind not only that competition is a driving force in economic activities but also that it pervades our personal life in every respect. The character of all our human relationships is molded by a more or less outspoken competition. It is effective in the family between siblings, at school, in social relations (keeping up with the Joneses), and in love life.

In love, it may show itself in two ways: the genuine erotic wish is often overshadowed or replaced by the merely competitive goal of being the most popular, having the most dates, love letters, lovers, being seen with the most desirable man or woman. Again, it may pervade the love relationship itself. Marriage partners, for example, may be living in an endless struggle for supremacy, with or without being aware of the nature or even of the existence of this combat.

The influence on human relations of this competitiveness lies in the fact that it creates easily aroused envy toward the stronger ones, contempt for the weaker, distrust toward everyone. In consequence of all these potentially hostile tensions, the satisfaction and reassurance which one can get out of human relations are limited and the individual becomes more or less emotionally isolated. It seems that here, too, mutually reinforcing interactions take place, so far as insecurity and dissatisfaction in human relations in turn compel people to seek gratification and security in ambitious strivings, and vice versa.

Another cultural factor relevant to the structure of our neurosis lies in our attitude toward failure and success. We are inclined to attribute success to good personal qualities and capacities, such as competence, courage, enterprise. In religious terms this attitude was expressed by saying that success was due to God's grace. While these qualities may be effective—and in certain periods, such as the pioneer days, may have represented the only conditions necessary—this ideology omits two essential facts: 1) that the possibility for success is strictly limited; even external conditions and personal qualities being equal, only a comparative few can possibly attain success, and 2) that other factors than those mentioned may play the decisive role, such as, for example, unscrupulousness or fortuitous circumstances. Inasmuch as these factors are overlooked in the general evaluation of success, failures, besides putting the person concerned in a factually disadvantageous position, are bound to reflect on his self-esteem.

The confusion involved in this situation is enhanced by a sort of double morality. Although, in fact, success meets with adoration almost without regard to the means employed in securing it, we are at the same time taught to regard modesty and an undemanding, unselfish attitude as social or religious virtues and are rewarded for them by praise and affection. The particular difficulties which confront the individual in our culture may be summarized as follows: for the competitive struggle he needs a certain amount of available aggressiveness; at the same time, he is required to be modest, unselfish, even self-sacrificing. While the competitive life situation with the hostile tensions involved in it creates an enhanced need of security, the chances of attaining a feeling of safety in human relations—love, friendship, social contacts—are at the same time diminished. The estimation of one's personal value is all too dependent on the degree of success attained, while at the same time the possibilities for success are limited and the success itself is dependent, to a great extent, on fortuitous circumstances or on personal qualities of an asocial character.

Perhaps these sketchy comments have suggested to you the direction in which to explore the actual relationship of our culture to our personality and its neurotic deviations. Let us now consider the relation of this conception to the views of Freud on culture and neurosis.

The essence of Freud's views on this subject can be summarized, briefly, as follows: Culture is the result of a sublimation of biologically given sexual and aggressive drives—"sexual" in the extended connotation Freud has given the term. Sublimation presupposes unwitting suppression of these instinctual drives. The more complete the suppression of these drives, the higher the cultural development. As the capacity for sublimating is limited, and as the intensive suppression of primitive drives without sublimation may lead to neurosis, the growth of civilization must inevitably imply a growth of neurosis. Neuroses are the price humanity has to pay for cultural development.

The implicit theoretical presupposition underlying this train of thought is the belief in the existence of biologically determined human nature, or, more precisely, the belief that oral, anal, genital, and aggressive drives exist in all human beings in approximately equal quantities.[1] Variations in character formation from individual to individual, as from culture to culture, are due, then, to the varying intensity of the suppression required, with the addition that this suppression can affect the different kinds of drives in varying degrees.

This viewpoint of Freud's seems actually to encounter difficulties with two groups of data. 1) Historical and anthropological findings[2] do not support the assumption that the growth of civilization is in a direct ratio to the growth of instinct suppression. 2) Clinical experience of the kind indicated in this paper suggests that neurosis is due not simply to the quantity of suppression of one or the other instinctual drive, but rather to difficulties caused by the conflicting character of the demands which a culture imposes on its individuals. The differences in neuroses typical of different cultures may be understood to be conditioned by the number and quality of conflicting demands within the particular culture.

In a given culture, those persons are likely to become neurotic who have met these culturally determined difficulties in accentuated form, mostly through the medium of childhood experiences; and who have not been able to solve their difficulties, or have solved them only at great expense to personality.

1. I pass over Freud's recognition of individual constitutional difference.

2. Ruth Benedict, *Patterns of Culture;* Margaret Mead, *Sex and Temperament in Three Savage Societies.*

14

Understanding Personality Difficulties
in a Period of Social Transition (1938)

The typescript of this address was in Harold Kelman's papers at the Post-graduate Center for Mental Health. According to the title page, the address was given on 26 February 1938 at the Hotel Pennsylvania in New York City. Internal evidence indicates that it was given to an audience of progressive educators. I have included the abstract that preceded the talk, which may have been intended for a printed program, because it contains material not contained in the talk and presents its thesis with greater clarity. The typescript appears to be an unrevised draft, and I have edited it for usage, readability, and succinctness. As was typical of Horney's thought at this time, her cultural concerns seem to be superimposed on her greater interest in and feeling for the impact of family dynamics on psychological development.

Abstract
One of the most striking differences between the older generation and the younger one is that previously the emphasis lay on duty, work, or submis-

sion to authoritative standards or persons, whereas now it is on the right of the individual to seek his own happiness and live his own life. The question is whether the contrast is as definitive as it seems to be. Have boys and girls attained the goal of independence and happiness? If not, what factors are interfering?

Notwithstanding their noisy self-assertion, the younger generation does not appear to be happy. They are full of fears. While they search for pleasure, their capacity for enjoyment is impaired, and they are much too vulnerable to have good human relationships. Although they are freer from authoritarian pressure from without, their lives are often determined by a system of relentless inner demands and prohibitions. Instead of being led by their own spontaneous wishes and ideals, they are often driven by ego-alien goals without being aware of it.

Various factors in childhood may be responsible for these ego-alien goals. Children may have to live up to standards imposed by their parents because they have been made to feel that they are not acceptable unless they fulfill other people's expectations. Lack of warmth and appreciation may make them insecure. They may feel that they are being treated unjustly and need to render themselves unassailable to unfair reproaches and demands by striving for rectitude and perfection. This striving makes them constantly dissatisfied with themselves, and they become afraid that others will be dissatisfied with them also. A further result is that they do not have a nurturing, constructive love either for themselves or for other people.

The difference between a constructive love for the self and an anxious concern for the self will be discussed. The cultural ideal of unselfishness suggests that one must choose between loving oneself and loving others. In reality, we tend to have the same attitude toward others that we have toward ourselves, whether it be positive or negative.

Some of the difficulties being experienced by the younger generation can be understood as the result of unresolved conflicts between the old cultural ideology of unselfishness and subordination and the new goal of unrestricted individual freedom.

Address

"Understanding personality difficulties in a period of social transition" is so broad a topic that I have had to choose between a wide range of problems that could be discussed. If I were neurotic, this would have brought me into the most disastrous difficulties. I would have had a dreadful time deciding what I should talk about, because any error in judgment would have meant a blow to my prestige and, more important, to my self-respect. I would have anticipated the danger of feeling entirely worthless or stupid if I made any mistake.

If I were neurotic, not only would the choice of topic be difficult, but I would have a dreadful time organizing the material because every word, every thought would have to be unassailably right, so that no one could possibly attack me. I would feel compelled to know everything you could possibly ask me. If I presented a difficulty, I would be afraid you would ask: "What are you going to do about it?" I would feel like a dullard if I couldn't immediately give you an all-embracing, definitive answer.

If I were neurotic and you told me that I had given a nice lecture, I would say that you said that only to please me; it really was not so good, and someone else would certainly have done it better. All my inner demands on myself would have put me in agony. On top of that, I would be annoyed with myself for being anxious, because one shouldn't have anxiety, and if one has anxiety, one should be able to relax and pay no attention to it. Also, not being aware that these were demands I had put on myself, I would project them onto you and would think: "What do these darned people expect of me?" As a consequence, I would have worked with a feeling of inner protest or even of defiance. Because of this defiance, I would not have been able to do good work, and then I would have a realistic basis for my inferiority feelings.

With this picture I have tried to suggest one of the greatest difficulties you encounter in your endeavors in progressive education. Your goals are to make a child free to choose his own way, to think his own thoughts, to pursue his own happiness. The youngsters have the same goals. They don't want to be dependent on authority; they want to be free; they want to live their own lives. But it is difficult to achieve these goals because of the kinds of merciless inner demands I have described.

Sometimes the origin of these demands is easy to see. Children may come out of puritanical families with inexorable standards. They may have parents who are too much engaged in the pursuit of righteousness and perfection to be able to give the child real affection and who make the child feel that he is not acceptable unless he is perfect. Often, however, there is a need for perfection in children whose parents are quite liberal and do not subject them to any explicit pressure. But these parents are still under the influence of former generations and often, in spite of their best intentions, are incapable of giving the child real affection. They may treat him unfairly without meaning to.

Let me give you some examples of what I mean by unfair treatment. Because he has a preferred brother or sister, a child will become nagging and then will be criticized for not being amiable. A parent may betray a child's secrets after having been taken into his confidence and then blame the child if he shows anger at this betrayal. Or a parent may fail to keep promises and then scold the child if he insists that they be fulfilled. In other words, parents often scold children for attitudes that they find inconvenient but that are the result of their own behavior. Naturally, children resent this. If they rebel, perhaps only by raising an eyebrow, they will be regarded as disagreeable.

At the same time, however, a development may set in that saves the child from being submerged in feelings of unworthiness or resentment. He may escape into feelings of superiority and believe that others do not understand him because he is so far above them. Without being aware of it, he sets out to prove the others to be wrong in their evaluation of him. Or he may respond to a sense of having been treated unfairly by trying to make himself so perfect that no one can criticize him again. By doing this, however, the child becomes unfair to himself. He tries to measure up to goals he cannot possibly attain.

At bottom, the compulsive need for perfection is driven by anxiety. There is the anxiety of not being acceptable unless one is flawless, the anxiety of having to prove oneself and feeling worthless if one cannot, and the anxiety of being unjustly criticized and hence of having to make oneself unassailable.

While a child's compulsive need for perfection arises because of disturbed relationships with others, it is apt to disturb these relationships further because the youngster will be convinced that others criticize him as inexorably as he criticizes himself and expect as unreasonable things of him as he expects of himself. Just as important is the impairment of his relationship to his own self. While his perfectionistic goals have arisen because of an impaired self-esteem, they are bound to impair self-esteem further because, as I tried to show at the beginning, he will become mercilessly critical and condemnatory toward himself.

As you may have noticed, what I call compulsive needs for perfection have some similarity to what Freud calls superego demands. Freud teaches that these demands differ only in quantity from what we usually call ideals. I believe compulsive demands for perfection, which are adopted under the stress of bitter necessities, to be the opposite of ideals. The individual tries to fulfill them formalistically, as one fulfills an imposed duty. Ideals, on the other hand, are goals which the individual loves and wants to attain. Compulsive needs for perfection are not only different from ideals, but they prevent ideals from developing.

Because they give rise to constant self-condemnation, strivings for perfection contribute to the incapacity of youngsters to love themselves. You may ask: "Should one love oneself? Is that not selfish? Has not Freud said, 'The more you love yourself the less you love others?'" What Freud meant is that the more egocentric a person is, the less he can love others. Being egocentric, however, means being anxiously concerned with the self. It is a sign not of self-love but of an essentially hostile, derogatory attitude toward the self.

There is no opposition, but a correlation, between a good attitude toward oneself and a good attitude toward others. You can love others only if you love yourself. We have to be clear, however, about what we mean by "loving oneself." We certainly do not mean an indiscriminate self-admiration and self-indulgence. We have in mind, rather, the attitude that a very good friend might have toward us, someone who wants us to have everything that contributes to our development and thereby ensures our happiness. Loving oneself means appreciating our strengths and virtues and having a critical but constructive attitude toward our shortcomings.

What has all this to do with the transition in social life? At first sight it seems as though the younger generation has goals and attitudes that are the extreme opposite of those of the older generation, the generation of the grandparents. In the older generation you find an emphasis on submission to the authority of established patterns or persons. In the younger generation and their teachers the emphasis is on the development of inner freedom and independence. If we look more closely, however, the difference is not as great as it seems, because the younger generation has to bear the brunt of difficulties it has inherited from the older generation.

Although the new goals of youngsters and of progressive education represent progress, we have to be aware that the progress is not as great as it seems, that the old factors still have a powerful influence. It is important for educators to know that the excessive demands that youngsters put on themselves may help them to a superficial "adaptation" but prevent them from developing autonomous ideals and good relationships with themselves and other people.

15

The Achievement of Freud (1938)

This undated typescript was in Harold Kelman's papers at the Postgraduate Center for Mental Health. It appears to be a talk Horney gave to a lay audience. It was probably written in 1938, while Horney was working on *New Ways in Psychoanalysis*. Many of the ideas in the talk are more fully developed in that book; but as I have said in the introduction, the talk conveys a much more appreciative attitude toward Freud. It is therefore an important corrective to the prevailing view of Horney as unremittingly hostile to the master. I have edited the text for usage, succinctness, and readability.

As we all know, there is much controversy about the value of psychoanalysis. At one extreme are serious people in and outside the psychiatric profession who tend to regard it as a series of baffling and sensational contentions that hamper rather than further the understanding of human personality and that are harmful rather than helpful in the therapy of neuroses. At the other extreme are equally serious people who tend to adhere religiously to every doctrine ever propounded by Freud.

Here, as elsewhere, the search for truth is not simple. People will be qualified to make an objective appraisal of Freud's work only when several decades have passed. Today, it is a matter of individual judgment. Thus, what I have to say about Freud's achievement is to be taken as my personal opinion, as it has crystallized during many years of psychoanalytical experience.

Today opinions are divided not only about the value of psychoanalysis but also about which psychoanalytical doctrines are the basic and important ones. Different analysts, including Freud himself, would present entirely different aspects as the essential ones.

If educated people were asked in a questionnaire what they deemed to be the specific contributions of Freud, what would they answer? Many would point to the doctrine that our strivings and character trends are determined by sexuality — that, for example, submissive tendencies in men can be understood as an expression of feminine wishes, or ambition in women as an expression of the wish to be a man. Others would add Freud's theory of the Oedipus complex, his contention that tragedies of passionate love, jealousy, and disappointment as we see them in adults, and as they are described over and over again in literature, originally occur in the child's early life and concern primarily his own parents. Still others would point to the doctrine that each later development is determined by early experiences and that later experiences are an almost direct repetition of earlier ones — that, for example, jealousy and rivalry in later life are repetitions of feelings felt toward one's brother or father, or that when a grown man feels easily rebuffed by women it is because he was rejected by his mother.

Personally, I would say that all these doctrines contain valid and constructive observations. To have made the observation fifty years ago, in the Victorian age, when sexuality was so heavily tabooed that sexual repression could produce neurotic disturbances was certainly courageous. It was surely a great finding that the child-parent relationship is of far-reaching importance for our further development, and also that early experiences mold our character and hence have to be taken seriously. Nevertheless, if asked what I believe to be Freud's achievement, I would not cite any of these formulations, nor others such as the dualism between the ego and the instincts or the concept of the superego. I shall indicate later why I believe that despite their being based on excellent underlying observations, these concepts are essentially erroneous.

Let me present first what to my mind are Freud's most important and, if I may venture to predict future development, imperishable contributions. To begin with, Freud has made us realize that our actions and feelings can be determined by unconscious motivations. We may make our most important decisions without knowing our real reasons for doing so; we may be torn by conflicts without being aware that we have any, much less what they are;

we may have profound grievances against someone without being aware that we do.

The concept of unconscious motivations has been generally accepted, but its implications are often not fully understood. Those who have not had the experience of discovering within themselves attitudes or strivings of whose power they were unaware will have difficulty coming to a deep understanding of this concept. Two aspects of it are of particular importance. The first is that to thrust strivings out of awareness does not prevent them from existing and exerting an influence. This means, for example, that we may entirely repress our desire for human closeness, adopt a "don't care" attitude, and yet suffer intensely from being lonely. Although we may repress our hostility toward someone, it may nevertheless arouse a panicky feeling within us.

The other aspect of unconscious motivation that is particularly important is the fact that we suppress feelings and strivings because we are vitally interested in not being aware of them. If an intimidated child feels safe only when giving his mother the blind reverence she expects of him, he must suppress whatever hostile feeling or critical thoughts he may have toward her. If it is imperative for a person always to be unassailably right, then he must never allow himself to be aware that he has done something wrong and must blame others instead. This process can be observed in groups as well. If, for example, a government is set on persecuting a minority group, it is vitally interested in eradicating all notions that this group consists in reality of human beings not much different from others. Because of our interest in suppressing awareness of our deeper motivations, we will put up a struggle if an effort is made to unearth unconscious factors. This accounts for what we describe as "resistance," which is a key concept for therapy.

It was only after Freud had recognized unconscious processes and their effects that he was able to arrive at another basic hypothesis — namely, that psychic processes are strictly determined. Naturally, your wife has recognized, without having read Freud, the meaning of your forgetting to think of a present for her birthday. But it is a huge step from such occasional intuitive understanding to a systematic application of a principle.

A few examples will illustrate the importance of psychic determinism. Whereas dreams, fantasies, and errors of everyday life were formerly regarded as merely accidental, today we would not be content to say that John had a nightmare because he ate too much pumpkin pie but would ask ourselves whether he is not being torn by some conflict without being aware of it. He could keep it under cover during the day, but in his dream he was searching for a solution to his problem and awoke with anxiety when he was unable to find one. We would not believe that a depression has befallen Mary out of the blue, even though she may be convinced that this is so. Rather, we would patiently ask why she became depressed at this particular time. We may find that her principal at school has criticized her and that she has taken it more to heart than she realized. In that case, we would have to go deeply into her character structure in order to understand why a criticism which actually was of no consequence has had the power to throw her into a depression. We would no longer merely commiserate with Paul when he tells us that each time he is about to complete a brilliant plan something interferes, or that it seems to be his fate to bestow help on others and always to be rewarded with ingratitude. Instead of believing in a mysterious fate, we would look for factors in his personality responsible for his repetitive experiences.

It is scarcely an exaggeration to say that without adopting the principle that psychic factors are strictly determined, we could not take a single step in our daily psychotherapeutic work. If, for example, an insignificant provocation, such as a slightly impatient tone in our voice, leads to a considerable increase in the patient's anxiety, then the disproportion between cause and effect will raise in the analyst's mind questions like these: If a slight and momentary impatience on our part can elicit such intense anxiety, does this mean that the patient feels basically uncertain about our attitude toward him? What then accounts for this degree of uncertainty? Furthermore, why is our attitude of such paramount importance? Does he perhaps feel utterly dependent on us, and if so, why? Is as great an uncertainty present in all his relationships, or have particular factors increased it in his relation to us? In short, the assumption that psychic processes are strictly determined encourages us to penetrate more deeply into psychological connections.

Freud not only revealed the importance of unconscious processes, but he taught us a great deal about how these processes operate. As we have seen, to repress a feeling does not keep it from influencing us. It merely means that we are no longer aware of it and that it cannot appear under its own flag but must take on some disguise. We may be irritable toward others, for example, while in reality and without knowing it we are angry with ourselves for not having stood up for our opinion in an argument. This Freud would call a displacement of affect. We may feel that another person is disloyal, unfriendly, or unfair toward us, while, in reality and without knowing it, we are harboring unfair reproaches toward him. This is what Freud calls projection. Most important of all is the concept of rationalization. Repressed feelings or drives may be expressed if they are made to seem rational, or according to Erich Fromm, who has put it more correctly, if they are made to appear in socially accepted forms. For instance, a tendency to possess or to dominate may be presented as an expression of love. A mother who mistakes her tendencies to domineer for love will reproach her child for a want of love, while in reality the child merely has failed to comply with her demands. Or we may believe that we love someone, while in reality we are merely clinging to them for the sake of reassurance. We may characterize personal ambition as devotion to a cause, a tendency to disparage as intelligent skepticism, or hostile aggression as an obligation to tell the truth. Although in crude ways the process of rationalization has always been recognized, not only has Freud shown its extent and the subtlety with which it is employed, but he has taught us to make use of it systematically for the purpose of uncovering unconscious drives in therapy.

Repressed wishes or impulses may reappear in dreams and fantasies. A boy who is almost choked by the smothering love of his domineering father may develop a fantasy in which he is the commander of a fortress where he sits in a watchtower and orders everyone who approaches to be shot. He thus creates a situation in which he is not only safe from any intrusion but also superior to all around him and can enjoy a vindictive triumph over those who would oppress him.

Recognizing the function of dreams and fantasies will probably prove to be even more fruitful than it has been thus far, particularly if we also include unconscious illusions about ourselves, how superior we are mentally or morally. From the point of view of therapy, what is described as a patient's reluctance to get well is often his unwillingness to abandon his illusions.

The achievements I have mentioned so far all pertain to the understanding of human personality in general. Freud gained these insights from his endeavors as a physician to understand and cure neuroses — that is, personality disorders. I wish I were eloquent enough to impress on you the full import of Freud's discovery that neuroses are not inexplicable but accessible to understanding. They are not mysteriously sent by God or by demons; they do not indicate hereditary degeneracy or an indulgence in bad habits. They are an illness like other illnesses; only, instead of concerning the body, they concern the soul, and they can be treated. Thus Freud did away with the wavering between regarding neuroses as incurable and appraising them too lightly, to be cured by advising the patient to pull himself together. Freud discovered that neuroses result from inner conflicts which are unconscious in nature and cannot be resolved without a change in the entire character structure.

That neuroses could be treated through therapy was a wonderful discovery, to be compared with the deeds of great scientists who discovered the cause of chronic bodily diseases like tuberculosis or diabetes and thus enabled us to find ways to fight them effectively. Freud's discovery is all the greater because it concerns all of us. Although we are not all neurotic, we all suffer from conflicts similar to those of neurotics, since we all live under the same difficult cultural conditions that are, in my opinion, ultimately responsible for neuroses. Quite apart from providing relief from suffering, the understanding of human conflicts that has been opened up by Freud has expanded our horizon in a way that is similar to the contribution of the greatest writers and philosophers, such as Shakespeare, Balzac, and Nietzsche.

As to the understanding of neuroses in detail, it would merely confuse you if I were to begin enumerating Freud's findings. Suffice it to say that there is almost no problem in the psychology of neuroses that Freud has not seen, although he may not have solved it.

As to therapy, Freud has given us some basic tools with which to work, the two most important of which are transference and free association. In essence, transference is the doctrine that the patient's emotional reactions to the analyst provide the most direct way of understanding his personality, and consequently his difficulties. Transference is the most powerful tool of analytic therapy. Indeed, if I were to be asked which of Freud's discoveries in the realm of therapy I value most highly, it would be his finding that one can utilize the patient's emotional reactions to the analyst and to the analytical situation for therapeutic purposes. It is a mark of Freud's inner independence that he regarded the patient's emotional responses as a useful tool, instead of using his attachment or suggestibility as a means of influencing him or treating his hostile reactions merely as a nuisance.

I believe that quite apart from its value to therapy, much of the future of psychoanalysis depends on a more accurate observation and a deeper understanding of the patient's transference reactions. This conviction is based on the assumption that the essence of all human psychology resides in comprehending the processes operating in human relationships. The psychoanalytical relationship is a special one that provides us with unheard of possibilities for understanding these processes. Hence, a more accurate and profound understanding of this relationship will constitute the greatest contribution to psychology that psychoanalysis has to offer.

The specific factor in psychoanalysis that renders a more accurate observation possible is the practice of free association, in which the patient is asked to express everything he thinks or feels, regardless of any intellectual or emotional objections. Psychotherapy provides a unique situation in which one human being confides in another without reservations and with a reasonable hope of being understood. To my knowledge, that is something new in the history of mankind. Religious confession is not really comparable, for both priest and confessor focus only on guilt and atonement. Of course, many people are prone to believe that one's sins, or what one regards as such, are one's deepest secrets; and this may include Freud, who ascribes an enormous role to unconscious guilt feelings. But, in contrast to confession, psychoanalysis embraces the whole personality, with all its calamities, wishes, and fears. It enables the patient to be sincere to an otherwise unheard-of degree, partly because he can expect an equal sincerity on the part of the analyst.

All these immeasurably constructive concepts unfortunately became embedded in a theoretical system of debatable value. Two great limitations have hampered the development of psychoanalysis, both of which can be overcome. One is that Freud did not realize the complexity of the problems he himself laid open to research. As will happen to everyone opening a new vista in unknown territory, he was prone to simplify and to generalize. It is a simplification, for instance, to assume that experiences in later life are almost direct repetitions of infantile experiences and to harbor the expectation that neurotic disturbances will be cured by unearthing appropriate infantile recollections. It is a generalization to contend that peculiarities observed in neurotic patients have equal application to healthy persons.

The other limitation is that despite his unique ability to make pioneering observations, in his theoretical thinking Freud is deeply rooted in the mentality of the nineteenth century. Like many great thinkers of that century — William James, for instance — Freud was to a large extent an instinct theorist; that is, he believed that psychic peculiarities that occurred frequently were ultimately determined by biological drives of a physiological-chemical nature. Nowadays we would search primarily for the cultural conditions engendering these peculiarities.

Time does not permit a full discussion of the influence of his instinctivistic thinking on Freud's ideas, but I can give a few examples. His biological orientation is responsible for his regarding certain peculiarities of modern man — such as his alienation from others, his competitiveness, his acquisitiveness — as determined by universal instinctual forces, more or less independently of culture. It is responsible for his regarding sexuality, in its broadest sense, as the ultimate cause of good and bad character trends and disturbances in human relations. It is Freud's merit to have made us wary about taking our good qualities and judgments at face value, since our pity for others may be transformed sadism or externalized self-pity, and we may value a person highly because we are secretly in love with him. But to use his own words, Freud contends that "every praiseworthy and valuable quality is based on compensation and overcompensation" of instinctual drives. His contention that all judgment is a product of instincts is unsubstantiated and misleading. The fact that love, pity, generosity *may* be determined by some sexual or destructive drive does not *prove* that these qualities cannot also be genuine and exist in their own right. That we may criticize a person or a theory out of emotional resentment does not prove that criticism cannot spring from our judgment about what is right or wrong.

Since I judge some of Freud's premises to be debatable, I deem psychoanalytical theories to be debatable insofar as they are determined by them. But while there are justifiable objections to such psychoanalytical concepts as libido theory, the Oedipus complex, the superego, and so forth, it is neither justifiable nor constructive to discard the valid with the invalid or to fling our criticism of his theory as an accusation against Freud. He was a genius who was far ahead of his time in many ways but who in others could not help being influenced by its mentality. Moreover, one cannot possibly expect one man both to open new perspectives and to see all the intricacies involved in his discoveries. It is more constructive to be deeply appreciative of the foundations Freud gave us and to use them for further work.

As a result of both theoretical considerations and practical experience, I believe that we can understand a broader range of problems if we cut ourselves loose from certain historically determined premises and the ideas that are based on them. When we relinquish Freud's one-sided emphasis on childhood, the analysis of the actual character structure becomes the focus of our attention. When character trends are no longer explained as the ultimate outcome of instinctual drives that are only modified by environment, the emphasis falls on the life conditions molding character, and we have to search anew for the environmental factors responsible for creating neurotic conflicts. A prevailing sociological orientation takes the place of a prevailingly anatomical-physiological one, and disturbances in human relationships become the crucial factor in the genesis of neurosis. When we stop invoking the pleasure principle to account for behavior, the striving for safety assumes more weight, as does the role of anxiety in engendering this striving. The relevant factor in the genesis of neuroses is then neither the Oedipus complex nor any kind of infantile pleasure striving but all the adverse influences that make a child feel helpless and defenseless and lead him to conceive of the world as potentially menacing. It is the safety devices a child is compelled to develop to cope with the basic anxiety created by the environment that constitute the nucleus of neuroses.

There will be other shifts in perspective as well. When sexual problems are no longer considered to be the dynamic center of neuroses, we shall regard them as the effect rather than the cause of neurotic character structure. Instead of attributing moral problems to "superego" and neurotic guilt feelings, which leads us nowhere, we shall take them seriously as genuine moral problems and help our patients to face them squarely and take a stand toward them. Finally, when the "ego" is no longer regarded as an organ merely executing or checking instinctual drives, such human faculties as willpower, judgment, and decision making are reinstated in their dignity. The ego Freud describes then appears to be a neurotic rather than a universal phenomenon. The warping of the spontaneous individual self must then be recognized as a paramount factor in the genesis and maintenance of neurosis.

We shall see then that neuroses represent a peculiar kind of struggle for life under difficult conditions. Their very essence consists of disturbances in the relations to self and others and of conflicts arising from these disturbances. The shift in emphasis on the factors considered relevant in neuroses enlarges considerably the tasks of psychoanalytical therapy. The aim of therapy, then, is not to help the patient gain mastery over his instincts but to lessen his anxiety to such an extent that he can dispense with his "safety-devices." Beyond this aim there looms a new therapeutic goal, which is to restore the individual to himself, to help him regain his spontaneity and find his center of gravity in himself.

I believe that by eliminating debatable elements and by working along the lines I have indicated with the tools Freud has given us, we shall enable psychoanalysis to develop fully its rich potentialities.

16

What Is a Neurosis? (1939)

This essay appeared in the *American Journal of Sociology* 45 (1939): 426–32. It seems to have been written after *New Ways in Psychoanalysis* and to contain some further thoughts on issues discussed there, particularly the question of whether it is possible to define neurosis independently of culture, in a nonrelativistic way. The essay is perhaps the final expression of Horney's cultural phase.

The need to define a neurosis has developed only recently. The psychic phenomena which in the latter part of the nineteenth century became an object of psychiatric curiosity concerned gross circumscribed disturbances, such as convulsions, functional paralysis, obsessional ceremonies, phobias, striking changes in mood, and gross sexual malfunctions. There was no doubt that they constituted an illness of a special kind.

Though we are not far removed in time from this state of blissful simplicity, we have emerged thoroughly from it and find ourselves confronted with much more puzzling problems. Several factors have combined to complicate the picture. To begin with, the gross disturbances mentioned have become comparatively rare and have given room to more diffuse disorders resisting psychiatric classification.

Moreover — mainly due to the pioneering work of Freud — our understanding of the neurotic processes has so far progressed that we are able to recognize expressions of them which formerly would have escaped attention. In this regard the development which has taken place is comparable to that of our knowledge of an organic illness, such as tuberculosis. Originally only the most conspicuous stages of the illness were known, giving rise to the name "consumption." Increased knowledge permitted us to recognize phases of the disease which formerly were not seen at all or which were not recognized as manifestations of the same underlying process.

Our better understanding of neuroses has taught us that the so-called neurotic "symptoms," such as phobias, depressions, fatigue, and impotence, can be absent altogether; that a neurosis may "merely" consist in character trends of a particular nature, the sum total of which interferes with the individual's proper functioning under given external conditions and thereby interferes with his happiness. As a result of these trends, his relationships with people are handicapped by a greater number of fears and hostilities than is warranted by the environment; he does not develop his potentialities as fully as he could under given conditions; his work is less effective, less successful, and, particularly, less creative than it might otherwise be; his capacities to assert himself and to enjoy whatever life offers him are impaired.

Thus the impression was created that two kinds of neuroses existed: symptom neuroses and character neuroses, the latter being roughly characterized by an apparent tendency to stand in one's own way. Such a definition, however, is misleading. It suggests that a symptom neurosis is not necessarily a character neurosis as well, while in reality every neurosis is essentially a character disorder, regardless of whether or not there are "symptoms." Symptoms, though often conspicuous and important to a person's life, do not constitute the essence of neuroses but are a by-product only.

This realization further adds to our confusion concerning the nature of neuroses, inasmuch as it introduces social viewpoints into a field which heretofore had been claimed by medical psychiatry. A fear of high places or a hysterical paralysis of the arm may be referred to as an illness. But a rigid and indiscriminate attitude of defiance or a compulsive compliance would involve social evaluations, though either could become an object of psychiatric treatment insofar as its consequences interfere with a person's life. The effect of such overlapping of social categories — social functioning, behavior, and attitudes — and medical-clinical ones represents the main difficulty in arriving at a definition of neuroses. The following remarks represent an attempt to clarify these issues and to understand their interrelations.

From a social standpoint a neurosis can be defined as a deviation from the "normal" in the sense of the statistically average in a given culture, as has been pointed out by Margaret Mead and other authors. Frigidity, for instance, will be suspect of an underlying neurosis only when the majority of women are not frigid. A compulsive perfectionism would strike no one as a problem in a rigidly puritanical group. This approach to neuroses is valuable because it shows that the evaluation of a phenomenon such as "illness" is dependent on social factors. It prevents us from making naive generalizations and value judgments. The limitations of this definition lie in that it necessarily deals with manifest behavior only and disregards the underlying processes. It does not and cannot give us any insight into the factors operating in these processes. It does not take into account the fact that people may be adapted to environmental requirements and yet suffer from severe psychic disturbances.

Moreover, regarding a neurosis as a deviation from the cultural pattern entails the danger of using a deceptive measuring rod concerning the value of such deviations. It enhances the temptation to regard the statistically average as right or superior, and neurotic manifestations as wrong or inferior. But it may be that a "problem child" who rebels against parental encroachments is essentially right and that the "well-adapted" parents are essentially wrong. It may be that a person who rebels against seeing the meaning of life in the acquisition of prestige and wealth has a better and deeper feeling for the values of life than has a society advocating these goals.

From a clinical viewpoint I would regard neuroses — chronic neuroses — as an attempt to cope with life under difficult internal conditions. In the center of these difficulties is a diffuse basic anxiety toward life in general. Such an anxiety — *Urangst* — is a fundamental human phenomenon. The basic anxiety of the so-called neurotic is more intense than is warranted by the environment for two main reasons. Owing to a combination of adverse influences in his childhood, he feels more isolated and more helpless toward the tasks and dangers of life. And likewise, owing to his early experiences, his anxiety is not only related to dangers of a more impersonal kind — illness, accidents, social or political vicissitudes, frightening events of nature — but in addition is specifically related to the hostilities of people around him, hostilities which he dimly senses as a permanent potential menace.

Since the objective of this paper is not to elucidate the genesis of neurotic phenomena but to elicit a feeling for what constitutes their essence, I shall merely indicate which early adverse influences I hold relevant in the generation of neuroses. I am thinking roughly of all those environmental attitudes and types of behavior which impair a child's capacity to assert himself and to fight and thereby render him helpless, which elicit a feeling of isolation, which provoke hostility, which in effect tend to crush the child's individuality. In this situation the child must find ways of dealing with the environment and of preserving the integrity of his own self. He develops trends which are subtly adapted to meet the particular difficulties with which he is confronted. Their main objective is not only to attain a measure of safety in life but also to find certain satisfactions attainable within the limits set by his overwhelming need for safety. It is their protective function which gives these "neurotic trends" their peculiar character of rigidity and which leads to their indiscriminate application. If for any reason the neurotic trends fail to operate, manifest anxiety may arise.

Mention may be made of a few of such neurotic trends frequent in our culture: to ward off one's real self and to overadapt one's self to environmental standards to such an extent as to become unassailable; to be unobtrusive and to become utterly dependent on others, expecting them to take one's life into their hands; to inflate an image of oneself and to strive for admiration and prestige.

Never does any change occur in any part of a living organism which does not influence the entire organism. Thus it would not be thinkable that neurotic trends develop while the personality as a whole remains unchanged. Invariably the neurotic trends have decisive consequences, varying in kind according to the type of neurotic trends which have developed. These consequences ensue in an elaborate system of avoidances and inhibitions; every trend or reaction not in line with the safety devices must be suppressed, since otherwise the safety devices would be jeopardized. If the emphasis is, for instance, on a passionate pursuit of rectitude and perfection, anxiety may arise at any failure to measure up to these standards. Hence, spontaneous expressions of all kinds must be checked. Personal feelings and wishes must be rigorously subordinated to the requirement of doing and feeling the "right" thing. Any activity must be avoided which entails the risk of failures. If safety is sought in a leaning dependency on others, anything must be avoided that might alienate them. Not only fights must be avoided but also critical thoughts and independent actions.

Furthermore, secondary anxieties will arise which in turn have their own consequences. Thus if the appearance of "rightness" must be maintained at any price, disparities existing between the immaculate façade and trends not fitting into the façade may give rise to an almost permanent fear of being "found out," with the resulting emphasis on secrecy and seclusion or with the resulting tendency to offer self-recriminations in order to ward off accusations on the part of others. Thus the hostilities which must be repressed in the leaning "symbiotic" type form a hidden source of explosive material which in turn adds to the individual's insecurity and requires new measures of precaution.

I shall mention, last, the sensitivities which develop and which render human relationships still more precarious than they were originally. Also any number of gross and subtle rationalizations will be built up in order to justify the behavior determined as it is by the neurotic trends.

Thus a whole intricate character structure develops around the neurotic trends. No feature in it is accidental. Every trait develops because of inexorable necessity and serves a necessary function. Peculiarities or "symptoms" emanate from this structure and must be understood on that basis.

It is this neurotic character structure that constitutes the essence of a neurosis. The "difficult internal conditions" under which a neurotic tries to cope with life are those inherent in his character structure.

Whether such a definition of neuroses is applicable to other civilizations than ours would require psychiatric observations in various cultures to decide. An offhand estimate is all the less opportune since the concept presented reckons most intimately with social and cultural factors. While the definition stresses individual character difficulties, these in turn have been engendered through environmental factors — that is, ultimately through cultural conditions. They are not only brought about through external conditions but also kept alive through these conditions, as is indirectly proved by the therapeutic effects of early changes of environment. Moreover, the kind of safety devices which are developed and the kinds of satisfactions which are attainable depend entirely upon the existing life conditions. It is hardly imaginable that a striving for the appearance of moral perfection would be used as a means toward security in a culture in which such perfection would meet with amazement and disapproval, in which, for instance, it would be regarded as inhuman. An attitude of helpless personal dependency would scarcely appeal as a safety device in a culture in which it would not elicit attention and protection, but would meet with ridicule.

Generally speaking, each of the safety devices we find in our neuroses has its factual security value and contains certain factual possibilities for attaining gratification. It is only their one-sided compulsive and indiscriminate application that lends them their precarious character. Thus a wish to achieve something and to obtain some recognition for one's achievement would appear as a "normal" striving in a competitive culture like ours. But if a wish for recognition becomes a devouring passion pursued at the expense of all other values in life, if simultaneously one's creative abilities are inhibited, and if, instead of putting one's energies into one's work, one tends to attain superiority through disparaging others, then we would call such an ambition "neurotic."

The latter considerations also suggest an approximate distinction between the "normal" and the "neurotic." Two ways of reasoning might lead to such a distinction. One would lie in the attempt to arrive at an absolute distinction valid everywhere. Then we might speak of neuroses whenever we meet with a basic anxiety and with neurotic trends in the above sense. Furthermore, we would then have to agree on a generally valid norm for what constitutes psychic health, such as, for instance, to be able to have a good attitude toward self and others and to have the free use of one's energies.

To adopt this way has, however, definite drawbacks. We could hardly avoid making ourselves the judge as to what is a "good" attitude toward self and others or as to what is a "free" use of energy. Moreover, we would find ourselves compelled to designate as neurotic a whole people or a large group belonging to it. This would be awkward because "neurotic," however we may define it, has the connotation of impairment of function. But the group as a whole and an individual belonging to such a group may function well within the given cultural limitations, as do others within other limitations.

The other way would be to abandon the search for an absolute meaning of neuroses and apply the term in a relative fashion only, to restrict it to mean the psychic conditions of individuals in relation to the statistically average psychic conditions in a given culture. Supposing every culture involves a measure of general anxiety toward life and provides for certain ways of coping with life safely; then we would call neurotic an individual whose anxiety surpasses the average and whose safety devices differ from the average in quantity or quality. Needless to say such a definition does not permit the drawing of a neat demarcation line between neurotic and normal (average) in a given culture. Here as everywhere in nature, we have to reckon with a great range of transitional phenomena. The decision whether or not to call an individual neurotic must ultimately be based on merely practical criteria, such as the degree of being handicapped or the degree of suffering.

This concept allows us to draw a bridge between a definition of neurosis which is merely socially oriented and one which is merely clinically oriented. We can agree with the anthropologist who holds a neurosis to be a deviation from the average, but we would add that the deviation does not primarily concern the manifest behavior but the quantity or quality of basic anxiety as well as that of the deviation developed for the sake of security.

17

Can You Take a Stand? (1939)

This essay appeared in the *Journal of Adult Education* 11 (1939): 129–32. I found a typescript of an earlier draft in Harold Kelman's papers at the Postgraduate Center for Mental Health. It was slightly different and bore the title: "Social Aspects of Feelings of Personal Inadequacy." The essay was, among other things, an attempt to explain the psychological appeal of totalitarianism. It did so in a way that anticipated Erich Fromm, with whom Horney was closely associated at the time (see Paris 1994). The essay was also strikingly personal, given that Horney identified the inability to take a stand as a problem she had had, and her description of childhood conditions that result in self-alienation is highly autobiographical.

Though the problem that I am going to consider in this article has its root in personal feelings of inadequacy, I shall not attempt to discuss at length the general psychology of such feelings, for the simple reason that the subject is inexhaustible. Only one introductory remark: We have to distinguish between two types of causes for distrust of self. It may be the result of self-minimizing tendencies, such as are present in individuals who have adopted a mouse-hole attitude toward life and who feel safe only when they are inconspicuous and unobtrusive. Or it may be caused by deficiencies that actually exist. The nature of these deficiencies varies. They are not necessarily indications of moral shortcomings or of traits that are so regarded; they may just as well be, and most frequently are, traits that betray a sense of insecurity or weakness, such as a diffuse fear of people, or a recoiling from risk, conflict, or responsibility.

I should like to consider in some detail merely one of the many deficiencies from which self-distrustful individuals suffer; namely, their incapacity to take a stand, to make evaluations of their own. I am choosing this particular subject because of its important social aspects. Upon the basis of my experience in and outside my profession, I have come to be somewhat skeptical in regard to the ability of most individuals to take a stand. More often than not, people seem to be unable to make up their own minds how to evaluate either persons or causes. Their judgments are determined either by emotional factors or by opinion prevailing in the environment. I am not thinking here only of obviously weak and compliant persons or of uneducated persons or of persons who are incapacitated by neuroses. I am thinking also of average, healthy, intelligent persons.

Most men and women are not aware that they cannot take a stand. Their weakness may be hidden under the cloak of objectivity. They pride themselves upon their ability to look at a controversial matter "from all sides," or to see both the virtues and the faults of any person of whom they are asked to form an opinion. Often their awakening to the true nature of this so-called objectivity is very much of a shock. It was so in my own case. I well remember taking a walk with a friend some ten years ago and talking about certain persons whom we both knew. I was utterly amazed when my friend made a remark to the effect that I was "wishy-washy" and did not form judgments of values. I retorted that he was wrong, that I was only being objective and trying to take into consideration both the good and bad qualities of the particular person of whom we were speaking. "Yes," my friend said, "that's all very well, but you do not take a stand toward him." I realized afterward that the criticism was just. I think that this realization was a milestone in my own development.

The shortcoming in question may also be hidden behind an assumption of tolerance, using that term in the sense implied in the frequently quoted dictum, *tout comprendre c'est tout pardonner.* But true tolerance is not incompatible with making a fair and honest judgment. I may fully understand why a person acts in an offensive way, and because of this understanding I may refrain from condemning him, but even the most tolerant understanding should not keep me from regarding this type of behavior as in itself a negative value.

It would appear that there are two main sources from which incapacity to take a stand arises: fear of others and failure to take oneself seriously. These traits are interdependent. By taking oneself seriously, I do not mean having no sense of humor in respect to one's own person. Still less do I mean insisting upon one's own importance. Curiously enough, there are many persons who demand a great deal of admiration and are grievously hurt if they do not receive it but who are honestly amazed if anyone takes them seriously. A few words about the genesis of this strange phenomenon may help to explain it.

A feeling of not mattering may begin in early childhood. A child may feel that he is not wanted or appreciated for his own sake, but that he is acceptable only if he lives up to the expectations of others, especially those of his parents. He may feel that he is acceptable only if he obeys blindly or if he uncritically adores one or the other parent. Or the child may feel that he is acceptable only if he measures up to the standards that are current in the family or fulfills the ambitions of his parents or satisfies their desire for showing off. Again, the child may become subservient to the excessive demands of a self-sacrificing mother. Different as these situations are, they all result in the child's feeling that he, his real self, is not understood or not wanted and that he, his real self, does not matter; that only the others and their expectations are important.

If the child is also intimidated in other ways, then he becomes alienated from himself. He decides, as it were — the process is, of course, unconscious — that in order to eliminate conflicts and to live at peace with the world, he had better conform to what is expected.

The desire to conform is born of fear and resentment. In effect the child says to himself: "I realize that you do not understand me; all right, I will do what is expected of me, but then please let me alone." But this compliance, it should be noted, is more than superficial. Nothing more or less than the complete shifting of the center of gravity from the self within to the world outside is involved. What the child himself feels, thinks, or means no longer carries any weight. Henceforth, only the opinions, feelings, and expectations of others count.

William James distinguishes between a material self, by which he means body and possessions; a social self, that is, the self dependent upon the opinion of others (my social self is what others think of me, he said); and the spiritual self, signifying the specific human qualities of judging and deciding. In the terms of James, one may say that an individual undergoing the process described above gives up his spiritual self and becomes more or less entirely his social self.

This type of conforming is a safety device that is most deceptive. It is frequently mistaken by the individual himself, as well as by others, for a good adjustment. I shall illustrate the nature of the resulting character structure by brief accounts of two of my patients. Both asserted, when they came to me, that they were all right, this being a typical attitude of such patients. The first admitted only that she sometimes felt badly depressed, ostensibly without cause.

When she was a child her father had treated her with an inhuman brutality, from which her mother could do little to protect her. Thus intimidated in her early years, she decided to adopt a course of believing that her father was always right. She held firmly and consistently to this conviction, though her father was often glaringly wrong. She had eliminated her real spontaneous self to the extent that she actually no longer had feelings or wishes or opinions of her own.

In time it came to be an unwritten law of hers that she should like everyone, without discrimination. She could not accuse anyone or even entertain feelings of reproach, no matter how badly she was treated. She had only apologetic words for any person who had hurt her. She would not ask for a job when she needed one. She could not assert herself in any situation. When, however, she was asked to do something for someone else, she could do it effectively, although she acted as if under compulsion. For instance, at a time when she had virtually no money, she was asked by a notorious gambler to lend him five dollars. And she did.

The other patient had had a less devastating experience in childhood, but she felt that her mother did not understand her. The mother was quite erratic. Sometimes she was overaffectionate, sometimes she flew at the child in a rage. In consequence, the bewildered child developed a strange attitude toward life. She played a sort of role toward herself and others. She appeared to be carefree, childlike, generous, sacrificing, with a little attractive touch of melancholia. This role, though determined ultimately by her underlying character structure, had nothing much to do with what she really felt or thought. Here, too, there was the deceptive appearance of "adaptation." But in reality the patient had become a marionette, automatically doing, feeling, and thinking what others expected of her. She no longer knew what her own feelings and thoughts were. She responded readily to every influence and could never arrive at any decision herself, no matter whether the issue was trivial or important.

Serious disturbances, such as those from which these two patients suffered, may be rare, but to recognize them and know something about them may help toward an understanding of the less pronounced forms of similar character deficiencies, which seem to be fairly common.

Let us conclude by examining some of the consequences of such a character structure as I have outlined, particularly those consequences that adversely affect society as well as the afflicted individuals.

First of all, a deep feeling of insecurity constrains these persons. They can never take a stand because their feelings and thoughts are largely determined by others. As a result, they are easily swayed, now this way, now that. For instance, the first patient, whom I described above, was asked by a friend to attend a Communist meeting. My patient knew nothing about Communism; she went to the meeting just to observe it. The next time I saw her — only a day later — she had joined the Communist Party!

The other patient had a similar experience, but one that led her in the opposite direction, politically speaking. She made a trip to one of the totalitarian states and came back an enthusiastic advocate of dictatorship. Again, I am convinced that the change was not due to any real understanding of the social philosophy so readily and enthusiastically adopted.

The second socially important consequence of individual feelings of inadequacy is that persons who are the victims of these feelings evaluate themselves entirely in terms of what others think of them. They feel unattractive if others appear to find them unattractive. All of them, therefore, are enormously susceptible to any kind of ideology that bolsters[1] up the ego.

Third, as their behavior and their feelings are wholly directed by expectations from the outside, they lose whatever power of initiative they may once have had. Hence, though they may preserve a semblance of independence, in reality they are lost if they are without guidance, and they naturally become easy converts to any ideology that promises guidance.

Although inferiority feelings of other types grow from other character structures, nevertheless, the results, as I have delineated them, are roughly similar in all cases. The traits described may be agreeable in relation to the immediate environment, but seen from a broader point of view, they constitute a danger. It is people with these traits who succumb most easily to fascist propaganda. Fascist ideology promises to fulfill all their needs. The individual in a fascist state is not supposed to stand up for his own wishes, rights, judgments. Decisions and judgments of values are made for him and he has merely to follow.

---

1. The *Oxford English Dictionary* says that "bolstering" has something to do with upholstering, padding, and that in its figurative sense the term means giving support to an object or a cause, implying, in addition, that the object or the cause is unworthy. — K. H.

He can forget about his own weakness by adoring the leader. His ego is bolstered up by being submerged in the greater unity of race and nation.

Democratic principles are in sharp contrast to fascist ideology. Democratic principles uphold the independence and strength of the individual and assert his right to happiness. It is important, therefore, that everyone who is convinced of the value of democracy do his utmost to strengthen individual self-confidence and willpower, and to develop individual capacity for forming judgments and making decisions. In the education of children, especially in "progressive education," these democratic aims have been emphasized. In adult education, it seems that, before we can stimulate self-confidence, we must first of all combat feelings of personal inadequacy and inferiority.

The question, then, that adult educators have to face in this connection is: What can adult education do to strengthen the weak and to develop in the citizens of this country a genuine capacity for self-government? I fear that I, personally, can be of very little help in finding an answer to this question. You are dealing with groups, and therefore you cannot make use of individual therapy, as I do. I can merely suggest that in your contacts with students you do everything in your power to impress upon the mind of each of them that he, as an individual, matters. Teach them that everyone should consult and express his own feelings and not blindly follow the leadership of others. Show them how imperative it is to take a stand upon all important questions. In a word, try both by precept and by example to give each of them the courage to be himself.

18

Children and the War (1939)

This essay was published in *Child Study* 17 (1939): 9–11. In 1942, Horney contributed a related piece, "Children in Wartime," to the series of war bulletins issued by the Association for the Advancement of Psychoanalysis. I have not been able to find any copies of this bulletin, but Jack Rubins quoted a passage from it in his biography of Horney:

> A child understands war in terms of his own home. War means that brother is away in the army, or that father is working on the swing shift and sleeps all day, or that mother is working in a defense plant and is not at home as she used to be. Alterations of the stability of family life and everyday routine are upheavals which are a disturbing force to children of all ages. A physical desertion of the child as a result of war has its emotional counterpart of deprivation and neglect. The full force of these events will be felt — not now — but in years to come. Mothers try heroically to keep things as much "like home" as possible. In trying to do so,

they overtax their own endurance and necessarily develop certain unin-
tentional resentments toward their children, adding to the anxieties they
are trying to allay. This is frequently seen where the mother feels she
must be both mother and father to the child. (Rubins 1978, 252)

The war is a reality which parents cannot, even if they would, keep from
their children. Attempts to keep it from them, like attempts to keep sex knowledge from children, are doomed to failure. And in both cases, the part of
wisdom is not to shield and to dissemble but to understand and to interpret.
Most of us instinctively try to present the world to our children as a gracious
and reasonable place. When they come to us complaining of the meanness or
injustice which they run into, few of us have the courage to let them know that
meanness and injustice are among the realities they will have to learn to cope
with. Invariably we try to justify the meanness, to explain away the injustice,
to insist on the silver lining in what is sometimes just a plain black cloud.
Perhaps we do all these things because the amount of ruthlessness and cruelty
apparent today in the expansion drives of nations the world over is genuinely
terrifying. We are frightened, moreover, because similar aggressive drives on a
personal plane exist within ourselves.

Probably the majority of children of a neutral nation face the fact of war
with far more equanimity than their parents. Why should they not? Their
experience is less, their feeling of responsibility less, their imaginations do not
extend greatly beyond their own homes. War has only a kind of story-book
reality. Bloodshed and killing are easily accepted by them, and the whole thing
is a pleasantly interesting and exciting game. For an American child, Europe
may seem as far away as Mars, and the younger child brought up in both
emotional and physical security is likely to believe that the wicked enemy will
be punished as surely as the bad witch in the fairy tale. Most children's interest,
we find, is keen but not excessive, and the excitement pleasurable rather
than painful.

There are some children, however, who feel the war as an immediate personal threat. Will their father have to go? Will enemy airplanes come in the
night and drop bombs on their own homes? Bad dreams, sleeplessness, fears of
the enemy lurking in every dark alley enter their world. News of a torpedoed
ship with loss of life preys on their sensibilities. They seem shaken as though
they were personally involved in every event. Parents of these children may try
to quiet them by finding ways of keeping the news away, by hiding the evening
paper, by limiting the use of the radio, by guarding their conversation. "He is

too afraid of the war," they say, or "He is such a sensitive child." These children seem unable to take the strong medicine that others tolerate easily, and it seems sensible to try at least to keep the dose within reasonable bounds.

Real censorship, however, is not only impossible to carry out but will fail because it does not recognize the central problem of these children. This problem revolves around the "why" of the child's fears. For in a country not at war, air raids and sudden attacks from the enemy are not real dangers and the war and its details are not real causes of fear. When simple explanations regarding our present safety are not effective in reassuring the child, we are forced to conclude that it is not fear of war at all, but other unconscious forces which are troubling him, and that war and its dangers are merely the external events which serve to stir to life those painful thoughts which lie beneath the surface of consciousness. For some children, thunderstorms, animals, loud noises, street accidents, and other details of their familiar environment perform exactly the same function, and these we must also regard purely as the symbol to which the child transfers the fear which has its sources in something quite different.

The problem then is, What are the real sources of the child's fears and anxieties, and how can they be understood and alleviated? This question cannot be answered with any generalizations. Each child is an individual case and must be studied individually.

For example: an American girl of sixteen became terribly agitated at the announcement of war in Europe. She lay awake at night in terrified anticipation of air raids, and in spite of quiet and reasonable discussions of the actual situation and the inescapable fact that she was nowhere near the war zone, she could not get over the expectation that she and her family might expect death at any moment. The extent of her fears was completely unrelated to the facts and therefore suggested at once that it was not the war at all, but something else which was the cause of her fears. Deeper knowledge of this girl's life experiences revealed that she had spent a childhood feeling choked by a mother who demanded perfection and who frequently humiliated her in connection with the inevitable faults of childhood. Not only did she feel humiliated by her mother's constantly disapproving attitude, but she never was able to shake off the feelings of culpability within herself which it gave rise to. She grew up with the conviction that she stood condemned before all decent people. Her mother was "good," she herself "bad," and throughout her life her attitude toward her mother was submissive and overadoring. Moreover, she constantly voiced an admiration of her mother which to a trained observer convicted the girl by its very vehemence and suggested that her protests masked a hatred which she was unable to admit to herself. Thus burdened with a sense of moral inferiority, this girl's life was characterized by a violent struggle for moral perfection. The least criticism from anyone threw her into a violent panic because it revived the feelings connected with her mother's early censure. Consequently, it was inevitable that this girl should regard herself as in imminent danger of punishment. In spite of the fact that she was surrounded only by people who, on the surface, were kind and gentle, punishment seemed none the less certain for her. And when it failed to come from humans, it could certainly come in the form of some cosmic event. The war served this purpose. It was for these reasons that events in Europe seemed to her to be the personal chastisement which she had always expected. And in addition, there was a further reason why thoughts of the war with its murder and bloodshed roused in her such terror. Just as it threatened to engulf and destroy her, so also was there a possibility of its destroying her mother. This thought, expressing as it did her own hostile wishes, was now far too near the surface of consciousness for comfort, and gave rise to her exaggerated war fears.

In young children fear of the war often has the same kind of significance as fear of thunderstorms or wild animals. It is essentially the fear of punishment descending out of the void to punish the unrighteous. It is built on the foundation of a guilty feeling foisted on them by parents in response to childish faults, with the resulting fear of punishment. There is also the further discomfort caused by bringing too near to the surface the angry wishes which the child bears toward his parents or toward his brothers and sisters. Only relief for the guilt at its original source can effectively banish the irrational fear. This is why the period of fears in early childhood is likely to correspond roughly to the period when nursery jealousies and hates are strongest, when sexual experimentation is frequent, and when the guilt which accompanies them is most acute.

A girl of seven, for example, suffered from night terrors and a belief that "wild animals," "burglars," and so forth, were coming to destroy her. In vain did her parents soothe and explain. The fears continued until the time when the child was induced to talk freely of her hostile feelings and death wishes toward her small brother. Once this was thoroughly expressed and her parents did not punish her or instantly withdraw their love, her development proceeded more normally and the fears abated.

Of course it must be remembered that most children in our society pass through certain infantile neuroses without any signs of a desperate crisis. The average child works through these difficult periods by himself, without the original sources of emotional conflict becoming conscious and without any special technique employed to help him. Nevertheless even in normal children, there are periods in which "bad" wishes, whether sexual or aggressive, play a considerable part in their inner lives and give rise to depressed moods, irritability, anger, and sensitiveness. Most parents are faced with these from time to time and are puzzled how to handle them. For these children, it seems sensible not to stimulate their conflicts by excessive talk of war and aggression, by stories or movies of horrors and cruelty. It seems wise to do some soft-pedaling of these powerful stimulants. Yet we should know that beneath the surface the child is disturbed not by the bombs, the villain, or the wicked witch but by his own hostile impulses. Realizing this, we give all the help that our understanding makes possible, but in most cases we leave the child to work the matter out for himself. Whatever censorship parents may exercise should of course be contrived so that it does not come in the form of direct and absolute prohibitions. Every bit of ingenuity to finding other more constructive occupations should be called into play. Family games instead of overexciting radio programs; stamp collecting, carpentry, "making things," instead of movies or horror stories; and whatever else the child can genuinely lose himself in are useful, not in removing the cause of the tensions, but in tiding the child over until a new period in his life proves less difficult.

It seems probable that for the adolescent boy the war presents special problems. He is bound to be faced with the problem of his own physical courage and with the inevitable doubts, therefore, of his ability to be a real man. This problem may play a large part during adolescence, since it is further complicated at this period by doubts concerning his sexual capacities or his ability some day to earn a living and the fears which he harbors on these scores. The imminent danger of war comes as an additional challenge and an additional source of painful self-doubting. This conflict will be heightened, of course, if his home is one in which the "sissy" is despised and physical cowardice regarded as shameful. But whatever his parents' attitude, that of society remains the same. In the world of today he cannot avoid the conclusion that a man, if called, must fight for his country. Can he meet the call? In his doubt of the answer to this terrifying question he is likely to do all manner of things to prove his virility and courage, from ordinary braggadoccio and various bullying attitudes to showing neurotic disturbances and apparent physical disorders less obviously connected with the real inner conflict. Here, too, the problem to be met must be met at its source. The boy needs help in facing his real fears and working out greater self-respect and assurance of his personal worth and of his dignity.

For most parents, the problems presented by the war are problems in moral education rather than in psychiatric technique. First of all, it is necessary that they think their way through these problems as best they can. How have we ourselves been able to cling to any standards of decency in a world where ruthlessness and cruelty not only are prevalent but seem at times to be victorious? Are we clear as to the meaning of the old warning, "What profiteth it a man if he gain the whole world, yet lose his soul," and can we help to make it clear to our children? This is the real problem, and if they grasp it, parents will not waste their time by moral preaching, by books describing the horrors of war and the beauties of peace, or by prohibiting war toys, guns, games, and stories of violence. These things never yet *caused* a child to become aggressive and warlike. They are merely the vehicles through which he expresses his need of aggression. Some of this need, as we have already seen, is to be expected in the normal course of things; and, if development proceeds as it should, will in time be spontaneously supplanted by other desires and activities. War and the need to hate and destroy can be eliminated not by learning to hate war but by learning to love life. And the love of life starts in the nursery. It is all-important that the parents' early relation to children should be free of elements which tend to arouse fears and feelings of hate which last throughout life. Such things as unfairness, favoritism, and neglect rouse a general crankiness in children which in turn provokes punishment or disfavor from the parent. Worst of all, perhaps, in its results on personality development, is the child's discovery that as far as his parents are concerned, his existence means little more than a means of satisfying their personal self-importance. A child who is rejected by his parents often cannot consciously hate *them* but he ends by hating Germans, Jews, or the "enemy," in whatever guise it is presented.

All children need adult conversation as a part of their lives, but it must be suited to their age and stage of growth as well as to their personal needs. There is no use trying to explain to young children the complicated motives and diplomatic moves of nations today. Our explanations must be simple, but in making them simple, we must guard against their becoming untrue. It does children no harm to be forced to realize that there are problems beyond their grasp — beyond adults' grasp, too, for that matter; and that there are certain things for which they will have to wait until they are older if they are really to understand.

Our older children, however, should be given a glimpse into the complexities of the scene and perhaps need training in something we call historic perspective. This is necessary if they are to have any orientation toward wars and recurrences of war. They need a gradual induction into the problems of the human race, which includes a realization of the cruelties and the follies which are inescapable but which also gives them a vision of the aspirations of man and a hope for something better. These are the lessons of a lifetime and cannot be imparted formally; they are implicit in the kind of family life of which the child is part and the kind of social attitudes to which he is subjected. If these are sound, children's values, too, are likely to develop soundly and parents will not be tempted to overstuff children with principles and information which they do not want and which fail to meet their needs. They will be able to listen more attentively to what their sons and daughters are really concerned with instead of rushing to tell them what they, the parents, think they ought to hear. Otherwise, they will shoot wide of the mark and have nothing to offer children in their struggle toward maturity.

19

Pride and Self-Hatred in Neuroses (1947)

In Part 1, I included lectures 8, 9, and 11 from the course "Pride and Self-Hatred in Neuroses" that Horney gave at the New School for Social Research in 1947 and 1948: "Influence on Human Relations," "Influence on Love Life," "Influence on Sex Life." Below are lectures 12 and 13: "Pride and Self-Hatred in Freud" and "Pride and Self-Hatred in Literature: The Devil's Pact." As in Part 1, I have edited Horney's detailed but somewhat fragmentary lecture notes to make them more readable, and I have deleted some portions that I found unintelligible. Horney compared her theory with Freud's once again in the concluding chapter of *Neurosis and Human Growth* ("Theoretical Considerations"), which overlaps somewhat with Lecture 12, on which she drew to some extent. Many of the references to literature in Lecture 13 reappear in *Neurosis and Human Growth,* some in conjunction with discussions of the devil's pact. Lecture 13, however, represents Horney's most concentrated discussion of literature and contains some material that appears nowhere else.

Lecture 12: Pride and Self-Hatred in Freud

RÉSUMÉ OF HORNEY'S THEORY

In all neuroses there is an element of self-destructiveness that ranges from various forms of self-frustration and self-contempt to self-mutilation and suicide. This self-destructiveness is not instinctual but is an expression of self-hatred. In trying to account for self-hatred, we encounter something that looks like its opposite, namely a reaching out for supernatural power and perfection. People search for glory because they feel helpless, are torn by inner conflicts, have no self-confidence, and regard themselves as unlovable and insignificant. By becoming perfect, they hope to gain a sense of strength and self-confidence and a basis on which to relate themselves to others. When they realize the impossibility of reaching their goals, they hate and despise themselves all the more. They are caught in a vicious circle in which feelings of nothingness drive them to pursue lofty objectives, and their failure to achieve these objectives makes them feel even more insignificant, which compels them to seek greater glory, and so on. Their sense of connection with their "real me," which has already been weakened by conflicts, is weakened further and further until it disappears.

COMPARISON WITH FREUD

Although their basic thinking is very different, Freud has seen most of the individual factors to which Horney points. He describes the kind of neurotic ambition that is involved in the search for glory in his accounts of sibling rivalry, the Oedipus complex, and penis envy in women. For him, self-glorification is a by-product of narcissism, with the person falling in love with himself or with his ego ideal (which is the same as Horney's idealized image) and then glorifying himself. Freud's followers have enlarged on self-glorification.

Freud attributes the need for perfection to the superego. He has a good description of shoulds but nothing about irrational claims on others. He sees self-destructiveness as the product of a death instinct that is concentrated in the superego, which is a self-prohibiting, self-condemning agency that subjects the individual to the pressure of many demands. The dictates of the superego arouse feelings of guilt, which may be either conscious or unconscious. Self-suppression is a way of "paying off" a severe superego. Others, such as Menninger and Alexander, have enlarged on this. Freud saw that people project their superego onto others, so that they believe it is others who are making harsh demands on them.

There is nothing corresponding to a "real me" in Freud's concept of the ego, since the ego is a weak, undynamic part of the personality that functions as an observer and mediator, cramped between the demands of the id (instincts) and those of the superego (idealized image).

We must admire the power of Freud's observations. It is true that poets and philosophers had observed many of the same things, but that is different from Freud's systematic search for these factors and application of them in medical therapy. Freud had to make his own discoveries, step by step, and he remains a pioneer of truly gigantic dimensions. It took tremendous courage to make sex a topic for scientific discussion and to subject moral questions to psychological scrutiny. Freud went against many age-old beliefs in his theories.

DIFFERENCES BETWEEN HORNEY AND FREUD

The differences between Freud and Horney are more than just a matter of terminology. Freud explained neuroses in terms of two factors, instincts and genesis in early childhood.

1. *Instincts*. Freud accounted for the aspects of human behavior he observed by attributing them to instincts, which are inherited biological drives. Thus, ambition is a by-product of sexual rivalry, the drive for perfection an expression of the instinct for self-preservation that is focused in the superego. The thinking of Freud's time was based on instincts. William James, for example, saw not only a sex instinct but also an antisex instinct.

What Freud calls an instinct Horney calls a compulsive drive. If we see these drives as instincts, it means that they are unchangeable. Freud said that these instincts could be modified or brought under better control only through sublimation or more conscious mastery. Horney believes that compulsive drives can be *changed* because they are *acquired*. The Freudian concept is static, while Horney's concept is dynamic.

2. *Genetic orientation*. Freud saw neurotic drives as instincts that have been reinforced by early experiences, and he tried to account for them by discovering their origins in childhood. This barred the way to an investigation of the real dynamics of the operative forces. Let me give some examples of the difference between Freud's and Horney's explanations.

Neurotic ambition: Freud explained great ambition and the need to excel and defeat competitors as the result of fixation on a childhood desire to outdo a parent or a sibling. For Horney, a person is driven to be ambitious by a feeling of nothingness and a need to justify his existence.

Penis envy: Freud believed that ambition in women is due to penis envy. According to Horney, when a woman loses her sense of herself as a person, her self-image becomes concentrated on her genitals, and she feels that she could be strong and assertive if she only had a penis.

Destructiveness toward others: Freud saw it as a death instinct which is turned outward. In Horney's view, the destructive person feels unlovable and has lost the capacity to love others. This results in a feeling of emptiness that needs to be filled by thrills and excitement. Someone like Hedda Gabler may try to destroy others for excitement and then hate herself so much that she destroys herself. Freud's instinct of self-destruction is different from Horney's conception of self-destructiveness as the result of self-hatred. This is important for therapy, in that for Freud we can only control the self-destructive instinct, whereas for Horney we can treat the self-hatred from which destructiveness springs.

Search for glory: for Freud, self-glorification is a by-product of narcissism, and the need for perfection is a by-product of self-destructiveness. Freud did not see the hunger for superiority in the need for perfection. This was poorly dealt with by Freud, in contrast to Adler, who emphasized the need for superiority.

Although he did not recognize the importance of self-hatred, Freud saw many aspects of the drives toward glory and self-destruction; but he did not bring them together. It is the awareness of interrelations that is the great therapeutic tool in Horney, because it allows us to relieve self-hatred by working on neurotic pride and the drive for glory.

In brief, Freud's thinking is instinctivistic and genetic, while Horney's is dialectical and focused on present dynamics.

CONCEPT OF MAN

Freud had much to say about the destructive forces in man but little about the constructive forces, the existence of which he usually denied. Failing to distinguish between the normal and the neurotic, he assumed many things he found in neurotics to be universal components of human nature. Neurotics have little feeling of the "real me." Freud generalized this as being the case with all human beings. Horney believes that this weakness and deadness of the "real me" is a neurotic product, the result of inner conflicts and self-alienation. The "real me" is the most dynamic part of the personality, the source of all energy, aliveness, decision, and responsibility. Freud considered the wish to grow and develop, emotionally as well as physically, to be narcissistic. It is true that this wish can be an expression of a neurotic desire for glory, but when the search for glory has been resolved through analysis, the person still wants to grow and develop and to be at one with himself. When the wish is constructive, it is an element of real maturity.

Freud denied authentic ideals and convictions. For him, ideals are residues of previous identifications or inner dictates of a destructive superego. Again, he was describing a neurotic state of affairs. Actually, it is not that the neurotic person has no ideals, but because of inner conflicts his ideals are contradictory and have no binding power. This does not mean that there are no real ideals that are important to life and give it direction and purpose. For Freud, moral goals are the result of the self-destructive drive, and this view is tantamount to a denial of morality and values. He makes no distinction between genuine guilt and the neurotic guilt that results from self-hatred.

In Freud's view, man is destructive of self and others by nature, and therefore war, cruelty, greed, and so on, are inevitable. A belief in goodness and constructive factors is just wishful thinking. Horney does not argue that man is by nature good but contends that if children are brought up under favorable conditions — that is, given real love, made to feel wanted, respected, and so forth — they will become constructive adults. It is neurosis that makes man destructive. As people progress in analysis, their wish for constructiveness emerges more and more clearly.

DIFFERENCES IN RELATION TO THERAPY

Freud is easier on the patient, because he allows the patient to blame his problems on his childhood and escape responsibility in the present. Horney: "I am nasty because I can't stand someone else being wiser or happier." Freud: "I am nasty because of my childhood experiences." The former is tougher on the self but more effective. Freud's emphasis on genesis was based on his belief in the repetition compulsion, and he felt that in the course of analysis the patient repeats his childhood experiences. Horney believes that there is no real repetition, that not all people have to re-experience early stages to arrive at an understanding and resolution of adult personality difficulties. Her emphasis is not on the past but on the present character structure of the patient.

Freud's theories created a series of barriers to therapy. His emphasis on instinct created a barrier, since problems deriving from instinct are insoluble. There are no barriers in Horney; in most patients, all problems are in the end accessible to treatment. If destructiveness is the result of a death instinct, it is ineradicable, but if it is the result of defenses that have been generated by our particular experience, we can do something about it. Freud's pessimism about the nature of man gave him a feeling of hopelessness, and because of this he never saw the hopelessness of his patients as a neurotic problem. Since Freud felt hopeless himself, he could not see a way of helping others with this feeling. For Horney, hopelessness is a result of the person's being caught in his conflicts and is therefore a condition that can be tackled and changed. Freud's denial of constructive forces in human nature meant that the patient's desire to get better was dependent on the transference, that he wanted to improve for the sake of the analyst. This is an unreliable incentive because the patient may turn against or away from the analyst, and this reaction would put an end to the drive for improvement. In Horney's view, the patient should want to get well for his own sake, to enhance his own creativity and productivity. It is important for him to discover his own goals and not simply to adopt those of the analyst. The analyst must liberate constructive forces in the patient, which will then combat the destructive forces of his neurosis.

Lecture 13: *Pride and Self-Hatred in Literature: The Devil's Pact*

INTRODUCTION

Poets and philosophers have known a lot about the curse of the drive for glory, as evidenced by stories of the devil's pact. These are stories of people in distress — material, as in Stephen Vincent Benét's *Devil and Daniel Webster,* or psychic, as in *Faust* — who are willing to sacrifice their souls in order to escape their unhappiness. In Oscar Wilde's *Picture of Dorian Gray,* the self-alienated protagonist values himself only for his beauty and is therefore terrified at the thought of growing old. Faust is in spiritual distress because he cannot stand limitations on his knowledge and wisdom and seeks to transcend the human condition.

I am talking not about vanity or a shallow wish for superiority but about a profound distress that leads to the search for glory. While the protagonist is in distress, the devil, or some version of him, enters the scene. In *Faust,* he actually appears and offers a way out if Faust will sell his soul. Afraid of aging, Dorian Gray is willing to give anything if he can remain young while the image of himself in his portrait grows old. The price of glory is always the loss of one's soul (that is, one's real self), which consigns one to a hell within. The protagonist first exults in his powers but then is overcome by a terror of death or damnation. In the end, he wants to break his contract and get rid of his powers, but it is usually too late.

SEARCH FOR GLORY

Poets also know about the ways in which the search for glory manifests itself. It often takes place in imagination, as in Ibsen's *Peer Gynt* and *John Gabriel Borkman,* in *Don Quixote,* or in the wishful thinking of fairy tales. Glory may be experienced through another person, as in Balzac's *Père Goriot.* There is the glory of perfection, as in Pearl Buck's *Pavilion of Women,* where Madame Wu must be the perfect wife and mother, or the glory of love, as in *Madame Bovary.* Emma Bovary dreams of a wonderful life but then marries a simple country doctor and can't stand the limitations of her existence. She seeks a solution by losing herself in glamorous love affairs. In Zweig's biography of Balzac, we see a similar longing for wealthy, glamorous lovers who will provide protection and the luxuries of life. In *The Red and the Black* by Stendhal, Julien Sorel seeks glory through his seduction of glamorous women.

Glory can also be pursued through aggression, as in *Don Giovanni,* where the protagonist has to prove his irresistible powers and find a perfect love. Something similar occurs in *Peer Gynt.* There is glory in the search for a vindictive triumph, as in *Moby Dick,* where Captain Ahab is driven by his desire for revenge on the whale. Hamlet, too, becomes obsessed by one goal after the ghost gives him the task of taking revenge. Dorian Gray takes a sadistic delight in driving others to despair and suicide; and Hedda Gabler, bitter, empty, and consumed by unfulfilled claims, lives for nothing except her vindictive need to destroy others.

RESULTS OF THE SEARCH FOR GLORY

The search for glory leads to a shrinking of the personality, for the individual becomes entirely egocentric, with nothing mattering except this one drive. Peer Gynt develops a gospel of self and takes pride in his idealized image, while Ahab's only interest in life is his pursuit of Moby Dick. There is also a shrinking of the emotions, which are deadened by the person's obsession. Hamlet reproaches himself for his lack of feeling. John Gabriel Borkman doesn't care for anybody and sacrifices his only companion because she doubts his glorious future.

People who are searching for glory have impaired human relationships. Their attitudes range from indifference to coldness to cruelty to destructiveness. They cannot see others realistically or have genuine relationships, because they are concerned with them only as means or obstacles to their pursuit of glory. Madame Wu comes to realize that she had no feelings for anyone and only pretended to be interested in them. Captain Ahab sacrifices his whole crew in his search for vengeance. Don Giovanni plays with the feelings of others, and Faust toys with the life and happiness of Gretchen. Dorian Gray takes a wicked delight in corrupting others.

The search for glory leads to a sense of futility (Hedda Gabler feels empty and bored) and to a hell of self-torture and self-condemnation. Hamlet is caught between contradictory shoulds: he should both execute his revenge and be gentle and good. Dorian Gray experiences great inner anguish when he contemplates the despised image of himself that is reflected in the increasingly disgusting portrait. The individual's self-hatred may result in a loss of interest in himself or, more severely, in self-frustration and self-destruction. Balzac ruined himself because of his self-hatred. Madame Bovary ruined herself through her love affairs and ended up a suicide. Dorian Gray destroyed his dignity and integrity. Such stories tend to conclude tragically, with the protagonist either committing suicide or being struck down by fate.

Some stories do not end in tragedy, however, but show the protagonist freeing himself from the search for glory and achieving a kind of redemption. Faust makes a pact with the devil, but he overcomes his misery in becoming constructive, acknowledging what he has in common with others, recognizing the value of simple human strivings. The Ancient Mariner feels psychically dead after he shoots the albatross but turns toward life when he sees the beauty of the water snakes. His feelings revive, and he is freed from the albatross. In Hans Christian Andersen's "Snow Queen," the boy is frozen in the cold glamour of the queen's castle, but his icy heart is melted by Gerda's love and tears. Before she can free him, however, Gerda must overcome the obstacles that prevent her from loving. Madame Wu gains understanding through the priest, after which she is able to take a constructive approach to life and love. Daniel Webster decides to fight the devil's jury with an appeal to the simple human things we all have in common. Acknowledging that there is some good and some bad in all of us, he appeals to the constructive forces in human nature and turns the jury's hearts.

When people sell their souls to the devil (that is, when they sacrifice their real selves in the pursuit of glory), they are doomed to suffer inner torment. Some never emerge from their torment, but it is a redemptive force in others, turning them toward love, belonging, and healthy human strivings. Because Freud did not recognize and make use of the constructive forces in human nature, he had little success in curing neurotics.

20

Inhibitions in Work (1947)

This essay was published in the *American Journal of Psychoanalysis* 7 (1947): 18–25. It was an expansion of Lecture 10, "Influence on Work," from Horney's course "Pride and Self-Hatred in Neuroses," whose plan it followed very closely. Horney used a few paragraphs from the essay in chap. 13, "Neurotic Disturbances in Work," of *Neurosis and Human Growth,* but her organization there was quite different. Instead of focusing on the prerequisites for doing creative work — gifts, consistency, self-confidence, and love of the work — she discussed the way in which each of the major solutions — narcissism, perfectionism, arrogant vindictiveness, self-effacement, and resignation — interferes with the individual's ability to be productive. In her chapter, Horney drew most heavily on "Inhibitions in Work" in her discussion of the work difficulties of the resigned personality. She had a particular interest in problems at work because she had suffered severely from such problems when she was a young woman but had overcome them to become extraordinarily productive in the last twenty-five years of her life (see Paris 1994).

Most neuroses affect our work life in one way or another. In this paper, I shall deal with some of the work impairments which stem directly from neuroses. I shall not refer to difficulties which are due to economic pressures, or to peculiarities due to cultural attitudes toward work (compare, for instance, the New Englander with the Mexican Indian); nor shall I consider the many impairments of work which are related not to the work itself but rather to disturbed relationships with the people for whom or with whom the work is done.

The range of neurotic difficulties in work is great. There is the prodigious worker with seemingly inexhaustible energies, but the quality of his work remains far beneath his real potential. There are those who work frantically and consider wasted every hour not given to work. There are many who cannot concentrate. There are gifted persons who take up one pursuit after another, starting with enthusiasm, but soon dropping it. There are those who make sporadic efforts but lack consistency; those who scatter their energies in various directions; those who conceive brilliant ideas or projects but never get around to doing anything about them.

All kinds of distress may be connected with work: from strain and exhaustion to fears and open panics. Such distress may arise in the process of work or at public performances. The capacity to work, finally, may be linked up to rigid conditions: to hours in the morning or at night; to the absence or presence of outside pressure; to strict solitude, or to other people being around — and so on and so forth.

The disturbances, as a rule, are all the greater, the more personal faculties are required for the particular work. There is a sliding scale from routine work to creative work; from factory work to social work, teaching, scientific, or artistic work. The difficulties usually increase with the amount of initiative, responsibility, self-reliance, courage, and creativity required. I shall restrict my comments to those kinds of work for which we have to tap our personal resources — creative work in the broadest sense of the word.

Four Factors in Work

What, then, are the conditions for doing creative work in the above sense? Four main factors are necessary which we shall discuss in detail:

1. Gifts
2. Consistency of interest and of effort
3. Self-confidence
4. A positive emotional attitude toward the work — genuine interest, love, devotion, faith

Gifts. Undoubtedly people are not equally endowed with gifts. Recent educational ventures have shown, for instance, that most people can paint when properly encouraged, but not everybody can be a Rembrandt or a Renoir. On the other hand, gifts are often regarded too much as an absolute and mysterious property which one has or has not, while actually many psychological factors enter into it. It would be difficult to say, for instance, whether a person has a gift for teaching or whether his personality and his interest — from whatever source — make him a good teacher. Has somebody an undefinable flair for psychological matters, or is it his interest — again from whatever sources — that makes him an astute observer or a good psychotherapist? Also, we cannot determine the extent of abilities before a person puts them to the test in the way of active work in the particular field. As long as he is inhibited to put them to the test, he is free to imagine either that he has supreme gifts or that he has none whatever.

Consistency. By consistency I do not mean the restriction of interest and effort to one field. This would merely make for the narrow-mindedness of the "specialist." Whatever our work is, it can only be done well against a broad background of a wide scope of interests. But for us to achieve anything in any field, there must be a clear hierarchy of interest. We must decide where our main interest, our main ability, lies. Also we must have the self-discipline necessary for putting in consistent effort in the chosen field. Needless to say, no productive work can ever be like the regularity of a machine. Relaxation will be necessary. Tolerance will be necessary for periods during which something is quietly growing within ourselves without anything being produced.

Self-confidence. Any work that is not mechanical routine requires a measure of self-confidence. Emerson expressed it in negative terms when he said: "It is because we minimize ourselves that we do not accomplish." It takes self-confidence to take one's work seriously; the more so when the effort does not show immediate results. The more so, the less we are backed up by approval, but work alone or against opposition. The more so, the more decisions are to be made, risks to be taken. The more so, the more creative a work is. It takes supreme and unerring assertion for the creative artist to express his feelings and experiences.

The fact that any productive work requires self-confidence is another reason that renders it difficult to appraise gifts. Is, for instance, the fact that women by and large are less productive than men due to their being less endowed by nature or to an impairment of their self-confidence through various outside pressures?

Genuine Interest (love, devotion, faith). A teacher, a minister, or an analyst may be interested in doing things for others; but in order to be a good teacher, minister, or analyst, he must believe in the work he is doing, he must love the work itself. For a work to be valuable, it must be not only a means to an end, no matter whether this end is to help, to earn money, or to gain prestige. What John Macmurray says about the artist's relation to his object is true for any productive work: "Without such an interest in the object for its own sake, it is impossible to grasp any reality at all." Success is dependent on many factors, largely outside ourselves; it is the work itself that must have meaning and value for us. Then, and then only, can we give ourselves to it with all our sensitivities, intelligence, imagination, energies.

All these basic requirements to work are well known. Each single detail has been said a thousand times by philosophers, poets, educators. But apparently it remains a fairly abstract knowledge, that is, a knowledge we do not apply to ourselves. Or else how can we account for the innumerable complaints about inhibitions in work without the question ever raised: Do I fulfill the necessary requirements? If not, why not? And this is why I started enumerating the preconditions for productive work: I want to discuss what exactly are the neurotic difficulties interfering with the healthy attitudes toward work.

Gifts

Let us start with frequent neurotic attitudes in regard to *gifts*. The existence of special faculties may be emphatically denied. A highly intelligent person, for instance, may insist on being stupid. A person with great understanding for painting may deny the possibility that he could paint. Such an attitude may be an integral part of a pervasive self-berating; in addition there is usually an unconscious preference of resigning rather than exposing himself to ridicule. The fear of ridicule, in turn, is an expression of a felt discrepancy between superlative imagined achievement and realistic possibilities. On the opposite extreme are the patients who emphasize and aggrandize their potentialities, bask in them, but in actual fact never get beyond having brilliant ideas or projects. These are people who, to use a term of Kierkegaard's, flounder in possibilities and shirk facing the necessity of down-to-earth work. In their imagination potentialities *are* the accomplished product and usually they claim the same recognition as if they had actually done the imagined deeds. Their pride is so overweening and so much based on sheer possibilities, that it does not permit of any putting to the test.

Consistency

Concerning *consistency* there are frequent difficulties. One of them is scattering of interests and energies in many directions. There is the woman, for instance, who has to be the perfect mother, housewife, hostess; she also has to be the best-dressed woman, to be active on committees, to have her hand in politics, to be a great writer. The person himself, when realizing the existence of such a disorder, usually ascribes it to the multitude of his gifts. With an ill-concealed arrogance, he may express his envy of those less fortunate fellow-beings who are endowed with just one gift. The diversity of faculties may actually exist, but it is not the source of his troubles. The background usually is an insistent refusal to recognize limitations. Against all evidence to the contrary, he feels that others may not be able to do so many things, but he can, and can do them all to perfection. To restrict his activities for him is not wisdom but would smell of defeat and contemptible weakness. The prospect of being a human being like others, with limitations like others, is degrading and thus intolerable. It almost goes without saying that he is not really related to any activity. He is consumed with having to prove his unlimited powers and unlimited excellence and is enslaved by these drives.

Many neurotics, otherwise inertly wasting time with trivialities, are able to make *sporadic* efforts. Real emergencies may dispel the psychic paralysis. Usually sloppy and disorganized, a housewife may swing a big party, or do a big housecleaning. Here it is the glory of the dramatic, of the unusual, that captivates her imagination, while the humble tasks of daily living are resented as humiliation or coercion. Others can start pursuits with frantic energy and enthusiasm. They make big outlines for a book, work at an invention, have business projects, set an organization going—but soon after, their interest peters out. Several things may interfere, all of them stemming from a similar background. An individual may have never thought realistically of doing any-thing, but his imagination may have simply indulged in producing glittering soap-bubbles. He may feel that it behooves him, the genius, to evolve plans, but the "detail" work should be done by the ordinary run of people. He may be unable to bear suspense as to failure or success, because failure would threaten him with total self-condemnation and, therefore, he tends to give up at the first difficulty. He may be impatient of immediate results because he feels he should be able to perfect the great invention, or to write the book in no time. Other-wise he is no good at all. The premature giving up, then, seen from the angle of pride, is a face-saving maneuver. If he holds out a little longer, each obstacle turns into an ordeal. Because again, he feels he *should* be able to overcome it perfectly and instantaneously otherwise he is just a poor fool.

Sporadic efforts, thus, rather feed the pride than detract from it. Consistent efforts are an insult to neurotic pride. Every Tom, Dick, and Harry can get somewhere with plodding work! As long as no efforts are made, the pride is protected. There is, then, always the reservation that he would have accom-plished something great if he had put in real efforts. The most hidden aversion against consistent efforts lies in the threat to the illusion of unlimited powers. Suppose you want to cultivate a garden. Whether you want to or not, you will soon become aware that the garden does not turn into a blossoming paradise overnight. It will progress not more and not less than the amount of work you put in. You will have the same sobering experience when consistently working at reports or papers, when doing publicity work or teaching. There is a limit to your time, your energies, and to what you can achieve within these limits. As long as the neurotic holds on to his illusions of unlimited energies and un- limited achievements, he must by necessity be wary of exposing himself to such disillusioning experiences. Or, when he does, he must chafe under them as under an undignified yoke. Such resentment in turn will make him tired and exhausted.

Self-Confidence

Self-confidence, as we know, is always impaired in neuroses for many reasons. Self-idealization and glorification, while giving a feeling of impor- tance, actually add to the inner uncertainty. They rob the neurotic of a solid base to stand on, alienate him from himself, and — even worse — make him in- evitably turn against his true self with hatred and contempt. The kind of dis- turbance varies according to the whole structure. A spurious self-confidence may be in the foreground. Self-doubts are rigidly suppressed. The person in his imagination *is* his idealized image. There is nothing he cannot do. The mere possibility of failure is eliminated. Failures that do occur hardly register. Whatever is done appears to be wonderful. People of this type are often ad- mired for their seemingly unlimited capacity for work. But I wonder whether their glib facilities to write, paint, speak, and so on, actually assume the dig- nity of work. Since they, too, are unrelated to their activities and since they have an endless craving for prestige, their work is easily a means to opportu- nistic ends.

Overconfident people of another category likewise do not become aware of existing inhibitions toward work. They paint masterpieces, write mas- terbooks, make world-rocking inventions — in their imagination. Their self- contempt is not as effectively blotted out as in the previous group. Though hardly perceived in conscious awareness, a crushing dread of failure lurks around the corner. This dread, though mostly unconscious, works as a power- ful deterrent from putting any abilities to the test of reality. Their pride, in- vested in limitless potentialities, is so brittle that it must be safeguarded by inactivity. As any weak position it requires further defenses. Thus they will often develop a secondary pride in the very fact of *not* working. They feel that they are above competition, above ambition. So they get more entrenched in their inertia. Then a third fortification becomes necessary. Any comparison with others achieving something—particularly others in their own age-group—threatens to demolish the whole lofty structure. So they have to avoid such contacts by withdrawing into an ivory tower.

In both categories mentioned not much of the inner battle between pride and self-contempt appears on the surface. Whether producing in a glib opportunistic fashion or producing in imagination only, the person does not become aware of existing difficulties. These make themselves felt in all those who keep trying to work. Sometimes, then, the individual is obviously pulled and pushed between exacting demands for absolute and immediate perfection on the one hand and destructive self-contempt on the other. A painter, for instance, struck by the beauty of a certain object, visualizes a glorious composition. He starts to paint. The first statement on the canvas looks superb. He feels elated. But it has not yet reached the ultimate perfection of his first vision. He tries to improve. It turns out less good. At this point he gets frantic. He keeps "improving" but the colors become duller and deader. And in no time the picture is destroyed and he gives up in utter despair. After a while he starts another picture, only to go through the same agonizing process. What happens? His own demands for excellence are so inexorable that without knowing it, he turns violently against himself as soon as he is faced with the possibility of not reaching the peak of his expectations. With patient work he might come close to it.

Similarly, a writer may write for a while fluently, carried by visions of greatness. But then he runs up against a difficulty in phrasing, in organizing the material. He gets listless, cannot get himself to work for some days, and in a fit of rage tears the last pages to shreds. Nightmares occur in which he is caught in a room with a maniac who is out to kill him—a pure and simple expression of murderous rage against himself.

Not always is the self-destructiveness so obvious or so violent. More frequently a subtle undermining, berating, doubting saps the energies without the person's being aware of what he is doing to himself. All he notices, then, is a lack of concentration, a restlessness. He becomes fidgety, doodles, plays solitaire, makes some phone calls which could just as well wait, files his fingernails, catches flies. He gets disgusted with himself, makes heroic efforts to work, but in a short time is so deadly fatigued that he has to give up.

It may take quite some analysis to realize that here, too, the person is expecting the impossible and beats himself down if he cannot measure up to it. He expects, for instance, to write a paper without having thought it through previously. He expects one thought to flow out after the other without his having made an outline. He expects the perfect verbal expression of a thought without the thought itself's being clarified in his mind. Inevitably running into difficulties because of such implicit expectations, he does not sit down to think it over—no, he starts to call himself an idiot, a dope, so that the little self-confidence he has sinks below zero. Being consumed with anger at himself, he then actually loses his capacity to think clearly.

The compulsive nature of these processes prevents him from learning from his mistakes, from developing feasible working habits. He may have realized ten or twenty times that it is better to make an outline prior to writing a paper. But his unconscious insistence that he should be able to write without such preparatory work prevents him from acting on his better knowledge.

The more responsibility a work requires, the more personal it is, the more the lack of self-confidence shows in still two other ways. We know that as a result of his divided self-evaluation the neurotic loses sight of his real self. He does not know what he really wants or believes. Hence he cannot or does not dare to make decisions. But in any personal work, decisions have to be made constantly. If I write a paper, for instance, I must decide what I feel to be more important and what less. I must decide what to elaborate and what to leave out. I must decide on the sequence of material presented. I must decide whether a sentence or a paragraph does say what I wanted to express. I must commit myself to a conclusion.

Also, because of the fading out of the real self, the neurotic often does not know or does not dare to know his own feelings. But for any creative work it is essential to be true to one's feelings, to express one's own experiences. No artist can create anything worthwhile with a glass wall between himself and his feelings. It is not only the intellectual sincerity that counts but even more so the emotional sincerity.

Sometimes people feel quite all right except for their inhibitions in work. That can hardly be true, because the factors operating here are bound to operate elsewhere. What it means is that the inhibitions in work disturb them most palpably. This is so for healthy and for neurotic reasons. There is no fulfillment of ourselves without constructive work. And the inhibitions may be a stumbling block in the compulsive search for glory. There is, however, another problem involved. Many neurotics can function fairly well when dealing with people; they can also work with people. But when it comes to doing something on their own, by themselves, they feel utterly lost. There is the anthropological field worker who can be most resourceful in contacting the natives but is utterly lost when it comes to formulating his findings; the social worker who is competent with clients or as supervisor but gets panicky over making a report or an evaluation; the art student who paints fairly well with his teacher around, but forgets all he has learned, when alone. How are we to account for such marked discrepancies? If self-contempt is strong and close to the surface, it has full sway when we are alone. It pulls us down into a feeling of nothingness or of ineffectualness. The others, then, keep us above water. They strengthen us by approval, attention, any kind of response. They may strengthen us even when they are hostile, because their very hostility allows us to thrust outside some of the hostility directed against ourselves.

What detracts further from self-confidence is a berating self-discrediting. A scientist could not get himself to read his own previous publications because through his self-disparaging they were burnt to ashes in his own mind. When he had to read them, he anticipated a humiliating experience and each time was surprised to find them to his liking. A music student is asked whether she works systematically. She becomes embarrassed and answers with an "I don't know." For her, to work systematically means to sit fixed before the piano for eight straight hours, working intently all the time, hardly taking a few minutes off for lunch. Since she cannot give this ultimate of concentrated, sustained attention, she turns against herself, calls herself a dilettante who will never get anywhere. Actually she studies hard at a piece of music, studies the reading, the memorizing, the structure, the fingering, the pedaling, the speed, the move-ments of the right and the left hand—in other words she could have been entirely satisfied with the seriousness of her work.

Genuine Interest

In spite of all difficulties, some neurotic people can feel *genuine interest* in their work. Many detached people, for instance, emotionally isolated from others, can be entirely devoted to the work they are doing. Others may frankly love at least some aspects of their work. These are areas in which they function well *despite* neuroses or *because* they satisfy certain neurotic needs. A neurotic person may transfer his self-glorification to his work and on these grounds develop an almost fanatic faith in its greatness and significance. It would be interesting to examine more accurately the individual constellations allowing for a comparatively free flow of emotions into work.

More frequently, however, such a positive attitude is marred by the neurotic entanglements; his inner conflicts may have led to a general numbness of feelings, which in that case also would include work. He may be so pre-occupied with his difficulties and, therefore, become so egocentric that his capacity to love is badly impaired. His very inhibitions in work may be felt as such a blow to his pride that he withdraws interest or even develops a vindic-tive hatred for his work. Finally the tension and turmoil he feels while working may be so great that he cannot possibly love the work. In the latter case, he often asks himself desperately whether perhaps his whole interest in his field is just pretense. But that is not necessarily so. The very fact of his sticking to it despite pains and panics points to a persistent existing interest. In that case, he will feel free to love his work as soon as he gains a measure of faith in himself.

Most frequently an existing alive interest for a work is deadened by the feeling of doing it under coercion and by the concomitant resentment. This process may be so deeply buried that merely its results show in the form of listlessness, fatigue, exhaustion. Others may at least start to wonder why they behave toward a work they cherish like a schoolboy playing hooky, as if it were a tedious task from which to get away. In many instances the feeling of coercion is fully conscious. It is referred, then, to outside pressures, such as a costumer expecting the delivery of a design, a speech required for a meeting, a publisher expecting a manuscript. Closer examination shows that the expectations of others may exist but do not account for the reaction. The expectation of the others often is the very thing the person himself wants. However minimal or legitimate the expectations are, they arouse a blind defiance and an entirely disproportionate resentment. Existing pressures, such as a deadline to be met, may even be helpful in sweeping aside the inhibitions toward work because they may temporarily silence the inner battle. All of which points to the reason for the hypersensitivity to coercion lying within the person himself. And here he chafes indeed under a merciless tyranny of inner dictates, under the "tyranny of the should" which is born from an unconscious presumptuous drive to be godlike and to attain the impossible. This inner tyranny is so cramping that as a means for escape he dreams of and craves unlimited freedom. This "freedom" is not a constructive freedom *for* but merely a negative freedom *from* all coercion. It entails the mistaken motive that freedom consists in doing whatever you please at any moment. This wish, understandable considering its origin, usually turns into a claim: he is entitled to a life without any pressures, without any necessities. Any expectation from the outside, then, is felt as an unfair imposition and is met not only with anger but with indignation and with an irresistible impulse to frustrate all intents to "enslave," regardless of his own interest in the matter. The blind rebellion is directed not only against persons, institutions, circumstances, but also against any necessity inherent in the process of work. Thus he may start a job or a piece of creative writing with quite some zest but blindly rebel against the necessity to put in disciplined work in order to achieve something. Working, then, against inner resistances makes him listless and unproductive. His love for the work is tainted with distaste.

Besides these general factors there are two specific ones counteracting a genuine interest in work. One of them we find in those people who on account of their self-hatred not only feel unlovable but try to blot out of their lives any hope for love. They feel it too much out of reach and throw all their energies into a pursuit of success. Psychologically they devote their lives to triumphing vindictively over others. These people logically, then, cannot love their work, partly because they cannot and do not want to love anything, partly because work for them is merely a means to an end.

On the opposite extreme are those who conversely tend to recoil from ambitious pursuits because they feel them too much fraught with psychic danger. And while they, too, feel at bottom unlovable, they nevertheless have gone on a frantic search for love, hoping that love would be an overall solution for all their neurotic troubles. Work for them is too closely knitted with vindictive triumph, thus appears as a direct threat to attaining love, and hence is resented. In Freudian literature those two extreme developments are understood as an unconscious decision for masculinity or femininity. But actually they have nothing to do with biology. Culturally the search for love as a solution is favored in women. If love is overemphasized, a vicious circle keeps operating, since with a suppression of the need for triumph usually all aggressive impulses are checked. People of this type feel weak and for this reason doubly need the direct affirmation of themselves through love.

Knowing the conditions for doing productive work, we could almost predict in a neurotic individual the kind of difficulties he is likely to have in his work — provided we are familiar with his character structure. Generally speaking, the conditions being as they are and the neurotic structure being as it is, we must expect to find some difficulties in work in every neurosis. These may loom large and present the main complaint, or they may have not been noticed by the patient — but some of the great range of disturbances will be operating. They — like any other neurotic trouble — cannot be tackled in an isolated fashion. But they will become understandable and disappear to the extent to which the whole personality is straightened out.

Cost of Work Inhibitions

It is difficult to convey the amount of suffering engendered by most of the inhibitions in work. Perhaps only an artist could describe the silent ordeals of those who in their attempt to work run up against intangible but unsurpassable odds, time and time again. I call them silent ordeals because they are often felt as such a disgrace that people do not like to talk about them, even to their best friends. We have said that the neurotic is averse to efforts, that he craves "effortless superiority" — to use a good term coined by Alexander Martin. That is right up to a point. As I mentioned, many neurotics scorn efforts; many of them go to great length to avoid anything resembling real work. But why should they like efforts if these are fraught with torments, and if, in addition, they do not believe they could ever achieve anything? If they were able to make healthy efforts, would they not enjoy them as much as anybody else? Most certainly they would, and as a matter of fact, they do, as soon as an effort is not loaded with self-torture and anxiety.

There are ways, however, to avoid suffering. As indicated before, many neurotics are not even aware of having inhibitions in work. But there is no way to avoid the losses the inhibitions entail. Whether or not they are aware of it, they are prevented from tapping all their resources and, hence, cannot fulfill themselves in an essential area of life. Multiplying the individual loss by the thousands, the inhibitions in work become a loss to mankind. They constitute a waste of human energies and should open everybody's eyes to the necessity of combatting neurosis more seriously than is now being done.

21

The Value of Vindictiveness (1948)

This paper was read before the Association for the Advancement of Psychoanalysis at the New York Academy of Medicine on 24 March 1948 and published in the *American Journal of Psychoanalysis* 8 (1949): 3–12. It was subsequently reprinted in *New Perspectives in Psychoanalysis* (Kelman 1965). As I indicated in my introduction, Horney used parts of the essay in her account of the arrogant-vindictive personality in *Neurosis and Human Growth,* but the essay deals with more than just the arrogant-vindictive personality.

There is a passage in the Bible that has puzzled me for a long time. In his letters to the Romans, Paul says: "Avenge not thyself; vengeance is mine, says the Lord, I will repay." We understand that God will repay and does repay, indeed. In terms of psychological laws: the consequences of our pretenses, our egocentricity, or whatever faulty attitude, invariably come home to roost. Contrary to neurotic expectations, we do not "get by" with the wrong solutions of our inner conflicts. But why the explicit warnings against revenge? Is it another way of asking us to offer the other cheek? No, we can hardly discard it that easily. We feel a deeper wisdom in it that is important for all our lives.

Another question arises: Does it not mean asking the impossible? Are not impulses to get back for injuries done universal? Are they not even culturally sanctioned in many civilizations? In Japan, for instance, elaborate rules exist for restoring injured pride by retaliatory measures.[1] But there is another way of looking at such institutions. While they implicitly acknowledge the general existence of needs to retaliate, they also take these needs psychologically out of the hands of an individual by rendering them a civic duty. In this sense, they rather confirm the principle expressed in the Bible.

And finally: Does it not clear the air if we express a vindictive anger? Do we not thereby forestall the danger of piling up resentment? Is it not, on the contrary, harmful to repress such impulses? Have we not all heard of the beneficial effect in therapy of "liberating aggressiveness?" Sure enough, to repress vindictiveness is harmful. But is there only the alternative between repression and acting out? When we agree on the desirability of becoming aware of whatever vindictive drives are operating, would we not ask: Desirable for what end? Is it not for the chance to take a turn toward the constructive? Furthermore, questions like these are unprofitable because they leave out a distinction which leads us to the core of the problem. Two people, A and B, both give a sharp answer to an unfair attack in a discussion. But with A it is a rational anger, proportionate to the provocation, that flares up and subsides with its expression. He also could have controlled it, but in the particular situation he preferred to express it. With B it might be the expression of a vindictiveness that pervades his whole personality. Considering this latter possibility gives us an understanding for the warning in the Bible.

In neuroses, vindictiveness can become a character trait; it can amount to a vindictive attitude toward life; it can become a way of life.[2] It can be as strongly compulsive as, for instance, the neurotic need for affection.[3]

In this paper I want to contribute to a more complete understanding of neurotic vindictiveness, its components, its sources, and its functions.

Aims of Vindictiveness

Most expressions of vindictiveness have been described, by others and by myself, as sadistic trends. The term "sadistic" focuses on the satisfaction to

---

1. Ruth Benedict, *The Chrysanthemum and the Sword,* 1946.

2. Harold Kelman spoke of a vindictive way of life in reference to traumatic neuroses in his paper, "The Traumatic Syndrome," *Am. J. Psychoanal.* Vol. VI, 1946.

3. Cf. Muriel Ivimey, "Compulsive Assaultiveness," summarized in *Am. J. Psychoanal.* Vol. VII, 1947.

be gained from the power to subject others to pain or indignity. Satisfaction — excitement, thrill, glee — undoubtedly, can be present in sexual and nonsexual situations; and for these the term "sadistic" seems to be sufficiently meaningful. My suggestion to replace the term "sadistic," in its general use, by "vindictive" is based on the contention that for all so-called sadistic trends vindictive needs are the crucial motivating force.

The aims of vindictive trends in neuroses are as manifold as the possibilities to hurt or injure others. To simplify for the sake of an easier orientation, we may, roughly, divide them into three groups:

To humiliate: to expose to ridicule; to cause feelings of guilt and inferiority; to make a person dependent and subservient; to defeat and to triumph over the defeated offender.

To exploit: to make use of others as a means to an end; to subject them to insatiable demands; to outwit.

To frustrate: to kill joy; to tease and disappoint; to ignore the wishes, desires, needs, hopes, ambitions of others.

A person may be fully aware of the fact that individual impulses or actions are vindictive. These conscious impulses, or actions, however, are experienced as just punishment, as perfectly rational responses to injury done. But I have not yet seen a neurotic person who is aware of the pervasive vindictiveness ingrained in his personality, or of its compulsive nature, although this characteristic may be blatantly obvious to an outsider. The untrained observer sometimes finds it hard to believe that the vindictive person is unaware of what he perpetrates on others. It is a fact, however, that even in these instances of seemingly uninhibited vindictiveness it may take long analytical work until in this particular instance, as well as in others, he is ready to face himself as he really is, instead of seeing himself as he feels he should be.

Forms of Vindictiveness

The ways in which vindictive aims are attained vary within a wide range. Roughly, we can distinguish an openly aggressive, a self-effacing, and a detached vindictiveness. We would be inclined to correlate these different forms to the original basic neurotic attitudes a child may assume toward others, to a moving toward, against, or away from people. Such a correlation, however, is approximately correct only if we include all the sources from which the basic attitudes are reinforced in the later development.

Openly aggressive vindictiveness looks uninhibited in action. The person may aggressively strike out at others. He is openly exploiting. He is usually proud of this capacity, although, as mentioned, he does not experience the vindictive character of these actions. He may feel that he is simply more honest and straight than the others, that he merely is doling out justice, that his dignity refuses to be insulted with impunity.

Self-effacing vindictiveness operates subversively and indirectly. Suffering is used unconsciously to make others feel guilty. Emphasis on needs, suffering, appeal to pity, and sacrifices serve as unconscious bases on which to make demands. The person himself puts less stress on justice than the aggressive type, but rather experiences himself as a particularly good person who is constantly abused by the others. The vindictiveness in this instance is by no means less great or less effective, but it evokes the puzzling impression of being done at the person's own expense.

Detached vindictiveness is the least dramatic of all. If I may say so, the sins are of omission rather than commission. Quietly but effectively, the detached person may frustrate others by not listening, by disregarding their needs, by forgetting their wishes, by making them feel like disturbing intruders, by withholding praise or affection, by withdrawing psychically or physically.

Vindictiveness Is Compulsive

After these preliminary remarks, we now proceed to raise some questions which in the end may lead to a better understanding. My first contention is that mere vindictiveness is compulsive. Therefore my first question is: How does the compulsive character of these trends show?

To begin with, the irresistible urge to get back at others is frequently open to direct observation in and outside the analytic situation. Often there is no more holding back a person driven toward revenge than an alcoholic determined to go on a binge. Any reasoning meets with cold disdain. Logic no longer prevails. Whether or not the situation is appropriate does not matter. It overrides prudence. Consequences for himself and others are brushed aside. He is as inaccessible as anybody who is in the grip of a blind passion. One of the best illustrations in literature is in Stendhal's *The Red and the Black* in Julien's frantic rushing to shoot Mme. de Rênal after having seen the denunciations which a priest forced her to write. We can most frequently observe the blind vindictive passion in instances of morbid jealousy which is mainly determined by hurt pride. Though the husband's interest in another woman may be a matter of the past, though it may merely consist in insignificant attentions, a wife may torment him and keep tormenting him in such a blind fury—sometimes against her own better judgment—that she may seriously jeopardize the whole marriage.

But we can observe the compulsive drive toward revenge not only in acute situations. This drive can be the governing passion of a lifetime to which everything is subordinated, including self-interest. All intelligence, all energies, then, are dedicated to the one goal of vindictive triumph. Great writers know about this phenomenon and have presented it in more impressive forms than a psychiatrist can hope to do. I am thinking, for instance, of *Hamlet*, *Moby Dick*, Heathcliff in *Wuthering Heights*. We see it in patients who, too inhibited to carry out revenge, seem to live for the "day of reckoning." This seems to be the flame sustaining their lives. It may originally be attached to one of the parents but may, later on, be one of the determining factors in every relationship that is of long duration, including the one with the analyst.

The compulsive character of the vindictive drives shows in their overriding prudence, happiness, ambition, and even life itself. The enigma of the self-effacing revenge begins to clear up, because also in aggressive vindictiveness the expenses to self count for little if anything.

Conversely, if a neurotic is prevented from getting back, he may become sleepless, irritable, fatigued, depressed. He may have headaches, stomach upsets, and so forth. These effects occur regardless of the reason for his not retaliating. The situation may have been prohibitive. Or inhibitions may have delayed or frustrated vindictive measures.

Sometimes the connection between frustrated revenge and symptomatic disorders is transparent. One patient was quite aware that his relapse of stomach upsets dated from his incapacity to get back at a porter who treated him with disregard. If fantasies could kill, this porter would have died twenty deaths. Sometimes the reaction is delayed. The "insult" has not been experienced as such; vindictive impulses, hence, remain under cover. But the person is irritable, wakes up in the middle of the night with a full-fledged rage at the insulter as well as at himself for, as it were, having slept on the all-important job of defending his pride by counterattack.

Among the inhibitions befogging the issue, two are outstanding. One is the pride in enduring something with equanimity, which prevents hurts from being consciously felt. The other one consists in numerous inner taboos on vindictiveness, such as an idealized image of absolute goodness, fairness, broadmindedness, rationality. The patient, then, cannot see the connection between frustrated revenge and his disturbed condition before these factors have been worked through.

A third observation pointing to the compulsive force behind vindictiveness is the so-called negative therapeutic reaction.[4] Briefly they are acute impairments of conditions occurring after a constructive move ahead. This may be a

4. Cf. Sigmund Freud, *The Ego and the Id*, 1927. Karen Horney, "The Problem of the Negative Therapeutic Reaction," *Psychoanal. Quart.* 5 (1), (1936). Muriel Ivimey, "Negative Therapeutic Reaction," *Am. J. Psychoanal.* 8 (1948).

realization of some important unconscious factors, it may be a stirring of friendliness, sympathy, or gratitude; a helpful deed; any turning toward life such as a greater enjoyment of things. The impairment may consist in a resurgence of symptoms, in sudden spells of despair and discouragement, in panic, or simply in a renewed upsurge of vindictiveness. The reasons for such negative reactions are complex. But we must always consider that any forward move the patient makes threatens to undermine his vindictive structure.

The negative therapeutic reaction, however, is but the peak of defensive battle carried on throughout analysis. Only the smallest part of this defense is explicit and direct. The patient may, then, declare frankly that he is determined not to relinquish his vindictiveness. "You won't take that away from me; you want to make me a goody-goody; it gives me a thrill; it makes me feel alive; it is strength." Most of the battle is subversive. And it is of the greatest clinical importance for the analyst to know the forms it may assume because it may not only delay the analytic process but wreck it altogether. It can do so in two main ways. It can greatly influence, if not govern, the analytic relationship. To defeat the analyst, then, may seem more important than a cure. And, what is less well known, it can determine the interest in problems to be tackled. Speaking again of extreme instances, the patient is interested in everything that might, in the end, make for a bigger and better vindictiveness — for a vindictiveness that at the same time would be more effective and be carried out without expense to himself, with superior poise and serenity. This selective process is not done by conscious reasoning but by dint of an intuitive sense of direction which operates with the unfailing certainty of a sixth sense. He is, for instance, keenly interested in removing compliant trends, or his feeling of having no rights; he is interested in getting over his self-hate because it weakens him in the battle against the world. On the other hand, he is uninterested in diminishing his arrogant claims, or his feeling abused by others. He may hold on with curious tenacity to his externalizations showing others to be the offenders. He may be unwilling, indeed, to analyze his human relations altogether, emphasizing that all he wants in this regard is not to be bothered. The whole analysis, then, may easily confuse the analyst until he grasps the formidable logic of the selective process.

The Uses of Vindictiveness

What, then, accounts for the compelling nature of vindictiveness?

In trying to answer this question, our natural propensity would be to deem it identical with another question: What is it that renders the hostility thus relentless? I call it a natural propensity because the hostility involved strikes the eye. But it is just the merging of these two questions that has blurred the issue for a long time. For instance, it has led Freud to the contention of a destructive instinct. Of course, anybody tackling the problem of vindictiveness has to scrutinize the magnitude of the hostility and its sources. But even so it would leave us with the problem: Why has this hostility such a sway over a person? Why is it so precious to him that he defends it with every fiber of his being?

In order to find a more satisfactory understanding we must raise the following questions:

What are the sources of hostility?

What are the positive functions of vindictiveness?

Which alternative roads can a person take?

What is the general mentality of a person in the clutches of vindictiveness?

The three main sources of *hostile retaliatory impulses* are: hurt pride, externalization of self-hate, and *Lebensneid*. I can be brief about them because I have dealt with this topic in other publications and lectures. Neurotic pride is an exalted self-esteem that is built not upon existing assets but upon an imaginary superiority. The more a person's whole being has come to rest on such pride, the more vulnerable is he actually, no matter how much he tries to hide this fact from himself by putting on a proud mask of invulnerability. He feels, then, easily humiliated and reacts to it with vindictive impulses. These, in turn, may be repressed so that mere flickers of irritability appear in awareness. But he may feel so deeply humiliated by so many things that he actually harbors within himself, without knowing it, a seething cauldron of vindictive fury. Any frustration of his fantastic claims, anything that he feels as a lack of appreciation or deference, any difference of opinion, any comparison with others that is not in his favor, any request made, any expression of sympathy for him — an endless chain of humiliations — may provide ever-new fuel for vindictiveness.

Externalization of self-hate means experiencing all intrapsychic destructive attitudes and intents as emanating from others. Others hate me, despise me, accuse me unfairly, drag me down, frustrate me, in short, prevent me from living. If life is experienced this way, it is but logical that a person acquires a desperate vindictive attitude toward others.

Despite the feelings of abuse stemming from pride and externalization of self-hate, both attitudes are tenaciously adhered to, or, as it were, unconsciously cultivated, because the vindictiveness, once established, calls for justifications. For a long time, many patients, while giving lip service to the irrationality of their hostility, keep pointing out the good reasons they have to be angry. A vicious circle, then, operates, and the reasons for anger become a position to be defended vigorously.

The intensity of hostility can be reinforced from a deeper source, the patient's hopelessness about his life. We will understand it better when we consider the general mental background of vindictiveness. Only this much here: hopelessness need not necessarily lead to a vindictive attitude toward life. It can also lead to resignation, and may, then, reversely dampen and actually diminish vindictive stirrings. But for reasons which to expound here would lead too far astray, it often does generate a vindictive hostility. It can do so in two different ways. One is the vindictive envy, stemming from feeling excluded. Through his entanglements the neurotic may be actually excluded from everything that makes life worth living: from joy, happiness, love, creativeness, growth. The constructive way to react to such a calamity would be to examine his own handicaps. As long as this avenue is closed to him, he may respond with unreasoning claims. He feels, then, mostly unconsciously, that he would be entitled to a better life, that it is unfair that the good things are not coming to him. Everybody else, he feels in his bitterness, is better off than he. And why should they be? It hurts his pride. They humiliate him by flaunting their happiness in his face. Experiencing things this way not only gives rise to such a vindictive impulse as wanting to kill their joy but may produce a curious kind of callousness by choking his sympathy for their suffering. Ibsen's Hedda Gabler is a good illustration for such vindictive callousness.

The other way in which hopelessness may feed vindictive hostility is in the blaming of others for failure and misery. The premise is the same as for envy: an incapacity to shoulder responsibility for whatever shortcomings have developed. "They" have ruined me beyond repair. If I go to pieces, it is "their" fault. They should feel guilty for it, or pay for it, this or that way. "They" refers originally to the parents. But as long as the inner condition remains the same, it may be experienced likewise in reference to teachers, physicians, marriage partners, business associates, society, life circumstances. Here, too, a vicious circle is operating. While this attitude stems from an inability to make constructive efforts in one's own behalf, it also, in turn, further paralyzes such efforts, because the energies thus become focused in a way destructive for self. More than that: it is most tempting, then, to remain an invalid, because with his improvement he would lose the bill to be presented.

We now shall discuss the second question: What are the *positive functions of vindictiveness?* Or: What, in the framework of neurosis, are its subjective values? Which inner needs does it fulfill? Which are the inner premises on the grounds of which vindictiveness appears not only right but also necessary and desirable?

In the first place vindictiveness serves as *self-protection* against the hostility from without, as well as against the hostility from within. A few comments may suffice to help understand the inner necessity for such self-protective measures. The basic anxiety is considerably reinforced in a neurotic development leading to compulsive vindictiveness. As such a person experiences it, the others are not only potentially but factually hostile. He harbors an ironclad conviction, which may or may not be conscious, that "they" are not to be trusted, that friendliness is merely a deceptive maneuver, that they are out to exploit or humiliate him, to cut his throat, to clip his wings, to drag him down. He would be a fool, thus, not to be on his guard, not to muster his energies for a defensive warfare. He must be always prepared to strike back. Or, since he must be either hammer or anvil, he feels it safer to anticipate the attack and strike out first. If such an attitude is or has become fairly conscious, he may defend it as "self-interest." Actually he has at such a period not the remotest real interest in himself. The self-interest he is talking about is merely a defensive one. And this latter must appear to him not only important but utterly "realistic." Any slackening of his suspicious vigilance would be pure foolishness.

When speaking of the sources of vindictive hostility, I mentioned the externalization of self-hate. Going a step deeper at this point, we arrive at an even more stringent need for self-protection. Vindictiveness against others is a safety valve, protecting a person against his self-destructiveness. I cannot discuss here the psychology of self-hate. Though my concept differs from Freud's theory of the death instinct, both not only acknowledge the existence of the self-destructive forces, but agree in the estimate of their intensity. Self-condemnation, self-deprivation, self-contempt, self-tormenting can reach such formidable proportions that they constitute a real danger for the individual. They may actually ruin every vestige of inner freedom and happiness, even if they do not lead to physical self-destruction. If a person, therefore, experiences all the harm he is inflicting upon himself as coming from others and then responds vindictively toward them, he thereby intuitively protects himself. The connection between self-hate and vindictiveness often comes into relief during analysis. Accusations against others . . . realization of their being unwarranted . . . violent self-destructive impulses — these moves may appear in clear sequence. An error in judgment or a plain lie being exposed may be followed by a vindictive outburst against the person who has "viciously" exposed him. Conversely, a spell of vindictiveness will often evaporate if the underlying condemnatory self-accusations are brought to awareness.

A second important function of vindictiveness is *to restore injured pride.* In the last analysis, this, too, is a self-protective function. For the neurotic individual, pride is not just an adornment shining in more or less bright colors; it is a life force sustaining him. And if it becomes injured gravely, he may collapse psychically. By getting back at the offender, he averts this very danger. This process is all the more compelling, the more his estimate of self is dependent upon others. An episode in Somerset Maugham's *Of Human Bondage* may serve as an illustration. Philip's pride is hurt by the insulting behavior of the waitress, Mildred. He feels driven to return to her in order to put her in her place. But he is defeated by her disinterested aloofness. At this point his pride is broken and the miserable dependency on Mildred starts. He becomes self-effacing and makes endless futile sacrifices for her, knowing full well that she is not worth his efforts. True enough, Philip's reaction is extreme, but it would be erroneous to discard its general validity for this very reason. What happened to Philip is in essence the lurking danger which the neurotic person senses if he fails to vindicate himself by a vindictive action.

Because the power to take revenge, then, acquires such vital importance, it is, in turn, invested with pride. Of course, the neurotic will mostly not say outright that he is proud of his vindictiveness. He will glorify it in some way or other. He is proud, for instance, of being "frank," of "asserting himself," of being "above common prejudice and hypocrisy," of being "just," "fearless," or — to refer again to Stendhal's character, Julien — of feeling "duty bound to his pride." When Julien says that his life is determined by duty, he refers mainly to the duty of never allowing anybody "to insult him with impunity." This glorification of vindictiveness is one of the factors contributing to a transformation of moral values. All that pertains to vindictiveness is honest, strong, realistic, while on the other hand many reasons combine to turn friendliness into hypocrisy, or generosity into being a "sucker." Particularly as long as such reversal of moral values is not out in the open, analyst and patient may easily pull on opposite ends of a rope or, as it were, talk a different language.

The functions of vindictiveness so far discussed are defensive in nature. They alone would account sufficiently for the compulsive character. We see here the same principle at work as everywhere in neurosis. Every compulsive phenomenon, in the last analysis, is determined by an underlying anxiety and the need for safety in the face of it. But these functions do not account for another element which so often is present in vindictive impulses, fantasies, or actions: the excitement, the thrill, the passion. We feel it compelling for the sake of safety to buy insurance or to obey traffic regulations, but to do so is by no means thrilling. This quality of excitement, of passion, stems from the hope for or the sensation of a *vindictive triumph*.

The need for a vindictive triumph stems from many sources. There is mostly an early history of having suffered thoughtless or openly cruel humiliations. There are later experiences felt as humiliations on account of neurotic pride.

All of these, consciously or unconsciously, make a person long for an ultimate triumph over his offenders. Together with his hopelessness in regard to a constructive development of his own life, triumph may become the only goal worth striving for. It may take fairly benign forms, where every trace of vengeance is eradicated from the conscious mind. There are Cinderella's dreams of the Prince Charming who will single her out. Mother, sister, or companions, then, will realize how blind they have been toward her superior beauty and goodness. But she will not bear any grudge and in the bigness of her generous heart [will] become their benefactress. This "I'll show you" and the wish to vindicate oneself in the spirit of defiant triumph can be the determining force in any drive for success, prestige, or sexual conquest. Finally the need for triumph is an integral part of all the vindictive drives mentioned before. To have power, to humiliate, to exploit, to frustrate, essentially means triumph.

The fascination that the prospect of triumph may hold for a person rests in two factors. Feeling mostly excluded, unwanted, disregarded, abused, frustrated while—in his imagination—being entitled to all the earth's glory, he must deem it most desirable or gratifying to reverse the roles. Perhaps nothing short of triumph can restore his boundless pride. In addition, the emotional experience itself—elation, thrill—is immeasurably precious to him, because it often constitutes one of the rare alive feelings he is capable of having. The excitement Hedda Gabler feels when destroying vindictively the irreplaceable manuscript is the only oasis of life in the midst of a desert of boredom. So, when the neurotic person defends his vindictiveness in pointing out its emotional value, he makes a correct statement of facts. It harbors, though, the germ of its own deterioration, because being addicted to chasing the phantom of triumph means being caught in a vicious circle. New and sharper stimuli are necessary to arouse him. Also, the very pursuit of triumph is bound to choke off his springs of life—a process that goes on insidiously and imperceptibly until after years he wakes up to the fact of his emotional deadness and starts to be puzzled by it. If, in every pursuit—love, sex, relation to children, social matters, work—the driving force is the prospect of triumph, then the activity or the relation itself becomes a mere means to an end. Then he can no longer enjoy his children or their growth. His interest in them narrows down to the one question whether or not they serve his ambition. He no longer cultivates his home or his garden for their own sake but for the sake of showing off. If he writes a paper, his interest in the subject matter evaporates as soon as he is blindfolded by the possible success of the end product. He loses the genuine pride in craftsmanship, the simple joy of being with a friend, the stimulating effect of an exchange of opinion in a discussion—in short his genuine interest

the patient's mind. He may know people who seem strong without being vindictive, but they are too far removed from his own world to puzzle him seriously. When it finally does dawn on him that there is a constructive way out, his reactions are mixed. He would like to have all the benefits accruing from becoming constructive: the peace of mind, the inner freedom, the emotional aliveness. But the road toward these goods does not seem at all appealing. To begin with: it would entail much work—work at his pride, at his externalizations, at all the factors entailed in his human relations. But if need be, he would do the work if it were not for one deterring factor. Taking this road would mean—heaven forbid—his becoming more human. It would mean giving up his isolated grandeur, his uniqueness, and becoming an ordinary human being like everybody else without any special privileges; becoming part of the swarming mass of humanity he so despises. To have limitations, to feel sorrow, tolerance, sympathy, and last but not least to assume responsibility not in the grand style of playing providence for others, but, to start with, just for his own life—all of this seems like a distasteful comedown. And it does take quite some reorientation until he can reverse his values and until just this "becoming human" will feel like the most desirable goal toward which to strive. Until that time the healthy alternative, too, is a danger to guard against and thereby rather adds to the rigid holding on to vindictiveness.

Therapy

While surveying all the factors contributing to the compulsive nature of vindictiveness, we realize that we cannot tackle or change it directly. It is the ultimate outcome of many conditions. As long as they persist, a person is bound to be vindictive. It would then be a symptom—a character symptom—indicating hidden disorder. This is one way of looking at it; but it does not do justice to its dynamics, because vindictiveness also keeps the more hidden disorders going. A simple mental experiment will elucidate the meaning of this statement. Think of a neurotic individual of the type described and then imagine him stripped of every trace of vindictiveness, including also the hope for triumph, but leave unaltered his hostility, his pride, his externalizations. His hopelessness and his inner tensions would mount to such an unbearable degree that he would collapse. In this sense we can well regard vindictiveness as a *neurotic solution*. It is a way of life that allows for a measure of balance, safety, and satisfaction while keeping intact his neurosis. This is the overall formulation for the functions of vindictiveness, for the reasons why the neurotic person adheres to it as for dear life. Conversely, in therapy it constitutes a retarding force of prime order. As long as he clings to this solution, the patient is neither willing to nor capable of going after his disturbances in a constructive way.

In general terms the difficulties which a vindictive attitude toward life presents in *therapy* are of three kinds. As in any other major neurotic solution, one of them resides in its subjective values. The greater these are, the more intense his resistance to constructive insight and change. In addition, the constructive forces themselves are weakened—the more so, the more pervasive the vindictiveness. To compare it with cancer eating up healthy tissues would be correct for extreme cases only. We must realize, however, that the more energies are consumed by the vindictive drives or by the necessity to control them, the more undernourished are the constructive forces. And it is with these latter ones we work in therapy.

A third difficulty comes not from the vindictiveness itself but from the *general mentality* which is its background. Its main feature is a strong alienation from self. Though always a severe problem, it would hardly deserve special mention because of its ubiquity in more severe neurosis, if it were not for certain specific factors. Being hostile and interested in accusing others, the patient must make his own position unassailable. He believes he needs every ounce of energy for the battle without and, hence, cannot jeopardize it by admitting either fault or weakness. Unfortunately, this strategical necessity often compels him to take a further step which is not even to *feel* either weak or wrong. We shall stop here for a while to realize the grave implications this has for his inner life. It means that he automatically tries to stifle all inner experiences that arouse any doubt in these two regards. It leaves but few feelings he can own. The inner necessity never to be wrong would mean not only to deny errors but to disown anything in himself that is irrational, contradictory, or compulsive. The resulting self-righteousness, then, is not so much a matter of vanity but of self-preservation, reasonable on his premises.

The necessity never to feel weak may involve the whole range of positive feelings toward others or toward life as such: tenderness, affection, sympathy, love, gratitude, joy, enthusiasm. What is left, often, is merely righteous indignation, anger, and highly distilled aesthetic feelings. Sometimes feelings for animals go scot-free. Here is the deepest source of the emptiness, the boredom, and the hopelessness we previously mentioned. The extent of disowning feelings accounts for the fact that in people whose neurotic development heads toward vindictiveness, alienation from self is greater than in other neurotic structures. The *cogito ergo sum,* though a correct logical inference, seems psychologically misleading. It is not primarily thinking and reasoning that gives us the sensation of "I," but feeling. From the vantage point of this background, we can more fully appreciate several aspects of neurotic vindictiveness. I mention but two of them. One is the egocentric callousness, resulting from the stifling of positive feelings. Outright cruelty toward others — in imagination or action — does not allow for a direct conclusion of a corresponding magnitude of hostility prompting it. Nor is it always determined by a sadistic satisfaction in the suffering of others. To put it differently: It is not correct to say that though a sadistic satisfaction is not observable, it must always operate. A considerable part of the cruelty may stem from eliminating [one's recognition of] the other fellow as a feeling human being. We would not feel our stepping on an ant as an act of cruelty.

The vindictive person thus is egocentric not because he has so many naive wishes for himself which he considers all-important, but because he has more or less severed his emotional relations to other human beings. On the other hand, because of his inner emptiness, he does not feel that anything originates in himself. He does not, for instance, experience a wish to be with others — he merely yields to outside pressure. Any work he starts soon imperceptibly turns into a coercion. The analysis he does is no longer his analysis but entirely the interest, business, and responsibility of the "expert." He may go to analysis as he would go to a dentist to have a tooth pulled. Even his getting better is not his experience; some magic trick of the analyst has done it. An anxiety dream does not emerge from his own depth but is "somehow" conjured up by the analyst.

Perhaps the best way to describe this condition is to call it an emotional paralysis. It is the ultimate basis for the tenacity of externalizations which we have pointed out. The patient may have seen in many instances that he feels others look down on him, while, in reality, it is he who despises himself. He may have discovered that he feels others interfere with his work, while it is his own inhibition — and so on and so forth. He will learn to catch on to an externalization and to correct it intellectually. But such correction can be only superficial, as long as he actually does not experience what is going on within himself.

Summary

To summarize some of the points made in this paper from the vantage point of therapy: Its main contention is that neurotic vindictiveness is an exquisitely compulsive phenomenon. The very grasp of this simple fact has a direct bearing on therapy. It will keep the analyst from being overimpressed by the patient's hostility. He will know that among the factors accounting for the compulsion, hostility and the need to discharge it — revenge pure and simple —

play a part but not the most important one. He will rather take it for granted that for the time being the patient cannot react but with animosity. His attitude toward the patient thus will be noticeably fairer than that of the patient's environment. The focus of his attention will be to penetrate through the shell of defensive hostility to the functions of vindictiveness and to the underlying structure which makes these functions necessary.

In addition, it helps the patient to recognize the compulsive character of vindictiveness. Such realization does not in any way diminish this quality. But it does diminish the secret pride in vindictiveness, if the patient sees himself driven instead of being the proud driver. It elicits thereby some incentive to tackle the whole problem. This incentive, to be sure, is still mostly on a neurotic basis, but we want to mobilize whatever is available, considering that the essential motivation for change, the constructive self-interest, is almost lacking at the beginning.

Another way to awaken an incentive for analytic work on the self, here as in other problems, is the sharp focus on the adverse consequences vindictiveness has for the person himself. This is particularly important in those cases in which the vindictiveness itself is glorified and healthy goals are scorned. In this paper we have not specifically elaborated on the consequences but merely mentioned them whenever it was necessary for the understanding of the whole process. In the simplest terms the vindictive person inflicts suffering not only on others but even more so on himself. His vindictiveness makes him isolated and egocentric, absorbs his energies, makes him psychically sterile, and, above all, closes the gate to his further growth.

This finally brings me back to the beginning, to the warning against revenge expressed in the Bible. The more we understand of neurotic vindictiveness, the more this warning reveals its profound wisdom. The self-effacing — "masochistic" — vindictiveness is merely more obviously at the person's own expense. Every vindictiveness damages the core of the whole being. Repressing it makes it worse. Not "liberating vindictive aggression," but overcoming it, is our therapeutic goal.

22

On Feeling Abused (1951)

Horney read this paper before the Association for the Advancement of Psychoanalysis at the New York Academy of Medicine on 28 February 1951. It was published in the *American Journal of Psychoanalysis* 11 (1951): 5–12, and subsequently reprinted in *Advances in Psychoanalysis,* edited by Harold Kelman (1964). The essay reflects Horney's clinical preoccupations at the time (see Horney 1999).

When speaking of feeling abused, I refer to a neurotic phenomenon which is well known to psychoanalysts in all its multiple facets. Patients may dwell on the harm done to them by previous psychotherapists, by other physicians, by their boss, wife, or friends, and, going all the way back, by their parents. In more diffuse ways, they may also feel themselves to be victims of social institutions, or of fate in general.

The particular content of such complaints varies infinitely. The emphasis may be on the general iniquity of fate. The patient may be convinced, then, that everybody is better off than he. Others find a better job, get a raise in salary; their clocks always keep the correct time, their cars never need repairs, their sorrows are negligible. More specifically, the emphasis may be on injustice done to him. He, the patient, has been cooperative, efficient, helpful, understanding; he has, in fact, done more than his share. But he got an unfair deal. The others failed to be grateful, to help him, to consider him, or even to show a minimum of decency. The emphasis may be on others' criticizing and accusing him, imputing motivations that were quite alien to him. He may feel exploited and imposed upon. Everybody seems to want something from him, or, indeed, to expect the impossible of him and to make him feel guilty if he does not measure up to expectations. The emphasis may be on being frustrated by others: "They" frustrate him; they keep him down; they squelch every joy he may have; they put every possible obstacle in the way of his achievements, or of his career. They begrudge every advantage he has, or every step ahead he takes. They humiliate him, slight him, despise him, disregard him. They betray and deceive him. There are but fine transitions from this state to that of the paranoid psychotic who feels spied upon, imperiled, persecuted, or ruined beyond repair.

As the neurotic patient gradually reveals these experiences, we are struck not so much by their kind, but by their frequency and intensity. We all not only *may have,* but in fact *have had* similar experiences. We all have been used as a means to an end. We have been deceived or disappointed. We have without exception had unfortunate human experiences in our early childhood which were painful and have left their traces. In other words, such experiences seem to belong to the human suffering we must bear and accept. And they may help us to become more discerning and more tolerant and to develop more compassion for the suffering of others.

The more entangled in unsolved inner conflicts a person is, the more do these experiences change in quantity and quality. Generally speaking, the main difference is one between external provocation (factual affronts, offenses, and so on) and emotional responses. To begin with, the neurotic person himself often elicits inconsiderate or offensive treatment by his behavior without being aware of it. He may be so compulsively compliant, helpful, and appeasing that he inadvertently invites others to run all over him. He may alienate others by his irritability and arrogance, but, being unaware of his provocative behavior, he may experience only that they reject or slight him in an entirely undeserved manner. This factor alone renders the frequency of factual abuse greater than for the relatively healthy person.

Disproportionate Responses

Furthermore, the patient's emotional responses to factual trespasses or mishaps are quite out of proportion. Because of his irrational claims, his demands on himself, his neurotic pride, his self-contempt, and his self-accusations, he is so diffusely vulnerable that he is bound to feel hurt more often and more deeply. Minor occurrences, such as requests made of him, friends not accepting his invitation, disagreements with his wishes or opinions, are experienced as major tragedies.

Finally, even when there is no particular provocation from the outside, even with his knowing full well that his life situation is a favorable one, he nevertheless may feel abused. He will, then, in subtle and gross ways — unconsciously — distort the actual conditions and give them in his mind a little twist, so that he appears as the victim, after all. This observation indicates that feeling abused is not only a patient's subjective response to existing difficulties in life. It is, in addition, prompted by some inner necessity which irresistibly *pulls* him to experience life the way he does.

The sum total of these factors often makes for a diffuse feeling of abuse. When speaking thus of feeling abused, I mean a person's rather pervasive experience of being the victim — a feeling which in its extent and intensity goes beyond, and is out of proportion to, actual provocations and may become a way of experiencing life.

All these various feelings of being unfairly treated stem from different sources within the individual and must be traced individually. For instance, a neurotic person so easily feels accused by the analyst, or someone else, because he is constantly accusing himself without knowing it; or, at any rate, without knowing the extent and intensity of his self-accusations. Or he feels easily slighted because his insatiable need for recognition lets anything short of unequivocal agreement or admiration appear to be a slight. He feels coerced so easily by others because he is so little aware of his own wishes or opinions and is relentlessly driven by his own demands on himself. All these individual connections must be traced and worked through in analytical therapy. But it is also important to see the totality of the picture because only by so doing — as we shall see presently — can we recognize the general background of feeling abused or victimized. This is the reason why I shall neglect the individual sources in this paper, and why I lump together under the heading of "Feeling Abused" all experiences of the kind mentioned so far.

Unawareness of Feeling Abused

The *awareness* of feeling abused varies, which in itself is a rather astonishing fact. Whatever the conditions, reasons, and functions for feeling abused may be, it always has the one function of making others, or circumstances, responsible for what is wrong in one's own life. This would entail an unconscious interest in emphasizing the fact of being abused and lead us to expect that the experience as such would always be conscious. This, however, is not generally true, because a person may also have strong reasons for not being aware of it. The following three main reasons may militate against awareness.

Since feeling abused always breeds resentment, a person may be afraid of experiencing this resentment and its disrupting effect on human relations and may therefore tend to keep it from awareness. Thus, the unconscious interest in these instances lies not in suppressing the experience of being abused as such, but in removing reasons for resentment.

In other instances, a pride in invulnerability and in inviolability leads people to suppress the experience. Nothing should happen — and therefore does not happen — that is not initiated by them, or under their control.

A third reason lies in the pride in endurance. They should be so strong — and therefore they *are* so strong — that nothing and nobody can hurt them. They should be able to put up with everything. They should have the unruffled serenity of a Buddha. Conversely, the very feeling of being hurt, injured, humiliated, rejected is a blow to their pride and, hence, tends to be suppressed.

Variations in Attitudes

The attitudes toward feeling abused, or the emotional responses to such feeling, also vary. People with predominantly self-effacing trends tend to suppress the resulting resentment and develop a more or less concealed pride in suffering under a world which is morally inferior to them. Predominantly aggressive and expansive people, while not owning up to hurt feelings, tend to respond with plain anger, moral indignation, and vindictiveness. The predominantly resigned person tends to assume a philosophical, detached attitude toward it. He takes it for granted that people are not to be trusted and withdraws from them.

Notwithstanding these variations in awareness and response, feeling abused has in itself some characteristics which are always present: The abuse is felt as real.

It goes with a feeling of being not only the victim, but the innocent victim.

It entails the feeling of, "It happens to me."

It feels real: People *are* unfair, ungrateful, condemnatory, demanding, deceitful, and therefore the patient's feeling abused is an entirely rational response. He will dwell on those situations in which realistic harm was done to him, whether in childhood or later on. He tends to maintain this attitude even though he may have recognized in many individual incidents that the vulnerability of his own pride or the externalization of his self-abuse were the incisive factors in bringing about his feeling abused by others. But such isolated insights do little to undermine the whole phenomenon. They still leave him with the feeling that by and large he *is* the victim of others, or of circumstances. In fact, a silent battle goes on between the analyst and the patient on this very score: the analyst stressing the subjective factors; the patient in ever so many versions emphasizing the stark reality of the abuse. He may at best admit that his reactions to unfair treatments are exaggerated.

The fact of such a struggle against evidence to the contrary permits the assumption that the patient must have a strong unconscious interest in seeing the sources as outside of, rather than inside, himself.

He is the innocent victim: In more or less articulate or subtle forms, the patient will stress how undeserved are the mishaps which have befallen him. His own virtue and rightness, his purity, his goodness, his fairness appear to him in striking contrast to the deal he receives from others or from fate.

Passivity and Abuse

"It happens to me": The patient experiences himself as the passive recipient of wrongs done to him. Passivity in this context does not always mean the emphasis on his helplessness. The expansive "types," as we know, abhor any admission of helplessness. They may be determined to prevent, by their vigilance and their planning, the perpetration of any harm. Or they may be most active in getting back in a punitive way at anyone injuring them. The general implication of passivity here is rather the person's feeling that the abuses have nothing whatever to do with him, that they hit him like rainstorms, cold, or heat. One of the results is that his major energies may be engaged in a battle with outside hostile forces, warding them off, appeasing them, or withdrawing from them.

Implications for Therapy

With the therapeutic aim of bringing patients back to themselves, the analyst will try to show them the extent to which their pride, their claims, their self-accusations, their self-contempt, their self-frustration, and so on, are responsible for their experiencing life as we have described it to this point. But these endeavors, although undertaken conscientiously, often meet with difficulties. The complaints may be driven underground, but the patients keep feeling wary, vindictive, appeasing. My contention is that these difficulties are due to an insufficient understanding of the whole phenomenon.

The analyst has no doubt whatever that the individual connections which he uncovers between the subjective factors in the patient and his feeling abused are true. What is more important, neither has the patient any doubts about their validity. But the patient does not *experience* these factors. He may, in fact, not experience much of anything that is going on within himself. He will, for instance, recognize that his feeling frustrated can be but a result of his own pride or irrational claims, or that his feeling disregarded and despised can be but a result of his self-contempt. But as long as he does not *experience* his claims or his self-contempt, these explanations must remain for him probable deductions which, of course, carry hardly any weight. If the analyst mistakes such intellectual agreements for real acceptance, he starts to walk on quicksand with every further step he takes.

The patient may not feel himself at all an active factor in his own life. He lives as though his life were determined by outside forces. While on the one hand there is a paucity of inner experiences, which often shows in a physical feeling of emptiness, or in compulsive hunger, his vision and energies are, on the other hand, all outward bound. While he may be consciously convinced that heaven and hell are within ourselves, this is *not* what he feels and how he lives. On a deeper level of his being, good and evil all seem to come from outside. He expects the solutions to his problem, or his fulfillment, through a change in external factors: through love, through company, success, power, prestige. Having no real feeling for his own value, affirmation of himself can come only by the approval or recognition of others. As long as his interest is thus outward bound, he cannot, despite his best intentions, be interested in his difficulties, but must primarily be interested in what others think of him, or in the ways in which he can manipulate others. It does not matter, in this context, whether this manipulation is being done by charm, appeasement, impression, intimidation, or domination.

Looking Out, Not In

Also, as long as he does not experience *his* feelings, *his* thoughts, *his* actions, he cannot possibly feel responsible for himself, or for his life. Whatever difficulties arise can be brought about only by others. "They" keep him down, disregard him, take advantage of him, coerce him. So, energies must be directed outward not only for attaining good, but for warding off evil, or for vindictively getting back at others. It is important for the analyst to realize not only that the patient may externalize this or that inner factor, but that his whole way of living is an *externalized living*. As a patient put it succinctly: "He looks out and not in."

When we understand the whole extent of such externalized living, with all its implications, it then becomes clear that feeling abused is but part and parcel of such living. For therapy this means that we cannot hope to make much headway with analyzing individual incidents of feeling abused before having exposed his externalized living as such.

We must look at the externalized living in two ways. As I have described it, it is a result of a paucity of inner experiences, of the loss of feeling a center of gravity in oneself and the absence of feeling oneself as a determining factor in one's own life. Briefly, it is one of the results of the alienation from self. But it is not only a result. It also acquires a function. It becomes an effective means for preventing a person from ever facing his problems, or even from being interested in them. Externalizing living, in other words, becomes a *centrifugal* living, characterized by active and often frantic moves away from self. The more a person emphasizes in his own mind the reality of others' unfairness, impositions, or cruelty, the more effectively can he evade facing his own vulnerability, the tyranny of his own demands on himself, the relentlessness of his self-abuse; the more the responsibility for self becomes meaningless in his mind.

In this sense, feeling abused becomes an overall defense against owning up to any neurotic drive or conflict within himself.

This is the reason why he not only experiences himself as the victim but feels irresistibly pulled in this direction. In other words, he not only feels easily humiliated because of many factors in his inner constellation but has a definite unconscious interest in emphasizing and exaggerating such "humiliations." This is why the patient's feeling abused is such an intricate mixture of facts and fancy. There is factual abuse, invited or uninvited. And there is abuse fabricated out of thin air, which seems as real to the person suffering it as the table he can grasp with his hands. It may create intense suffering, out of proportion to the provocation—and may barely touch the conscious mind, although it will be stored in deeper layers. Modifying Voltaire's words on the existence of God: if there were no abuse, the patient would have to invent it.

In certain phases of analytical therapy we can observe and uncover rapidly this defense function of feeling abused. But after the tendency has subsided to some extent, it may suddenly re-emerge with an impact brushing aside all reason. The patient may bring forth one association after the other, concerning the wrongs done to him, or he may be suddenly swept away by a huge wave of vindictiveness produced by a massive feeling of abuse. All of these complaints or rages, then, can be readily dispelled by the simple question: "Have you not come close to facing a problem in yourself, and are you not trying to ward off its realization?"

Defense against Recognition

Patients who are familiar with this defense function may themselves catch on quickly to any emergence of feeling abused. Instead of wasting much time justifying the reproaches felt against others, they may take them as a signal, indicating their need to avoid a realization of some emerging problem of their own. Conversely, as long as the patient has not yet recognized this defense function, he will bitterly resent as an unfair imposition any suggestion of self-scrutiny. He is the one who is harassed by his boss, his wife, his friends, so why should he, in addition to all the wrong done to him, go through the humiliating process of self-examination and change? This is a reaction which again demonstrates his intrinsic lack of interest in outgrowing his difficulties. He may not be able, however, to experience and express this response of resentment to the analyst and the whole analytic procedure. But under the stress of having to be rational and having to appease, he may cover it up with a polite intellectual interest in the analyst's suggestions. The inevitable result is that nothing sinks in and nothing changes!

When, thus, we see feeling abused as an expression of centrifugal living and as a patient's overall defense against facing his own problems and assuming responsibility for them, the phenomenon assumes a crucial importance in the neurotic process and in analytical therapy. It is, indeed, one of the main factors in perpetuating neurotic attitudes. It is like a heavy iron door that blocks access to the recognition of inner problems. But when analyzed sufficiently, it is also a gateway making possible an approach to them.

Does analysis of feeling abused, as described above, help immediately? In some ways its therapeutic effect is visibly beneficial. It does improve the patient's human relationships. He can relate himself better to others, to the extent that he realizes they cannot possibly give him what only he himself can do, and that he cannot make them responsible for things which are his responsibility alone.

In that he feels himself the responsible agency in his life, his feeling of "I" also becomes stronger. Even though owning up to his difficulties is painful, he nevertheless gains a greater feeling of solidity and aliveness. And since he is less preoccupied with what others are, do, or don't do, he can direct more interest and energies toward himself and use them for constructive self-examination.

Experiencing Difficulties

On the other hand, the very process of coming closer to himself entails being in for a troublesome and upsetting time. It would give a wrong impression if one were to say that he starts only now to see his difficulties. He has already seen many of them. But he saw them, as it were, as possibilities, as assumptions — likely to be, but not really, pertinent to his life. Now he begins to *experience* them and this sets going all his still-existing needs to justify or condemn them, with the result that he feels more divided than he did before. This inner battle can subside only gradually, as his interest in how he *is* increases and his focus on how he *should* be dwindles. At the same time, his real self emerges and he has to defend it against the onslaught of the pride system. All of this means that the symptomatic picture may be temporarily impaired. In simple terms, the patient may at times feel worse than before. Nevertheless, these upsets are constructive because of their being expressive of moves in a constructive direction, a direction toward finding himself and toward self-realization.

If, conversely, feeling abused is not sufficiently analyzed, the therapeutic process is bound to suffer. Though the patient may make efforts to get at his problems, these efforts are bound to be half-hearted. Briefly, we could say that nobody can find himself if he keeps running away from himself. The patient cannot possibly be interested in himself and his difficulties as long as — consciously or unconsciously — he makes outside factors responsible for them. He will use whatever superficial insights he gets about himself, to understand, manipulate, or change *others*. In addition, he is bound to resent, unconsciously, that he should be the one to change, since, as he experiences it, the others are the ones who make life difficult for him. The analysis thus is bound to be delayed and to move in circles until the analyst wakes up to the fact that the changes which may take place in the patient lag considerably behind the efforts put in, because some invisible forces prevent insights from taking root. Going after these invisible forces, he still may be able to get at their sources, but much precious time is lost.

Or, the analysand may have gained sufficient insight into certain aspects of himself, particularly in his relations to others, to function more smoothly. In that case, the analysis may peter out when the patient's obvious troubles are diminished. The patient may feel quite satisfied with what the analysis has done for him and decide to terminate it. His incentive to come to terms with himself for the sake of a more productive life is not great enough when he no longer feels driven by the whip of manifest disturbances.

Rise of Self-Hate

Finally, the patient's destructiveness may get out of hand. He may take a definite turn for the worse by becoming both more openly vindictive against others and more self-destructive. The greater vindictiveness against others cannot be explained simply by the patient's increasing freedom to feel and express it. The main danger precipitating such an unfortunate outcome lies in a rise of self-hate, often barely perceptible, but steady and relentless. For quite some time the analysis seems to go on satisfactorily. The patient seems to gain more and more insight into his neurotic structure. He also seems to be better able to cope with many situations. The analyst feels, nevertheless, on precarious grounds. The patient seems eager to learn a few things about himself, but his insights lack depth. He does not follow up on his own any connections he has grasped. His emotional life seems to remain rather barren. His relation to the analyst does not gain in solidity and his tendency to externalize abates but little, though he may be more cautious about expressing it. The patient keeps feeling interpretations as accusations and tends to justify himself automatically.

Among the factors the patient has seen within himself are also some of the sources of feeling abused: his pride, his irrational claims, his fear of self-reproaches and the subsequent tendency to put the blame on others, his need to use the others as scapegoats for his not measuring up to the height of his inner dictates. And with such realizations, the feeling abused, too, seems to recede.

Externalizing Self-Abuse

But as the analysis goes on, the patient's defenses start to wear thin and some of his problems begin to hit home. He begins to realize that his having problems is not merely a construct, but an existing fact, and he responds to such growing realization with an equally growing self-hate in one form or another — self-condemnation, self-contempt, self-destructiveness. This process, though painful, is not dangerous if the patient has developed sufficient constructive self-interest to help him to retain a healthy perspective on the onslaught of self-hate. If, however, such interest has not developed, he then has nothing to set against the impact of self-hate, and he feels threatened with total collapse or total disintegration. At this point, that part of feeling abused which is, briefly, an externalization of self-abuse comes into the foreground. He may turn against others — including, of course, the analyst — with a more or less violent vindictiveness. This process which has been described as a simple and rather mechanical "turning outward of aggression" is a desperate attempt on the part of the patient to make the others — and not himself — appear as the evil ones. They — and not he — deserve every imaginable punishment, defeat, and destruction. He is, however, usually not successful in his effort to ward off self-hate, but on the contrary, is caught in a vicious circle. His greater vindictiveness against others is likely to increase the very self-hate he is so anxious to tune down. The resulting inner turmoil makes him panicky and he may break up the analysis in a state of panic. Even at this stage, if it is not so far advanced that the patient is inaccessible, the analyst has still a chance to save the situation, provided he is alert to the impairment of the patient's relation to himself and to a rise of the patient's vindictiveness in general. In tackling it, the analyst must be extremely careful to avoid anything that might feel to the patient like an accusation. The best way to do so is not to take it at its face value, that is, as retaliatory hostility, but as an expression of inner distress, caused ultimately by his externalized living. If, on the other hand, self-hate and vindictiveness rise to an unbearable degree, the dangers of psychotic episodes or attempts at suicide are fairly great.

Role in Therapy

Feeling abused plays a more crucial role in therapy than is usually assumed. Even if the phenomenon is not obvious, it is important for the analyst to be alert to any signs of it, particularly in any case of a pervasive tendency to externalize. Or, even more generally, in any case of a dearth of inner experiences because of externalized and centrifugal living. It remains necessary — at the appropriate time — to trace all the individual connections with intrapsychic factors. The analyst must be aware, however, that these connections cannot mean much to the patient as long as he has shut himself off from his inner experiences. As long as he does not feel them, the whole realm of inner experiences remains to him uncanny, weird, mysterious. A too early unraveling of intrapsychic factors, therefore, is a waste of time. When the feeling of abuse is sighted, the analyst must proceed from there to lay bare all the aspects of externalized living — that is, the ways in which the patient lives for, through, and against others. The therapeutic effect of this step is a lessening alienation from self. As the patient gradually realizes how his feeling of his own value, his hopes, concerns, fears, resentments, and activities are determined by others, or by factors outside himself, he begins to wonder where *he* is. He wonders how little he *is* in his own life, how little he is the captain of his ship. This wondering is the beginning of an interest in himself and a search for himself.

Summary

To summarize with regard to the phenomenon of feeling abused, it is important to see both the *diversity* of content, form, and individual sources,

23

The Paucity of Inner Experiences (1952)

Horney read this paper before the Association for the Advancement of Psychoanalysis at the New York Academy of Medicine on 27 February 1952. It was published in the *American Journal of Psychoanalysis* 12 (1952): 3–9, and subsequently reprinted in *Advances on Psychoanalysis*, edited by Harold Kelman (1964). Jack Rubins made the following comment on the paper in *Karen Horney: Gentle Rebel of Psychoanalysis:* "Although Karen seemed to be influenced by existentialist ideas in this paper insofar as she cited Kierkegaard's 'fear of nothingness' and Tillich's 'fear of non-being' as a source of anxiety, this influence was more apparent than real. . . . She did not see her concepts of being, or of anxiety, as ontological states but rather as emotions and forms of consciousness, therefore as psychological functions" (1978, 330).

All of us have an interest in not being aware of certain feelings, drives, conflicts, qualities within ourselves. The particular content of such unconscious factors depends upon the whole personality structure. A person, for instance, who persistently keeps himself down is unconsciously interested in being unaware of his assets; a person who needs to keep others at a distance is unconsciously interested in being unaware of his need for affection. Briefly, this is one of the basic tenets with which we work in psychoanalytic therapy. The paucity of inner experiences to be discussed here is a more pervasive haziness of all, or most, inner experiences. The entire threshold of awareness is lowered.

Neither is the paucity of inner experiences restricted to the emotional life — feelings of pain, of joy, of hope, of disappointment, of likes or dislikes. It also includes thinking, willing, wishing, believing, doing. In short, it means living in a fog.

It is not identical with an alienation from the real self, but concerns the whole actual self: the awareness of pride and self-hate, triumph and defeat, hurts, illusions. Even anger, though unmistakably shown, may not be felt as such.

One last point to define the nature of the problem: the world of inner experiences is not shriveled or extinct. Dreams that the memory retains are like the rumblings of distant volcanoes or thunderstorms and reflect the depth and aliveness of inner battles, of destruction, of despair, of attempts at some solution. But this inner world is not accessible to conscious experience. We can describe the condition by analogies only, analogies which are not artificially constructed, but are taken from symbols as they may appear in dreams. It is as if the person had turned his back on his inner life; as if it all was covered by fog; as if he had closed an airtight or soundproof door; as if he had walled off everything. It may be a glass wall through which he still can observe what is going on without experiencing it. The fog is usually not always equally thick; it may lift at times and at others become impenetrable. Then feelings of unreality may result. All of a sudden some hurts, some loss, some work of art may penetrate and elicit a response. Some areas may be relatively free, like a relation to nature or music.

The problem can be tackled from various angles, such as its genesis and development in the individual, or its role in the neurotic process. I want to focus on the questions which have a rather direct bearing on therapy: the manifestations by which to recognize it; its influence on life and on therapy; the patient's awareness of it and his attitude toward it, and ways to tackle it.

Though inconspicuous and, as it were, undramatic, the paucity of inner experiences is a fairly crucial neurotic phenomenon. It is crucial both in the sense that many currents converge to create it and also that in turn it gives rise to or reinforces several neurotic disturbances. The currents which contribute to its formation are of a general nature, inherent in every neurotic process. Hence the dearth of inner experiences itself also is not restricted to any special kind of neurotic development, which means it seems to occur independently of so-called types.

The subsequent disturbances, manifold as they are, in principle can be put into two categories. One of these categories can be understood as substitute functions. The unawareness of inner experiences is after all a severe deficiency. It impairs not only a person's aliveness but also his functioning in daily life. It is to be compared perhaps with the loss of eyesight, jeopardizing his orientation. One might even call it a kind of inner blindness. This analogy allows for a further step. If somebody becomes blind, he will find other ways to orient himself in his surroundings. The person who is numbed to his inner experiences likewise must find other ways, and he does so automatically. The most important one is to shift emphasis from the inner to the outer life. Ordinarily we do not care to make much of a distinction between the inner and outer life, because they are indeed an interwoven texture. But just as the inner life comes into full focus when attention is withdrawn from externals — as in meditating or dreaming — so, conversely, externals dominate the picture when the inner life is dimmed out. If such one-sided emphasis on externals is rather pervasive, we speak of "externalized living."[1]

Nature of Externalized Living

Roughly, that entails the following characteristics: intrapsychic processes are experienced as interpersonal ones. For instance, a person does not feel that he despises himself, but he is aware of despising others, or being despised by them. His own wishes and his own compulsive demands on himself fade out and are replaced by the real or imagined expectations of others. The expectations of others, then, have the same compulsory character as his own "shoulds," that is, he must meet them or rebel against them. He is what others think of him; prestige or success may become the only measuring rods for his value. In conjunction with such delegating of his rights to others, the emphasis shifts from *being* to *appearing*. What counts then is proper behavior, proper functioning, physical looks — in short, the role he plays or the impression he makes on others. A feeling of anxiety, for instance, becomes alarming only if it shows in perspiring or in trembling of the hands. In moral terms, this shift from being to appearing means that he can do anything — lie, steal, cheat, be promiscuous — provided he "gets by" with it. Vigilant observation of others becomes a supreme necessity and is cherished as a precious asset.

If a person is aware of his feelings, wishes, fears, beliefs, and ideals, he is provided with an orientation for his personal life. If all these inner experiences are dimmed out, he has, as it were, no directive. The expectations of others or, in a more general way, any kind of rules, regulations, or routines supply him with substitute means of orientation. He clings rigidly to these directives and feels lost, anxious, or irritable if they are not available. He may be apprehensive, for instance, in any situation when he does not know what is expected of him.

From Being to Thinking

Another shift of functions — likewise of far-reaching importance — is that from *being* to *thinking*. To speak in terms of Zen Buddhism: "Life is not a problem to be solved but an experience to be realized." The more remote a person is from his inner life, the more abstract his thinking. The less alive he is, the more he may turn into a thinking machine. The more he is cut off from a spontaneous contact with the world around him, the more the subjectivity of his thoughts becomes self-evident truth. The greater his need for superiority (for whatever reasons), the more imperative the necessity of foresight and omniscience.

Not only the faculty of thinking but also that of willing may assume, as it were, a life of its own. Separate from the context and the reality of the whole living person, it may soar into the fantastic and turn into sheer magic. The belief in the omnipotence of the mind or in its magic powers stems from other sources, but it is perpetuated and reinforced by the unavailability of inner experiences.

The other category of subsequent disturbances is constituted by reactive anxieties. The unawareness of inner experiences gives a person a feeling of emptiness or nothingness, which in itself may or may not be conscious. But whether this feeling is conscious or not, it is in any case frightening. On the grounds of our clinical experiences we can understand those philosophers who contend that anxiety ultimately *is* the fear of nothingness (Kierkegaard) or the fear of nonbeing (Tillich). Though I am not prepared to regard it as the only and ultimate source of anxiety, it is at any rate one of the deep and essential wells from which anxiety springs. This dread of nothingness may appear in rather direct forms, such as a gnawing and painful feeling of bodily emptiness; as a pervasive feeling of the futility and boredom of life; as dread of darkness and aloneness; in nightmarish dreams such as being terror-stricken by seeing a light on an empty bed or becoming blind with terror about being in an empty and dark cave. More often this dread does not appear as such but shows in the attempts to run away from it. There are many ways to do so, such as compulsive and hectic activities to prohibit any breathing spell in which a feeling of futility could make itself felt; compulsive avoidance of ever being alone; compulsive eating or drinking. Blind destructiveness may ensue when a person becomes aware of the futility of life.[2]

Factors of Awareness

The *awareness* of such impoverishment varies and depends upon the following factors: to begin with a rather self-evident fact, a person can miss his own depth only if ever — even for a short period in the past — he has been alive and alert; he may, for instance, in his teens have played with heart and soul at some sport, enjoyed dramatics, or politics; he may have gone through a turbulent time with his first love affair, and his emotional deadness may have set in after such periods. Hence he knows by contrast the difference between a meaningful life and an empty one. Speaking of the present, even a fairly healthy individual is not always equally alive. He, too, knows by contrast when the beauty of a tree merely registers or is actually felt as such; when he is productive or merely works under pressure. The same holds true for many less healthy people. Here the times of aliveness are rarer, and they are more often tied to conditions of questionable value such as the thrill of conquest, power, triumph, sadistic pursuits.

Furthermore, a person's awareness of his feeling of inner emptiness depends upon the extent of his success in running away from it. He may have such a multitude of social contacts, so many committees to attend, so many "friends," so many cocktail parties, so much shopping or house cleaning, such an amount of business to attend to, that he remains unaware of how meaningless everything is to him.

Finally, we have to consider whether a person is consciously or mostly unconsciously interested in being aware or unaware of the paucity of inner experiences. (The question of the unconscious interest is crucial in *any* attempt to account for awareness or unawareness of *any* factor; the interest being determined by the whole inner constellation.) Does he want to be alive, or is he afraid of it? Is he proud of deep feelings or convictions; or is he proud of being above wants, needs, passions, beliefs? In the latter case he would speak of being "unsentimental," "unemotional," "dispassionate," "poised," "stoical," "detached," "objective," "impersonal."

The suffering that may be entailed in the inner retrenchment — leaving out the subsequent anxieties — is as undramatic as the phenomenon itself: a more or less vague feeling of missing out on something, of yearning or discontentment. Although we can understand the reasons for this relative unconcern, we may, nevertheless, from a broader perspective wonder about it, because the disturbance strikes at the very root of our existence. It means, after all, nonliving, missing out — not on this or that factor, like success or sex or material assets — but on life itself. Whatever he does or gains, good, bad, or indifferent, life passes him by, he is excluded from it.

Resultant Problems

In psychoanalytic therapy the paucity of inner experiences essentially makes for two main difficulties, the combination of which amounts to a severe impasse. On the one hand, as long as the condition persists, in its turn it perpetuates many neurotic processes, part of which were mentioned as substitute phenomena. It means for therapy that the patient keeps externalizing and intellectualizing; that he keeps expecting to solve his difficulties by knowing the reason why they exist—that is, by looking at them and talking about them; often enough by looking at the difficulties of others and talking about these. He insists on overcoming his difficulties by sheer willpower from one day to the other, or depends upon the analyst's having the magic key to set him free. He keeps running away from his feeling of inner emptiness.

On the other hand, the very wall that separates him from his inner experiences also prevents any insight from penetrating this wall. We are more and more convinced that in therapy only that counts which is felt and experienced. Realizing something intellectually is merely the first step and without much therapeutic value if it does not stir up some emotional response. The patient must feel his conflicts,[3] live with his self-contempt, experience how unrelated he is to anything. As long as the patient remains remote from himself, he may now and then have a short-lived emotional response, but he closes up soon after. He may talk about a problem intelligently, glibly, or even enthusiastically—which is very deceptive—but his apparent interest peters out quickly. In the next hour he may have forgotten all about it, although he may have made conscious efforts to retain the content in his memory. It is like the well-known sensation of a dream vanishing, no matter how hard the dreamer tries to keep it in awareness. He then may pick up another thread, and the same sequence of rising interest and fading out occurs. This results in the analysis easily becoming disconnected and repetitious. Some superficial improvement may take place, but the changes that occur are entirely incommensurate with work put in.

Recognizing the Blockage

Naturally, it is important to recognize the condition and the blockage it represents to therapeutic progress. This is not always easy, because the picture may be obscured by the patient's intellectual eagerness and the intellectual grasp of his problems. It is often difficult indeed to distinguish in any direct way what the patient realizes by dint of an intellectual vision—often quite accurate and productive—and what he experiences emotionally. But there are many signs which point indirectly to the nature of the blockage. The safest of these is the petering out of interest in whatever problem emerges. Besides, there are all the disturbances which in some way or other are connected with the condition, like pervasive and tenacious externalizations, compulsive eating, incapacity to be alone, and so on. Finally there are dreams which unmistakably may depict inner emptiness or emotional deadness: dreams of marble statues, corpses, empty frames, empty rooms, loss of identity, and the nightmares mentioned before.

Tackling the Problem

An early recognition of the blockage gives the analyst a vision of the odds against which the analytical work will have to militate, odds which at first sight look like an impasse because the very paucity of inner experiences that keeps neurotic processes going also keeps him from reaching the patient. Such recognition prevents the analyst from getting bewildered and discouraged as the analysis goes on, or from deceiving himself about seeming progress. Nevertheless, an early recognition is of no immediate help. He cannot possibly confront the patient with his feelings of nothingness as long as he has nothing to fall back on. The analyst's first aim, therefore, is to help the patient toward some measure of self-knowledge, toward some measure of inner relatedness to himself. He will tackle whatever is available of his neurotic structure, like various kinds of power drives in an expansive person, or aspects of self-doubts, self-berating, or appeasing in a self-effacing type.

Though insights thus gained are on an intellectual level only, they nevertheless help the patient to recognize certain outlines of his structure, or to get a notion of forces operating within him. Even in this initial work it is advisable to make attempts to convey to the patient the distinction between intellectual interest and emotional grasp, between talking from the top of his head and from the bottom of his heart. Perhaps it boils down to the distinction between glibness and sincerity.

The patient who thus has gained some inner strength and some solid ground on which to stand is then ready to be confronted with his feeling of inner emptiness. When he shows in his associations or his dreams signs of interest in the problem, it is profitable for him to become aware of how great this feeling of futility or meaninglessness toward life actually is. His reactions may be more on the positive side, which means that he feels and expresses a longing to come to life, or his prevailing mood may be a defensive one. Pursuing the latter, we realize sooner or later that it is prompted by two kinds of dreads: the dread of the very emptiness itself and the dread of coming to life. These fears are present even though the particular patient may have complained bitterly about his emotional deadness. In any case the patient's feelings are different from the analyst's. The analyst is convinced that a merely perfunctory living is altogether undesirable, that it means vegetating instead of living, that it is altogether desirable to be alive in one's inner experiences. The patient has at best divided feelings. The prospect of greater aliveness is more or less appealing, though because of his dreads he may consciously adopt a "don't care" attitude. But on the other hand, he is reluctant or averse to taking any steps leading in this direction.

The next objective thus becomes to examine the nature of the dreads. One of them is the dread of *facing* his feeling of nothingness, instead of running away from it. It is to the credit of Dr. Ralph Harris to have first seen the therapeutic importance of this step. As in so many steps leading to some decisive discoveries, the underlying idea here was perfectly simple: apparently nothing can happen as long as the patient finds sufficient means to avoid the issue. If, however — and only if — he fully experiences his feeling of emptiness, then the possibility opens up for something constructive growing out of such a step. The aspect of this problem which is accessible to him varies. To some patients, for instance, the word "emptiness" does not mean much, but the word "futility" or "unrelatedness" does. The process goes from fleeting, vague, or localized feelings of futility to a clear or comprehensive experience of how little meaning all or most aspects of life have for him. He may have had doubts before whether he was really interested in his work; or he may have been concerned about feeling bored so easily, or about short-lived enthusiasms, leaving him flat and empty. Now he begins to feel that at bottom he is not related to anything. Such experience, naturally, is terrifying. It feels like life evaporating, like losing the ground under his feet, like being lost in a fog of nothingness.

Penetrating the Wall

But such experience, coming at a time when a patient is ready for it, has a constructive effect. Somehow it has the power to penetrate through the wall to his alive core; he feels closer to himself. To put it differently, he begins to realize feelingly that his emptiness is not a plain, unalterable fact, but that there is an alive core of himself that wants to live and that reaches out for a meaning. Several factors account for such a fact. In intellectual terms I would say that one must first recognize the spurious or tenuous nature of one's relatedness to things and people before something real and genuine can grow. Such a description, however, is inadequate for the simple reason that this is not an intellectual process. Probably we come closer to the truth when we consider that a person's experience of emptiness or unrelatedness is so contrary to the meaning of life that it elicits a countermove of a positive nature.

To illustrate this process with an experience of a different kind: during a difficult period of his life, a patient had incurred a near-fatal accident. Soon after this event he almost succumbed to an acute organic disease. Then a friend of his, who knew about his precarious life situation and felt worried about his nearly dying twice in a brief period, said to him: "Why do you want to die?" The patient contended that this question actually saved his life. Because in a flash he feelingly recognized that he wanted to die, indeed. And it was the recognition of this danger that mobilized his will to live.

Perhaps our view of such experiences will be clearer when we compare it with the view J.-P. Sartre has expressed in his writings. Sartre likewise stresses the importance of facing nothingness. He also is aware of such a step requiring greater than average courage. But he does not see the feeling of emptiness as the outcome of a neurotic process. In his opinion life *is* meaningless, and it is better to do away with illusions about it and avoid their inevitable repercussions by facing the fact of its futility.

Fear of Life

The second major dread that counteracts the patient's emerging wish to overcome his emotional deadness concerns the prospect of coming to life. This dread is clearly illustrated by a patient's dream of a vegetable coming to life and his feeling terrified at this sight. This dream occurred at a time when the patient started to realize the meaninglessness of his life; it was a condensed expression of the realization of his wish to come to life. In this dream he explicitly takes a stand by calling his present way of living a mere vegetating. In a condensed form he expresses both his wish to come to life and his dread of it.

In order to understand this dread, we must consider that the general lowering of awareness has important functions. It keeps a person from recognizing contradictions, discrepancies, and pretenses in his personality, or, generally speaking, from recognizing an existing disorder. It makes it possible not to let his left hand know what his right hand does. He may remain unaware, for instance, that his actions toward employees are contrary to his fine social sentiments, or that his amiability is artificial and not in accord with his using people as stepping-stones toward his own glory. In short, unawareness protects illusions and unconscious pretenses.

Furthermore, it is an overall protection against all *painful* inner experiences. Scrutinizing the nature of these painful experiences, we will be inclined to focus on this or that particular factor. We may do so not only with different patients, but also during various periods of *one* analysis. It often looks as though the patient was "really" running away from experiencing his conflicts or his self-hate or his failure to measure up to his demands, or his claims and their frustrations. Actually he avoids *all* of these experiences. Even this comprehensive answer is not yet fully satisfactory because there are after all many patients who at the proper time are capable of experiencing their conflicts, their self-contempt, and so on. Therefore, we must seek the reason that renders such experience unbearable.

The patients of whom I am talking harbor an unconscious but firmly entrenched belief in their omnipotence and omniscience. While such belief is inherent in every neurosis, its intensity varies. Leaving out its individual development, there seems to be a correlation between the paucity of inner experiences, on the one hand, and an unconscious reliance upon unlimited powers of the mind on the other. The more removed a person is from his inner experiences, the more rigidly does he adhere to the belief in his omnipotence, the more this belief becomes a vicarious source of strength — yes, a vicarious ground on which to live. It would need more observations to see whether or not this correlation is a regular one. I can only say at this point that it seems plausible and that I have not yet seen one exception.

The reverse side of this belief in omnipotence is a profound dread of anything connoting helplessness. Any experience of helplessness is not only felt as utter disgrace and humiliation, but like an earthquake shattering the very ground on which he stands.

Value of Unawareness

Let us consider now the influence which this whole problem of omnipotence-helplessness has on the patient's experiencing his difficulties in analysis. To feel any force in himself that is compulsive means that — far from being all-powerful — he is not even master in his own house. But to come to life would include feeling in his blood and bones the grip some compulsive drive has on him.

It is a disgraceful admission of "weakness" that he cannot dispel any difficulty as soon as he recognizes it as such, by the magic wand of knowledge and willpower. To accept himself with his "failures" would expose him to a shattering experience of impotence. Similarly, he must avoid facing his claims as irrational demands upon the world around him. If he experienced them for what they are, he would be in the ludicrous position of a person clamoring for rights and privileges without any power to enforce them.

To experience a conflict, any conflict — which is painful anyhow! — becomes unbearable because it conjures up the humiliating prospect of having to stoop down to make a choice. Moreover, since most neurotic conflicts cannot even be solved by making a choice, the emotional participation in a conflict means the dreaded experience of being helplessly caught in a dilemma from which he cannot extricate himself by magic or violence.

It is this specter of ridicule, disgrace, and impotence that accounts for the patient's stringent interest in maintaining a cloak of unawareness. As long as he is not willing or able to relinquish the belief in his magic powers, his budding and growing wish to come to life will be checked by this dread of impotence. And for quite a while the yearning for life and the fight to maintain the belief in omnipotence may alternatively have the upper hand.

Retreat from Life

Whenever there is a lurking dread of some inner danger, many means are automatically resorted to which would keep such anxiety from emerging, or allay it in case it emerges. The general lowering of awareness is the most pervasive protection in this regard. The most crippling one is a retreat from realistic activity. It proceeds along the principle: "If you don't try, you won't fail." This retreat corresponds to an even more insidious inner restriction which is a consistent tendency to keep oneself down; to develop, as it were, pervasive taboos against any expansive desires, either healthy or neurotic. It entails unconsciously cultivating the feeling of "I can't," "I have no rights," "I don't care." Such attitudes may look like abdicating omnipotence, but they actually help to preserve it. They prevent a person from testing his belief in omnipotence and omniscience and thereby allow him to retain it.

The way out of this impasse in principle is the same as the one that leads away from the dread of emptiness. Nothing is gained, nothing can happen as long as we run away from an inner ordeal. The belief in omnipotence and the havoc it causes goes on and on under cover. The patient must experience all that has registered in him as humiliation, disgrace, impotence. He must experience his humiliation of not being the master over life and death; of being subject to laws of cause and effect; of harboring unwarranted fears of so many people or things; of not understanding everything at first glance; of having "to put up with" imperfect people, and so on and so forth. He must experience his willing the impossible. He must feelingly realize that he has beaten his head against the stone wall of the impossible. Then, as he accepts the confines of his limitations as a human being, he also can gradually accept and experience himself as he is. The wall between him and his inner life wears down. To put it in terms of Kierkegaard: it seems that *only if we do no longer will the impossible do we have a glimpse of the possible* — which gives us a sense of inner freedom. It seems that caught in the wheels of neurotic processes we have to go through the purgatory of experiencing our inner dreads in order to find the path toward freedom and inner growth.

Notes

1. K. Horney, On Feeling Abused, *Am. J. Psychoan.* 11 (1951); N. Kelman, Clinical Aspects of Externalized Living, *Am. J. Psychoan.* 11 (1951).

2. Cf. the play by the Swiss author Max Frisch *Graf Oederland.*

3. A. R. Martin, The Body's Participation in Anxiety and Dilemma Phenomena. *Am. J. Psychoan.* 5 (1945).

24

Human Nature Can Change (1952)

Karen Horney originally presented the following remarks at the symposium "Human Nature Can Change," held at the town hall in New York City on 19 March 1952, under the auspices of the Auxiliary Council to the Association for the Advancement of Psychoanalysis. The other participants were Harold Kelman, Paul Tillich, and Frederick A. Weiss. The papers were subsequently published in the *American Journal of Psychoanalysis* 12 (1952): 62–68. The text given here is based largely on the published version, but it incorporates material from two other sources. The symposium was broadcast on the radio, and a recording of the broadcast was made. I have obtained a copy of the recording that was transferred to tape from the American Institute for Psychoanalysis. In addition, Renate Horney Patterson, Horney's youngest daughter, has provided me with a typed version of the talk, which is headed "A Lecture by Karen Horney, M.D., transcribed from a record." Given that this typed version does not correspond in all respects to the taped version, I am uncertain about its source. The passages I have placed within brackets were not in the published version of the paper but were on the tape and in the typescript. I have used the tape to correct the typescript in a few places, and I have edited some ungainly sentences in both the published and unpublished portions.

Those people who are convinced that human nature cannot change usually have not only a static but a pessimistic view of man. In simple terms, their conviction is that man has always been and always will be greedy, envious, cruel, vindictive, and destructive. They usually contend that those who disagree with this viewpoint merely lack the courage to face unpleasant truth and try to cover it up with a rosy haze of flattering self-deception. Many others consider this a one-sided view. In short, they see in human nature the possibility for good and evil, the latter being expressed in Christian terminology in the symbol of the original sin.

Being in the position to study human beings intimately, we as analysts agree with this latter viewpoint. We see clearly both possibilities, but with one significant distinction. The constructive and destructive possibilities do not stem from the same forces; they are not on the same level; we cannot put them side by side. They are different in origin and different in kind. Briefly, our belief is that the constructive possibilities stem from man's essential nature, from the core of his being, from what we call his real self. Conversely, we believe that man turns unconstructive or destructive if he cannot fulfill himself — that it is an unfulfilled life which makes him barren or destructive. This belief is not mere speculation, but is based on evidence of three kinds.

1. The first kind can be seen by anyone who keeps his eyes open — it has to do with a child's development. Just as a tree needs certain conditions for its growth, so does a child. If the environmental conditions are favorable, a child develops whatever particular potential he has. He does so because, like every other living organism, he has the innate urge to grow. These observations are supported by educators and anthropologists.

However, under conditions unfavorable to his growth, his development can easily go astray. Then he may become wary, hostile, withdrawn, or overdependent. If, however, his environmental conditions, in the sense of human relationships, change for the better in early years, he loses his wariness, suspiciousness, and resumes or embarks upon healthy growth. If the unfavorable conditions persist, a developmental process sets in — which we call neurotic — which is complicated and essentially unconscious. As a *result* of this neurotic process he develops all kinds of unconstructive or destructive attitudes, the main features of which are pride and conceit, unconscious pretenses, and irrational hostility in its many forms, such as suspiciousness, egocentric callousness, vindictiveness, ruthless ambition.

The conditions under which such a process sets in are manifold but describable. You could not call the results of this process his essential nature, any more than you would do so with a tree. If a tree, because of storms, too little sun, or too poor soil becomes warped and crooked, you would not call this its essential nature.

2. The most convincing evidence for our belief stems from our clinical experience. We see that a person who is power- or prestige-ridden or who is arrogant and vindictive or who is compliant to the point of making meaningless self-sacrifices is *driven* to have such attitudes by powerful unconscious forces. He cannot be other than aggressive or appeasing: he develops anxiety if he cannot be that way. The drivenness is what we call compulsive and what in medieval terms was called being possessed by demons. He does not what he wants to do but what he must, as determined by inexorable unconscious necessities.

A person who is dominating, irritable, and vindictive has become that way and remains so because [he has experienced life as an unending sequence of abuses and humiliations. Can we call such hostility part of his inherent nature? No, we cannot. In the old controversy about whether hostility is innate or acquired, we can most definitely say that it is acquired. This brings me to the heart of our question today, because what is acquired can be changed.]

3. The third kind of evidence is in the changes that occur during psychoanalytical therapy. For instance, as a hostile person experiences the compulsive nature and intrinsic futility of his drive for power, his vindictiveness, his use of other people as a means to an end, he begins to change. The change I am referring to is not just a better control or channeling of these drives but something far more radical. It involves giving up of irrational, destructive drives and functioning in an increasingly more self-realizing way.

[As the inner compulsive forces lose their grip on him, the person's hostility actually becomes meaningless, just as it would be meaningless for him to have a revolver at hand if he no longer needed to defend himself. When he sees how he has been driven toward this or that feeling or attitude, he begins to ask himself: Who am I? What do I feel? What do I want? What do I believe? He starts to come home to himself. He begins to taste how it feels to be alive, and since feeling alive is the most precious thing that we have on this earth, he wants more of it. Something constructive and creative starts to grow in him. He develops an increasingly strong wish to fulfill himself and to have a meaningful life.]

We have too little faith nowadays in the power of constructive forces, and one of the ways in which this lack of faith shows is in the frequency with which the following question is raised: Granted that you can help a person, but if this person remains in or returns to the environment or culture that originally made him sick, will he not succumb to the adverse influences again? Actually, just the opposite holds true. A person who has acquired a positive, productive attitude toward himself and life in general through analytical work will in turn exert a positive influence on the people around him.

Our experience as analysts has convinced us that the alternative to a pessimistic view of human nature is not the belief that man is good by nature but that he has, as do all living beings, an innate urge and capacity to realize his given potentialities. The hope of mankind for a more constructive living together is not an illusion but a realistic possibility. We must recognize, however, that this possibility will not materialize without serious and concerted effort on the part of every single one of us.]

25

Abstracts, Symposia, and Other Brief Items

This review of the American edition of Otto Rank's *Modern Education* was published in *Psychoanalytic Quarterly* 1 (1932): 349–50. It must have been written, in English, before Horney left Germany. Although she characterized Rank's book as retrogressive and saw it as part of a reaction against Freud's ideas that was as yet incapable of "orderly critical thought," she felt that "a critical review of the body of knowledge which is embraced by psychoanalysis could undoubtedly be of great value." She later undertook such a review herself in *New Ways in Psychoanalysis*.

On Ranks's Modern Education: *A Critique of Its Fundamental Idea*

After the resistances with which a new discovery is at first met are overcome and followed by an enthusiastic response, a reaction usually sets in; this reaction, as yet incapable of self-conscious and orderly critical thought, presents as a rule a critical devaluation of the new idea and an overevaluation of the older and even oldest principles which have been abandoned.

The new book by Rank dealing with modern education may be viewed as being essentially an exposition of this return to the past. Thus, if Freud's new concepts postulated that character formation is essentially determined by experiences related to the first few years of one's life, Rank brings to the foreground the emphasis on the important factors of later life, such as accidental occurrences, profession, success in life, and so on. If Freud broadened our vision by his new understanding of the instinctual life of the child, Rank lays stress on other feelings of the child: he avers the child racks its brain much less over sexual problems than over the general mysteries of life, that is, over problems of a philosophic or religious nature. If Freud taught us to appreciate how important it is that the child understand more fully certain things, Rank points out the dangers involved in the tendency to understand everything. If Freud gives extraordinary insight into the psychology of the individual, Rank comes to point out how relatively irrelevant this insight is as compared with the importance of broad sociological factors.

However, to point out that the book is an expression of a retrogressive trend does not mean that its value is thus properly estimated. One may ponder over those things which gifted men before Freud have known well and yet produce a welcome and valuable contribution: also, it is beyond any doubt that a critical review of the body of knowledge which is embraced by psychoanalysis could undoubtedly be of great value. It is therefore a matter of regret that both the critical part of the book and the somewhat muddled firework of some old and some new ideas which are presented in the positive part fall short of even the most modest requirements for scientific thoroughness. Thus, among the ideas offered, there are a number of highly questionable scientific value, as for instance the theory of the development of feelings out of inhibited "impulsive life." On the other hand, one finds a series of interesting views, like those attempting to throw new light on the Oedipus drama of Sophocles from the sociological standpoint of the earlier stages of the patriarchy. Yet nowhere in the book can one find any solid basis for or clearly conceived formulations of the author's contentions.

This undated abstract was in Harold Kelman's papers at the Postgraduate Center for Mental Health. The paper appears to have been addressed to an audience of physicians and to have been delivered sometime before Horney wrote *The Neurotic Personality of Our Time*. I have tentatively dated it 1933, the year in which Horney gave a series of lectures to gynecologists. For some of her later thoughts on neurotic suffering, see "The Meaning of Neurotic Suffering" (1948) here and *Neurosis and Human Growth,* chaps. 9 and 10.

B. Illness and Suffering as a Form of Gratification

This paper deals with the type of patient who during some period of life keeps falling from one illness into another and is continually in need of medical care. In contrast with hypochondriac patients who are also in never-ending need of medical reassurance, these patients really go through a startling number of diseases, of which some have an organic basis and others are merely of a functional nature.

These patients offer serious practical problems, particularly if they lack financial support, partly in regard to their own lives, since they spend most of their time and energy suffering from diseases and curing them, and partly in regard to the clinics and hospitals charged with their medical care. Hence the problem, if there are factors that make these persons more susceptible to diseases, is not only of theoretical but of distinctly practical importance. Approaching the problem from the psychological side is only one of several possibilities, but this approach is rather encouraging, for careful nonanalytical observations of the behavior of several such cases already suggests the possibility of contributing psychic factors.

These patients show some striking similarities in their attitudes. The more obvious ones are these:

1. They have an excessive need for attention and affection. In spite of these yearnings, they usually have no close friends and no satisfactory personal relations. They will, however, attach themselves readily to physicians and nurses and easily become emotionally dependent upon them. They cannot stand being alone.

2. Their interpersonal relations are not satisfactory because they always seem to be the ones who are neglected, rejected, or maltreated. They will complain about this in a more or less disguised way. If their relationship with the physician or nurse lasts long enough, the same emotional situation is bound to arise — in other words, they will also feel neglected or offended if an extraordinary amount of care and time is not continually devoted to them.

More accurate observation leads to the discovery that their unsatisfactory relationships are brought about in four ways:

a. They seem to have an intuitive capacity for picking out persons with a distinct streak of cruelty.

b. They provoke attacks by being overdemanding or by complaining and nagging in a way that insinuates some kind of reproach toward the other party.
c. If they are treated offensively or are injured, they suffer to quite a disproportionate degree.
d. Their sexual life is unsatisfactory, and the manifestations of it may be practically negligible.

In sum, these patients give the impression of wanting to suffer at any price and in any situation. People who have much to do with them sense that an element of satisfaction is hidden in the suffering. They will say, for instance, that "X is not satisfied if he doesn't have something to complain about." Yet even surface observation, if accurate enough, shows opposing trends also. Not only do these patients seem to indulge in all forms of suffering, but they also are quite aggressive, though in a veiled, surreptitious way.

In the long run, despite their emotional clinging, these patients prove to be extremely disagreeable and irritating. I have already mentioned the provocative attitude, which, though aimed at inducing an attack, is certainly also a release of hostility. Furthermore, though consciously feeling modest and unworthy of attention, they are in reality very demanding. One will feel a secret menace behind their yearning for affection. Finally, they turn easily against other people, again not openly but in suddenly refusing cooperation or getting worse or leaving without giving any clue to what has caused the change.

Psychoanalysis allows us to make these observations in a more orderly fashion and thereby reveals the dynamic structure of what is going on. One recognizes that the patients are in the dilemma of craving affection but at the same time being convinced of being absolutely unlovable. This dilemma is produced by excessive but vague guilt feelings: because they feel so guilty, they cannot possibly believe that anyone can like them. At the same time, receiving affection is of vital importance to them because it is the only way in which they can obtain reassurance against the free-floating anxiety that issues from their guilt feelings.

The sources of the guilt feelings may be traced — as in other neuroses — to intense, repressed feelings of hostility. The fear of letting any of these hostile impulses find expression is so great that usually even normal, adequate aggressiveness becomes checked. The patients feel paralyzed in asking for things for themselves, standing up for their rights, defending themselves against unwarranted claims, and fighting where it is necessary to fight.

All these aims are achieved indirectly, however, by suffering and illness. On the basis of being ill and helpless they can claim care and consideration. Moreover, the illness serves as a weapon to carry out defense and attack. Because of their guilt feelings, they very readily feel criticized, neglected, and rejected and react with an intense hostility which they again have to repress, being overly apprehensive about every feeling and expression of antagonism. They can express it, however, with an increase of their symptoms or with a new illness, which then has the implication: "Look at how you have made me suffer." This implication, which is expressed quite frankly during analysis, allows them to feel that they are the innocent martyrs and to put all the blame on others. In the analytical situation this reaction can be made conscious and worked out in its various ramifications, but outside analysis these vindictive impulses often are lived out naively, for instance against physicians by whom these patients feel mistreated. Finally, they use the alleged injury as an excuse for demanding particular attention and care.

For these patients, sexual relations are disturbed in the same way as other interpersonal relations, or else they anticipate so much cruelty and violence in sexuality that they recoil from it altogether. Analytically, one can show convincingly that illness and suffering are also substitutes for sexual gratification.

Summing up, we see that suffering fulfills a variety of needs: it provides reassurance against anxiety, is a means of living out repressed hostility, and serves as a substitute for sexual gratification. Since all these needs are of vital importance for the persons concerned and could not be attained otherwise, it is not improbable that these psychic factors play a role in making them more susceptible to illness.

When Horney first came to the New York Psychoanalytic, such colleagues as Adolph Stern, Lawrence Kubie, Fritz Wittels, and Gregory Zilboorg perceived her as a threat to classical theory. They also feared such other "dissidents" as Sandor Rado, Abraham Kardiner, David Levy, and Clara Thompson. In 1939, therefore, the Educational Committee of the institute revised the curriculum to ensure that candidates were well-grounded in Freud before being exposed to unorthodox teachers. According to the dissidents, candidates who were working with them were subjected to discrimination, and other candidates were discouraged from taking their courses or choosing them as training or supervising analysts. Horney became a particular target because of her critique of Freud in *New Ways in Psychoanalysis*—which was acrimoniously discussed at two meetings in 1939—and because she wanted to teach courses that would evaluate psychoanalytic concepts from her point of view.

Horney was demoted from instructor to lecturer in 1941 and told that she could still offer elective courses but could no longer participate in the basic curriculum. As a result, she resigned from the New York Psychoanalytic Institute and Society, accompanied by Clara Thompson, Bernard Robbins, Harmon Ephron, and Sarah Kelman. Soon thereafter, fourteen candidates also withdrew, proclaiming their action to be the inevitable result of the unscientific spirit and undemocratic attitude of the Educational Committee. Those who resigned formed the Association for the Advancement of Psychoanalysis, which then founded the American Institute for Psychoanalysis, with Karen Horney as dean, and the *American Journal of Psychoanalysis,* with Karen Horney as editor. They sent the letter below to each member of the American Psychoanalytic Association and published it in the first issue of the *American Journal of Psychoanalysis* (1941), 9–10. (For further details of Horney's conflict with the New York Psychoanalytic Association and its consequences, see Rubins 1978, Quinn 1987, and Paris 1994.)

C. Letter of Resignation from the New York Psychoanalytic Society

Dear Colleague:

When five individuals, all members of a professional society, feel impelled, for reasons not of a personal nature, to resign their membership in that society, an explanation to their professional colleagues is an obligation upon them and a matter of fundamental importance to those interested in the profession.

The resignations are a response to a situation which constitutes a crisis in psychoanalytic education. Psychoanalysis is a young science, still in an experimental stage of its development, full of uncertainties, full of problems to which anything approaching final and conclusive answers is still to be sought. As in all sciences, the solutions of these problems are directly dependent upon more voluminous and keener observations, as well as upon further weighing and consideration of observations already made.

Education in any field consists in a passing on from an older to a younger generation of the truth that the older generation believes it has learned, as well as a bequeathing to the younger generation of the problems left unsolved by their elders. In psychoanalysis as it is today, we cannot afford to subject the younger generation to any dogmatism; we should not mislead it with the illusion of certainty, where none actually exists.

There are two antithetical attitudes toward psychoanalysis today. One of these is based upon the awareness that psychoanalysis is still in an experimental stage of its development. The other attitude regards psychoanalysis as having in many respects passed beyond this stage and holds that training in psychoanalysis should begin with the learning of certain concepts and techniques which are, as they sometimes term it, "classical," and which represent psychoanalysis as they conceive it to have been handed down by Freud. No two of these "classicists" have precisely the same notions of what "classical" psychoanalysis is. But they seem to be agreed that something which passes under the name of "classical" psychoanalysis should be first inculcated in the student, and that after this certain "deviating" notions of psychoanalysis may be taught to the student, if he so elects.

The educational program which is based upon the conviction that psychoanalytic therapy — and therefore theory — is still in an experimental stage, and which, for want of a better term, might be called "non-classical," is considerably less crystallized than the "classical" one. Its advocates hold that the student at the beginning of his training in psychoanalysis may choose whether he will first be exposed to "classical" or to "deviating" or "non-classical" concepts. They likewise hold that the student who elects to be personally analyzed by a "non-classicist" should be taught "classical" concepts in the course of his training and that the student who chooses a "classical" type of personal analysis should learn "deviating" notions as a part of his later training.

Thus while the "classicists" are very positive about what the beginning of psychoanalytic training should be and are willing to enforce this view where they have the power to do so — as in the case of the disqualification of Dr. Karen Horney as a training analyst of the New York Psychoanalytic Institute — the "non-classicists," realizing that any crystallization of this nature is in the present circumstances premature, are of the opinion that the decision should in each case be left to the individual student.

There can be no doubt that there is here drawn a real issue in psychoanalytic education: Shall policy in psychoanalytic training be decided upon the basis of the number of votes that can be mustered in favor of this or that theory; or shall we frankly admit that it is much too early to attempt a definite decision of policy? There is no question in the minds of the undersigned that to choose the first of these alternatives will delay rather than accelerate progress, not only in psychoanalytic education but in psychoanalysis itself. Scientific issues cannot be decided by votes or by political power in any form; one would have thought that the experience of Galileo with the Church had determined this truth once and for all.

We have tried for many years now to combat this dogmatism in psychoanalytic education. Our efforts have increasingly met with frustration; the "classicists" within the New York Psychoanalytic Society and its Educational Committee have become more and more strongly entrenched in their dogmatism, and recent developments have convinced us of the impossibility of persuading them to take a more liberal attitude toward this issue.

We have therefore felt it essential for the future of psychoanalysis and psychoanalytic education to dissociate ourselves from a professional organization a majority of whose members are under the impression that scientific issues may legitimately be decided through the possession of political power, and to create a new center for psychoanalytic work, devoted to truly liberal and scientific principles, in psychoanalytic training, investigation, and discussion. We invite freely all those of our colleagues who are likewise devoted to such principles to join with us in this endeavor.

(signed)
Harmon S. Ephron
Karen Horney
Sarah R. Kelman
Bernard S. Robbins
Clara Thompson

When the United States entered the Second World War, the Association for the Advancement of Psychoanalysis formed the War-Efforts Committee, which issued a series of war bulletins based partly on panel discussions held at the New School for Social Research in March and November 1942. The first five of these bulletins were published in the *American Journal of Psychoanalysis, 2* (1942): 31–41. There were further bulletins, but none have survived. The fifth bulletin, "Understanding of Individual Panic" (40–41), was by Karen Horney. The other bulletins dealt with psychological warfare, first aid treatment of panic, group factors in civilian morale, and the dynamics of group panic. In addition to Horney, contributors were Meyer Maskin, Edward S. Tauber, and Alexander Reid Martin.

D. *Understanding of Individual Panic*

Experiences in England indicate that only those persons react with excessive anxiety to war emergencies who are predisposed to do so, or as one might say, persons who are neurotic. Fortunately, not all such people react with panic. Many of them are effective and courageous in the face of real emergencies or even improve considerably under such conditions. For instance, if they have felt inferior hitherto and then during war find a task which gives them the feeling of being useful, their self-esteem is thereby lifted.

The statement then that a person develops panic because he is "neurotic" is too general to be useful. In order to understand individual panic we must be more specific.

To begin with, we must be aware of two facts. One is that panic is not a response to realistic danger. People reacting with panic to bombing or war news are no more afraid of these dangers than their more serene or more self-controlled neighbors. The other fact is that the real source of anxiety is not the same with everybody but varies from one person to another. Ostensibly, three people are seized by an identical panic provoked by an identical cause; the terror that each of the three experiences, however, is different in quality. Most of us, though adjusted to reality on the surface, harbor certain hidden dreads. Generally we are not aware of their existence or of their depth. One person, for instance, dreads the limelight, while another one is equally afraid of not being admired. One is terrified at having to assume hardships, while another is equally afraid of losing any vestige of power. Still another one is terrified at being alone and feeling unwanted, while the other feels safe only in his ivory tower and dreads any closeness. These anxieties often are dormant but can flare up in a fit of panic when touched off by external circumstances, just as dynamite may explode when shaken up or kindled. War emergencies may provoke an explosion if they happen to touch off these specific anxieties in any person.

Two examples observed during the first air raid alarm in New York may illustrate this process. The first concerns a person of the perfectionistic type. His unconscious attitude toward life was that of living under a sword of Damocles which might fall at any moment, and believing that he could ward off menacing catastrophes by being the ultimate in correctness. The air raid alarm caught him off guard while he was on an errand of his own during office hours. The incorrectness of his behavior would not have ordinarily worried him, all the more so since he would have made up amply for the lost half hour. But because of his unconscious attitudes the alarm at this point meant the dreaded catastrophe and he reacted with panic.

The other example concerned a writer who by and large was well balanced. But he had an insatiable and compulsive need for personal admiration. He too experienced a feeling of panic at the alarm. The dread uppermost in his mind was that in case of bombing he would not appear as a hero and thereby not gain the admiration indispensable for his psychic existence. It was this dread and not the fear of the realistic danger that made him panicky.

What are the practical conclusions?

1. Understanding the nature of individual panic will be of no help in the immediate situation, because people are not accessible to reason in a state of acute panic.

2. If sufficient psychiatric help were available in clinics or in first-aid stations, people seized by panic could be treated there after the emergency. It will hardly be possible to treat their neuroses under such conditions, but it appears reasonable to expect that in a large number of cases one might find out the real sources of the acute anxiety. The result would be to fortify them against the stress of actual emergency because their anxiety would no longer be so strongly attached to the external danger.

3. As to prevention of individual panic, we might anticipate that well-organized psychological information would be helpful. The best way to do so would be to explain and discuss the nature of panic to groups.

4. Prevention on a large scale would encompass everything that tends to diminish the frequency and severity of neuroses. Roughly, such a plan would include every measure apt to improve human relationship; psychological education of people; a much larger number of psychiatric clinics all over the country than is available at present; and so forth. This latter plan would require considerably more expenditure than we are accustomed to making for psychiatric prophylaxis and treatment, and would hardly be justified merely for war emergencies. It is justified, however, if we take a long view of our future development.

This abstract was in Harold Kelman's papers at the Postgraduate Center for Mental Health. Probably dating from 1942, it may have been an abstract of one of the bulletins issued by the War-Efforts Committee of the Association for the Advancement of Psychoanalysis. Horney was talking here about people whom she would describe in *Our Inner Conflicts* as aggressive and detached.

E. *Psychological Remarks on Hoarding*

I. It is important to know that hysterical buying is *not* based on rational fears of deprivation, such as fears of being without food or shoes.

II. The reasons for hysterical buying are irrational in nature and vary from one person to another. The following elements may be involved:

    a. A blind rebellion against anything faintly resembling coercion. This would be similar to people's drinking more alcohol during prohibition. A defiant attitude of this kind is found in people who have misconceived notions of independence. Independence for them means freedom from any obligation or responsibility. Furthermore, those persons are hypersensitive to "coercion" who, without being aware of it, want to dominate and manipulate others. These people tend to accuse others of being dominating and resent bitterly anything which might constitute an interference with their own wishes.

    b. An irrational fear of impoverishment, which drives people to take exorbitant precautions against such danger. This fear operates in persons who at bottom are out to exploit others and to take advantage of them. They tend to feel it as a triumph if they can fool others or take advantage of a situation. Conversely, they feel it as a disgraceful defeat if they are deprived of anything. They are obsessed by a fear that they might come out at the short end, that others might outwit them; they resent having to give or to sacrifice anything.

III. Both factors mentioned operate in people who are essentially egocentric and isolated. They regard the world around them as potentially hostile and are primarily engaged in being on their guard against others. Hence, the idea of cooperation is entirely alien to them.

This is an abstract of a paper Horney presented at the scientific meeting of the Association for the Advancement of Psychoanalysis held at the New York Academy of Medicine in 1946. The abstract was published in the *American Journal of Psychoanalysis* 6 (1946): 56. The ideas presented in the paper had not appeared in Horney's previous writings, but, as Jack Rubins has observed, they were "incorporated as a central concept into the final version of her theory" (1978, 189). See especially chap. 1 of *Neurosis and Human Growth*.

F. The Role of Imagination in Neurosis

Imagination is a function of the mind which can serve constructive or destructive ends. The normal individual uses it for constructive planning or consolation in adversity; the artist consciously remolds reality through his imagination. The neurotic individual develops a need to live in the imagination when the inner psychic pressure becomes intolerable. Hence, he transforms his ideas about himself and the world in accordance with his unconscious needs, and thus achieves a sense of equilibrium. Although he may possess real potentialities for what he idealizes in himself, the main purpose of this self-idealization is its function as a solution for conflicts.

Living in the imagination is carried out in two different ways. Some neurotic individuals are excessively optimistic and find satisfaction in the belief that magic fulfillment is always just around the corner. Regarding themselves as omnipotent, they feel exempt from death. Others are resigned to the burden of themselves and of living. They ask little from reality and confine their satisfactions to the imagination. Considering themselves worthless, they often think of suicide.

As a consequence of these attitudes, the neurotic individual experiences marked feelings of unreality. He is also easily hurt by contact with reality and readily humiliated when not accepted at his imaginary self-evaluation. At times he reacts with explosive anger. For the most part he is alienated from self and others and unable to assess realistically his personality assets and weaknesses. The concept of time has little meaning for the neurotic individual. His values are reversed, and therefore reality appears as unreality and unreality becomes reality.

This is an abstract of a paper Horney presented at a scientific meeting of the Association for the Advancement of Psychoanalysis held at the New York Academy of Medicine in 1946. The abstract was published in the *American Journal of Psychoanalysis* 6 (1946): 57. In 1945–46, Horney, in conjunction with Harold Kelman, offered a course called "The Meaning of Dreams" at the New School for Social Research, and she may have offered other such courses of which no record has survived. She addressed the topic of dreams in her courses on analytic technique in 1950 and 1951, and a reconstruction by Wanda Willig of her lecture was published in the *American Journal of Psycho-*

analysis 19 (1959): 127–37 and reprinted, in edited form, in *The Therapeutic Process* (Horney 1999). Horney believed dreams to be important, but she did not write about their function and interpretation in any detail. Apart from her lecture, the fullest discussion of dreams from a Horneyan perspective can be found in Harold Kelman, *Helping People: Karen Horney's Psychoanalytic Approach* (1971), chaps. 15–20.

G. Criteria for Dream Interpretation

The validity of an interpretation is judged by the effect it has on the patient. If the latter presents confirmatory evidence which opens new avenues for discussion or work, it is felt that the interpretation was valid. Sometimes the explanation confirms or clarifies previous interpretations. A second criterion is found in the symbolism. One should ask oneself, "Does the explanation of the symbol coincide with the emotions operating in the patient?" and "Is there evidence that the symbol expresses exactly that which goes on in the patient?" A third criterion is whether or not one can establish a connection between the conflict in the patient and the solutions he uses in the dream. We should speak of plausibility of dream interpretations rather than of validity.

The following is an abstract of a paper Horney gave at a scientific meeting of the Association for the Advancement of Psychoanalysis held at the New York Academy of Medicine in 1947. The abstract was published in the *American Journal of Psychoanalysis* 7 (1947): 68–69. Horney was lecturing on this topic at around the same time in her course "Pride and Self-Hatred in Neuroses." See Lecture 8, "Influence on Human Relations," in Part 1 of this volume, and chap. 12 of *Neurosis and Human Growth,* "Neurotic Disturbances in Human Relationships."

H. Self-Hate and Human Relations

We have reason to be dissatisfied with ourselves when we fail to aspire to or do not achieve our potentialities as human beings. Healthy dissatisfaction leads to constructive action. However, when our claims for ourselves are irrational, we have contempt for our real achievements and succumb to destructive self-hatred. Self-hate also results when the irrational claims we make on others are not fulfilled.

All neurotic individuals strive toward irrational goals of superiority. Some drive toward unlimited power, recognition, or success; others achieve superlative heights in their imagination; and others indicate their supremacy strivings by perfectionistic goals. In all of these drives are seen a need for vindictive triumph and an enormous pride.

These superiority strivings originate in early childhood, are defenses against basic anxiety, and serve as a means of survival in the face of a severely injured self-esteem, which is then replaced by a false pride. In the pursuit of phantoms of supremacy, the individual suffers in two ways. He sustains a greater loss of self-confidence since he looks down at his real self from the heights of imaginary superiority. This self-contempt may take the form of hostility toward others, toward himself, or may be felt as contempt from others. This interferes seriously with his capacity to love or to believe in his own lovability, makes him feel vulnerable, and results in disturbance in his relationship to himself and others.

The individual in the grip of these drives is faced with two dilemmas. On the one hand, he needs the love of others badly yet feels unlovable and cannot believe that anyone can really like him. On the other hand, he needs people to affirm his vast superiority yet cannot relate himself to them because of his diminished capacity to give love.

To get out of these dilemmas he may resort to any number of neurotic solutions. He may exclude love and consciously drive himself toward goals of supremacy, since he feels that he could never be liked anyhow. Or he may do nothing in reality and attempt to achieve satisfaction by living in reflected glory or the admiration which may come to him through a partner or through children. Or he may envelop himself in a thick armor of righteousness which protects him from self-doubt. Or the individual may be resigned to never getting anything for himself and so look around for someone to take over for him. In this instance, he needs the partner for survival and may become seemingly self-effacing.

In treating this dilemma of irrational pride and self-hatred, it is most important to work through the attitudes toward self. These may become apparent only in the light of the individual's human relations. For the restoration of real self-esteem, it is necessary to get out of the vicious circle of false pride, to relinquish illusions, and to modify the search for absolute success. When an individual stops looking down on himself from the false heights of great imaginary superiority and ceases invidious comparison, his healthy self-confidence increases. When the false pride is loosened and the illusions are dispensed with, the individual can begin to develop.

This talk was given by Karen Horney as part of the symposium "Mature Attitudes in a Changing World," held at the Hotel Pennsylvania in New York City on 5 May 1947. It was published in the *American Journal of Psychoanalysis* 7 (1947): 85–87. The symposium marked the fifth anniversary of the Auxiliary Council to the Association for the Advancement of Psychoanalysis. In addition to Horney, Margaret Mead spoke, on "Maturity and Society," Edwin Lucas on "Maturity and Crime," and Eduard C. Lindeman on "Maturity and Culture." Horney's paper is striking for its advocacy of a "constructive toughness toward ourselves." This means not blaming other people, our childhoods, or our unconscious for our problems but taking responsibility for our thoughts, feelings, and actions, our growth as human beings, and the development of our talents. If others keep us down, it is up to us to fight them.

I. Maturity and the Individual

As an analyst, I shall speak of the individual, the individual who is influenced by world changes and who in turn can influence them. He can influence them for the better, the more mature he is.

Maturity is no faculty which we have or have not but it is rather a goal toward which we strive. It is not well defined at that. It is a kind of receptacle into which everybody puts his personal ideals.

However, you would hardly disagree with me if I emphasized as essential two ingredients of maturity. One is the ability to see the stark reality of persons or situations outside ourselves and to base our judgments and observations on the factors actually operating.

This is part of wisdom, a wisdom which everybody could approximate, given sufficient insight. I gather that in certain so-called primitive tribes — who know much more about the art of living than we do — the old man or old woman not only is regarded as wise but actually *is* so. In our civilization, getting older is by no means identical with getting wiser. Why not? I would say simply that we do not get wiser because we do not learn from our experiences; and we do not learn from our experiences because we are too neurotic, too rigid. More specifically, we are too confined by the misty and narrow horizon of our subjectivity. That is part of what neurosis does to us. It makes us too preoccupied with ourselves, whether we are aware of it or not, whether we want it or not. On top of our insecurity, we build a lofty edifice of arrogance which makes us believe that we are the only ones to be fair, intelligent, to understand and solve absolutely everything. In order to protect the vulnerable pride which goes with such arrogance, we see the mote in another's eyes and fail to see the beam in ours.

For instance, we saw clearly Hitler's anti-Semitism but we fail to see our attitude toward Jews and Negroes.

If our pride is hurt — which it is, easily — we turn vindictive to restore it; but again we believe that it is the other who is aggressive and that we are just on a legitimate defensive. We idealize ourselves and disparage others, see dangers where there are none or exaggerate them, while we fail to see the dangers where they actually are. We harbor the illusion of being utterly realistic, while actually and constantly we falsify reality around us because of our egocentricity. Particularly those pride themselves on being realistic who invariably assume underhanded, hostile motives in others. Actually they are just as one-sided as those who insist that everybody is good and rational.

The other essential ingredient of maturity is the ability to assume responsibility for ourselves. I know from personal experience that many people do not even understand the meaning of the term. The word "responsibility" evokes in them the same response as it does in the landlord when he grants a lease. Let us assume that most of us are responsible in this sense. But what does it mean to be *responsible for ourselves?* It involves two main things:

First, I (and nobody else) am responsible for my life, for my growth as a human being, for the development of whatever talents I have. It is of no use to imagine that others keep me down. If they actually do, it is up to me to fight them.

Second, I (and nobody else) am responsible for what I think, feel, say, do, decide. It is weak to blame others, and it makes me weaker. It is useless to blame others, because I (and nobody else) have to bear the consequences of my being and my doing. It is harmful to shirk responsibility, because I deprive myself of the possibility of growing as a human being. And I can grow only if I realize my difficulties, learn from them, and eventually overcome them.

I will illustrate what I am talking about with a difference I saw in a patient. This patient occasionally drank too much and he would come and say, "Well, I don't know how it happened. They offered me too much, too many mixed drinks." Or, at best, he would say, "I drink because I feel uneasy with people." It meant a tremendous progress when some time later he came and said to himself, "I am Jimmie Jones. I (nobody else) am responsible for my actions. I should know enough not to mix drinks. I should know how to stop. I am the one who has the hangover, or who bears the loss of being late for the analysis." In his first reaction, it was placing the blame and the fault on the other person.

"I don't feel at ease with people," with the implication that the analyst should have cured him of that.

In the second reaction it is: "*My* doing and *my* responsibility, *my* consequence." Only in the latter case can the individual get interested in examining his own difficulties.

This example shows how we avoid responsibility. One is to put the blame on others. For instance, somebody may say, "I blew up, but I was provoked by something." That may be so, but it leaves out the only constructive question: What about my own vulnerability in the matter, to get so easily provoked — and what can I do about it? A favorite trick in this regard — particularly since Freud — is to put the blame on one's parents. "I am suspicious and cannot trust other people and am easily humiliated because I couldn't trust my father or because my mother humiliated me when I was a child." That is a half-truth and all the more dangerous because it leaves out the only thing which is constructive: "What is the matter with me that keeps me from outgrowing these early injuries?"

A second and frequent way of avoiding responsibility is to feel, "It happened, I had no say in it." That may be said not only in the case of failure but also in the case of achievement. "It was just good luck." But what about our self-confidence if we don't give ourselves credit for achievement? Self-confidence is the basis for all we are doing.

A last evasion I would mention is a more sophisticated way — to put the blame on the unconscious. To say, "Well, I may prevaricate a bit, I may frustrate others, but that is unconscious. You can't blame me for it." That is true enough, but it isn't a question of blame; it is a question of fact. Am I prevaricating? Am I frustrating others? We often behave as if warding off the blame settled the matter, but it does not. Whether it is conscious or not, I have to bear the brunt of my unconscious forces, and so I had better put my effort into becoming aware of them, thus being able to assume responsibility for them.

Now, this inability to assume responsibility for ourselves — what does it do to us?

First, it makes for plenty of irrational hostility against others.

Second, it alienates us from ourselves.

Third, it prevents us from growing and from tapping all the resources we actually have. And, with all of that, it prevents us from growing mature. In the most simple terms, the inability to assume responsibility for ourselves is a lack of constructive toughness toward ourselves. It is not because we are too sensitive or too weak by nature but because of our neurosis. It is here that psychoanalysis comes in and where the educational work of the Auxiliary Council comes in. It is just as important to combat neurosis as it is to combat cancer. We do not die from neurosis, but it makes us weak and it robs us of the possibility of overcoming our egocentricity, of assuming responsibility for ourselves, and with that the possibility of becoming mature and bringing order into a chaotic world.

Do not think it is up to the leaders only. It is not only the leaders, it is every single individual that counts!

This is either an unusually full abstract or a short paper that Horney gave at a scientific meeting of the Association for the Advancement of Psychoanalysis held at the New York Academy of Medicine in 1948. The piece was published in the *American Journal of Psychoanalysis* 8 (1948): 75–77. In it Horney introduced "the self-effacing character as a clinical entity" for the first time and tried to explain the relationship between "compliance," the term she used in *Our Inner Conflicts,* and "self-effacement," the term she was to use in *Neurosis and Human Growth,* by presenting compliance as an earlier stage of self-effacement.

J. On Self-Effacing Attitudes

The term "self-effacing" is used to mean blotting out oneself. This is sometimes called masochism, but this term, with its specific sexual connotations, is misleading. The following remarks will include a general survey of self-effacing attitudes and an evaluation of them as a clinical entity.

A self-effacing person is one who makes strenuous and often pathetic efforts to win another person over, but at the same time feels afraid of that person and abused by him. In these attitudes he has positive expectations. Just as the aggressive person expects danger or trickery from others, and the detached person expects nothing but wants only to be let alone, the self-effacing person expects everything good from others — love, admiration, protection, sympathy, tolerance, appreciation, and stimulation. He goes about eliciting these things by expressing no wants of his own, seeking to fulfill the expectations and wishes of others, being available for services, being understanding, staying out of all competition, and never being resentful. In addition he may make appeals for sympathy and pity by showing his needs, his weakness, and his suffering; and he may try to evoke guilt feelings in the other person by showing how he has been made to suffer and how he deserves better treatment.

There is another reason for his need to win others over. He actually can't demand anything openly or fight for himself. He may not even realize how badly he actually is being treated but may persist in endless appeasing maneuvers and endless "understanding" of the other one. But he puts his suffering to neurotic use. Since he cannot endure reproaches, he wards them off by making anyone who reproaches him feel despicable and mean. If his appeasing overtures are not accepted, he will feel abused, unappreciated, victimized, exploited, or even injured beyond repair. Another alternative is to feel abject and no good.

There are three main sources of abused reactions: 1) the person actually lays himself open to being abused by his abjectness or by pressing attentions and services that are not really wanted; 2) he feels abused if the returns he secretly counted on are not forthcoming; 3) he feels abused if his pride in the idealized qualities of understanding, sympathy, and being of service is injured or if his motives are questioned.

Typical abused reactions may be to blow up in rage, which is not understood by others, since they do not know his unexpressed expectations; to feel an intensification of suffering, becoming ill, more depressed, and more miserable; to become more vindictive through suffering in a manner particularly likely to make others feel guilty. This combination of helplessness, self-sacrifice, and defenselessness makes for morbid dependency on others. Feelings are emphasized, in contrast to the [reactions of the] detached person who hides feelings or the aggressive person who distrusts them.

Another characteristic of the self-effacing person is his attitude toward difficulties in life. He takes them lying down. He feels unable to cope with difficulties which he really feels he should master, such as those connected with his work, and he is prone to use suffering as an alibi — "I really couldn't." Feeling so abused, he actually stands in his own way. He is afraid to get stronger, to improve things for himself. He feels abuse where none is intended, he invites abuse, and he is assailed from within by his own self-disparaging attitudes toward himself, which he is prone to attribute to others. In advanced stages a person can only reproach himself or talk interminably of what has been done to him. He is in great despair and wants to commit suicide. There is real danger of this, since he remains entirely inaccessible to help as long as he dwells entirely on his suffering.

We would regard this picture as a clinical entity. The various factors included in it have been ascribed by other analytic writers to a variety of causes. Freud spoke of certain phases of it as derived from the death wish, as related to feminine tendencies, to oral drives, or to homosexuality — generally speaking, a somewhat scattered view. Viewing the self-effacing character as a clinical entity, we would look for a compliant individual with strong inverted sadism, an idealized image of being a saint, with extensive unfulfilled unconscious claims. Why is this character syndrome a clinical entity? We see some individuals who are openly quite unassertive, martyrized, self-sacrificing, abused. This is the more self-effacing type. In other individuals these characteristics exist as one side of a conflict, on the other side of which are vindictiveness and exploitiveness. In still others both of these sides are present, but one may be largely repressed. The advanced stages present a very clear picture with a prevalence of self-reproaches, despair, repetitious recounting of what they have suffered, suicidal ideas, and real negativism to all constructive suggestions. They want help on their own terms, but do not realize what these terms are.

These attitudes arise of necessity out of another attitude. The beginning is a moving toward others in order to cope with anxiety, with appeasing tendencies in order to make oneself likable. But a child who feels so driven comes to feel hostile to the environment which seems so threatening. He then tries to eliminate this side of the arising conflict and to stifle resentments. This makes him more helpless and from being compliant, of necessity he becomes self-effacing. But conflicts persist and he then has to idealize himself, to make a virtue out of necessity, to raise himself safely above intolerable conflicts. The traits he will idealize are the patient, long-suffering, unselfish qualities, and he is no longer aware of these as painful needs but sees them as morally superior characteristics. His needs now turn into claims, he feels entitled to rewards, and in order to get them, he uses the sufferings of the blameless person he believes himself to be more than ever.

However, when a person idealizes himself, he also starts to despise himself for any failure to live up to the idealized image. He feels he is never sacrificing enough. He also sees that others override him, that he comes out at the small end of things, and that others fail to notice and appreciate him because he is constantly self-effacing. This puts him on a seesaw of uncertainty about himself. He cannot be sure whether he is superior to others or whether he is no good. A person has to have some certainty about himself. The aggressive person puts himself on the side of feeling superior to others. The self-effacing person allies himself with feelings of worthlessness and guilt feelings. He has to do this because he is afraid of being expansive. He has always felt safer in second place; he has always stood in the shadow of others; he is afraid of winning; he has to depreciate himself when complimented; he is terrified of the limelight, even a favorable limelight. He does not dare feel he really has successes; he feels this only as fear of making himself ridiculous. To be conspicuous seems like inviting exposure.

When, during analysis, the feeling of being abused diminishes, self-reproaches continue and are usually externalized. The individual becomes more dependent on what others do for him or think of him. If he has retained some vestige of expansiveness, he will be proud of suffering and of the amount and severity of it, but he will see himself as a saint who is a martyr. The severely self-effacing person may function in a certain measure and may even achieve a feeling of unity and satisfaction. If the life situation is favorable, he may get considerable [satisfaction] out of life by living for others. This can look like a healthy capacity to help others, but the difference becomes apparent when there is a loss, through death or other changes, of the object of these services. Thrown back upon himself, he may develop a psychotic episode.

Individuals who have a compulsive need to live for others have made an adjustment in a measure healthier than those who have succeeded only in losing or submerging themselves through alcohol, for instance, or in some other kind of oblivion. The most frequently sought and the most satisfactory oblivion is that of "love." The person is sure of losing himself in this manner; he is sure he can give a partner all the desired things and that he can be loved in return. The final form of seeking to lose oneself is suicide, with the conviction that death is the ultimate rest, the only friend.

In this degree of hopelessness and despair we find individuals who become panicky over minor physical symptoms. If they are dizzy, they feel they have a brain tumor; a cold in the head is certain tuberculosis; a stomachache means cancer; severe anxiety means the beginning of insanity. In such persons we are often able to trace earlier signs of resignation, just giving up. This means a preference to disintegrate under the blows of a cruel world rather than to give up one atom of the idealized image. "I am just too pure and fine, and so I must suffer." In connection with these phantasies, we occasionally find masochistic activities, a predilection for being coerced, beaten, and otherwise misused.

Adler was aware of the use of suffering to get attention, to get back at others, or to get something out of others. This is quite clear, but it does not go far enough. Freud recognized the depth, power, and intensity of suffering when he called it instinctual. If we assume it is instinctual, our curiosity about how it develops and from what sources is left unsatisfied. To regard it as instinctual has certain erroneous implications, such as the idea that the neurotic always wants to suffer. Here no distinction is made between neurotic suffering which is used to gain specific advantages and the kind of suffering to which a person is driven and which has no strategic value. The difference is great. Neurotic or strategic suffering will never help a person in his development, while suffering not used for strategic purposes makes one more sensitive, more refined, more patient and understanding. The self-effacing individual must have some way of asserting his claims; the neurotic use of suffering is the consequence of this need. Freud said, pessimistically: "Men will always want to suffer." If we look upon suffering as a consequence of neurosis, we can hope to help a person to find himself, instead of effacing himself.

These are either unusually full abstracts or two short papers that Horney gave at scientific meetings of the Association for the Advancement of Psychoanalysis held at the New York Academy of Medicine in 1948. The pieces were published in the *American Journal of Psychoanalysis* 8 (1948): 78–80. Horney pointed out that people with different solutions have different attitudes toward suffering and focused on the meaning of suffering for the compliant individual. She explored the relation of suffering to compliant peoples' idealized image and its interpersonal and intrapsychic functions. This was a continuation of her exploration of the self-effacing solution, which culminated in chaps. 9 and 10 of *Neurosis and Human Growth*. For an earlier treatment of neurotic suffering, see "Illness and Suffering as a Form of Gratification" earlier in the section.

K. The Meaning of Neurotic Suffering

Every neurosis entails actual suffering, such as physical discomforts — headaches or fatigue — or mental suffering — anxiety or despair regarding inhibitions and blockage in work and in relations with others. There is, however, considerable difference between the actual suffering and the individual's attitude toward realistic unhappiness and limitations. One individual makes little of them, may even deny them, will be embarrassed or angry at any mention of them, thinks of them as weakness which inevitably exposes him to the contempt of others. He is wary of any evidence of sympathy and prone to interpret it as patronage or ridicule. He will rarely refer to the actual misery he is in but on the contrary can discuss his neurotic pride and superiority drives with ease.

An entirely different type of individual complains constantly, displays continuous undisguised self-pity, and appeals urgently to others for help. He relishes misery as a connoisseur and tends to feel grandiose about the hopeless character of his personal suffering. He is pessimistic about everything, pessimistic about the probable outcome of anything that befalls him, and pessimistic about the ability of anyone to help him. He is absorbed in his own feeling or lack of feeling and dramatizes his emotional state. His pride is particularly easily hurt, and when it is hurt, he comes abject and cringing and throws himself on the mercy of others.

What function has this emphasis on suffering? Suffering has been recognized and studied by psychoanalysts of every school of thought. To put it very briefly, Freud would have called it instinctual and related it to masochism. Adler would have said it served to get attention because of inferiority feelings. W. Reich would interpret it as a reproach to others. Alexander would feel it was to punish others. We would be inclined to examine the attitudes and values associated with it, that is, to look at this kind of behavior in relation to the compliant individual's idealized image.

The subjective values of this attitude toward suffering seem to be to make accusations against others through suffering, to make unconscious claims through suffering, and to externalize responsibility. The idealized image here is one of goodness, unselfishness, and helpfulness. Such a person tends to do what he wants to do, but under the flag of self-sacrifice. He feels virtuous, he modestly takes it for granted that he is morally superior, but he would never talk about it, because that would be pride and he feels he has no pride. His huge claims on the basis of his self-glorification cannot be made openly, but they appear in the form of needs and suffering which point to what he feels should be done for him. Suffering has the value of a moral victory over others. No one should expect anything of him because of his suffering. Self-contempt is apt to be great but it is externalized. It is felt only as the low opinion others have of one. Such people tend to wallow in the feeling of being just stupid, incapable, miserable, and they have no spontaneous interest in bringing about any real change in these conditions. Efforts to make life endurable follow along the line of immersing oneself in love, if possible, or in work.

In general they feel that all their renunciations and sacrifices should be repaid in full. The inner unconscious functions of suffering are apparently as a safety device against self-destruction, as a way of justifying claims, as a way of revenge for disappointments and deprivations, as confirmation of the ideal of unselfishness, and as a preoccupation which serves to shut out hatred and vindictiveness from awareness.

General discussion of Dr. Horney's paper brought out the following points: an individual who presents a persistent dramatic tableau of "how I suffer, how horrible it was, how scared to death I was" generally is quite deaf to suggestions that he remedy matters, particularly if they involve any effort on his part. He apparently regards his part as complete when he has made a convincing presentation of his suffering. He also tends for a long while to regard the analyst in two typical ways: as having enormous powers, and able, if he wishes, to give or withhold the magical cure; and as a coldhearted monster unable and unwilling to understand the patient's suffering.

Neurotic suffering appears in the form of a persistent complaining attitude which may and often does rest on the unrealistic basis of neurotic claims and phantastic, inflated ideas of what one is entitled to. Although we may see clearly the unreality, the lack of sound logic, or the exaggerated nature of the patient's complaints, still they must be respected because of their reality to him. They must be studied with great care because of what we can learn about his inner structure of values.

One function these sufferings serves is in the individual's relations with others. There they may be used to impress others with the courage with which he bears this huge and undeserved burden; or to win the liking of others on this basis; or to extort their help, which he feels would not be forthcoming without this overwhelming display of his need; or to excuse him for escaping responsibilities; or to demonstrate his innocence and blamelessness in the face of any reproach. For these individuals their sacrifices can represent something which they mistake for love. In an active sense they feel they are giving real love when they are compulsively giving to others and doing for them. On the passive side they expect and try to extort continual pity, sympathy, and charity from those who are fond of them, since these qualities, for them, stand for love.

Suffering also serves an intrapsychic function in which the burden of misery may be of great inner value as a way of appeasing the onslaughts of self-contempt. It is a sort of inner excuse of "I can't help it" or "I am too small and weak to do anything about it." It serves as a way of pleading guilty for defensive purposes as the quickest and even the only way of putting a stop to bitter self-reproaches.

Maintaining suffering and the feeling of helplessness is indispensable as a protective measure against self-hatred. An example of this can be seen in neurotic pessimism in which one chooses to dwell only on the disappointments and losses in one's past life. This is used as a neurotic proof that hard work or confidence in oneself or others should not be expected of one. This merges into the feeling that nothing at all should be expected of one.

Conflicts may be present between a drive to self-sacrifice and a feeling of godlike virtue and purity. Each subtly reinforces the other without the individual's being aware of the contradiction between them or of the conflict into which he is forced. Or a person may really grovel before others, feel fearful, not dare to ask anything of anyone, but he may have an inner conviction of being entitled to all rights. This conflict may show in giving and taking. Here there would be great apparent generosity, but accompanied by an actual callous egocentricity. Often in such conflict one side is stronger than the other; usually the individual is totally unaware of the other side. A striking example of this occurs in a person who actually grovels in his excessive esteem of others, but remains unaware of the fact that he holds some individuals in such contempt as to feel actually contaminated by them. Where the conflict between compliance and aggression is quite open and acute, one sees an individual who, if he makes any sacrifice, tells himself he is a weakling; but if he is callous and reaches for what he wants, he feels he is obnoxious. This kind of conflict makes one unable to take any stand, and one remains lukewarm. Pride and self-hatred do not in themselves constitute conflict, but these incompatible attitudes toward the self lead to conflicts strong enough to tear a person apart when his drives toward compliance and toward aggressiveness compel him toward opposite goals.

This was either an unusually full abstract or a short paper that Horney gave at the scientific meeting of the Association for the Advancement of Psychoanalysis held at the New York Academy of Medicine on 22 September 1948. It was published in the *American Journal of Psychoanalysis* 9 (1949): 84–86. Horney was primarily interested in shallow living as an aspect of the neurotic solution of resignation, a solution she explored most fully in chap. 11 of *Neurosis and Human Growth*. She found the syndrome to be so widespread in modern civilization that it is "difficult for people to see that there is anything pathological in it."

L. Shallow Living as a Result of Neurosis

The problem of shallow living first struck me when a writer consulted me as to why he had become completely unproductive after having written one quite good book. At that time I eliminated the possibility of conflicts about subject matter, then found progressively that he had greatly diminished interest in any subject at all, then began to see that he had turned entirely away from any serious work and had for years simply pursued pleasure. When I pointed out that he had turned wholly to the periphery of life and spent all his energies there, and that as a result all his feelings had flattened out, he was able to tackle this with real seriousness, get to work again, and make some progress.

Later Erich Fromm wrote of this problem in individuals who had been crushed quite early in life — and who then started simply to adapt themselves, like automatons, never undertaking any life of their own. He made the point that this condition should be distinguished from a condition of "defect." Problems similar to this are described in Jackson's *The Outer Edges,* in which a brutal murder can be experienced by those around only as a sort of thrill, and in George Eliot's *Romola,* in which a slight weakness of character slowly develops into a real deterioration of the whole personality.

These examples show different parts of the same syndrome: A person who was originally normal, capable, full of life, later shows loss of moral values, of feelings, and of real appreciation of life. By definition, this is a kind of living that lacks depth and intensity; lacks direction, autonomy, and real meaning. This I would call shallow living.

Concerning feelings and interests, we can say that feelings in such people are very shallow. Words of praise or warmth appear easily with little meaning and no marked sincerity. They have personal conversations but no serious discussions, and they seek diversions more vigorously than anything else. Their interests are directed almost entirely to external values, such as money, entertainment, or gossip. Although they may talk of art, music, social questions, or politics, these talks are apt to develop more by contagion than spontaneous interest. They show failure to form judgments of their own and are influenced more by current opinion or by what others will think of them. Interest in their own growth and self-development is lacking and their talk of values is shallow. There is drifting because of few real convictions or serious direction of their own lives — which alone can steer and guide one's life.

One group is interested only in pleasure. One might call their theme, "Oh, give me a home where the millionaires roam," but it would be a mistake to think this refers only to the leisure classes. It is as true of those who go to the movies as of those who make up theater parties. It may also take special forms, such as collecting stamps, fancying oneself as a gourmet, or reading mystery stories. These people will protest, "But it's so much fun being with people where nothing happens but drinking and talking." This can be quite deceptive. It may look like zestful living, freedom, and broadmindedness, whereas it is nothing more than an escape into talking and lack of standards. What is called "doing the right thing" may cover deceptively a lack of real moral fiber. Then there are the opportunistic people, whose real goal is to avoid friction or pain and always to get by. Overlapping with this group are the prestige-seekers — prestige not through work but through being in the right group, with the right people, doing things likely to bring success.

In all these groups is a profound feeling of futility, although it is usually largely repressed. The prognosis for the individual is better if this feeling comes to the surface, because it indicates there is some capacity for seriousness still alive. Among all these people there is an aura of something impersonal, even in such intimate relations as marriage. There is little real investment of themselves in anything they do, and a very great overemphasis on external values.

Do such people come to analysts? Rather rarely, because they specialize in seeking easy methods and quick cures. The easier the life they have created for themselves, the less they will go into serious discussion of themselves. This kind of living is seen so frequently in modern societies that we tend scarcely to realize how unhealthy and unnatural it actually is. Further, the actual character of the problem is often obscured by the convincing externalizations offered by them: that their unhappiness comes from a wrong spouse, climate, or diet. It is typical of those who externalize a great deal that they tend to be so alienated from themselves as not to feel things as caused by themselves, but in general to look around the external world for explanations.

Some of these people are not wholly deadened, and a part of themselves may feel futile and distressed, while others become aware of disappointments and distress about themselves only as it is manifested in psychosomatic illnesses. If they come into analysis, they are prone to stop early upon relief of one symptom, or to find excuses for stopping abruptly when their values, standards, and goals start to look uncomfortably clear.

Erich Fromm has raised the question whether this is innate or acquired. In my own experience, the analytic data indicates that such patients have been much more alive around adolescence. They have had ambition, have wanted and acquired things, have had deep feelings of love or despair, or were real leaders in their groups. Then they went through some serious disappointment, despair, or depression, after which there was apparent recovery. Later they seemed duller and slid into a pattern of shallowness offered by the environment. For example, a New Englander may become quite bohemian, or perhaps go after only earning money, or become stuffily pompous. On the surface, they may then show a glib, smooth behavior, but in their dreams one will find depth of feeling, despair, hope, self-hate, anxiety. And in the course of analysis, in connection with some memory, something very alive will appear again, in which depth and intensity of feeling are shown to be really there.

But there is another factor which shows they are really present: there is an anxious moving away from the real self, from their real depth. When these appear in dreams and are pointed out, they move away from the dream. When they are brought back to it, they leave again and go on in an impervious manner to something quite far from it. There is a tenacity to this process which indicates the effectiveness of externalization as a way of letting nothing touch one. This is a deliberate moving away from life, toward the surface—not one turning away but a continual one. This means that this movement must be of great value to them. If we remember the functions of the real self as an inner spring, as a source, a directing power, a judicial power which decides our values for us as a basis for our electing or rejecting, then we find a high degree of alienation from the real self in shallow living. If this is pointed out to the patient, he sees it but is not interested, or will reply that he feels what he is doing is all right and is a better way of living. Upon trying further and pointing out to the patient that he could make much more of his life and have much more happiness, one meets complete failure. But it becomes clear then that this patient doesn't really expect anything. He is not hopeless, he just doesn't want to be pulled into any maelstrom. If he is more sophisticated, he may bring up something of oriental philosophy, or some sort of philosophy of seeking peace. But there is a determined resignation from active and productive living of his own life.

The leading role here is not the search for glory, because, although there is a definite idealized image, the resignation means the patient has actually given up active efforts to achieve anything in reality, in actual achievement. It is much like a person who can do good work but settles for simple tasks because it is easier. Even the members of the prestige group, from whom one might expect more activity, have actually the same attitude. They look to gain not from real work but through association with others.

The most serious consequence occurs in their own lives, as a restriction on real achievement requiring active efforts. This may be very unsatisfactory and may be possible to change, but they do not see this. Instead, they evolve a kind of endless patience which is actually a neurotic resignation.

Often they can be quite active in helping others. They will then make many excuses for doing nothing for themselves. This is also resignation. They do not want friction, fight, or pain. They may call this compliance. It is not compliance but resignation, which is deeper. This neurotic resignation is a recoiling from inner struggles. Those who take this curious and fatal step choose it as a solution to keep from suffering too much from their own internal conflicts. By this means they find a certain kind of peace. If they resent any fighting, it is because they have given up and recoiled from any inner struggle. The external struggle is only an extension of the internal ones.

But there can be other outcomes. There may be a profound inertia as a cover for inner resignation, or an enormous restriction of activity as a consequence of resignation. A still further step may be the feeling of not wanting anything at all for one's self—that is, eliminating one's self entirely, with an attempt to live wholly for others. This is sometimes fairly successful and satisfying for a while, and such a patient is apt to come to our attention only when this solution has broken down. If we look on this condition as a result of an active neurotic process, then the outlook is quite hopeful compared to regarding it as an innate or hereditary defect.

Analysis of such patients may end unsatisfactorily because of unrecognized resignation, in an open or hidden form. This needs to be recognized and tackled quite early and can never be lost sight of. This tackling is particularly difficult because the patient is so averse to pain, efforts, and change in general. He has found peace of a sort, and he doesn't want to risk changing from these narrow confines. The success of analytic work will depend on the amount of constructive interest still alive in the patient.

I selected this subject as an opportunity to discuss resignation as a destructive force of the first magnitude, then secondly because this syndrome occurs so frequently in modern civilization. It is even more apparent that this condition cannot be innate, since it is so widespread among intelligent and able people and involves such serious loss.

It is interesting to speculate to what extent cultural factors may be involved in its occurrence. Sociologists could undoubtedly produce evidence of this. For individuals, however, these social factors are less important. The individual needs to come out of this crippling condition, then be prepared to help others to free themselves from it. He must also be prepared to work through the personal factors in himself, rather than look to the culture for an understanding of it.

Social approval of this kind of living makes it more difficult for people to see that there is anything pathological in it and makes it harder for psychiatrists to work against it. The more clearly the psychiatrist understands the dynamics of it, the better he will be equipped to deal with it.

This is an abstract of a paper Horney gave at an interval meeting of the Association for the Advancement of Psychoanalysis held at the American Institute for Psychoanalysis on 13 March 1949. The abstract was published in the *American Journal of Psychoanalysis* 9 (1949): 94–95. Horney's topic here was aggressive individuals who use their intellectual powers "to promote a kind of self-idealization in which the belief in the supremacy of the mind and compulsive efforts to mold oneself into intellectual perfection are prominent features." The themes Horney sounded here were taken up again in *Neurosis and Human Growth,* particularly in chap. 8.

M. Man as a Thinking Machine

We find in many neuroses something in the nature of an elaborate philosophical system. One such system is founded on the belief in the power of the mind in which an enormous pride is invested. Thinking then takes on special importance, since it is used in the service of the neurotic pride system as distinguished from the service of healthy and constructive purposes. Those who invest thinking with neurotic pride tend to talk endlessly and will intellectualize everything without any involvement of their true feelings or their true beliefs.

Thinking powers are used to promote a kind of self-idealization in which the belief in the supremacy of the mind and compulsive efforts to mold oneself into intellectual perfection are prominent features. This is seen most frequently in aggressive individuals. It is accompanied by marked alienation from themselves and little awareness of anything else about themselves, their feelings, or their bodies. In vindictive individuals feelings are undervalued and disparaged. Such people end by having nothing to live for except their minds. With this comes a kind of retirement into the intellect, detachment from others, and a high degree of alienation from the self.

They may be quite dead emotionally, and they often feel lucid and clear only when they think or read. They frequently say, "I have no existence apart from my thoughts." Intellect is used as their only standard for gauging superiority, and they expect and require themselves to be supreme in that area. Any failure to achieve that is regarded as total failure at the moment and in life in general. The intellect is used in the service of power over others — outwitting, outmaneuvering, and confusing others by complicated language which, frequently, no one can understand. Sadism is always present. They size up others in respect to intellectuality exclusively. They prefer highbrow talk and evaluate others according to their capacity for this kind of talk in a spirit of competition and disparagement. They try to maintain a godlike self-sufficiency because of the inner dire necessity to confirm the idealized image and the pride system. They need to regard their own thinking as infallible. Since they have nothing else, their lives — apart from intellectualizing — are usually quite barren.

What does this do to the individual's attitudes toward himself? He loses respect for himself as he really is. He cultivates a passion for getting by, or getting around everything quickly. In analytic treatment, wanting to get by may be a serious retarding force. When a patient sees a conflict, he at once asks: "How do I get over it?" which stalls him in actually working at a problem. In addition to wanting to get by, he also takes pride in getting by very fast.

Pride in intellect has a constricting effect on the ability to enjoy anything, since nothing can be enjoyed that hasn't been approved by the intellect. Is it rational, does it measure up, is it perfectly acceptable to my thinking? Only if it passes can it be enjoyed.

The opposite is found in the self-effacing person who feels he never thinks as well as others do, never has any ideas, and quickly calls himself stupid. There is an anxious need to make no claims to having a good mind, in order to avoid disappointments.

Intelligence can be turned wholly to the service of neurotic pride, rather than toward enriching life and the enjoyment of being wholly one's real self. In other cases beauty or sex can likewise be turned to the service of pride with the same consequences. Analysis would aim to achieve synthesis with the real self as a whole, using knowledge not just for pride in knowledge but for understanding and in order to increase the appreciation and enjoyment of oneself and others.

This was Horney's contribution to the symposium "Psychoanalysis and Moral Values," sponsored by the Auxiliary Council to the Association for the Advancement of Psychoanalysis and held at the Henry Hudson Hotel on 5 April 1950. Other participants were Harold Kelman, Muriel Ivimey, Alexander Reid Martin, and Frederick A. Weiss — all colleagues of Horney's at the American Institute for Psychoanalysis. The papers from the symposium were published in the *American Journal of Psychoanalysis* 10 (1950): 63–69. Horney's paper was derived in part from the introduction to *Neurosis and Human Growth,* "A Morality of Evolution."

N. *Psychoanalysis and Moral Values*

When we speak of analysts in therapy operating with moral values, some people may be concerned that the analysts' particular values may exert influence on the patient and, therefore, interfere with the patient's autonomy. An analysis without interference or influence by the analyst is impossible. In every human relationship one person influences another.

The analyst needs a set of values to operate as a psychoanalyst. These will determine what he takes up with the patient and what he discourages or encourages. The analyst needs a set of values related to the patient's problems and of a kind to help the patient with his neurotic difficulties.

What is analytical therapy? Is it only a process of gaining awareness? Is it only a process of gaining self-knowledge? Its aim is actually toward reorientation. Self-knowledge which does not lead to a reorientation is of no value. Analysis itself is essentially a disillusioning process in large part. This disillusionment is necessary but has been overrated for a long time — for it is not enough. In O'Neill's play *The Ice Man Cometh*, the deteriorated alcoholics gain disillusionment which only leads to further misery, as they are no longer able to summon up constructive forces to utilize the insights gained.

Neurotic development is the opposite to healthy human growth. In every human being there is the urge to grow and develop his human potentials, according to his special gifts and environment. He may become more cautious, hard, self-reliant, contemplative, active, or dependent, but the healthier he is, the more the individual tends to develop his own potentialities. The neurotic gives up development of his real self to establish a glorified self, being driven toward absolute perfection by various tyrannical shoulds and claims.

We can understand the main process going on in neurosis by seeing that energies are used to prove one is a unique, superior being rather than to promote true self-realization. This results in the building up of false pride, and eventually the neurotic turns against himself if he doesn't live up to the impossible demands he makes on himself. This is a moral problem.

Granted that neurotic inner dictates lead to a cramping of our spontaneity and are a whip which we use to drive ourselves into perfection, don't we still need these inner dictates which push us toward healthy moral conduct? The answer depends on the kind of belief one has in human nature. Three groups would answer this question in different ways:

1. Man by nature is primitive, sinful, instinct-ridden, and bad. With this belief one must adhere to superimposed moral dictates and sanctions to insure moral conduct.

2. It is taken for granted that there is something essentially good and also something essentially bad in human nature. The responsibility rests on the individual to place a check on his own bad, sinful drives. It implies that man needs help from outside sources, like "grace," to be good, which is the hope for salvation. It implies that the bad in man may be inhibited by fears and the goad of moral conscience.

3. We believe that there are constructive forces inherent in human nature and that man, on his own, wants to grow and develop his own potentialities.

Each person has within him what I would call the morality of evolution. Efforts go spontaneously toward the liberation of constructive forces.

The work of eliminating obstructive forces is one of our moral obligations. Any kind of righteousness is obstructive to growth. We must realize our mistakes and try to correct them. One must begin by facing and understanding and solving his own inner conflicts before trying to solve conflicts between self and mankind.

Self-analysis with healthy self-fulfillment becomes, then, our chief moral obligation to ourselves and to others. Truthfulness toward ourselves is an absolute necessity. Mutuality toward others is important as we must have good relations with others to realize ourselves.

These moral values and goals do not interfere with the patient's autonomy, but help him to find and express his own moral autonomy.

This is an abstract of a paper Horney gave at a scientific meeting of the Association for the Advancement of Psychoanalysis held at the New York Academy of Medicine on 1 March 1950. The abstract was published in the *American Journal of Psychoanalysis* 10 (1950): 80–82. The paper seems to have been based on the chapter of the same title in *Neurosis and Human Growth* (chap. 13), and the abstract provides a condensed account of how each of the five major solutions (self-effacement, narcissism, perfectionism, arrogant vindictiveness, and resignation) affects people's ability to work, the degree of their satisfaction, and the quality of their performance.

O. Neurotic Disturbances in Work

Neurotic disturbances have a profound effect on the ability to work. These disturbances may affect the attitude toward the work actually done, as in overrating or underrating it, or they may make the conditions under which work can be done far more rigid and constricted than is usual. They can affect the ability to start or to finish work. There may be underrating or overrating of the extent to which internal difficulties are a disturbing factor. They result in varying abilities to plan, to take risks, to take help, or to delegate to others. Wide differences will exist in individual awareness of there being difficulties, and also in the amount of suffering that occurs.

In the aggressive-expansive individual, there will be a feeling of being superior, a complete identification with the idealized image; the appeal of life will be a desire for mastery. His desire will be to overcome every obstacle, that is, to do the difficult task immediately, and the impossible a little later. Such individuals regard their work as superior, and feel that anyone who disagrees is jealous, or is attacking because of hostility. They cannot allow doubts to arise on this score, so must ward off criticism. They can't give credit to others, and no one's achievements can be praised in their presence. They must attack any job and are sure they can do it. There is no illness they cannot diagnose and no paper they cannot write. There is a general overrating of their capacities and of the quality of their own work. They remain oblivious to any disturbances in regard to work.

The aggressive-narcissistic type, in contrast, can be the most productive of all the aggressive individuals. He is, however, swayed by his own imagination and may scatter his talents by having too many irons in the fire. If he has any failure, he feels it is because he has too many gifts, and he will say he envies duller people. Or he may start, but drop, too many things, stopping at the slightest obstacle. He won't want to see that he has difficulties, and his seeming lack of interest is a face-saving device. He feels he hates details. Ordinary people should do such things. His pride resides in effortless superiority and in the glory of the dramatic and the unique. Sporadic efforts feed his pride, but regular efforts are demeaning. Regular effort threatens his feeling of unlimited power. The quality of his work is often disappointing.

The arrogant-vindictive individual who has had terrific early humiliations survives by stifling softer feelings. His driving force in life becomes that of vindictive triumph. His assets are that he is a prodigious worker with a real passion for work. He has a relentless ambition, but an empty life; for him an hour not spent on work is an hour lost. He works like a well-oiled machine but often stays on the fringes of a field, since his interest is in method and results, rather than in content. In speaking, he will be sure to cover every side and every point but contribute nothing of his own. He plans well and carefully but is dictatorial, intimidating, and exploitive. He will never delegate anything, as he believes only he, or others like him, are fit to take charge. He can take small losses, because of long-range planning, but real trials are frightening.

Somewhat different is the aggressive-perfectionistic individual, who is often prevented, if his perfectionistic needs are very powerful, from ever accomplishing anything at all.

The prevailingly self-effacing type is quite different. He sets his aims too low. He underrates his gifts. He is plagued by self-berating criticisms and constantly has the feeling, "I can't." The quality of his work may not suffer, but *he* does. He may do better if he works with or for other people. In general he can work well with people, since he feels most helpless when alone. He may really enjoy a kind of work which is beneath his real capacities. But he may eventually get into speaking or writing where he begins to work at the real level of his gifts. His demands on himself will be as high as those of the expansive individual, but his self-contempt will require actual fulfillment of them, while his self-berating goes on at every instant. If he is aware of winning or of doing things well, he can become quite paralyzed. He will be hampered by a self-destructive contempt, and may at any time be seized by inertia.

Where the self-effacing trends are more chronic and more seriously inhibiting, there can be a lack of concentration, with a feeling of the mind going blank. Instead of working, this person will fritter the time aimlessly away, or doodle, until he becomes intolerably disgusted with himself and tries to work, although actually too tired. He is blocked by his self-minimizing and his inefficiency in attacking anything. He is undermined by doubts but actually isn't aware of them. He frequently forgets. Things are not available to him when he needs them. He feels weak, with an oppressive sense of impotence and insignificance. He may be quite apologetic about his work. Feeling quite helpless about his ideas, he is full of taboos about starting anything. Certainly, he has ideas, but he is unable to operate with them. Work actually is torment for him, being, as he is, driven by the need for ultimate perfection. The quality should be perfect and the methodology, as well. There are obviously unavoidable errors in thought, style, and organization, but his self-contempt cannot bear them.

Any approval must come from others, and he wants and needs approval, advice, and comfort. He sees the relatedness of human beings as a long chain in which each one does something for others, never for himself. He has to tell others of his intentions, but then feels that a great deal is expected of him, and that he can't live up to these impossibly high demands. He is unable to use his own inner values and standards in his work; because of this he craves constant sympathy, appreciation, and encouragement from above. Much that he tries to do ends in disappointment, humiliation, and vindictiveness. His anxiety is quelled by work but rises again when the job is done and presented. He has his greatest difficulty if he strikes a really hard problem, if he has had some success, or if he receives severe criticism.

Although love affairs don't bring him happiness, he hopes, in earlier life, that they will and plunges into them. He flees from work difficulties into these love affairs, and alternates between work and unsuccessful attempts at love as a solution.

In the resigned type of individual, the difficulties are principally inertia and hypersensitivity to coercion. The latter may drive him to rebel against inner, as well as outer, dictates, so that he cannot ever do what he himself wishes to. He may, though, find some expression of his artistic gifts, if he has them, in a rather defiant spirit. But he is more likely to degenerate into being not much more than a rugged individualist, or simply doing everything differently than other people.

These difficulties are understandable only through studying the neurotic structure, and they can be predicted if the particular individual neurotic is well understood. Some of these conditions entail great suffering, others certainly do not, but all are alike in preventing the individual from developing in one of the essential areas of his life.

Artistic gifts occur in individuals quite independently of neurosis, but their expression can be seriously diminished by neurotic incapacity. The question of artistic work being contingent on neurosis arises frequently, but most often in the aggressive type. The expansive and rebellious types fear they may, through analysis, lose their angry, arrogant drive, and become self-effacing automatons. Along with this, they fear that they will begin to consider someone else's criticism, which might weaken their self-confidence and destroy them. They also fear they might be too content after analysis to want to bother to create. Realistically, there are sufficient sources of drive and feeling and real interest without recourse to neurotic stresses, but to be able to tap these sources, the individual must be sufficiently alive to operate in spite of conflicts.

The self-effacing individual does not have this fear of analysis endangering his ability to create. He knows too well how much his conflicts clip his wings.

Real gifts, and the desire and capacity to express them, have to be free to approach self-realization. Artists, like others, work in spite of neuroses.

The following was based on Horney's lecture of 1 March 1950, "Neurotic Disturbances in Work." It originally appeared in the 20 March 1950 issue of *Newsweek* and was reprinted in the *American Journal of Psychoanalysis* 51 (1991): 245–47. Although it was based on the same lecture as the preceding abstract, it gave greater emphasis to Horney's ideas about the relation between artistic creativity and neurosis, ideas that were developed most fully in chap. 13 of *Neurosis and Human Growth*. My study of literature has led me to conclusions that are somewhat different from Horney's. Although neurosis usually interferes with a person's ability to work, it often seems to fuel the creativity of the great literary geniuses, who frequently use their writings as a means of expressing their conflicts, glorifying their predominant defenses, and maintaining their precarious equilibrium.

P. Karen Horney on Work, Art, Creativity, and Neurosis

Nullified Neuroses

A famous American writer, sunk in emotional distress, once confessed to his psychiatrist: "I suppose I do need psychotherapy . . . but I'm afraid of it. It might destroy that something in me which is my own."

The writer was one of the 9,000,000 Americans who are said to have neuroses (disorders of the psyche) to some degree. By "that something" he meant his peculiar talent which had lifted him to the top of his profession. Resting on the theory that "misery loves company," he and the other neurotics had found satisfaction in such catch phrases as "of course, every genius is a neurotic," and "be grateful for your neurosis," which, they believed, might help in any effort from holding a routine job to creating a masterpiece of art.

To Dr. Karen Horney, the handsome, gray-haired dean of the American Institute for Psychoanalysis, this stand is neither practical nor scientifically correct. Speaking at the New York Academy of Medicine, the 64-year-old Norwegian-Dutch psychoanalyst bluntly discounted the value of a neurosis for the creative person. "An artist," she concluded, "can create not because of his neurosis, but in spite of it."[1]

BLOW HARD AND GIVE UP

No matter how self-assured or realistic the neurotic may seem, his self-confidence, "probably the most crucial prerequisite for creative work," is always shaky, Dr. Horney pointed out. He is rarely able to make an adequate appraisal of what is expected of him: he either underrates or overrates the job he sets out to do.

When working conditions are fairly rigid, the neurotic pays a tremendous price in physical and emotional effort. He seldom works up to his maximum

1. In rebuttal, just published is a book called "The Writer and Psychoanalysis," by Dr. Edmund Bergler, which states that writers write to compensate for infantile frustrations. (Footnote from the *Newsweek* article.)

capabilities, and the quality of the work actually performed suffers. Nor is there much satisfaction to him from creative or congenial work. He is too driven, too loaded with conflicts and fears of failure to enjoy it.

Dr. Horney divides neurotic workers into three groups. They are: (1) the expansive, (2) the self-effacing, and (3) the resigned.

Generally, the expansive worker feels superior to others and desires to triumph over them. He "tends to regard the particular work he is doing as uniquely significant and to overrate its quality."

Because of the need to deny self-doubt, the expansive neurotic responds to the slightest criticism of his work as though it were a malicious, hostile attack. At the same time, his ability to give credit to others within his own field and age group is limited.

This worker's superiority stems from the implicit belief that there is no obstacle which he cannot overcome through his will power and superior faculties. To prove his mastery, he may become very resourceful, with an incentive to attempt tasks which others may shy away from. But he scatters his interests and energies in too many different directions. Stopping and starting one pursuit after another, he loses interest when real difficulties arise. His enthusiasm peters out before the job is accomplished.

Despite good potentialities, this type is often disappointing in the caliber of his work. Dr. Horney explained. "For neurotic reasons, he simply does not know how to work."

Another example of the expansive neurotic is the perfectionist who works methodically and attends to details too meticulously. He is the slow and unproductive worker, who turns out a piece of "unspirited work" at great cost to himself. He has a tremendous need for respect from others, and a failure may bring him close to collapse.

The self-effacing neurotic sets his aims too low and underrates his natural gifts as well as his work's importance. His motto: "I can't do anything, but I must." He is the helpless one, plagued by self-doubt and self-berating criticism, who does his best work under some kind of supervision.

This type frequently complains of lack of concentration. He becomes fidgety when working. He doodles, plays solitaire, makes telephone calls, and files his fingernails after sitting down at his desk to work. Then, disgusted with himself, he makes a heroic effort, feels deadly fatigue, and gives up. "In any case," said Dr. Horney, "there is great likelihood of this type not accomplishing too much."

The resigned neurotic is distinctly different. He may "settle for less than his faculties warrant, as part of his pattern of general resignation from active living." When forced to work for others, he becomes listless, without initiative, and slow in physical and mental action. Because of his detachment, he works better alone. If his real self is sufficiently alive, he may be able to break his ties with other people and accomplish genuinely creative work on his own.

ART VS. NEUROSIS

With cool sympathy, Dr. Horney dissected the "silent ordeals" of the neurotic who in his attempt to work runs up against "intangible but unsurpassable odds."

Many are not even aware of these difficulties, she observed. Others are disquieted by the possible relation between their creative ability and their neuroses. "Granted," they will say, "that a neurosis makes for suffering in general and for hardship in work in particular, is it not the indispensable condition for artistic creativity? Would it not curtail or even destroy this creativity if an artist were analyzed?

Dr. Horney's answer is no. Analytic experience will show in greater detail the neurotic factors which can be a hindrance to creative work. To the neurotic who fears that analysis will flood him with self-doubt and plunge him into self-contempt, she counsels: "He will have to see and experience self-contempt or the tendency to comply, but he will certainly not stay with such attitudes for good."

Further argument against analysis is raised by the neurotic. "Assuming analysis can resolve neurotic conflicts and make a person more happy, would it not also remove so much inner tension that he would simply be content with being and lose the inner urge to create?"

"The value of neurosis for creative activity is unfounded," Dr. Horney reminds him. "The large majority [of neuroses] have an untoward effect on the artist's work. He can create only to the extent that his real self is alive."

The tenth anniversary of the founding of the Association for the Advancement of Psychoanalysis was marked by a gala reception in June 1951 at the St. Moritz Hotel in New York. The remarks Karen Horney delivered on that occasion were then published at the beginning of volume 11 (1951) of the *American Journal of Psychoanalysis*. The association and the American Institute for Psychoanalysis were badly damaged by the splits that occurred in the early 1940s, but they prospered after the war, when interest in psychoanalysis burgeoned. By 1950, there were more than sixty candidates at the institute, along with a teaching staff of twenty-five, eleven of whom were training analysts. Nonetheless, there were a great many internal tensions, as one can infer from Horney's remarks. For fuller accounts of the splits and internal tensions, see Rubins 1978, Quinn 1987, and Paris 1994.

Q. Tenth Anniversary Address

Ten years ago a small number of analysts separated from the New York Psychoanalytic Society and founded a new analytic group—the Association for the Advancement of Psychoanalysis—in order to provide for the possibility of training psychiatrists along lines which in many ways deviated from Freud's theories.

The separation evolved from ideological differences which had gradually become too crucial for constructive work. Any cooperative effort, to be productive, needs diversity and unity—the unity consisting of a common base of essential issues and a willingness to explore in a scientific spirit the validity of one's concepts. It must be remembered that all members of the seceding group had been trained in and worked for many years with the traditional concepts of Freud. Thus, a common base existed then and exists today. The recognition of unconscious forces, of dreams being meaningful, the belief in the importance for therapy of the patient-analyst relationship, of recognizing and dealing with the patient's defenses, and the value of "free associations" are all part of a common heritage which forms the groundwork of psychoanalytic theory and method.

In other regards, however, we had in fact lost a common base. Our philosophic premises had changed in decisive ways. These concerned, above all, our belief in the nature of man. Man for us was no longer an instinct-ridden creature, but a being capable of choice and responsibility. Hostility was no longer innate but reactive. Similarly, egocentric and antisocial cravings like greed or the lust for power were not inevitable phases of man's development, but an expression of a neurotic process. Growing up under favorable conditions, we believed, man would develop his inherent constructive forces, and like every other living organism, would want to realize his potentialities. Human nature was no longer unalterable but could change.

The reason we decided not merely to withdraw but to develop a new group was primarily the obligation felt toward the younger generation of psychiatrists to teach them what we believed to be more constructive ways in theory and therapy. This step required some courage because it veered toward an uncertain future. We started as a small group, without money, without prestige. What is more important, we did not yet have a firm theoretical ground to stand on. Many of the old concepts with which we were used to working had lost their meaning; our own theories were just beginning to emerge; all we had was a rather clear perception of the direction we wanted to go.

Our meetings and courses were held in our private homes. Only subjects which were of interest to allied fields were being taught at the New School for Social Research. Furthermore, during these first years we had to struggle not only with all the difficulties of a pioneering group, but also with disruptive friction within the group which resulted in two subsequent splits. At bottom, these were due to the fact that the group was initially too heterogeneous. Not all those who separated from the New York Psychoanalytic Society did so because of the search for new territory. Some joined the new group as a protest against dogmatic rigidity. The concrete issues precipitating the splits were the questions of lay analysis and of an affiliation with a medical school. Though all of us felt in close touch with medical science and the medical profession, the majority felt that for our development in research and teaching, involvement with a larger institution was not timely.

The splits left us in a weakened condition. All the teaching and the organizational work had to be done by a handful of people. However, the remaining members became a more solid group. Each one of us did his ample share of the work according to his abilities, whether these were predominantly in scientific writing, in teaching, or in organizing. In all of these areas we have made satisfactory progress.

In the scientific field much work has been done on particular problems of psychoanalytic theory and therapy—too much, in fact, to enumerate within such a brief survey. It may suffice to say in general that we did gain considerable understanding of the neurotic development and its difference from healthy human growth. In addition, we got a clearer perception of the goals of therapy and of the means to attain them. Inevitably, the more we understood, the more keenly we realized the magnitude of the subject, and the more desirable became the productivity of the whole group. So, we encouraged in every way possible the spirit of free inquiry and the capacity for critical thinking in our "Interval Meetings" and in the courses. We encouraged original thinking in the papers written by members and candidates. We sponsored such experimental enterprises as group analysis.

We put in incessant work at improving our teaching methods. We profited in this regard from the experiences of progressive educators. We have tried to make better teaching a concern not only of the teachers but of the candidates as well. We have, for instance, encouraged their making more and more relevant evaluations of the courses and have taken them into serious consideration in planning the curriculum.

The organization of the association, the institute, and the Candidates Association became increasingly solid and effective. We fostered the growth of a lay organization, ACAAP, for the important task of community education and mental hygiene. In contrast to our first headquarters, which had space only for small meetings and for the office, we now have space for all teaching except that done at the New School, for our library, and for the considerably increased office activities.

Naturally, with different personalities working closely together, frictions were unavoidable. Here, too, we had to learn from experience. We learned and are still learning that in human relations which are focused on work to be done, personal factors such as righteousness, ambition, vulnerabilities, and resentments have to recede before the task at hand. At the same time, we could have the confidence that each one of us was working at himself and his personal difficulties. And in this most inconspicuous work, a work done by the individual for himself and his self-realization, lies the greatest assurance for the further growth of the group. To be sure, we need creative minds, good teachers and organizers. But the productivity of these very activities and their benefit for the whole group depend upon the aliveness and the integrity of all the individuals composing the group. For knowledge may freeze into dogmatism; teaching may fall on barren soil, and organizing may deteriorate into bureaucracy unless a group is pervaded by a spirit of aliveness and an interest in the individual growth of all its participants.

On 23 April 1952, the scientific meeting of the Association for the Advancement of Psychoanalysis, held at the New York Academy of Medicine, took the form of a panel on neurotic anxiety, moderated by Karen Horney. The panelists were Kurt Goldstein, Paul Hoch, Rollo May, Frederick A. Weiss, and Harry Gershman. Abstracts of the presentations, along with Horney's opening remarks, were published in the *American Journal of Psychoanalysis* 12 (1952): 89–95.

R. Neurotic Anxiety

The large audience here tonight is evidence of the widespread interest in the subject we are discussing. We believed it was a good idea to have people discuss this subject who come from quite difference disciplines and whose conclusions are based on different kinds of research.

Because there are such widely divergent ideas about anxiety, there are only a few points about which most everyone agrees. One point is that anxiety is a response to danger. For many the focal question then is, "What is the nature of the danger?" My friend Dr. Paul Tillich would say "anxiety" is the fear of nonbeing, or of the meaninglessness of life.

For all psychotherapists, for all those who have to work with anxiety, there are three questions we have to account for:

1. What is the nature of the danger or what has been endangered? We would all agree that what is endangered is an essential value (or what the person feels is an essential value).

2. What is endangering? What is the threatening factor?

3. Since helplessness is an essential part of every anxiety, what accounts for the helplessness? Is the helplessness objectively real or subjectively felt as real?

The subject for this evening has been announced as "Neurotic Anxiety" to narrow down the vast subject of anxiety. But speaking of neurotic anxiety presupposes the existence of healthy anxiety or an anxiety which we all have by virtue of our being human beings, healthy or otherwise. If we think of the existence of these two forms of anxiety, we are again faced with some pertinent questions:

What do these two types of anxiety, healthy and neurotic, have in common? Are they different qualitatively? Are they different quantitatively?

What about our attitudes toward anxiety — our attitude as the observer and our attitude as the physician?

Is anxiety something paralyzing, or is it constructive? We know it can be both a moving or paralyzing force. Is it better to ask under which conditions it is a moving force and under which it is paralyzing? Is it valuable to experience, endure, and stick through anxiety under all conditions or only under certain conditions? I hope we will touch upon some of these and other questions this evening.

Writings of Karen Horney

1915. *Ein kasuistischer Beitrag zur Frage der traumatischen Psychosen* [A case history contributing to the question of traumatic psychoses]. Published doctoral thesis. Berlin: H. Bode.

1917. Die Teknik der psychoanalytischen Therapie. *Zeitschrift für Sexualwissenschaft* 4. The Technique of Psychoanalytic Therapy. *American Journal of Psychoanalysis* 28 (1968): 3–12. Reprinted in *The Therapeutic Process*, 11–23.

1923. Zur Genese des weiblichen Kastrationskomplexes. *Internationale Zeitschrift für Psychoanalyse* 9: 12–26. On the Genesis of the Castration Complex in Women. *International Journal of Psycho-Analysis* 5 (1924): 50–65. Reprinted in *Feminine Psychology*, 37–53.

1925. Review of *Zur Psychologie der weiblichen Sexualfunktionen* by Helene Deutsch. *Internationale Zeitschrift für Psychoanalyse* 11: 388–94. Review of *On the Psychology of Female Sexual Functioning* by Helene Deutsch. *International Journal of Psycho-Analysis* 7 (1926): 92–100.

1926a. Die Flucht aus der Weiblichkeit. *Internationale Zeitschrift für Psychoanalyse* 12: 360–74. The Flight from Womanhood: The Masculinity Complex in Women as Viewed by Men and by Women. *International Journal of Psycho-Analysis* 7: 324–39. Reprinted in *Feminine Psychology*, 54–70.

1926b. Gehemmte Weiblichkeit: Psychoanalytischer Beitrag zum Problem der Fridigität. *Zeitschrift für Sexualwissenschaft* 13: 67–77. Inhibited Femininity: Psychoanalytical Contribution to the Problem of Frigidity. In *Feminine Psychology*, 71–83.

1927a. Der Männlichkeitskomplex der Frau. *Archiv für Frauenkunde* 13: 141–54. The Masculinity Complex in Women. In *The Unknown Karen Horney*.

1927b. Psychische Eignung und Nichteignung zur Ehe. *Die Ehe: Ihre Physiologie, Psychologie, Hygiene und Eugenik,* ed. M. Marcuse. Berlin: Marcus & Weber, 192–203. Psychological Fitness and Unfitness for Marriage. In *The Unknown Karen Horney.*

1927c. Über die psychischen Bestimmungen der Gattenwahl. *Die Ehe: Ihre Physiologie, Psychologie, Hygiene und Eugenik,* ed. M. Marcuse. Berlin: Marcus & Weber, 470–80. On the Psychological Determinants of the Choice of a Marriage Partner. In *The Unknown Karen Horney.*

1927d. Über die psychischen Wurzeln einiger typischer Ehekonflikte. *Die Ehe: Ihre Physiologie, Psychologie, Hygiene und Eugenik,* ed. M. Marcuse. Berlin: Marcus & Weber, 481–91. On the Psychological Roots of Some Typical Marriage Problems. In *The Unknown Karen Horney.*

1927e. Diskussion der Laienanalyse. *Internationale Zeitschrift für Psychoanalyse* 13: 203–6. Discussion on Lay Analysis. *International Journal of Psychoanalysis* 8: 255–59 [with S. Freud, E. Jones, H. Sachs, C. Oberndorf, J. Rickman, A. Brill, S. Jelliffe, F. Alexander, C. Muller-Brunschweig, T. Benedek, T. Reik, G. Roheim, H. Nunberg, F. Deutsch, W. Reich, E. Simmel, R. Waelder]

1928a. Die monogame Forderung. *Internationale Zeitschrift für Psychoanalyse* 13: 397–407. The Problem of the Monogamous Ideal. *International Journal of Psycho-Analysis* 9 (1928), 318–31. Reprinted in *Feminine Psychology,* 84–98.

1928b. The Problem of the Monogamic Statute. *Psychoanalytic Review* 15: 92–93.

1930a. Die spezifische Problematik der Zwangneurose im Lichte der Psychoanalyse [Specific problems of the compulsion neurosis in the light of psychoanalysis]. *Archiv für Psychoanalyse* 91: 597–601.

1930b. Die Einrichtungen der Lehranstalt: Zur Organisation [The establishment of the educational program: On organization]. *Zehn Jahre Berliner Psychoanalytisches Institut.* Vienna: Internationaler Psychoanalytischer Verlag, 48–52.

1931a. Das Misstrauen zwischen den Geschlechtern. *Die Ärztin* 7: 5–12. The Distrust Between the Sexes. In *Feminine Psychology,* 107–18.

1931b. Die prämenstruellen Verstimmungen. *Zeitschrift für psychoanalytische Pädagogik* 5: 1–7. Premenstrual Tension. In *Feminine Psychology,* 99–106.

1931c. Der Kampf in der Kultur: Einige Gedanken und Bedenken zu Freuds Todestrieb und Destruktionstrieb in *Das Problem der Kultur und die ärztliche Psychologie* [The problem of civilization and medical psychology]. *Vorträge, Institut für Geschichte der Medizin, Univ. Leipzig* 4: 105–118 (Leipzig: Thieme-Verlag). Culture and Aggression: Some Thoughts and Doubts About Freud's Death Drive and Destruction Drive. *American Journal of Psychoanalysis* 20 (1960): 130–38. Reprinted in *The Unknown Karen Horney* as Culture and Aggression: Some Thoughts and Doubts About Freud's Theory of Instinctual Drives Toward Death and Destruction.

1932a. Die Angst vor der Frau: Über einen spezifischen Unterschied in der männlichen und weiblichen Angst vor dem anderen Geschlecht. *Internationale Zeitschrift für Psychoanalyse* 18: 5–18. The Dread of Woman: Observations on a Specific Difference in the Dread Felt by Men and by Women for the Opposite Sex. *International Journal of Psycho-Analysis* 13: 348–60. Reprinted in *Feminine Psychology,* 133–46.

1932b. Zur Problematik der Ehe. *Psychoanalytische Bewegung* 4: 212–23. Problems of Marriage. In *Feminine Psychology,* 119–32.

1932c. On Rank's *Modern Education: A Critique of Its Fundamental Ideas* (Review). *Psychoanalytic Quarterly* 1: 349–50. Reprinted in *The Unknown Karen Horney.*

1932d. On the Manifestations of Repressed Female Homosexuality (lecture). In *The Unknown Karen Horney.*

1932e. Behavioral Patterns of Repressed Homosexual Women (lecture). In *The Unknown Karen Horney.*

1933a. Die Verleugnung der Vagina: Ein Beitrag zur Frage der spezifisch weiblichen Genitalangst. *Internationale Zeitschrift für Psychoanalyse* 19: 372–84. The Denial of the Vagina: A Contribution to the Problem of Genital Anxieties in Women. *International Journal of Psycho-Analysis* 14: 57–70. Reprinted in *Feminine Psychology,* 147–61.

1933b. Psychogenic Factors in Functional Female Disorders. *American Journal of Obstetrics and Gynecology* 25: 694–703. Reprinted in *Feminine Psychology,* 162–74.

1933c. Maternal Conflicts. *American Journal of Orthopsychiatry* 3: 455–63. Reprinted in *Feminine Psychology,* 175–81.

1933d. The Misuse of Psychoanalysis. In *The Therapeutic Process,* 24–31.

1933e. Common Deviations in Instinct Development: Homosexual Women and Boy-Crazy Girls (lecture). In *The Unknown Karen Horney,*

1933f. The Problem of Frigidity (lecture). In *The Unknown Karen Horney.*

1933g. Psychogenic Factors in Menstrual Disorders (lecture). In *The Unknown Karen Horney.*

1933h. Psychogenic Factors in Problems Relating to Pregnancy (lecture). In *The Unknown Karen Horney.*

1933i. The Uses and Limitations of Analytic Knowledge in Gynecological Practice (lecture). In *The Unknown Karen Horney.*

1933? Illness and Suffering as a Form of Gratification. In *The Unknown Karen Horney.*

1934a. The Overvaluation of Love: A Study of a Common Present-Day Feminine Type. *Psychoanalytic Quarterly* 3: 605–38. Reprinted in *Feminine Psychology,* 182–213.

1934b. Restricted Applications of Psychoanalysis to Social Work. *The Family* 15 (6): 169–73. Reprinted in *The Therapeutic Process,* 45–51.

1934c. Concepts and Misconcepts of the Analytic Method. *Archives of Neurology and Psychiatry* 32: 880–81.

1935a. The Problem of Feminine Masochism. *Psychoanalytic Review* 22: 241–57. Reprinted in *Feminine Psychology,* 214–33.

1935b. Personality Changes in Female Adolescents. *American Journal of Orthopsychiatry* 5: 19–26. Reprinted in *Feminine Psychology,* 234–44.

1935c. Conceptions and Misconceptions of the Analytical Method. *Journal of Nervous and Mental Disease* 81: 399–410. Reprinted in *The Therapeutic Process,* 32–44.

1935d. Certain Reservations to the Concept of Psychic Bisexuality [Abstract of paper presented at a meeting of the American Psycho-Analytic Association]. *International Journal of Psycho-Analysis* 16: 510–11.

1935e. On Difficulties in Dealing with the Transference. *The News-Letter of the American Association of Psychiatric Social Workers* 5 (2), 1–5. Reprinted in *The Therapeutic Process,* 52–58.

1935f. Woman's Fear of Action [a talk delivered to the National Federation of Professional and Business Women's Clubs in July 1935]. In Bernard J. Paris, *Karen Horney: A Psychoanalyst's Search for Self-Understanding.* New Haven: Yale University Press, 1994, 232–38. Reprinted in *The Unknown Karen Horney.*

1936a. The Problem of the Negative Therapeutic Reaction. *Psychoanalytic Quarterly* 5: 29–44. Reprinted in *The Therapeutic Process,* 59–71.

1936b. Culture and Neurosis. *American Sociological Review* 1: 221–30. Reprinted in *The Unknown Karen Horney.*

1937a. *The Neurotic Personality of Our Time.* New York: W. W. Norton.

1937b. Das neurotische Liebesbedürfnis. *Zentralblatt für Psychotherapie* 10: 69–82. The Neurotic Need for Love. In *Feminine Psychology,* 245–58.

1938a. Understanding Personality Difficulties in a Period of Social Transition. In *The Unknown Karen Horney.*

1938b. The Achievement of Freud. In *The Unknown Karen Horney.*

1939a. *New Ways in Psychoanalysis.* New York: W. W. Norton.

1939b. Can You Take a Stand? *Journal of Adult Education* 11: 129–32. Reprinted in *The Unknown Karen Horney.*

1939c. What Is a Neurosis? *American Journal of Sociology* 45: 426–32. Reprinted in *The Unknown Karen Horney.*

1939d. Children and the War. *Child Study* 17: 9–11. Reprinted in *The Unknown Karen Horney.*

1941. Letter to American Psychoanalytic Association by Five Resigning Members of the New York Psychoanalytic Society. *American Journal of Psychoanalysis* 1: 9–10 [with H. Ephron, S. Kelman, B. Robbins, C. Thompson]. Reprinted in *The Unknown Karen Horney.*

1942a. *Self-Analysis.* New York: W. W. Norton.

1942b. Understanding of Individual Panic [Summary of contribution to a symposium on panic at the New School for Social Research] *American Journal of Psychoanalysis* 2: 40–41. Reprinted in *The Unknown Karen Horney.*

1942c. Remarks made at a meeting of the Auxiliary Council of the Association for the Advancement of Psychoanalysis in 1942. Dedication (to the Twentieth Anniversary of the Karen Horney Clinic), *American Journal of Psychoanalysis* (1975) 35: 99–100.

1942? Psychological Remarks on Hoarding. In *The Unknown Karen Horney.*

1945a. *Our Inner Conflicts.* New York: W. W. Norton.

1945b. Overemphasis on Love. In *The Unknown Karen Horney.*

1946a. Karen Horney, ed. *Are You Considering Psychoanalysis?* New York: W. W. Norton.

1946b. Introduction to *Are You Considering Psychoanalysis?* New York: W. W. Norton, 9–13.

1946c. What Does the Analyst Do? In *Are You Considering Psychoanalysis?* New York: W. W. Norton, 187–209. Reprinted in *The Therapeutic Process,* 97–109.

1946d. How Do You Progress After Analysis? In *Are You Considering Psychoanalysis?* New York: W. W. Norton, 235–57. Reprinted in *The Therapeutic Process,* 110–22.

1946e. The Role of Imagination in Neurosis [Abstract of paper presented at a meeting of the Association for the Advancement of Psychoanalysis]. *American Journal of Psychoanalysis* 6: 56. Reprinted in *The Unknown Karen Horney.*

1946f. Criteria for Dream Interpretation [Abstract of paper presented at a meeting of the Association for the Advancement of Psychoanalysis]. *American Journal of Psychoanalysis* 6: 57. Reprinted in *The Unknown Karen Horney.*

1946g. The Future of Psychoanalysis [Summary of an address, delivered in May 1946, celebrating the fifth anniversary of the Association for the Advancement of Psychoanalysis]. *American Journal of Psychoanalysis* 6: 66–67. Reprinted in *The Therapeutic Process,* 152–54.

1946h. Sadistic Love. Pamphlet of the Auxiliary Council to the Association for the Advancement of Psychoanalysis. Published in *The Unknown Karen Horney.*

1946?. Enslavement in Marriage. In *The Unknown Karen Horney.*

1947a. Inhibitions in Work. *American Journal of Psychoanalysis* 7: 18–25. Reprinted in *The Unknown Karen Horney.*

1947b. Foreword to the article "Gymnastics and Personality" by Gertrud Lederer-Eckardt. *American Journal of Psychoanalysis* 7: 48–49. Reprinted in *The Therapeutic Process,* 123–25.

1947c. Self Hate and Human Relations [Abstract of paper presented at a meeting of the Association for the Advancement of Psychoanalysis]. *American Journal of Psychoanalysis* 7: 65–66. Reprinted in *The Unknown Karen Horney.*

1947d. Pride and Self-Hate in Psychoanalytic Therapy [Abstract of paper presented at a meeting of the Association for the Advancement of Psychoanalysis]. *American Journal of Psychoanalysis* 7: 68–69. Reprinted in *The Therapeutic Process,* 154–55.

1947e. Maturity and the Individual [Contribution to the symposium Mature Attitudes in a Changing World]. *American Journal of Psychoanalysis* 7: 85–87. Reprinted in *The Unknown Karen Horney.*

1947f. Pride and Self-Hatred: Influence on Human Relations (lecture). In *The Unknown Karen Horney.*

1947g. Pride and Self-Hatred: Influence on Love Life (lecture). In *The Unknown Karen Horney.*

1947h. Pride and Self-Hatred: Influence on Sex Life (lecture). In *The Unknown Karen Horney.*

1947i. Pride and Self-Hatred in Freud (lecture). In *The Unknown Karen Horney.*

1947j. Pride and Self-Hatred in Literature: The Devil's Pact. In *The Unknown Karen Horney.*

1947k. Pride and Self-Hatred: Solution in Therapy (lecture). In *The Therapeutic Process,* 126–33.

1948a. The Value of Vindictiveness. *American Journal of Psychoanalysis* 8: 3–12. Reprinted in *The Unknown Karen Horney.*

1948b. On Self-Effacing Attitudes [Abstract of paper presented at a meeting of the Association for the Advancement of Psychoanalysis (see also abstract of the discussion of this paper with Karen Horney as moderator, same journal issue, 81–82)]. *American Journal of Psychoanalysis* 8: 75–77. Reprinted in *The Unknown Karen Horney.*

1948c. The Meaning of Neurotic Suffering 1 [Abstract of paper presented at a meeting of the Association for the Advancement of Psychoanalysis]. *American Journal of Psychoanalysis* 8: 78–79. Reprinted in *The Unknown Karen Horney.*

1948d. The Meaning of Neurotic Suffering 2 [Abstract of paper presented at a meeting of the Association for the Advancement of Psychoanalysis]. *American Journal of Psychoanalysis* 8: 79–80. Reprinted in *The Unknown Karen Horney*.

1949a. Finding the Real Self: A Letter with a Foreword by Karen Horney. *American Journal of Psychoanalysis* 9: 3–7. Reprinted in *The Therapeutic Process*, 134–42.

1949b. Shallow Living as a Result of Neurosis [Abstract of paper presented at a meeting of the Association for the Advancement of Psychoanalysis held at the New York Academy of Medicine on 22 September 1948]. *American Journal of Psychoanalysis* 9: 84–86. Reprinted in *The Unknown Karen Horney*.

1949c. Man as a Thinking Machine [Abstract of paper presented at a meeting of the Association for the Advancement of Psychoanalysis held at the American Institute for Psychoanalysis on 13 March 1949], *American Journal of Psychoanalysis* 9: 94–95. Reprinted in *The Unknown Karen Horney*.

1950a. *Neurosis and Human Growth: The Struggle Toward Self-Realization*. New York: W. W. Norton.

1950b. A Morality of Evolution. *American Journal of Psychoanalysis* 10: 3–4. (Reprint of the introduction to *Neurosis and Human Growth*).

1950c. Contribution to the symposium on Psychoanalysis and Moral Values held at the Henry Hudson Hotel on 5 April 1950. *American Journal of Psychoanalysis* 10: 64–65. Reprinted in *The Unknown Karen Horney*.

1950d. Neurotic Disturbances in Work [Abstract of paper presented a meeting of the Association for the Advancement of Psychoanalysis held at the New York Academy of Medicine on 1 March 1950]. *American Journal of Psychoanalysis* 10: 80–82. Reprinted in *The Unknown Karen Horney*.

1950e. Responsibility in Neurosis [Abstract of paper presented at a meeting of the Association for the Advancement of Psychoanalysis held on 11 December 1949]. *American Journal of Psychoanalysis* 10: 84–85. Reprinted in *The Therapeutic Process*, 155–56.

1950f. Psychotherapy [Abstract of a conference talk at the Institute of Living delivered on 22 March 1950]. *Digest of Neurology and Psychiatry* 18: 278–79. Reprinted in *The Therapeutic Process*, 156–57.

1950g. The Search for Glory, Part 1. *Pastoral Psychology* 1: 13–20.

1950h. The Search for Glory, Part 2. *Pastoral Psychology* 1: 31–38.

1950i. Karen Horney on Work, Art, Creativity, and Neurosis [Condensation of a 1 March 1950 lecture by Karen Horney at the New York Academy of Medicine] *Newsweek*, March 20, 1950, 44–46. Reprinted in *American Journal of Psychoanalysis* 51 (1991): 245–47. In *The Unknown Karen Horney*.

1951a. Tenth Anniversary [Address to the Association for the Advancement of Psychoanalysis, delivered in June 1951 on the tenth anniversary of its founding]. *American Journal of Psychoanalysis* 11: 3–4. Reprinted in *The Unknown Karen Horney*.

1951b. On Feeling Abused. *American Journal of Psychoanalysis* 11: 5–12. Reprinted in *The Unknown Karen Horney*.

1951c. The Individual and Therapy [Contribution to the symposium Psychoanalysis and the Constructive Forces in Man held on 4 April 1951]. *American Journal of Psychoanalysis* 11: 54–55. Reprinted in *The Therapeutic Process*, 158–59.

1951d. Ziele der analytischen Therapie. *Psyche: Eine Zeitschrift für Tiefenpsychologie und Menschenkunde in Forschung und Praxis* 5 (7): 463–72. The Goals of Analytic

Therapy. *American Journal of Psychoanalysis* 51 (1991): 219–26. Reprinted in *The Therapeutic Process*, 143–51.

1952a. The Paucity of Inner Experiences. *American Journal of Psychoanalysis* 12: 3–9. Reprinted in *The Unknown Karen Horney*.

1952b. Human Nature Can Change [Contribution to a symposium on this topic held at the town hall in New York City on 1 March 1952]. *American Journal of Psychoanalysis* 12: 67–68. Reprinted, with additions, in *The Unknown Karen Horney*.

1952c. Values and Problems of Group Analysis [Contribution to the symposium Group Analysis: Some Problems and Promises held in New York on 7 October 1951]. *American Journal of Psychoanalysis* 12: 80–81. Reprinted in *The Therapeutic Process*, 159–61.

1952d. Abstract of remarks by Karen Horney as moderator of a panel discussion on neurotic anxiety at a meeting of the Association for the Advancement of Psychoanalysis held at the New York Academy of Medicine on 23 April 1952. *American Journal of Psychoanalysis* 12: 89–90. Reprinted in *The Unknown Karen Horney*.

1953a. Abstract of remarks by Karen Horney as moderator of the round table discussion Constructive Forces in the Therapeutic Process at the annual meeting of the American Psychiatric Association held in Atlantic City, N.J., on 15 May 1952. *American Journal of Psychoanalysis* 13: 4.

1953b. Abstract of remarks by Karen Horney as moderator of a discussion of Dr. Kondo's paper on Morita Therapy at a meeting of the Association for the Advancement of Psychoanalysis held on 9 November 1952. *American Journal of Psychoanalysis* 13: 87–88.

1956a. Evolutionary Psychotherapy [An interview of Karen Horney by Werner Wolff, "Therapy of Interpersonal Relationships"]. In Werner Wolff, *Contemporary Psychotherapists Examine Themselves*. Springfield, Ill.: Charles C Thomas, 84–90.

1956b. Aims of Psychoanalytic Therapy [compiled by Ralph Slater from lectures on psychoanalytic technique given by Karen Horney at the American Institute for Psychoanalysis during 1946, 1950, 1951, and 1952]. *American Journal of Psychoanalysis* 16: 24–25. Revised version in *The Therapeutic Process*, 175–77.

1956c. Understanding the Patient as the Basis of All Technique [compiled by Emy A. Metzger from lectures on psychoanalytic technique given by Karen Horney at the American Institute for Psychoanalysis during 1946, 1950, 1951, and 1952]. *American Journal of Psychoanalysis* 16: 26–31. Revised version in *The Therapeutic Process*, 198–205.

1956d. Blockages in Therapy [compiled by Joseph Zimmerman from lectures on psychoanalytic technique given by Karen Horney at the American Institute for Psychoanalysis during 1946, 1950, 1951, and 1952]. *American Journal of Psychoanalysis* 16: 112–17. Revised version in *The Therapeutic Process*, 215–21.

1956e. Interpretations [compiled by Ralph Slater from lectures on psychoanalytic technique given by Karen Horney at the American Institute for Psychoanalysis during 1946, 1950, 1951, and 1952]. *American Journal of Psychoanalysis* 16: 118–24. Revised version in *The Therapeutic Process*, 206–14.

1957a. The Analyst's Personal Equation [compiled by Louis A. Azorin from lectures on psychoanalytic technique given by Karen Horney at the American Institute for Psychoanalysis during 1946, 1950, 1951, and 1952]. *American Journal of Psychoanalysis* 17: 34–38. Revised version in *The Therapeutic Process*, 191–97.

1957b. The Initial Interview, Part 1 [compiled by Morton B. Cantor from lectures on psychoanalytic technique given by Karen Horney at the American Institute for Psychoanalysis during 1946, 1950, 1951, and 1952]. *American Journal of Psychoanalysis* 17: 39–44. Revised version in *The Therapeutic Process*, 178–85.

1958. Dreams, Part 1: Theoretical Considerations [compiled by Wanda Willig from lectures on psychoanalytic technique given by Karen Horney at the American Institute for Psychoanalysis during 1946, 1950, 1951, and 1952]. *American Journal of Psychoanalysis* 18: 127–37. Revised version in *The Therapeutic Process*, 222–31.

1959. The Quality of the Analyst's Attention [compiled by Morton B. Cantor from lectures on psychoanalytic technique given by Karen Horney at the American Institute for Psychoanalysis during 1946, 1950, 1951, and 1952]. *American Journal of Psychoanalysis* 19: 28–32. Revised version in *The Therapeutic Process*, 186–90.

1960. Evaluation of Change [compiled by Ralph Slater from lectures on psychoanalytic technique given by Karen Horney at the American Institute for Psychoanalysis during 1946, 1950, 1951, and 1952]. *American Journal of Psychoanalysis* 20: 3–7. Revised version in *The Therapeutic Process*, 242–47.

1967a. *Feminine Psychology*, ed. Harold Kelman. New York: W. W. Norton.

1967b. Mobilizing Constructive Forces [compiled by Morton B. Cantor from lectures on psychoanalytic technique given by Karen Horney at the American Institute for Psychoanalysis during 1946, 1951, and 1952]. *American Journal of Psychoanalysis* 27: 188–99. Revised version in *The Therapeutic Process*, 248–56.

1967c. Free Association [compiled by Sara Sheiner from lectures on psychoanalytic technique given by Karen Horney at the American Institute for Psychoanalysis during 1946, 1951, and 1952]. *American Journal of Psychoanalysis* 27: 200–208. Revised version in *The Therapeutic Process*, 232–41.

1980. *The Adolescent Diaries of Karen Horney,* ed. Marianne Eckardt. New York: Basic Books.

1987. *Final Lectures,* ed. Douglas H. Ingram. New York: W. W. Norton.

1999. *The Therapeutic Process: Essays and Lectures,* ed. Bernard J. Paris. New Haven: Yale University Press.

2000. *The Unknown Karen Horney: Essays on Gender, Culture, and Psychoanalysis,* ed. Bernard J. Paris. New Haven: Yale University Press.

References

Abraham, K. 1920. Manifestations of the Female Castration Complex. Reprinted in *Selected Papers of Karl Abraham*, trans. D. Bryan and A. Strachey. London: Hogarth Press, 1949.

Brown, J. F. 1939. Review of K. Horney, *New Ways in Psychoanalysis*. *Nation* 149 (23 September), 328–29.

Fleigel, Z. O. 1973. Feminine Psychosexual Development in Freudian Theory: A Historical Reconstruction. *Psychoanalytic Quarterly* 42: 385–408.

Freud, S. 1925. Some Psychological Consequences of the Anatomical Distinction Between the Sexes. Reprinted in vol. 5 of *Collected Papers*, ed. J. Strachey. New York: Basic Books, 1959, 186–97.

Kelman, H. 1971. *Helping People: Karen Horney's Psychoanalytic Approach*. New York: Science House.

———, ed. 1964. *Advances in Psychoanalysis: Contributions to Karen Horney's Holistic Approach*. New York: W. W. Norton.

———. 1965. *New Perspectives in Psychoanalysis: Contributions to Karen Horney's Holistic Approach*. New York: W. W. Norton.

Paris, B. J. 1974. *A Psychological Approach to Fiction: Studies in Thackeray, Stendhal, George Eliot, Dostoevsky, and Conrad*. Bloomington: Indiana University Press.

———. 1978. *Character and Conflict in Jane Austen's Novels: A Psychological Approach*. Detroit: Wayne State University Press.

———. 1991a. *Bargains with Fate: Psychological Crises and Conflicts in Shakespeare and His Plays*. New York: Insight Books.

———. 1991b. *Character as a Subversive Force in Shakespeare: The History and Roman Plays.* Rutherford, N.J.: Fairleigh Dickinson University Press.

———. 1994. *Karen Horney: A Psychoanalyst's Search for Self-Understanding.* New Haven: Yale University Press.

———. 1997. *Imagined Human Beings: A Psychological Approach to Character and Conflict in Literature.* New York: New York University Press.

———Paris, B. J., ed. 1986. *Third Force Psychology and the Study of Literature.* Rutherford, N.J.: Fairleigh Dickinson University Press.

Quinn, S. 1987. *A Mind of Her Own: The Life of Karen Horney.* New York: Summit.

Rubins, J. L., 1978. *Karen Horney: Gentle Rebel of Psychoanalysis.* New York: Dial.

Westkott, M. 1986. *The Feminist Legacy of Karen Horney.* New Haven: Yale University Press.

———. 1989. Female Relationality and the Idealized Self. *American Journal of Psychoanalysis* 49: 239–50.

Index

Abortion, 112, 114

Abraham, Karl, 1, 3, 185

Adaptation, 206, 225–26

Adler, Alfred: influence of, 193; on masculine protest, 7, 38; on penis envy, 30–31; on sex-role uncertainty, 55; on suffering, 319, 321; on validation, 45

Advances in Psychoanalysis (Kelman), 271, 283

Affection, compulsive need for, 163, 198–99, 301. *See also* Love

Age issues, 120–21, 202–203, 206, 313–14

Aggression: in dreams, 76, 89; feeling abused and, 274; guilt and, 91–99, 96–97; intellectualism and, 328–29; non-erotic type of, 160–61, 186; role of, 182–91; source of, 170, 179–80, 233, 297; vindictiveness and, 257–58; work difficulties and, 332. *See also* Arrogant-vindictiveness; Sadism

Agoraphobia, 34, 73

Alcoholism, 148–49

Alexander, Franz, 1, 236, 321

Ambition. *See* Competition

American Institute for Psychoanalysis, 1, 124, 304, 337–40

American Journal of Obstetrics and Gynecology, 13, 80

American Journal of Psychoanalysis: abstracts in, 160, 309, 310, 311, 323, 331, 340; lectures in, 124, 141, 313, 334, 337; papers in, 182, 243, 255, 271, 283, 295, 316, 320, 323, 329; resignation letter in, 304; war bulletins in, 306

American Journal of Sociology, 216

American Psychoanalytic Association, 304

American Sociological Review, 163, 192

Andersen, Hans Christian, 242

Anxiety: competition and, 197–200; concept of, 182–84, 340–41; effects of, 165, 318; factors in, 148–49, 162; in

Daughters: and conflicts with mother, 77–78, 87–90, 96–97; and disappointment in father, 87–89; and fear or hatred of mother, 10–11, 75–79, 85–87, 89–90, 95–97, 230–31; fear of father, 6–7, 34–36, 51; and identification with father, 36, 77–78, 88–89; and identification with mother, 88, 107–108; and love for father, 70–71. *See also* Girls

Death instinct: role of, 160–62, 181–91, 237–38, 261; sex act and, 34

Death wishes: toward mother, 10–11, 77, 86, 87, 231; toward self, 317, 319; toward sister, 87

Defense: against anxiety, 163, 165; enslavement feelings and, 23; feeling abused as, 278; strategies of, 20–21; structure of neurosis and, 2, 19, 168; in therapy, 260; against unfair treatment, 164–65. *See also* Arrogant-vindictiveness; Narcissism; Perfectionism; Resignation; Self-effacement

Dependency: overvaluation of love and, 22–23, 137–40; sadism and, 132; sources of, 25, 118, 122, 264, 301, 317–19

Destructiveness: neurosis and, 236–40; source of, 160–62, 186–91; in vindictiveness, 175. *See also* Sadism

Deutsch, Helene, 8, 28

Devil and Daniel Webster, The (Benét), 172, 240, 242

Devil's pact, 24, 172–73, 240–42

Don Giovanni, 241

Don Juanism, 17, 25, 57, 152

Don Quixote (Cervantes), 240

Dreams: aggressive impulses in, 76, 89; castration impulses in, 91, 94; death wishes in, 87; externalization and, 284, 289, 291; fears expressed in, 34, 75–76, 103; function of, 166; interpretation of, 311; masculinity wishes in, 31, 84–85, 92; source of, 209, 211; of vampire, 98; wishes for child in, 111–12

Drives: for affection, 163; compulsive phenomena vs., 184; definition of, 171, 189, 201, 237; destructive, 186–91, 297; externalization and, 292–93; giving up, 180; for love, 22–23, 150–51, 198–99, 312; for marriage, 71–73, 76; for pregnancy, 106; suppression of, 164, 190; vindictiveness and, 258–60

Education, 227, 299–300, 304–306

Educators, lectures for, 202–206

Ego, 214–15, 226, 236–37

Egocentricity, 44, 146–47, 205–206, 269, 323

Egotism, 130

Emerson, Ralph Waldo, 245

Enslavement, 23, 142–43, 252

Ephron, Harmon S., 304, 306

Escape from Freedom (Fromm), 169

Externalization: awareness of, 287, 292–93; concept of, 277, 283–85; in feeling abused, 177–78, 276–82; manifestations of, 285–86; in pride and self-hatred, 147–48; recognition and resolution of, 288–94; shallowness and, 324–25; in vindictiveness, 261, 263, 269

Family dynamics: competition in, 199; emphasis on, 13, 170; female homosexuality and, 75; neurosis and, 19, 40, 164–65, 168–69; parents' role in, 162, 190–91; in wartime, 229–34; women's roles and, 122–23. *See also* Childhood; Daughters; Fathers; Marriage; Mothers; Siblings; Sons

Fantasies: in competition, 197–98; of marriage, 71–73, 76; of masculinity, 30–32, 35–37, 84–85, 92; with masturbation, 184; of pregnancy, 105, 109–10; of prostitution, 94–96; of rape, 104–105, 114; as real, 35; source of, 209, 211; of suicide, 114, 317, 319

Fathers: commandment to honor, 62–63; conformity and, 225–26; daughter's